Disliking Others

LOATHING, HOSTILITY, AND DISTRUST IN PREMODERN OTTOMAN LANDS

Ottoman and Turkish Studies

Series Editor
HAKAN T. KARATEKE (The University of Chicago)

ACADEMIC
STUDIES
PRESS

Disliking Others

LOATHING, HOSTILITY, AND DISTRUST IN PREMODERN OTTOMAN LANDS

Edited by
HAKAN T. KARATEKE
H. ERDEM ÇIPA
HELGA ANETSHOFER

Library of Congress Cataloging-in-Publication Data:

The bibliographic data for this title is available from the Library of Congress.

ISBN 978-1-618118-80-6 (hardback)
ISBN 978-1-618118-81-3 (electronic)
ISBN 979-8-897830-94-7 (paperback)

Book design by Kryon Publishing Services (P) Ltd.
www.kryonpublishing.com

Cover design by Ivan Grave.

On the cover: The "Jewish shaykh" (fragment). Qazwīnī, *ʿAjāʾib al-Makhlūqāt* (Ottoman Turkish), Baghdad, mid-17th century. Jerusalem, The National Library of Israel, Ms. Yah. Ar. 1113, fol. 140a. Courtesy of the National Library of Israel, Jerusalem.

Published by Academic Studies Press in 2018.
Paperback 2025.

press@academicstudiespress.com
www.academicstudiespress.com

Table of Contents

Acknowledgments vii

Author Bios viii

Introduction xi

Changing Perceptions about Christian-Born Ottomans: Anti-*ḳul* Sentiments in Ottoman Historiography 1
H. Erdem Çıpa

Circassian Mamluks in Ottoman Egypt and Istanbul, ca. 1500–1730: The Eastern Alternative 22
Jane Hathaway

Dispelling the Darkness of the *Halberdier's Treatise*: A Comparative Look at Black Africans in Ottoman Letters in the Early Modern Period 43
Baki Tezcan

The Jew, the Orthodox Christian, and the European in Ottoman Eyes, ca. 1550–1700 75
Bilha Moor

An Ottoman Anti-Judaism 107
Hakan T. Karateke

Evliyā Çelebī's Perception of Jews 128
Hakan T. Karateke

Ambiguous Subjects and Uneasy Neighbors: Bosnian Franciscans' Attitudes toward the Ottoman State, "Turks," and Vlachs 148
Vjeran Kursar

"Those Violating the Good, Old Customs of our Land": Forms and Functions of Graecophobia in the Danubian Principalities, 16th–18th Centuries 187
Konrad Petrovszky

The Many Faces of the "Gypsy" in Early Modern Ottoman Discourse 215
Faika Çelik

Gendered Infidels in Fiction: A Case Study on Ṣābit's *Ḥikāye-i Ḫᵛāce Fesād* 244
İpek Hüner-Cora

"The Greatest of Tribulations": Constructions of Femininity in Sixteenth-Century Ottoman Physiognomy 264
Emin Lelić

Defining and Defaming the Other in Early Seventeenth-Century Ottoman Invective 296
Michael D. Sheridan

"Are You From Çorum?": Derogatory Attitudes Toward the "Unruly Mob" of the Provinces as Reflected in a Proverbial Saying 321
Helga Anetshofer

Index 334

Acknowledgments

The majority of the articles in this book are revised and expanded versions of the papers originally presented at a symposium titled "Xenophobia and Alterophobia in Pre-Modern Ottoman Lands" held at the University of Chicago on October 22–23, 2015. From its inception, this project benefitted from the support of several units and individuals at the University of Chicago and the University of Michigan, who not only found the concept of the symposium intriguing and worthy of support but also helped with the organization of the symposium and the publication of this volume. At the University of Chicago, the editors are grateful to the following units for their financial support: Franke Institute for the Humanities; Center for Middle Eastern Studies; Center for Jewish Studies; Division of the Humanities; Humanities Visiting Committee; Center for the Study of Gender and Sexuality; and Norman Wait Harris Memorial Fund administered at the time by the Center for International Studies. The heavy load of e-mail traffic and various other logistical details were competently administered before, during, and after the symposium by Thomas Maguire and Brittany Ciboski, both of the Center for Middle Eastern Studies. İpek Hüner-Cora and Tunç Şen, then doctoral students at the Department of Near Eastern Languages and Civilizations, provided the organizers with their on-site help. At the University of Michigan, the College of Literature, Science, and the Arts; the Office of Research; the History Department, and the Near Eastern Studies Department provided financial support necessary for the copyediting and indexing this volume.

We are also thankful to those who assisted in the production of this book. We owe a great debt of gratitude to Alessandra Anzani, acquisitions editor at the Academic Studies Press, for accommodating our manuscript for publication in an exceptionally expeditious manner, and to Kira Nemirovsky, production editor at the Press, who oversaw its production with great care.

Author Bios

Helga Anetshofer (PhD, Vienna University) is Lecturer for Ottoman and Turkish at the University of Chicago. Her publications include her recent article "Folk Etymologies and Stories of Toponyms from Danishmendid Territory in Evliya Çelebi's Seyahatname" (2015) and "The Hero Dons a Talismanic Shirt for Battle: Magic Objects Aiding the Warrior in a Turkish Epic Romance" (forthcoming in 2018).

Faika Çelik (PhD, McGill University) is Assistant Professor of Political Science and International Relations at Manisa Celal Bayar University. Her recent publications are "Civilizing Mission in Late Ottoman Discourse: The Case of Gypsies" (2013) and "Probing the Margins: Gypsies (Roma) in the Sixteenth Century Ottoman Society" (2007).

H. Erdem Çıpa (PhD, Harvard University) is Associate Professor of Ottoman history at the University of Michigan. He is author of *The Making of Selim: Succession, Legitimacy, and Memory in the Early Modern Ottoman World* (2017) and co-editor, with E. Fetvacı, of *Writing History at the Ottoman Court: Editing the Past, Fashioning the Future* (2013).

Jane Hathaway (PhD, Princeton University) is Professor of History at Ohio State University. She is author of *The Arab Lands under Ottoman Rule, 1516–1800* (2008). Her book *The Chief Eunuch of the Ottoman Harem: From African Slave to Power-Broker* will be published in 2018.

N. İpek Hüner-Cora is a doctoral candidate at the Department of Near Eastern Languages and Civilizations of the University of Chicago. Her work focuses on the history of Ottoman literature, gender, and sexuality. She published an article titled "Travelling within the Empire: Perceptions of the East in the Historical Narratives on Cairo by Mustafa Âli and Evliya Çelebi" (2013).

Hakan T. Karateke (PhD, Bamberg University) is Professor of Ottoman and Turkish Culture, Language, and Literature at the University of Chicago. He is author of *Evliya Çelebi's Journey from Bursa to the Dardanelles and Edirne* (2013) and forthcoming article titled "The Rosy History of Jews in the Ottoman Empire: A Critical Approach to Jewish Historiography."

Vjeran Kursar (PhD, University of Zagreb) is Assistant Professor of History and Hungarian, Jewish, and Turkish Studies at the University of Zagreb. His publications include "Being an Ottoman Vlach. On Vlach Identity(ies), Role and Status in Western Parts of the Ottoman Balkans (15th–18th Centuries)" (2013) and "Non-Muslim Communal Divisions and Identities in the Early Modern Ottoman Balkans and the Millet System Theory" (2013).

Emin Lelić (PhD, The University of Chicago) is Assistant Professor of History at Salisbury University. He has recently published "Physiognomy ('ilm-i firāsat) and Ottoman Statecraft: Discerning Morality and Justice" (2017) and is currently working on "*Firâsa* as an Investigation of Nature and Politics at the Ottoman Court," which will appear in the forthcoming *Routledge Handbook on Science in the Islamicate World.*

Bilha Moor (PhD, Hebrew University of Jerusalem) was the Andrew W. Mellon Postdoctoral Fellow of Islamic Art and Architecture at Northwestern University, Department of Art History from 2014 to 2017. "Shahnama Kings and Heroes in *'Aja'ib al-Makhluqat* Illustrated Manuscripts" (2012) and "Mosque and Church: Arabic Inscriptions at Shivta in the Early Islamic Period" (2013) are among her publications. At present she is writing a book tentatively titled *The World in Muslim Eyes: Illustrated Cosmographies, 1550–1700.*

Konrad Petrovszky (PhD, Humboldt University) is a research associate at the Institute of Modern and Contemporary Historical Research at the Austrian Academy of Science. He is author of *Geschichte schreiben im osmanischen Südosteuropa: eine Kulturgeschichte orthodoxer Historiographie des 16. und 17. Jahrhunderts* (2014) and co-edited (with

A. Helmedach, M. Koller, and S. Rohdewald) *Das osmanische Europa: Methoden und Perspektiven der Frühneuzeitforschung zu Südosteuropa* (2014).

Michael D. Sheridan (PhD, Bilkent University) teaches humanities and literature at Bilkent University and TED (Türk Eğitim Derneği) University in Ankara. His recently completed dissertation focuses on rivalries, factions, and power relations among the early seventeenth-century Ottoman elite as viewed through the lens of the period's invective (*hicv*) corpus and in relation with the contemporary advice literature. He has an upcoming publication, with Robert Dankoff and Nuran Tezcan, entitled *Ottoman Explorations of the Nile*.

Baki Tezcan (PhD, Princeton University) is Associate Professor of History at the University of California, Davis. He is author of *The Second Ottoman Empire: Political and Social Transformation in the Early Modern World* (2010). His recent publications include "The Memory of the Mongols in Early Ottoman Historiography" (2013) and "Law in China or Conquest in the Americas: Competing Constructions of Political Space in the Early Modern Ottoman Empire" (2013).

Introduction

Historians know well that post-nationalist societies are not unique in nurturing dislike—or even hatred—of foreigners and members of marginalized subcultures. The perception of certain groups as outsiders, or as alternative groups within a society, is a salient feature of bygone societies as well. In fact, it would be fair to say that dislike of others has been a persistent condition of society throughout history. This volume explores that theme within the premodern Ottoman context.

Recent historical studies on the Ottoman Empire, as well as a contemporary political rhetoric that glorifies the Ottoman enterprise, have taken for granted that subjects of the Ottoman polity flourished under a so-called *Pax Ottomanica*. This widely—but uncritically—accepted view posits that the economic and social stability of the sixteenth and seventeenth centuries made the Ottoman lands a relatively safe and secure environment for trade, the flourishing of arts and crafts, peaceful coexistence and settlement, particularly for groups—for example, Jews—for whom the situation in Ottoman lands compared favorably to that in other parts of the world. Whatever the validity of such a supposition, the relative stability of Ottoman lands at that time did not preclude established or even formal antipathies among groups of people within Ottoman society. Some prejudices stretched back to the Middle Ages and earlier; others arose from contemporary social and political tensions. Religious convictions and affiliations were no doubt a factor in the formation of mutual antipathy, but conflicting economic interests played a significant role as well. Thus, historical sources suggest that the social and cultural realities of the premodern Ottoman world were far more complex than is assumed by the proponents of *Pax Ottomanica*—a phenomenon that, plausibly, can be explained and appreciated by historians within its limitations but certainly represents a myth in the way it is understood, especially by conservative masses, and utilized by populist politicians and neo-Ottomanist demagogues alike.

The critical scholarly evaluation of this myth constituted the principal objective of a symposium at which most of the articles in this volume were first presented. Organized by the editors in October 2015 at the University of Chicago, this symposium aimed to explore two related themes in the context of premodern Ottoman lands: xenophobia (dislike of foreigners) and alterophobia (dislike of "the other," that is, members of alternative groups within the same society). Defining these terms as "irrational or unreasoned" fear of outsiders and foreigners, scholars have noted the socially and religiously stratified structure of Ottoman society. A systematic analysis of antipathies among communities has not yet been attempted, however. Most studies that investigate controversies stemming from antipathy between groups within the Ottoman context have focused on the nineteenth century, exploring enmities that resulted from varied expressions of nationalism as well as religious identities underscored by nationalistic ideals. These findings, while valuable for the present project, have limited relevance to an effort to understand social antipathies in early modern Ottoman society.

Of course, "dislike" takes a multitude of forms and degrees. Whereas systematic state persecution, forced migration, and violence are located at one end of the spectrum, general contempt or distrust in business dealings can be situated at the other. The editors opted to focus on antipathies among groups of people within Ottoman society. As such, this volume features several essays that contribute to the development of a historical approach to classifying forms of social antipathies and contextualizing them in early modern Ottoman society.

We do not mean to suggest that dislike or distrust was the primary defining characteristic of Ottoman society—or of any past society, for that matter. On the contrary, we are well aware that the cosmopolitanist nature of a multiethnic and multireligious empire allowed for the nonconfrontational coexistence of, and various forms of amicable relationships among, diverse communities. We further emphasize that the Ottoman polity represents a particularly fascinating and fruitful field of historical inquiry because, as an empire, it by necessity allowed not only for the existence of a multitude of officially recognized religious, ethnic, and linguistic groups but also for the coexistence of competing claims held by these subject communities. This volume, therefore, explores forms and expressions of dislike within the early modern Ottoman context, adding nuance to an otherwise uncritically accepted narrative that presumes the uninterrupted peaceful coexistence of various communities under the aegis of a tolerant imperial polity.

Undoubtedly, an interest in reconstructing such sentiments faces significant difficulties. The authors whose works are presented here were asked to reconstruct, to the extent possible, the mind-set of people living in sixteenth- and seventeenth-century Ottoman lands. We hoped to explore patterns in expressions of dislike in literature, historiography, and religious texts, particularly in those texts that one would classify as "ego documents," such as memoirs or otherwise personalized accounts. By studying a range of historical narratives, the contributors to the volume were able to develop rare insight into the self-described perceptions of individuals. Perceptions are necessarily difficult to delineate and can be open to multiple interpretations. Moreover, delineating negative perceptions can prove particularly difficult, in part because alterophobic sentiments often were not explicitly presented. Rather, one must carefully read between the lines, sweeping through the adjectives used to describe a group of people and comparing them to expressions used to describe various other groups, in order to reconstruct a perception. Utilizing a range of historical narratives yields opportunities to identify people's perceptions, which can prove exceptionally useful for understanding the intricate workings of past societies. The line of inquiry should not center on perceptions alone; repercussions of antipathy felt between groups compose another important component of analysis. We must be cautious, however, not to conflate feelings of prejudice or dislike with actions, which are likewise not necessarily the result of enduring negative cognition and feelings. Our approach thus considers rhetoric of dislike and actions of hate as two separate analytical categories.

The articles in this volume challenge the received wisdom in the field of Ottoman studies in a variety of ways. Perhaps most importantly, they probe the concept and nature of diversity in premodern Ottoman lands, and focus on a variety of tensions within early modern Ottoman society, by using hitherto unexplored or underutilized historical sources. Some of the essays explore relatively familiar factional divisions; as such, they analyze forms of dislike between groups defined by their denominational belonging or scrutinize expressions of aversion toward traditionally marginalized and alienated groups of people—such as Jews, gypsies, women, or blacks. Several other contributions focus on forms of antipathy that, one could argue, were peculiar to the Ottoman context. Highlighting the the evolution of Ottoman attitudes toward Circassian Mamluks in Egypt and Istanbul, the dislike between freeborn Muslims and converts, and the one-off stereotyping of people from a central Anatolian town, these essays shed light on the nature and character of coexistence between inhabitants of a vast geography. Two articles in the volume contribute to the previously inadequate dialogue between Ottoman studies and the field of southeast European history by highlighting long-standing tensions among Christian communities in the Balkans. Last, but certainly not least, several essays bring forth original arguments based on fiction, poetry, and the rather well-known autobiographical travel account of the celebrated seventeenth-century explorer Evliyā Çelebī.

Collectively, the essays in this volume highlight that the dislike of others is not conditioned solely by religious affiliation. They also remind us that we should be cognizant of the inaccuracy of identifying large groups of people with overarching categories such as *the* Muslims, *the* Christians, *the* Jews, *the* Druze, and the like. In fact, the attribution of group identities or group perceptions to any of these larger communities over time is of limited analytical value—for such attributions are at least partially due to the historian's lack of the sources necessary to accurately reconstruct the intricate inner workings of these communities.

Therefore, we wish to offer the following research questions as a road map for further scrutiny of Ottoman diversities. We developed these questions in the early stages of our project, to envision potential directions for this edited volume and to serve as guidelines for establishing the specificity of various forms of dislike, either to Ottoman society or to the early modern era:

Can prejudices be traced to sacred religious texts, or to traditions emanating from them? What role can be ascribed to religious conviction and affiliation in the creation of cultures of aversion? Did religious traditions influence one another in creating collective antipathies toward third-party groups? What were the similarities and differences among the respective antipathies held by different religious communities? How can one compare and understand the antipathies felt by members of institutionalized religions toward communities, ideas, or the practices of syncretic religious groups, or by the marginal offshoots of a religion? How did political circumstances and effective state propaganda occasion new antipathies?

How did being a member of the majority or a minority group shape an individual's feelings about other communities? How did it effect his or her ability—and willingness—to express dislike in word or deed? How were sentiments of antipathy directed toward specific ethnic groups, regardless of their religious identities? What were Ottoman elites' common perceptions of foreign others, with whom they may have had little or no contact? How did such perceptions trickle down to the common people? How were negative attitudes toward the poor, homeless, and outcasts of society manifested? How did inhabitants of the imperial center of Istanbul, or of other established urban cultural centers, perceive people immigrating to their cities from the provinces? How can one characterize, generalize, or trace the particularities of antipathies based on gender or on sexual orientation within Ottoman society? Were the antipathies of religious or societal groups toward certain others particular to time periods (for example, the aftermath of a rebellion) or to certain geographies (for example, large cities or borderlands)?

Comparative studies to substantiate the forms and causes of dislike across premodern societies of similar configuration will no doubt open new avenues of research and help rescue historians from feelings of singularity. In offering our preliminary findings to the scholarly world via this volume, we hope that the questions above will also guide researchers as they explore and inquire into similar problems in their respective sources.

Changing Perceptions about Christian-Born Ottomans: Anti-*ḳul* Sentiments in Ottoman Historiography

H. Erdem Çıpa

Writing in the early 1590s, court historiographer Ṭaᶜlīḳīzāde Meḥmed (d. 1600) identified the peaceful coexistence of a diverse "collection of religious communities" (*terāküm-i milel*) under Ottoman rule as one of the qualities of the House of ᶜOs̱mān that rendered it superior to all Islamic dynasties, past and contemporary.[1] The cohabitation of ethnically and confessionally varied communities in the Ottoman realm is a theme addressed by non-Ottoman early modern authors as well. The bilingual treatise on the state of Ottoman affairs penned in 1672 by Jakab Harsányi Nagy (d. after 1679), an exceptionally versatile Transylvanian man of letters, provides a case in point.[2] A meticulous observer of Ottoman

1 Ṭaᶜlīḳīzāde Meḥmed, *Şehnāme-i Hümāyūn*, 7a–b/122: "Ṭoḳuzıncı ḫāṣṣa terāküm-i milel ve telāṭum-ı niḥeldür. Hīç bir salṭanat yoḳdur ki pāy-taḫt-ı pāyende-baḫtda millet-i Tersā ve niḥlet-i Mūsā terāküm eyleyüb ecnās-ı şettā ictimāᶜ ḳılmaḳ olmamışdur. İllā bu devlet-i ᶜālī-şān-ı raṣīnü'l-bünyānda vāḳiᶜ olmışdur." For a discussion of Ṭaᶜlīḳīzāde's list of twenty superior qualities (*ḫāṣṣa*) of the Ottoman dynasty, see Necipoğlu, *The Age of Sinan*, 30–35. Also see Krstić, "Conversion and Converts to Islam in Ottoman Historiography," 72.

2 Jakab Harsányi composed his *Colloquia Familiaria Turcico Latina* in Ottoman Turkish and Latin. A modern edition of the treatise, including a German translation

realities, Jakab Harsányi attempts to describe "the nature and mores of the Ottomans," but first cautions his readers that the Ottomans formed not a "pure" nation but one composed of the descendants of a great number of peoples, including "Germans, Poles, French, English, Dutch, Hungarians, Muscovites, Czechs, Rus, Cossacks, Serbs, Bulgarians, Albanians, Abkhazians, Georgians, Kurds, Persians, Arabs, Greeks, Armenians, Tatars, Wallachians, Moldavians, Circassians, Croatians, Italians, Jews, Indians, and many others." In a nuanced tone, he further notes that "those who are born Muslim have different customs than those who have converted from Christianity; the educated have their way, the uneducated theirs; people of the frontiers develop different customs than those who are born in the central lands of the empire; everyone learns both good and bad things from Christians and [other] neighbors."[3]

We do not know whether Jakab Harsányi considered the social relations among various ethnic and religious communities living under Ottoman rule—or the relationships between these communities and the Ottoman state—to be fundamentally peaceful. His remarkably non-essentialist attitude, however, suggests that he would probably not be as quick as Ṭaᶜlīḳīzāde Meḥmed to praise early modern Ottomans as the architects of a glorious "Pax Ottomanica." Moreover, judging by Jakab Harsányi's extraordinary breadth of knowledge about Ottoman affairs, it is highly unlikely that he was unaware of expressions of dislike and antipathy employed by Ottoman chroniclers, chancellors, and scribes to describe a great number of subject populations. Among such expressions were the euphonious religio-ethnic slurs referring to the "cursed, dishonorable Hungarians" (*engürüs-i menḥūs, engürüs-i bī-nāmūs*), "wicked Kurds" (*ekrād-ı bed-nihād*), "disunited, ignorant, Turks/Turkomans" (*etrāk-ı ḳalīlü'l-ittiḥād, etrāk-ı bī-idrāḳ*), and "despicable and scheming Laz" (*mezmūm-u-ġammāz*

---

of the text, was published by György Hazai in 1973. On Jakab Harsányi's life and career, see Kármán, *A Seventeenth-Century Odyssey in East Central Europe*.

3 See Harsányi Nagy, *Colloquia Familiaria Turcico Latina*, 162–64. For a discussion of the relevant segment of the text, including Jakab Harsányi's portrayal of the "Ottoman character," see Kafadar, "A Rome of One's Own," 14; and Kármán, *A Seventeenth-Century Odyssey in East Central Europe*, 220–21. The translations by Kafadar and Kármán include slight variations. Quoted here is Kafadar's more idiomatic translation (based on the Ottoman Turkish version of the text) rather than Kármán's more literal one (based on the Latin version of the text).

olan Laz),[4] not to mention the Ḳızılbaş, who were commonly depicted as evil-mannered (*bed-maᶜaş*) rabble-rousers (*evbāş*).[5] Last but not least, he surely was aware that Ottoman authors consistently referred to non-Muslims as "evil-doing infidels" (*küffār-ı bed-girdār*).[6]

Jakab Harsányi would also undoubtedly disagree with Ṭaᶜlīḳīzāde's modern—and mostly Turkish—counterparts, who uncritically accept an idealized version of the sixteenth- and seventeenth-century Ottoman imperial self-image as historical fact.[7] Produced in a politico-religious landscape shaped first by the predominantly secular nationalist ideology of the early Republic,[8] then by the official state doctrine of "Turkish-Islamic Synthesis,"[9] and more recently by the rise of the Sunnī Turkish variant of political Islam and a concomitant sentiment of neo-Ottomanism, this brand of scholarship posits that the (relative) economic and political stability of the early modern Ottoman enterprise rendered Ottoman lands a safe and secure environment for all subjects of a multi-confessional empire, regardless of ethnic or religious background.

Recent studies have moved away from this idealized portrayal of Ottoman realities. A number of works in (primarily) Euro-American scholarship, including the essays that comprise this volume, present nuanced readings of a wide range of historical narratives. In so doing, they identify areas of contention among various communities within Ottoman society

---

4 For references to the Kurds, the Turks, and the Laz, see, for example, Muṣṭafā ᶜĀlī, *Nuṣḥatü's-selāṭīn*, 1:23, 63 (translation), 139, 158 (transcription); and Celālzāde Muṣṭafā, *Me'āṣir-i Selīm Ḫānī*, 129.

5 See, for example, Luṭfī Paşa, *Tevārīḫ-i āl-i ᶜOs̱mān*, 214; and Celālzāde Muṣṭafā, *Me'āṣir-i Selīm Ḫānī*, 145.

6 See, for example, Luṭfī Paşa, *Tevārīḫ-i āl-i ᶜOs̱mān*, 196.

7 The titles of several recent publications demonstrate that Ṭaᶜlīḳīzāde's idealizing view of Ottoman rule has remained a fundamental component of a particularly durable historiographical current. See, for example, Çiçek, *Pax Ottomana*; and Ortaylı, *Osmanlı Barışı*.

8 For a critique of the "Kemalist view of Ottoman history," which has been characterized by "the imagined descent of an imagined 'Turkish state tradition' from the Orkhon inscriptions to the *ḳānūnnāme* of Meḥmed II," see Imber, "'An Illiberal Descent'".

9 Originally formulated in the 1970s by the right-wing nationalist Intellectuals' Hearths (*Aydınlar Ocakları*), the doctrine of the "Turkish-Islamic Synthesis" became a principal tenet of the Turkish Republic's official ideology after the 1980 coup, aiding the rise of a Sunnī-sectarian variant of political Islam in Turkey. See Eligür, *The Mobilization of Political Islam in Turkey*.

as well as spheres of conflict—and compromise—between individual communities and the Ottoman polity that governed them.[10] The aim of this article is to complement these studies by highlighting the dissonance between groups of people *within* the Ottoman military ruling elite (*ᶜaskerī*). Specifically, I intend to focus on the portrayal of the "slave-servants" of the Ottoman sultan—known as *ḳul*s—in Ottoman historiography of the early modern era. Paying particular attention to a number of Ottoman works of advice (*naṣīḥatnāme*), an impressive genre of ethical-political writing that flourished during the sixteenth and seventeenth centuries, I aim to demonstrate that the majority of freeborn Muslim Ottoman authors directed their frustration and resentment toward the sultan's Christian-born *ḳul*s. Finally, I argue that the expression of *ḳul*-critical sentiments in Ottoman historical writing was not the result of a religio-social conflict between Christian-born and Muslim-born individuals but rather the outcome of rivalry among members of a ruling class who competed for appointments and promotions in the military–administrative hierarchy of the Empire.

SLAVE-SERVANTS IN THE OTTOMAN MILITARY–ADMINISTRATIVE HIERARCHY

Originally an old Turkish word denoting a servant, vassal, or dependent, "*ḳul*" was used in a variety of ways in Ottoman historiography.[11] In some cases, the term specifically denoted a slave, an individual who could be bought and sold.[12] Per Süleymān I's ("the Lawgiver," r. 1520–1566) imperial order of 1531 decreeing that all of his subjects were *ḳul*s, the word could also refer to practically anyone who was not a member of the

10 The best examples in this regard are two book-length studies by Karen Barkey and Tijana Krstić. While the former defines empire as a "negotiated" enterprise and analyzes the social organization as well as the mechanisms of governance of the multiethnic and multireligious polity ruled by the House of ᶜOs̱mān, the latter provides a sophisticated analysis of interconfessional dynamics within the Ottoman context. See Barkey, *Empire of Difference*; and Krstić, *Contested Conversions to Islam*.

11 For the various meanings the term acquired over time, see *The Encyclopaedia of Islam* (second edition, henceforth "*EI*²"), s.v. "*Ḳul*" (C. E. Bosworth).

12 The authoritative study on various forms of slavery in the Ottoman world is Toledano, *Slavery and Abolition in the Ottoman Middle East*. On the holding of slaves during the early Ottoman period, also see Erdem, *Slavery in the Ottoman Empire and Its Demise*, 1–17.

dynastic family.[13] Most often, however, "*ḳul*" referred to members of the Ottoman military ruling elite who had been (almost exclusively) recruited through an elaborate system called *devşirme*, through which thousands of Christian-born subjects of the Empire entered the Ottoman military–administrative structure and became the sultan's slave-servants.[14] This practice entailed the forcible removal, in the form of a tribute, of the male children of non-urban, mostly Christian subjects of the Empire from their ethnic, religious, and cultural environments, along with their transfer into the Turkish-Islamic milieu, with the aim of employing them in the service of the palace, army, and imperial bureaucracy. As *devşirme* recruits, these children were, on the one hand, to serve the sultan as slaves and freedmen and, on the other, to eventually form the ruling class of the Ottoman state.

As Ehud R. Toledano notes, "slavery was *both* an important, albeit involuntary, channel of recruitment and socialization into the elite and a major, though forced, means of linking individuals into patronage networks."[15] Indeed, the majority of these recruits became janissaries (*yeŋiçeri*). Originally forming the sultan's household troops and imperial bodyguard, this standing corps of salaried infantrymen evolved to constitute the "indispensable operational core of the Ottoman army" by the early seventeenth century.[16] A great many others served the Ottoman enterprise as statesmen, bureaucrats, and administrators. The critical juncture in this regard was the reign of Meḥmed II ("the Conqueror," r. 1444–1446 and

13 The relevant section of the edict is quoted in Kunt, *The Sultan's Servants*, 35: "Those living in my domains, either officers or subjects, all of them are my servants" (Benüm memālik-i maḥrūsemde vākiᶜ olan eger sipāhīlerdür ve eger reᶜāyādur cümlesi ḳullarumdur). I am grateful to Cornell Fleischer for this reference.

14 In this study, the term will be used in this last, more common sense. Although most *ḳuls* were *devşirme* recruits, their ranks also included captives of war who converted to Islam and became *ḳuls* voluntarily. On this institution, see Ménage, "Sidelights on the *Devshirme* from Idrīs and Saᶜduddīn"; Ménage, "Some Notes on the *Devshirme*"; Palmer, "The Origin of the Janissaries"; Wittek, "*Devshirme* and *Sharīᶜa*"; and Kafadar, "The Ottomans and Europe," 603–606. Prominent sixteenth-century historian and jurist Saᶜdeddīn Efendi (d. 1599) estimates that this system of recruitment produced more than 200,000 converts to Islam over the course of more than two centuries. For this and other estimates, see *EI²*, s.v. "Devshirme" (Victor L. Ménage). For a discussion of the *devşirme* as a method of conversion to Islam, see Minkov, *Conversion to Islam in the Balkans*, 67–77.

15 Toledano, *Slavery and Abolition in the Ottoman Middle East*, 4. Italics in the original. On the legal status of the *ḳul*, also see Minkov, *Conversion to Islam in the Balkans*, 69n25.

16 See *EI²*, s.v. "Yeñi Čeri" (Rhoads Murphey).

1451–1481), who strategically promoted men of *devşirme* background to high offices.[17] In fact, until the late seventeenth century the Ottoman imperial administration was dominated by *ḳul*s.

This was certainly part of Meḥmed II's "imperial project,"[18] which entailed, among other endeavors, the establishment of Constantinople as the new Ottoman capital, the codification of fratricide,[19] and the transformation of privately owned lands (*mülk*), as well as lands that belonged to pious endowments (*vaḳıf*), into military fiefs (*tīmār*).[20] Meḥmed II also created a court culture in which royal patronage of the arts was further extended to "outsiders."[21] An anonymous author used poetry to express his resentment of the sultan's advancement of these "outsider" Jews, Christians, and Persians:

> If you wish to stand in high honor on the Sultan's threshold,
> You must be a Jew, or a Frank, or a Persian;
> You must choose the name Ḳābīlī, Habīlī, Ḥāmidī,
> And behave like a Zorzi; show no knowledge.[22]

---

17 Kafadar notes that between 1450 and the late 1600s, the great majority of Ottoman viziers were products of this system of recruitment. See Kafadar, "The Ottomans and Europe," 605.

18 For the original use of the term, see Yerasimos, *La fondation de Constantinople et de Sainte-Sophie dans les traditions turques*, 249. On Meḥmed II's "imperial project" and its critique as articulated in early Ottoman historiography, see Kafadar, *Between Two Worlds*, 96–97.

19 For a detailed discussion of the "fratricide clause" in Meḥmed II's *ḳānūnnāme* and the most recent argument for its authenticity, see, respectively, Özcan, "Fâtih'in Teşkilât Kanunnâmesi ve Nizam-ı Alem İçin Kardeş Katli Meselesi"; and *Ḳānūnnāme-i āl-i ᶜOsmān*, xxiii–xxxiv.

20 See Babinger, *Mehmed the Conqueror and His Time*, 447; and Beldiceanu, "Recherches sur la réforme foncière de Mehmed II." The fifteenth-century historian Ṭursun Beg states that Meḥmed II confiscated more than one thousand villages or estates and converted them to military prebends. See Ṭursun Beg, *Tārīḫ-i ebū'l-fetḥ* (Tulum edition, 197; İnalcık and Murphey edition, 169a). Earlier in the text, the number of confiscated estates is given as "twenty thousand" (Tulum edition, 22; İnalcık and Murphey edition, 18a).

21 For royal patronage of the arts at Meḥmed II's court, see Rogers, "Mehmed the Conqueror"; and Raby, "A Sultan of Paradox."

22 Translation, with minor modifications, as quoted in Raby, "A Sultan of Paradox," 8. The original poem, which is included in *Risāletü'l-leṭāʾif ve ḥikāyātü'l-Ḥācı Ṣabrī*, is quoted by Süheyl Ünver as "Gel dilerseŋ şāh eşiginde olasın muḥterem / Yā Yahūd ol gel bu mülke yā Frenk ol yā ᶜAcem / Adıŋı ḳo Ḳābīlī vü Habīlī vü Ḥāmidī / Żūrzīlikten ġāfil olma maᶜrifetten urma dem." See Ünver, *İstanbul Üniversitesi Tarihine Başlangıç*, 248.

While the anonymous poet's bitterness was directed toward non-Muslims (or Muslims of non-Sunnī background) who benefited from the sultan's literary patronage, the resentment of many other Ottoman authors who lived through at least part of Meḥmed II's reign was directed principally at Christian-born members of the Ottoman ruling elite, the majority of whom were *ḳul*s. Their resentment resulted from several factors. First and foremost, perhaps the most effective centralizing strategy employed by Meḥmed II involved the three interrelated processes of expanding the standing army, extending *devşirme* recruitment, and promoting *ḳul*s to the highest positions in the military-administrative hierarchy. The increasing ascendancy of the sultan's slave-servants to the pinnacle of the Ottoman imperial administration marked the end of an era when the frontier traditions of the early *ġāzī*-state reigned supreme. The centralization of political power also led to the marginalization of those who once constituted the vanguard of Ottoman expansion, including (but not limited to) frontier warriors, their hereditary leaders (*uc begi*), and the "colonizing dervishes" associated with them.[23] Because the authors of a number of early chronicles of the House of ᶜOs̱mān "were evidently dervishes or close enough to the gazi-dervish milieux to have been touched, either personally or through their patrons" by Meḥmed II's centralizing policies, it is not surprising that the earliest glimpses of anti-*ḳul* sentiments and/or resentment directed toward other Christian-born statesmen emerged in these dynastic histories written during the second half of the fifteenth century.[24]

One of the most revealing of such examples is included in ᶜĀşıḳpaşazāde Dervīş Aḥmed's (d. after 1484) chronicle of the Ottoman dynasty. Through his rather personal account of Meḥmed II's fiscal policies in the aftermath of the conquest of Constantinople, ᶜĀşıḳpaşazāde vehemently criticizes the imposition of an onerous "rent" (*muḳāṭaᶜa*) on the buildings of the newly conquered city that were inhabited by Muslim Ottoman settlers, including the chronicler himself.[25] ᶜĀşıḳpaşazāde's hostility is not, however, directed toward the sultan but toward Rūm Meḥmed

23 See Barkan, "İstilâ Devirlerinin Kolonizatör Türk Dervişleri ve Zâviyeler."

24 Kafadar, *Between Two Worlds*, 97.

25 See ᶜĀşıḳpaşazāde, *Menāḳıb ü tevārīḫ-i āl-i ᶜOs̱mān* (Yavuz and Saraç edition), 488–90. On the controversy regarding the imposition of that "rent," see İnalcık, "The Policy of Mehmed II toward the Greek Population of Istanbul and the Byzantine Buildings of the City," 240–47.

Pasha (d. ca. 1470), Meḥmed II's vizier. In his *Menāḳıb ü tevārīḫ-i āl-i ᶜOs̱mān*, ᶜĀşıḳpaşazāde refers to Rūm Meḥmed Pasha as a "son of an infidel" (*bir kāfirüŋ oġlıydı*), whose family and friends included "the old infidels of Constantinople."[26] He further argues that Rūm Meḥmed Pasha, in cahoots with "deceitful, accursed infidels" (*muġvī melᶜūn kāfirler*) and one other "nominally Muslim" (*adı Müsülmān*) person, schemed to prevent the restoration of the city by the "Turks" (*Türkler*), so that it would remain in the possession of Christians.[27] An even more direct attack on Rūm Meḥmed Pasha and his identity as a convert is expressed in the couplets at the end of the relevant chapter of the *Menāḳıb*, where the vizier is called an infidel rather than a renegade:

> If his [that is, the sultan's] vizier is an infidel
> He always seeks to cause harm to the faith [that is, Islam][28]

ᶜĀşıḳpaşazāde's animosity toward Rūm Meḥmed Pasha was undoubtedly the result of many frustrations. As a Muslim settler who had presumably benefitted from Meḥmed II's grant of houses as freehold, ᶜĀşıḳpaşazāde must have suffered financial losses due to the imposition of the *muḳāṭaᶜa*. As a learned dervish and a (potential) recipient of sultanic gifts customarily distributed to dervishes and sheikhs, he also appears to have reacted negatively to the Christian-born vizier's abolition of such rewards.[29] Besides, ᶜĀşıḳpaşazāde's statements undoubtedly exemplified the sentiments of many Muslim-born figures who yearned for a return to the "good old days" when they, and not the Christian-born *ḳuls*, served as decision-makers at the heart of Ottoman political power.

Feelings of resentment toward the sultan's servants and subjects with non-Muslim ancestry were not limited to those associated with the *ġāzī*-dervish milieu of the early Ottoman period, however. Similar

26 ᶜĀşıḳpaşazāde, *Menāḳıb ü tevārīḫ-i āl-i ᶜOs̱mān* (Yavuz and Saraç edition), 488.

27 ᶜĀşıḳpaşazāde, *Menāḳıb ü tevārīḫ-i āl-i ᶜOs̱mān* (Yavuz and Saraç edition), 488–90. In one of the editions of the text, *muġvī* (deceitful) is rendered as *maḫfī* (secret). See ᶜĀşıḳpaşazāde, *Menāḳıb ü tevārīḫ-i āl-i ᶜOs̱mān* (ᶜAlī Bey edition), 143. For a brief analysis of this episode, see Krstić, "Conversion and Converts to Islam in Ottoman Historiography," 66–67.

28 ᶜĀşıḳpaşazāde, *Menāḳıb ü tevārīḫ-i āl-i ᶜOs̱mān* (Yavuz and Saraç edition), 490: "Ḫuṣūṣā kim kāfir ola vezīri // Żarar ister olur dāᵓim īmānda."

29 On this point, see İnalcık, "The Policy of Mehmed II toward the Greek Population of Istanbul and the Byzantine Buildings of the City," 245.

anti-convert and anti-*ḳul* sentiments are discernable in the writings of numerous other Ottoman men of letters in the sixteenth century. The fact that *devşirme* recruits were converts to Islam was certainly not forgotten by Ottoman authors, including learned members of the House of ᶜOs̱mān. For example, in a lengthy treatise written in 1508, Sultan Bāyezīd II's (r. 1481–1512) erudite son, Prince Ḳorḳud (d. 1513), expresses his anxieties about moral, religious, administrative, and political troubles. He also produces a blistering critique of numerous Ottoman institutions and practices. Of particular significance for the purposes of this essay is the fact that Ḳorḳud considered the janissaries, as well as members of the military units of *devşirme* origin at the imperial palace, to be disorderly and violent, "as were their infidel fathers." He thus creates a causal link between the non-Muslim origins of a segment of the Ottoman military–political elite and their ostensibly unruly behavior.[30]

Even an intellectual like Muṣṭafā ᶜĀlī (d. 1600) could not hide his disdain when he referred to the Christian ancestors of the segment of Ottoman society that he called "Rūmīs"—despite the fact that ᶜĀlī himself descended from a *ḳul* family, he believed in the "transformative power" of Islam, and thus did not hesitate to consider converts to Islam to be faithful members of the Ottoman military–administrative elite.[31] In his discussion of the meritorious characteristics of these Rūmīs, ᶜĀlī singles them out "for their piety, cleanliness, and faith." When he refers to the "confused ethnic origins" of these notable figures, however, he points out that "either on their father's or their mother's side, the genealogy is traced to a filthy infidel."[32] In the context of a discussion of ideal members of scholarly–literary gatherings (*mecālis*), ᶜĀlī also states that "literate idiots," who are ignorant about Koranic interpretation and prophetic traditions, and "beasts," who recite inferior poetry or plagiarize

30 For an analysis of Ḳorḳud's *Daᶜwat al-nafs al-ṭāliḥa ilā al-aᶜmāl al-ṣāliḥa* (An Erring Soul's Summons to Virtuous Works), see Fleischer, "From Şeyhzade Korkud to Mustafa Âli," 71; and Al-Tikriti, "Şehzade Korkud (ca. 1468–1513) and the Articulation of Early 16th Century Ottoman Religious Identity," Chapter 5.

31 On the evolution of the Rūmī identity in the Ottoman context, see Kafadar, "A Rome of One's Own"; Krstić, "Conversion and Converts to Islam in Ottoman Historiography"; and Krstić, *Contested Conversions to Islam*, especially 3–6, 51–74.

32 For the translation and a brief analysis of the relevant passage, see Fleischer, *Bureaucrat and Intellectual in the Ottoman Empire*, 254–55; and Kafadar, "A Rome of One's Own," 12. Also see Krstić, "Conversion and Converts to Islam in Ottoman Historiography," 59–60; and Krstić, *Contested Conversions to Islam*, 3–5.

the poetry of others, should be excluded from such séances. He refers to these individuals as "sons of ᶜAbdullāh" (*ᶜAbdullāh oğulları*), a term most often denoting people of non-Muslim origin.[33]

Despite the prevalence of similar anti-non-Muslim and anti-convert sentiments in various genres of Ottoman historical writing, we find strikingly few such references in works composing the Ottoman variety of advice literature (*naṣīḥatnāme*)—possibly limited to Ḳorḳud's statement that the unruly janissaries resembled their "infidel fathers." I do not mean to suggest that Ottoman authors considered freeborn Muslims and Christian-born *ḳul*s as equals. On the contrary, evidence suggests that, especially from the second half of the sixteenth century onward, even the length of a convert's "tenure" in Islam gained new significance.[34] What I would like to emphasize instead is that most Ottoman writers considered the rivalry between *ḳul*s and non-*ḳul*s not a struggle between Christian-born and Muslim-born individuals, but a competition between privileged and disadvantaged members of an all-Muslim ruling elite regardless of their religions at birth.

ANTI-ḲUL SENTIMENTS IN OTTOMAN ADVICE LITERATURE—AND BEYOND

A distinctly Ottoman advice literature proliferated during the sixteenth and seventeenth centuries.[35] The composition of such works appears to

33 Schmidt, *Pure Water for Thirsty Muslims*, 216. Converts to Islam whose fathers remained non-Muslim commonly used as their father's name ᶜAbdallāh/ᶜAbdullāh (lit. "slave of Allāh"). On the use of ᶜAbdullāh as a patronymic by converts in the Ottoman context, see Ménage, "Seven Ottoman Documents from the Reign of Meḥemmed II," 112–18.

34 Krstić, "Conversion and Converts to Islam in Ottoman Historiography," 73.

35 While a definitive monograph on Ottoman *naṣīḥatnāme* literature is still wanting, numerous studies, some of them excellent, survey various aspects of Ottoman advice literature. For a detailed and annotated list of works of advice composed throughout Islamic history, with particular emphasis on the Ottoman experience, see Levend, "Siyaset-nameler"; and Uğur, *Osmanlı Siyâset-nâmeleri*. Discussions of a variety of aspects of the genre can be found also in Kafadar, "The Myth of the Golden Age"; Lewis, "Ottoman Observers of Ottoman Decline"; Lewis, "Some Reflections on the Decline of the Ottoman Empire"; Fodor, "State and Society, Crisis and Reform"; Sariyannis, "The Princely Virtues as Presented in Ottoman Political and Moral Literature"; and Sariyannis, "Ottoman Critics of Society and State." Two recent articles by Douglas A. Howard, which highlight the literary aspects of the genre,

have been impelled by the emergence of a historical consciousness of "decline" in Ottoman learned circles from the middle of the sixteenth century onward. The *naṣīḥatnāme* genre itself provides the most lucid expression of that consciousness.[36] Composed between the later years of Süleymān I's reign and the beginning of the eighteenth century, these works exhibit immense variety in terms of chronology, content, authorship, and target audience. They address a number of challenges and crises faced by the Ottoman state and society within the context of ever-changing historical circumstances during a particularly transformative period of Ottoman history. They also propose remedies. While *naṣīḥatnāme* authors are unanimous in their emphasis on justice and equity (*ᶜadālet*) as a precondition for the (re)establishment of the proper societal order (*niẓām-ı ᶜālem*), they differ in their suggestions as to how this can be achieved.[37] They also diverge in their identification of those responsible for these troubled times.

The principal reason for this divergence is that *naṣīḥatnāme* authors were learned men of diverse socio-cultural backgrounds, most of whom had served the Ottoman polity as statesmen, administrators, bureaucrats, or scholars (or, in most cases, a combination thereof); possessed varied skill sets; and benefited or suffered from different life experiences. While most were freeborn Muslims, their ranks also included Christian-born *ḳuls*.[38] Without doubt, influenced by all these factors, they expressed disparate, and at times conflicting, political and ideological viewpoints. They also had specific presentist agendas.

Quite a few *naṣīḥatnāme* authors, especially those who were Muslim-born, nevertheless ascribed primary responsibility for the

---

represent the most notable contributions to the scholarly literature on the subject. See Howard, "Genre and Myth in the Ottoman Advice for Kings Literature"; and Howard, "Ottoman Historiography and the Literature of 'Decline.'"

36 For a careful analysis problematizing the term "decline," see Kafadar, "The Myth of the Golden Age." For the uncritical usage of the term "decline," see Lewis, "Ottoman Observers of Ottoman Decline"; and Lewis, "Some Reflections on the Decline of the Ottoman Empire."

37 On the notion of the Ottoman "world order" (*niẓām-ı ᶜālem*), see Hagen, "Legitimacy and World Order," especially 55–57.

38 Renowned *naṣīḥatnāme* writers like Luṭfī Pasha (d. 1563) and Koçi Beg (d. ca. 1650), as well as the anonymous authors of advice works entitled *Ḳavānīn-i yeŋiçeriyān* (Laws of the Janissaries, ca. 1609–1617) and *Kitāb-ı müstetāb* (The Pleasant Book, ca. 1620), were *devşirme* recruits.

deterioration of the once-pristine Ottoman universal order (*niẓām-ı ᶜālem*) to the sultan's slave-servants (*ḳul*). Writing in the 1550s, grand vizier Luṭfī Pasha (d. 1563), himself a product of the *devşirme* system, objects to the increasing influence the janissaries exerted on the affairs of the state and argues that grand viziers should control the janissaries via the appointment of "prudent and restraining" commanders.[39] Writing in 1581, Muṣṭafā ᶜĀlī (d. 1600), a prominent and prolific man of letters and a freeborn Muslim bureaucrat, complains about abuses at the hands of the *ḳul*. Frustrated by (what he perceived as) a lack of recognition of his qualifications and a parallel lack of promotion to high office, ᶜĀlī goes so far as to declare the pivotal Ottoman institution *devşirme* "at variance with the Divine Law" (*şerᶜe muġāyır*).[40] Writing in 1596, just before Meḥmed III's (r. 1595–1603) Egri campaign, Ḥasan Kāfī el-Aḳḥiṣārī (d. 1616), a member of the religious establishment (*ᶜulemāʾ*) and a judge (*ḳāḍī*), comments on the sedition and destruction effecting the order of Ottoman society (*ᶜālemüŋ niẓāmında fesād ve bozġunluḳ*). He highlights as causes of the frequent setbacks suffered on the battlefield the technological inferiority of Ottoman armies vis-à-vis their enemies and the lack of discipline among Ottoman soldiers.[41] Aḳḥiṣārī also assigns blame for the "oppression and tyranny" (*ẓulüm ve taᶜaddī*) that imperial subjects suffered in the Anatolian provinces to the slave-servants of the Ottoman sultan (*ḫünkār ḳulı*) stationed in these provinces. He ultimately states that this was the reason why "God Almighty sent enemies to attack the [empire's] Rumelian frontiers."[42] One more example gives writing in 1608 Veysī (d. 1628), a prolific poet and prose writer who served the Ottoman polity as a judge (*ḳāḍī*), who complains about unruly and disobedient *ḳul*s of the Ottoman dynasty by using Sultan Aḥmed I (r. 1603–1617) as his mouthpiece: "If the *ḳul*, my *ḳul*, does not submit to me and obey my orders, how can I protect the tax-paying subjects

---

39 Luṭfī, *Āṣafnāme*, 245: "vezīr-i aᶜẓam olan *ḳul* ṭāʾifesine müdebbir ve żābıṭ kimesneleri aġa . . . itmek gerekdür."

40 Muṣṭafā ᶜĀlī, *Nuṣḥatü's-selāṭīn*, 2:30 (translation), 148 (transcription). ᶜĀlī continued to state that the method of *devşirme* "was only adopted in the past out of need as a means to increase the number of Muslims."

41 See Ḥasan Kāfī, *Uṣūlü'l-ḥikem*, especially 267–75. Egri: Hungarian Eger; German Erlau.

42 Ḥasan Kāfī, *Uṣūlü'l-ḥikem*, 275.

(*reᶜāyā*) with the sword of justice and equity, and control and govern the realm?"[43]

As these examples indicate that numerous Muslim-born *naṣīḥatnāme* authors, especially those who were members of the Ottoman religious establishment (*ᶜulemāᵓ*), were critical of the *ḳul*s. This does not mean, however, that Ottoman advice literature represented a monolithic block of anti-*ḳul* writing. On the contrary, textual evidence suggests that advice authors of *devşirme* background expressed sentiments that were critical of the freeborn Muslim "strangers" (*ecnebī*) admitted into their ranks.[44] The anonymous author of *Kitāb-ı müstetāb* (The Pleasant Book, ca. 1620), who apparently entered the *ḳul* establishment as a *devşirme* recruit, identifies the intrusion of foreigners (*ecnebī ḳarışub*) such as "Turkomans, Kurds, Gypsies, Tats, Iranians" (*Etrāk ve Ekrād ve Çingāne ve Tāt ve Aᶜcām*) as the principal factor leading to the breakdown of the Ottoman military organization.[45] Another noteworthy case written from the vantage point of the Christian-born *ḳul* is a treatise entitled *Ḳavānīn-i yeŋiçeriyān* (Laws of the Janissaries). Written during the reign of Aḥmed I by an anonymous veteran-janissary-turned-scribe, *Ḳavānīn* addresses the laws, regulations, and customs that governed the janissary establishment, a central part of the larger *ḳul* system. Written in an era when the abandonment of the practice of the levy of Christian children—coupled with the conscription of Muslim-born "intruders" in their place—led to the gradual disintegration of the traditional hierarchy of the janissary corps, *Ḳavānīn* calls for the restoration of time-honored conventions (*ḳānūn*) and a recruitment system based on merit. In this work, the anonymous ex-janissary complains about "innovations" (*bidᶜat*) that culminated in the weakening of the janissary corps by the first quarter of the seventeenth cen-

43 Veysī, *Ḫābnāme*, 46. For a brief analysis of Veysī's work as a representation of "declinist sensibilities" within the context of early modern Ottoman political consciousness, see Şen, "A Mirror for Princes, a Fiction for Readers," especially 46–48.

44 For an analysis of the nature and extent of the conflict resulting from the admission of Muslim (Turkish) subjects (*reᶜāyā*) to the privileged and exclusive community of the *ḳul*s or the ranks of the fief-holders, see Káldy-Nagy, "The 'Strangers' (*Ecnebiler*) in the 16th Century Ottoman Military Organization."

45 See Anonymous, *Kitāb-ı müstetāb*, 4. For the problem of the expansion of the ranks of Palace *ḳul*s by "eastern foreigners," see Fleischer, *Bureaucrat and Intellectual in the Ottoman Empire*, 154–59. On the identifier "Tat" and its various meanings, see *EI*², s.v. "Tat" (C. E. Bosworth).

tury. More significantly, he loathes the freeborn Muslim "Turks-Murks" (*Türk Mürk*) who joined the ranks of the janissaries contrary to established laws and practices.[46]

These cases suggest that the majority of *naṣīḥatnāme* authors writing in the sixteenth and early seventeenth centuries did not necessarily think highly of statesmen or soldiers of *devşirme* origin (*ḳul ṭāʾifesi*)—unless, of course, they themselves were products of the *devşirme* system. While, on one level, the non-Muslim origins of the sultan's *ḳul*s may have aggravated Muslim-born *naṣīḥatnāme* authors' anti-*ḳul* sentiments, the primary factor that led to these sentiments was the structure of the Ottoman military, administrative, and bureaucratic hierarchy, which was established—at least in theory—in accordance with meritocratic principles that governed Ottoman practices of appointments and promotions.

Most *naṣīḥatnāme* authors were freeborn Muslim madrasa graduates who entered the Ottoman elite as scholars, judges, scribes, or secretaries, hoping to rise to prominence in the Empire's legal, administrative, and bureaucratic hierarchy. Each author's degree of success in achieving his professional and political goals depended on his own efforts and merit as much as his personal connections and patronage networks. As Muslim-born individuals, they competed in particular against members of the Ottoman military ruling elite of *devşirme* origin. They thus voiced their most potent criticisms against *ḳul*s and against Ottoman monarchs who employed pro-*ḳul* recruitment strategies, thereby significantly restricting opportunities for freeborn Muslims to be promoted to bureaucratic and administrative high offices.

THE CASE OF THE MERDÜMZA-DE

Authors of advice works were not the only Ottoman men of letters with a *ḳul*-critical attitude. Beginning from the second half of the sixteenth century, when a critical historical consciousness of "decline" began to emerge in Ottoman learned circles, a number of other authors hailing from a freeborn Muslim background articulated remarkably similar anti-*ḳul* sentiments in works composed in a variety of genres.

Muṣṭafā ʿĀlī's aforementioned criticisms, directed at some of the sultan's slave-servants, were akin to those expressed by Celālzāde

46 Anonymous, *Ḳavānīn-i yeŋiçeriyān*, 16a.

Muṣṭafā Çelebi (d. 1567), a prominent Muslim-born bureaucrat and historian of the Süleymānic age. Celālzāde Muṣṭafā's *ḳul*-critical statements constitute part of his discussion of the commendable qualities of *merdümzādes*, whom the author portrays as accomplished and worthy Muslims of common or noble descent from Anatolia and Rumelia.[47] Celālzāde's references to *merdümzādes* appear in his (quite possibly apocryphal) account of a speech delivered by Selīm I (r. 1512–1520) as recorded in *Meʾāṡir-i Selīm Ḫānī* (Illustrious Acts of Selīm Khan). Composed in the *Shāhnāma* style, *Meʾāṡir* is not part of Ottoman advice literature. Yet, Celālzāde's rendering of Selīm's speech is highly relevant for the purposes of this essay, since it focuses primarily on Bāyezīd II's failure to appoint qualified statesmen to the upper echelons of the imperial administration:

> The meritless ones, the plunderers, and those who covet wealth and possessions at my father's threshold idolize presents and worship them. They are addicted to calamities. I heard that, since my great ancestors disregarded the promotion of *merdümzādes* and brave and distinguished champions and celebrated heroes who had been serving our threshold for ages, [since] they always favored *ḳuls* and did not appoint anyone other than *ḳuls* to high offices, brave members of the people of our province and country were inclined toward joining the Ḳızılbaş and attending their threshold. That is why I chose to raid (*aḳın*) the Georgian lands and that is why I summoned you. My benevolent gaze is upon your kind. Since the days of our grandfathers the advice given to us has been that our true servants at our threshold are our companions who faithfully risk their lives to accompany us in battle and to serve us. Exalted offices and valuable fiefs belong to them. If the praised and exalted God bestows the sultanate upon me, my benevolent gaze will be upon *merdümzādes*. The grace of my kindness is upon brave and distinguished champions who deal out blows with their swords. Our *ḳuls* are our true servants and it is necessary to promote those among them who are pious and virtuous Muslims. Promoting incapable, miserly and lowly ones just

47 On the life and oeuvre of Celālzāde Muṣṭafā, who served the Ottoman polity as chief chancellor (*nişāncı*) between 1534 and 1557, see Şahin, *Empire and Power in the Reign of Süleyman*. For a discussion of the concept of *merdümzāde* and its significance, see Çıpa, "The Centrality of the Periphery," 156–63.

> because they are *ḳul*s, however, is unbecoming of a sultan. It is not permissible to neglect *merdümzādes*. God willing, that is my firm intention.[48]

Selīm's address, as rendered by Celālzāde, is laced with acerbic criticism of Bāyezīd II's strategy of assigning high offices only to those members of the Ottoman military ruling elite of *devşirme* origin (*ḳul ṭāʾifesi*). Perfectly in line with a variety of *ḳul*-critical sentiments that were voiced in Ottoman works of advice and other historical narratives from the mid-fifteenth century onward, its principal argument is that an exclusively pro-*ḳul* recruitment strategy bore detrimental consequences for the House of ʿOs̱mān, both at home and abroad. What should be highlighted here, however, is the atypical terminology Celālzāde employs to refer to Selīm's target audience as *merdümzāde*s.

The general tenor of the narrative suggests that *merdümzāde*s belonged to a social category whose members were marginalized by Bāyezīd II's pro-*ḳul* policies. Indeed, at first glance, *merdümzāde*s and *ḳul*s appear to be mutually exclusive social groups.[49] Further references in *Meʾās̱ir*, however, indicate that Celālzāde simultaneously imagined two categorical distinctions. The first, horizontal distinction was based on pedigree, which could be defined by an individual's ethnic, social, or religious identity, noble descent, *devşirme* origin, or even the duration of his "tenure" in Islam.[50] The second, vertical distinction was based on merit and qualification. It was in respect to this second distinction that Celālzāde defined the social category of *merdümzāde*, which included Ottoman subjects of diverse backgrounds, even *ḳul*s, as long as they were "absolutely worthy and deserving."

---

48 Celālzāde, *Meʾās̱ir*, 54b–55a.

49 All three references to *merdümzāde*s are either preceded or followed by the mention of *ḳul*s, and Selīm's praise for the former is always coupled with criticism of the latter.

50 For a discussion of what Tijana Krstić calls "one-upmanship in religion" as an important facet of Ottoman political life in the sixteenth century, see Krstić, "Conversion and Converts to Islam in Ottoman Historiography," 70–71. On the significance of the ethnic and geographical origins of members of the Ottoman ruling elite as a source of socio-political cohesion, see Kunt, "Ethnic-Regional (*Cins*) Solidarity."

CONCLUSION

The resentment of the advancement of individuals considered "outsiders" already constituted an integral component of intra-elite competition within the highest echelons of the Ottoman military–administrative structure—and at the imperial court—by the time *naṣīḥatnāme* authors composed their works. As the aforementioned anonymous couplets composed during the reign of Meḥmed II suggest, these foreign elements included, among others, Jews, Franks, and Persians. The principal focus of dislike and resentment for most sixteenth- and seventeenth-century Ottoman authors, however, was the Christian-born *ḳul*.

This resentment is particularly, though not exclusively, visible in Ottoman works of advice composed in an era when a consciousness of "decline" emerged among the intelligentsia. This anti-*ḳul* sentiment did not lead to an argument for the categorical exclusion of *ḳul*s from government offices, however. Instead, this alterophobic language was often instrumentalized to express grievances regarding employment and promotion, to reject the privileged status of the *ḳul*s, and to call for meritocratic principles to govern all appointments and advancements within the administrative–bureaucratic hierarchy of the Ottoman polity. In other words, in most works written by Muslim-born authors, the articulation of *ḳul*-critical sentiments served as a key component of an overarching argument regarding the Ottoman variety of early modern empire-building. Despite the occasional use of anti-infidel rhetoric, statements critical of *ḳul*s more often than not acted as code for a presentist political argument in favor of meritocratic recruitment, appointment, or promotion in Ottoman imperial hierarchy.

BIBLIOGRAPHY

Sources

Anonymous. *Ḳavānīn-i yeŋiçeriyān*. Edited and transliterated by Tayfun Toroser. In *Kavanin-i Yeniçeriyan: Yeniçeri Kanunları*. Istanbul: Türkiye İş Bankası Kültür Yayınları, 2011.

Anonymous. *Kitāb-ı müstetāb*. Edited and transliterated by Yaşar Yücel. In *Osmanlı Devlet Teşkilâtına Dair Kaynaklar*, Part I. Ankara: Türk Tarih Kurumu Basımevi, 1988.

ᶜĀşıḳpaşazāde [Dervīş Aḥmed]. *Menāḳıb ü tevārīḫ-i āl-i ᶜOs̱mān*. (1) Edited and transliterated by Kemal Yavuz and M. A. Yekta Saraç, 319–586. In *Aşık Paşazade: Osmanoğulları'nın Tarihi*. Istanbul: K Kitaplığı, 2003. (2) Edited by ᶜAlī Bey.

In *Tevārīḫ-i Āl-i ᶜOs̱mān'dan ᶜĀşıḳpaşazāde Tārīḫi*. Istanbul: Maṭbaᶜa-i Āmire, 1332/1914.

Celālzāde Muṣṭafā. *Me'āṣir-i Selīm Ḫānī* (or *Selīmnāme*). Edited and transliterated by Ahmet Uğur and Mustafa Çuhadar. In *Selim-nâme*. Ankara: Kültür Bakanlığı, 1990.

Harsányi Nagy, Jakab. *Colloquia Familiaria Turcico Latina*. Edited by György Hazai. In *Das Osmanisch-Türkische im XVII. Jahrhundert: Untersuchungen an den Transkriptionstexten von Jakab Nagy de Harsány*, 33–199. The Hague: Mouton, 1973.

Ḥasan Kāfī [el-Aḳḥiṣārī]. *Uṣūlü'l-ḥikem fī niẓāmü'l-ᶜālem*. Edited and transliterated by Mehmet İpşirli. In "Hasan Kâfî el-Akhisarî ve Devlet Düzenine Ait Eseri *Usûlü'l-Hikem fî Nizâmi'l-Âlem*." *TED* 10–11 (1979–80): 239–78.

Ḳānūnnāme-i āl-i ᶜOs̱mān. Edited and transliterated by Abdülkadir Özcan. In *Fatih Sultan Mehmed: Kânunnâme-i Âl-i Osman (Tahlil ve Karşılaştırmalı Metin)*. Istanbul: Kitabevi, 2003.

Luṭfī Paşa. *Tevārīḫ-i āl-i ᶜOs̱mān*. Edited and transliterated by Kayhan Atik. In *Lütfi Paşa ve Tevârih-i Âl-i Osman*. Ankara: Kültür Bakanlığı, 2001.

Luṭfī Paşa. *Āṣafnāme*. Edited and transliterated by Ahmet Uğur. In *İslam İlimleri Enstitüsü Dergisi* 4 (1980): 243–58.

Mevlānā ᶜĪsā. *Cāmiᶜü'l-meknūnāt*. Leiden University Library, Or. 1448.

Muṣṭafā ᶜĀlī. *Nuṣḥatü's-selāṭīn*. Edited and translated by Andreas Tietze. In *Muṣṭafā ᶜĀlī's Counsel for Sultans of 1581*. 2 vols. Vienna: Verlag der Österreichischen Akademie der Wissenschaften, 1982.

Ṭaᶜlīḳīzāde Meḥmed. *Şehnāme-i Hümāyūn*. Transliterated and edited by Christine Woodhead as *Şehnāme-i Hümāyūn: A History of the Ottoman Campaign into Hungary, 1593–94*. Berlin: Klaus Schwartz, 1983.

Ṭursun Beg. *Tārīḫ-i ebū'l-fetḥ*. (1) Facsimile edition and summary English translation by Halil Inalcık and Rhoads Murphey. In *The History of Mehmed the Conqueror*. Minneapolis and Chicago: Bibliotheca Islamica, 1978. (2) Edited and transliterated by Mertol Tulum. In *Târîh-i Ebü'l-Feth*. Istanbul: Baha Matbaası, 1977.

Veysī [Üveys b. Meḥmed]. *Ḫābnāme*. Edited and transliterated by Mustafa Altun. In *Hâb-nâme-i Veysî*. Istanbul: MVT Yayıncılık, 2011.

Studies

Babinger, Franz. *Mehmed the Conqueror and His Time*. Revised edition of *Mehmed der Eroberer und seine Zeit* (Munich: F. Bruckmann, 1953) by William C. Hickman, translated by Ralph Manheim. Princeton: Princeton University Press, 1978.

Barkan, Ömer Lütfi. "Osmanlı İmparatorluğunda Bir İskân ve Kolonizasyon Metodu Olarak Vakıflar ve Temlikler I: İstilâ Devirlerinin Kolonizatör Türk Dervişleri ve Zâviyeler." *Vakıflar Dergisi* 2 (1942): 279–386.

Barkey, Karen. *Empire of Difference: The Ottomans in Comparative Perspective*. Cambridge: Cambridge University Press, 2008.

Beldiceanu, Nicoara. "Recherches sur la réforme foncière de Mehmed II." *Acta Historica* 4 (1965): 27–39.

Çıpa, H. Erdem. "The Centrality of the Periphery: The Rise to Power of Selīm I, 1487–1512." Ph.D. diss., Harvard University, 2007.

Çiçek, Kemal, ed. *Pax Ottomana: Studies in Memoriam Prof. Nejat Göyünç*. Ankara: Yeni Türkiye, 2001.

Eligür, Banu. *The Mobilization of Political Islam in Turkey*. New York: Cambridge University Press, 2010.

Erdem, Hakan. *Slavery in the Ottoman Empire and its Demise, 1800–1909*. New York: St. Martin's Press, 1996.

Fleischer, Cornell. "Of Gender and Servitude, ca. 1520: Two Petitions of the Kul Kızı of Bergama to Sultan Süleyman." In *Mélanges en l'Honneur du Prof. Dr. Suraiya Faroqhi*, edited by Abdeljelil Temimi, 143–51. Tunis: Fondation Temimi pour la Recherche Scientifique et l'Information, 2009.

Fleischer, Cornell. "From Şeyhzade Korkud to Mustafa Âli: Cultural Origins of the Ottoman *Nasihatname*." In *Third Congress on the Social and Economic History of Turkey*, edited by Heath W. Lowry and Ralph S. Hattox, 67–77. Istanbul: The Isis Press, 1990.

Fleischer, Cornell. *Bureaucrat and Intellectual in the Ottoman Empire: The Historian Mustafa Âli (1541–1600)*. Princeton: Princeton University Press, 1986.

Fodor, Pál. "State and Society, Crisis and Reform, in 15th–17th Century Ottoman Mirror for Princes." *Acta Orientalia Academiae Scientiarum Hungaricae* 40, no. 2–3 (1986): 217–40.

Hagen, Gottfried. "Legitimacy and World Order." In *Legitimizing the Order: The Ottoman Rhetoric of State Power*, edited by Hakan Karateke and Maurus Reinkowski, 55–83. Leiden: Brill, 2005.

Howard, Douglas A. "Genre and Myth in the Ottoman Advice for Kings Literature." In *The Early Modern Ottomans: Remapping the Empire*, edited by Virginia H. Aksan and Daniel Goffman, 137–66. Cambridge: Cambridge University Press, 2007.

Howard, Douglas A. "Ottoman Historiography and the Literature of "Decline" of the Sixteenth and Seventeenth Centuries." *Journal of Asian History* 22, no. 1 (1988): 52–77.

Imber, Colin. "'An Illiberal Descent': Kemalism and Ottoman Law." In *Warfare, Law and Pseudo-History*, 173–200. Istanbul: The ISIS Press, 2011.

İnalcık, Halil. "The Policy of Mehmed II toward the Greek Population of Istanbul and the Byzantine Buildings of the City." *Dumbarton Oaks Papers* 23 (1969–70): 229–49.

Kafadar, Cemal. "A Rome of One's Own: Reflections on Cultural Geography and Identity in the Lands of Rum." *Muqarnas* 24 (2007): 7–25.

Kafadar, Cemal. *Between Two Worlds: The Construction of the Ottoman State*. Berkeley: University of California Press, 1995.

Kafadar, Cemal. "The Ottomans and Europe." In *Handbook of European History, 1400–1600: Late Middle Ages, Renaissance, and Reformation*, edited by Thomas

A. Brady, Heiko A. Oberman, and James D. Tracy, vol. 1, *Structures and Assertions*, 589–635. Brill: Leiden, 1994.

Kafadar, Cemal. "The Myth of the Golden Age: Ottoman Historical Consciousness in the Post-Süleymânic Era." In *Süleymân the Second and His Time*, edited by Halil Inalcık and Cemal Kafadar, 37–48. Istanbul: Isis Press, 1993.

Káldy-Nagy, Gyula. "The 'Strangers' (*Ecnebiler*) in the 16th Century Ottoman Military Organization." In *Between the Danube and the Caucasus*, edited by György Kara, 165–69. Budapest: Akadémiai Kiadó, 1987.

Kármán, Gábor. *A Seventeenth-Century Odyssey in East Central Europe: The Life of Jakab Harsányi Nagy*. Leiden: Brill, 2016.

Krstić, Tijana. "Conversion and Converts to Islam in Ottoman Historiography of the Fifteenth and Sixteenth Centuries." In *Writing History at the Ottoman Court: Editing the Past, Fashioning the Future*, edited by H. Erdem Çıpa and Emine Fetvacı, 58–79. Bloomington: Indiana University Press, 2013.

Krstić, Tijana. *Contested Conversions to Islam: Narratives of Religious Change in the Early Modern Ottoman Empire*. Stanford: Stanford University Press, 2011.

Kunt, İ. Metin. *The Sultan's Servants: The Transformation of Ottoman Provincial Government, 1550–1650*. New York: Columbia University Press, 1983.

Kunt, İ. Metin. "Ethnic-Regional (*Cins*) Solidarity in the Seventeenth-Century Ottoman Establishment." *International Journal of Middle East Studies* 5, no. 3 (1974): 233–39.

Levend, Agâh Sırrı. "Siyaset-nameler." *Türk Dili Araştırmaları Yıllığı: Belleten* (1963): 167–94.

Lewis, Bernard. "Ottoman Observers of Ottoman Decline." *Islamic Studies* 1, no. 1 (1962): 71–87.

Lewis, Bernard. "Some Reflections on the Decline of the Ottoman Empire." *Studia Islamica Studies* 9 (1958): 111–27.

Ménage, Victor L. "Some Notes on the *Devshirme*." *Bulletin of the School of Oriental and African Studies* 29, no. 1 (1966): 64–78.

Ménage, Victor L. "Seven Ottoman Documents from the Reign of Meḥemmed II." In *Documents from Islamic Chanceries*, edited by S. M. Stern, 81–118. Cambridge: Harvard University Press, 1965.

Ménage, Victor L. "Sidelights on the *Devshirme* from Idrīs and Saᶜduddīn." *Bulletin of the School of Oriental and African Studies* 18, no. 1 (1956): 181–83.

Minkov, Anton. *Conversion to Islam in the Balkans:* Kisve Bahasi *Petitions and Ottoman Social Life, 1670–1730*. Leiden: Brill, 2004.

Necipoğlu, Gülru. *The Age of Sinan: Architectural Culture in the Ottoman Empire*. London: Reaktion, 2005.

Ortaylı, İlber. *Osmanlı Barışı*. Istanbul: Timaş Yayınları, 2007.

Özcan, Abdülkadir. "Fâtih'in Teşkilât Kanunnâmesi ve Nizam-ı Alem İçin Kardeş Katli Meselesi." *TD* 33 (1980–81): 7–56.

Palmer, J. A. B. "The Origin of the Janissaries." *Bulletin of the John Rylands Library* 35, no. 1 (1952): 448–81.

Piterberg, Gabriel. *An Ottoman Tragedy: History and Historiography at Play*. Berkeley: University of California Press, 2003.

Raby, Julian. "A Sultan of Paradox: Mehmed the Conqueror as a Patron of the Arts." *Oxford Art Journal* 5, no. 1 (1982): 3–8.

Rogers, J. M. "Mehmed the Conqueror: Between East and West." In *Bellini and the East*, edited by Caroline Campbell and Alan Chong, 80–97. London: National Gallery Company, 2005.

Sariyannis, Marinos. "The Princely Virtues as Presented in Ottoman Political and Moral Literature." *Turcica* 43 (2011): 121–44.

Sariyannis, Marinos. "Ottoman Critics of Society and State, Fifteenth to Early Eighteenth Centuries: Toward a Corpus for the Study of Ottoman Political Thought." *Archivum Ottomanicum* 25 (2008): 127–50.

Şahin, İ. Kaya. *Empire and Power in the Reign of Süleyman: Narrating the Sixteenth-Century Ottoman World*. New York: Cambridge University Press, 2013.

Schmidt, Jan. *Pure Water for Thirsty Muslims: A Study of Muṣṭafā ᶜĀlī of Gallipoli's* Künhü l-Aḫbār. Leiden: Het Oosters Instituut, 1991.

Şen, Ahmet Tunç. "A Mirror for Princes, a Fiction for Readers: The *Habnâme* of Veysī and Dream Narratives in Ottoman Turkish Literature." *Journal Turkish Literature* 8 (2011): 417–65.

Al-Tikriti, Nabil. "Şehzade Korkud (ca. 1468–1513) and the Articulation of Early 16th Century Ottoman Religious Identity." Ph.D. diss., The University of Chicago, 2004.

Toledano, Ehud R. *Slavery and Abolition in the Ottoman Middle East*. Seattle: University of Washington Press, 1998.

Uğur, Ahmet. *Osmanlı Siyâset-nâmeleri*. Kayseri: Kültür ve Sanat Yayınları, 1987.

Ünver, Süheyl. *İstanbul Üniversitesi Tarihine Başlangıç: Fatih, Külliyesi ve Zamanı İlim Hayatı*. Istanbul: İstanbul Üniversitesi Yayınları, 1946.

Wittek, Paul. "*Devshirme* and *Sharīᶜa*." *Bulletin of the School of Oriental and African Studies* 17, no. 2 (1955): 271–78.

Yerasimos, Stéphane. *La fondation de Constantinople et de Sainte-Sophie dans les traditions turques: Légendes d'Empire*. Istanbul: Institut français d'études anatoliennes, 1990.

Circassian Mamluks in Ottoman Egypt and Istanbul, ca. 1500–1730: The Eastern Alternative

Jane Hathaway

This essay traces the Ottoman encounter with the northern Caucasian population known as the Circassians (*Çerkes* in Turkish, *Jarkas* in Arabic), whose ancestral territory today lies mainly in southern Russia, on the northeastern shores of the Black Sea. During the early period of Ottoman expansion—the fourteenth and early fifteenth centuries—the Ottomans viewed the Circassians primarily as the chief pool of man- (and woman-) power for the late Mamluk Sultanate, which at the time ruled Egypt, Syria, the Hijaz, and southeastern Anatolia. After the Ottoman conquest of the Mamluk Sultanate in 1516–17, however, the Circassians and other peoples of the Caucasus gradually began to enter Ottoman territory as (both male and female) elite slaves (*mamlūks*). The prevailing reason for this influx was that Circassians offered a clear alternative to Balkan and Anatolian Greek personnel recruited through the *devşirme*, the "classical" Ottoman method of collecting Christian boys from the empire's provinces, converting them to Islam, and training them as either palace pages or janissaries. By the early eighteenth century, Circassians had become common elements in the Ottoman military–administrative hierarchy.

My study traces the diachronic evolution of Ottoman perceptions of Circassians. I attach particular importance to the ways in which these perceptions manifested themselves in Egypt, the seat of the Mamluk Sultanate and a site of especially heavy Circassian concentration under Ottoman rule. Shifts in attitude, it becomes clear, correspond to the changing nature of contact between Ottoman administrators and intellectuals, on the one hand, and Circassian elite slaves, on the other. We can identify three chief attitudinal phases between roughly 1500 and 1730. First, during the Ottoman confrontation with the Mamluk Sultanate, the Ottoman attitude toward Circassians was one of abhorrence, as the Mamluks represented a geopolitical rival who had sided with the Twelver Shiᶜite Safavids. Next, during the seventeenth century, as increasing numbers of Circassians and other Caucasian peoples entered Ottoman service as *mamlūks*, they began to compete with populations from the Balkans and Anatolia for key administrative positions, leading to what Metin Kunt has described as the "east–west" antagonism between the two population groups.[1] At the same time, Ottoman observers of Circassians in their native land, above all the well-known traveler Evliyā Çelebī, evinced a sort of ethnographic curiosity combined with a degree of shock at the Circassians' unfamiliar customs. By the early decades of the eighteenth century, finally, Circassians were one of numerous ethno-regional groups co-existing and even cooperating, rather than struggling for dominance, in the Ottoman Empire's military and administrative circles. In these less highly-charged circumstances, special mention of their ethnicity became rare in archival and narrative sources. Over the course of two centuries, then, loathing and alarm gave way to competition, then acceptance.

EARLY ENCOUNTERS WITH CIRCASSIANS: THE OTTOMAN–MAMLUK WARS

The Ottomans' first sustained encounters with *mamlūks* from the Caucasus, and from Circassia more specifically, came in the fifteenth century, when Sultan Bāyezīd II (r. 1481–1512) engaged in a series of rather inconclusive wars against the Mamluk sultan Qāytbāy (r. 1468–1496) in southeastern Anatolia, the contested border region between the Mamluk

1 Kunt, "Ethnic-Regional (*Cins*) Solidarity," 233–39.

domains and the expanding Ottoman Empire.[2] Following Selīm I's (r. 1512–1520) crushing 1514 defeat of the Shiᶜite Safavids, under their charismatic leader Shāh Ismāᶜīl (r. 1501–1524), at Çaldıran in far eastern Anatolia, the Mamluk sultan Qānṣūh al-Ghūrī (r. 1501–1516) reached an agreement with Shāh Ismāᶜīl to deploy an army to the Mamluk frontier in northern Syria in the event of further Ottoman aggression in the region.[3] Two years later, in 1516–17, Selīm, no doubt as a partial consequence of the Mamluk–Safavid defense pact, conquered Syria, Egypt, and the Hijaz, bringing the Mamluk Sultanate to an end.

To the hostility with which Ottoman intellectuals had regarded the Mamluks—as the tenacious antagonists of the Ottoman–Mamluk wars—during Bayezīd II's reign was now added a visceral abhorrence of a Sunnī Muslim regime willing to make common cause with the heretical Safavids against the Ottomans, their fellow Sunnīs. Nonetheless, Ottoman propaganda against the Mamluks during and immediately after Selīm's conquests—as reflected in *fetḥnāmes*, or celebratory conquest narratives; *Selīmnāmes*, or panegyric accounts of Selīm I's exploits; and early chronicles of Ottoman Egypt—focuses not on the Mamluks' religious proclivities but on their Circassian ethnicity, which these sources uniformly deride, as if the Circassians as a people were somehow inherently treacherous and untrustworthy. Ottoman chroniclers of the conquest of the Mamluk Sultanate never fail to modify the noun Çerkes ("Circassian") with the adjective *nākis* ("loathsome" or "vile"), except on those occasions when they substitute "treasonous" (*hāʾin*) or "devil" (*şeytān*) for "loathsome."[4] Meanwhile, they deride the Mamluk sultans as "slaves and sons of slaves," in contrast to Selīm, "sultan, son of sultan, son of sultan."[5]

A particularly visceral example of this anti-Circassian bias is the chronicler Keşfī Meḥmed Çelebī's description of the famous episode in which the Mamluk sultan Qānṣūh al-Ghūrī suffers an apoplectic fit

---

2 Petry, *Twilight of Majesty*, 88–103.

3 Holt, *Egypt and the Fertile Crescent*, 37.

4 Keşfī Meḥmed, *Selīmnāme*, 71a; and Celālzāde Muṣṭafā, *Selīmnāme*, 426.

5 Hathaway, "The *Evlād-i ᶜArab* ('Sons of the Arabs') in Ottoman Egypt," 209n29. The nineteenth-century British traveler George Ditson claims that the word "Çerkes" is a Tatar (i.e., Mongol) word meaning "highwayman" (Ditson, *Circassia,* 408n). Jaimoukha (*The Circassians*, 12) offers the alternative explanation of a Turkic corruption of the Greek word "Kerxetai." The Circassians' self-designation is "Adyghe" (Jaimoukha, *The Circassians*, 11–12).

and dies on the battlefield at Marj Dābiq, near Aleppo, in August 1516. The chronicler gloats over the spectacle of "the head of the loathsome Circassian under the hooves of his horse like an Abū Jahl watermelon" (*Çerkes-i nākis başı at ayağı altında Ebū Cehl ḳarpuzı gibi*).[6] As if "loathsome Circassian" were not enough of an insult, he compares the defeated al-Ghūrī to Abū Jahl ("the father of ignorance"), aka ᶜAmr ibn Hishām, a Meccan polytheist and an archenemy of the Prophet Muḥammad who was killed at the battle of Badr in 624 CE. The implication is clear: through their alliance of convenience with the Safavids, the "loathsome Circassians" have become enemies of Islam.

AFTER THE OTTOMAN CONQUEST OF THE MAMLUK SULTANATE

Following his conquest of the Mamluk Sultanate, Selīm I allowed members of the defeated Mamluk administration who swore allegiance to him to join the new Ottoman regime in Egypt and Syria.[7] Nonetheless, this magnanimous gesture did little to dispel antipathy toward the Mamluks, often expressed in narrative sources as anti-Circassian bias, which pervaded the administration of Ottoman Egypt in the years immediately following the conquest. The historian ᶜAbdullāh Çelebī Rıḍvān Paşazāde, recounting the events of 928/1522, mentions a former Mamluk *emīr*, Yaḥya İnāl, who served the Ottoman administration as a district governor, or *kāshif*; he tried to withhold revenue from the provincial treasury but was caught by the Ottoman governor of Egypt. Five years after the conquest, he was still considered *nākis-i Çerākise* ("one of the loathsome Circassians").[8] Even Khayrbāy, the Mamluk governor of Aleppo whose defection to Selīm at Marj Dābiq made the Ottoman victory possible, is described by the well-known late sixteenth-century Ottoman intellectual Muṣṭafā ᶜĀlī as an exception to the rule of Circassian treachery (although,

6 Keşfī Meḥmed, *Selīmnāme*, 78a; see also 68b; see also Süheylī Efendi, *Tevārīh-i Mıṣīr* [sic], 81a.

7 A number of historians have argued—erroneously, in my view—that Selīm's magnanimity paved the way for the continuation, or at least revival, of "the Mamluk system" in Egypt. See, for example, Ayalon, "The End of the Mamlūk Sultanate," 125–48; Holt, *Egypt and the Fertile Crescent*, 41–45, 71–73; and Winter, *Egyptian Society under Ottoman Rule*, 7–9, 47–54.

8 Rıḍvān Paşazāde, *Tārīh-i Mıṣır*, 128a.

of course, he betrayed Qānṣūh al-Ghūrī). When Khayrbāy, whom Selīm had made the first governor of Egypt under Ottoman rule, remitted the province's revenue to Istanbul in full, the sultan exclaimed, "Bravo, Circassian! You are not even that loathsome!" (*Āferīn bre Çerkes! Hele ḳaṭıᶜ nākis degil imişsin!*)[9]—a back-handed compliment with ethnic undertones.

Under Süleymān I (r. 1520–1566), the Ottomans took measures to incorporate the former Mamluk territories—not only Egypt but also Syria and southeastern Anatolia—firmly into the imperial administration and, in the process, to eliminate, or at least drastically reduce, surviving Mamluk usages.[10] In Egypt, Süleymān's grand vizier and personal confidant, Ibrāhīm Pasha, in 1525 implemented the *Ḳānūnnāme-i Mıṣır*, which specified the terms under which six regiments of Ottoman soldiery were to garrison the province and forbade the *mamlūk*s to take Circassian names resembling those of the *emīr*s of the defunct sultanate.[11] Later in the sixteenth century, additional administrative measures seemed designed to prevent any Mamluk revival.[12] A seventh regiment, the *müteferriḳa*, was introduced in 1554; essentially a mirror of the imperial *müteferriḳa* based in Topḳapı Palace, this was a combined infantry and cavalry unit attached to the governor's council (*dīvān*) and staffed with elite members of the palace soldiery and their sons. Before the eighteenth century, it was larger than any other regiment save the janissaries; its members commanded the highest salaries and enjoyed distinctive privileges.[13] In 1564, furthermore, an imperial decree stipulated that only members of the *müteferriḳa* regiment and the Çavuşān regiment—like the *müteferriḳa*, an elite regiment attached to the governor's *dīvān*—could be promoted to the rank of *ṣancaḳ beyi*, which in Egypt meant a sub-provincial gover-

9 Muṣṭafā ᶜAlī, *Muṣṭafā ᶜAlī's Description of Cairo of 1599*, 69, 70, 157. I have modified the orthography slightly. Andreas Tietze's translation (page 70) reads, "You are not even that stingy," but, given the resonance of *nākis* in other contexts, I think "loathsome" is more appropriate.

10 Hathaway, *The Politics of Households in Ottoman Egypt*, 8–11; Hathaway, *A Tale of Two Factions*, 3–4; and Hathaway, *The Arab Lands under Ottoman Rule*, 48–52. See also Peirce, *Morality Tales*, 27–36.

11 For the text of the *Ḳānūnāme*, see Barkan, "Mıṣır Ḳānūnnāmesi."

12 See note 7.

13 Hathaway, *The Politics of Households in Ottoman Egypt*, 11; and Shaw, *The Financial and Administrative Organization and Development of Ottoman Egypt*, 192–94.

nor or the holder of the office of pilgrimage commander (*emīrü'l-ḥacc*) or chief financial officer (*defterdār*).[14] This measure seemed designed to ensure that Egypt's beys, to say nothing of its highest regimental officers, would be largely products of the imperial palace—that is to say, they would belong to the population of "sultan's servants" known as *ḳul*s, who were overwhelmingly *devşirme* recruits from the Balkans and western Anatolia. Thus a resurgence of Circassian dominance would be prevented.

A SOLUTION WORSE THAN THE CIRCASSIAN PROBLEM: THE *ḲULS*

In attempting to solve the Circassian problem, however, the Ottoman central authority created a *ḳul* problem in Egypt. Sultanic orders to the governor of Egypt from the second half of the sixteenth century indicate the emergence of a new military–administrative elite in the province, with roots among the palace *ḳul*s. It was apparently common during these years for members of the imperial *müteferriḳa* to become beys in Egypt. One such individual was even a client of Sultan Süleymān's son, Prince Muṣṭafā, who was promoted to the rank of *ṣancaḳ beyi* after Muṣṭafā's execution, on the sultan's orders, in 1553. During that same year, the son of a member of Egypt's *müteferriḳa* regiment was promoted to imperial *silāḥdār*, or weapons-bearer, at the request of the future sultan, Selīm II (r. 1566–1574).[15] The great Ottoman naval commander Pīrī Reʾīs, it appears, assigned his own son Meḥmed to Egypt's *müteferriḳa* corps; on Pīrī's execution in 1555, Meḥmed replaced his father's *kethüdā*, or lieutenant, as commander (*reʾīs*) of the *müteferriḳa*.[16] In 1559, a different Pīrī, who had been a *ṣancaḳ beyi* in Yemen, joined Egypt's *müteferriḳa* at the request of Egypt's governor.[17] The sons or clients of governors of Egypt and Yemen might also be appointed beys or assigned places in Egypt's *müteferriḳa*

14 BOA, Mühimme Defteri (hereafter "MD") 6, no. 487 (Cemāziyülevvel 972/December 1564); BOA, MD 29, no. 9 (18 Cemāziyülevvel 984/13 August 1576); and Hathaway, *The Politics of Households in Ottoman Egypt*, 11.

15 BOA, MD 1, no. 1667 (962/1555); BOA, MD 2, no. 612 (17 Cemāziyülāḫir 963/28 April 1556); BOA, MD 2, no. 955 (6 Şaʿbān 963/15 June 1556); and BOA, MD 2, no. 1042 (20 Şaʿbān 963/29 June 1556).

16 BOA, MD 2, no. 2038 (7 Cemāziyülevvel 964/8 March 1557); see also *EI*², s.v. "Pīrī Reʾīs b. Ḥādjdjī Meḥmed" (S. Soucek).

17 BOA, MD 4, no. 380 (26 Receb 967/22 April 1560).

corps—or even placed among the imperial *müteferriḳa*.[18] Members of Egypt's *müteferriḳa* could acquire their own *ḳul*s, whom they could then place in other regiments.[19] The few Egyptian beys identified by name in the mid- to late sixteenth century, such as Pīrī and ᶜO̱smān Beys, must have come from such elite backgrounds.

This situation implies that a critical mass of *ḳul*s from the Balkans, Hungary, and Anatolia; their families; and their clients had established themselves in Egypt, displacing the previous critical mass of Circassians. By the early years of the seventeenth century, this population of *ḳul*s was regarded as a source of oppression and unrest. Both the early seventeenth-century Ottoman court chronicler Muṣṭafā Ṣafī (d. 1616) and the contemporary Egyptian chronicler al-Isḥāqī (d. ca. 1649) bemoan the brutal exactions of Pervīz "Mācār" ("the Hungarian"), *kāshif*, or administrator, of the Nile Delta sub-province of Gharbiyya, who was executed in 1609 by the governor Öküz Meḥmed Pasha (d. 1619).[20] In the long term, then, the orders of the mid-sixteenth century, in the course of warding off any attempt to "revive" the Mamluk Sultanate or otherwise establish an autonomous Circassian base of power, created a provincial "*ḳul* problem" that mirrored the situation that had begun to plague the capital.

In Egypt, the "*ḳul* problem" culminated in the murder of the governor Ibrāhīm Pasha in 1604 by disgruntled cavalry troops, seemingly in collusion with the *ṣancaḳ beyi*s, followed by a full-fledged rebellion by the cavalry troops. The above-mentioned governor Öküz Meḥmed Pasha responded brutally, executing the ringleaders of the revolt, banishing the remaining rebels to Yemen, and expelling thirteen of the twenty-four beys from Cairo; consequently, he came to be remembered locally as "Ḳul Ḳıran," or "Breaker of the *Ḳul*s."[21] In Istanbul fifteen years later, *ḳul*s murdered the eighteen-year-old Sultan ᶜO̱smān II (r. 1618–22), who had conceived a plan to supplement the imperial janissaries, at the time

18 BOA, MD 4, no. 644 (4 Şaᶜbān 967/30 April 1560); BOA, MD 4, no. 843 (10 Ramaẓān 967/4 June 1560); BOA, MD 4, no. 1214 (27 Zi'lḳāᶜde 967/19 August 1560); and BOA, MD 25, no. 260 (12 Ramaẓān 981/4 April 1574).

19 BOA, MD 2, no. 905 (21 Receb 963/31 May 1556). See also BOA, MD 4, no. 718 (18 Şaᶜbān 967/14 May 1560), where a *müteferriḳa* described as the "man" (*adam*) of a deceased bey of Egypt is given a *tımār*.

20 Muṣṭafā Ṣafī, *Zübdetü't-tevārīh*, 2:90; and al-Isḥāqī, *Akhbār al-uwal*, 167–68. In the Latin-alphabet transcription of *Zübdetü't-tevārīh*, "Gharbiyya" is erroneously rendered "ᶜAzbiyye."

21 Hathaway, "The '*Mamlūk* Breaker' Who Was Really a *Ḳul* Breaker."

composed largely of *ḳul*s, with an army of mercenaries recruited from Anatolia—and even to move the imperial capital to Bursa, Damascus, or Cairo.[22]

THE CAUCASIAN MAMLŪK ALTERNATIVE TO *ḲULS*

Clearly, the *ḳuls* of *devşirme* origin had spun out of control in both the imperial capital and the Ottoman provinces. In the wake of so much destruction and chaos perpetrated by *devşirme* recruits, Ottoman sultans and provincial grandees alike began to search for alternative sources of manpower. Anatolian mercenaries had proven instrumental to the Ottoman military effort during the Long War (1593–1606) against the Habsburgs. For officers and for palace personnel, however, the sultan, provincial governors, and, increasingly, provincial grandees (such as Egypt's beys) turned to *mamlūk*s from the Caucasus. Already by the late sixteenth century, increasing numbers of palace pages were being recruited from this region, notably from Circassia, Abkhazia, and Georgia.

Ironically, then, the *ḳul* problem led to a reintroduction of *mamlūk*s from Circassia and other regions of the Caucasus. Yet such a development was perhaps to be expected after the Ottoman conquest of the Mamluk Sultanate in 1516–17 and Ottoman successes against the Safavids of Iran in the early decades of the sixteenth century, which gave the Ottomans relatively easy access to the Caucasus, as well as control of the major routes along which Caucasian slaves were traded. In any event, by the 1620s *mamlūk*s from the Caucasus and their sons were emerging as an alternative, and occasionally rival, source of influence to the *ḳul*s within the imperial palace.

Sultan Murād IV (r. 1623–40), younger brother of the murdered Sultan ᶜOs̱mān II, was wary of the *ḳul*s; in fact, he abandoned the *devşirme* in 1635. (Over the next eighty or so years it was employed only very sporadically before being discontinued entirely.) His court featured a number of prominent *mamlūk*s and former *mamlūk*s from the Caucasus, including the future grand vizier Melek Aḥmed Pasha, an Abkhazian; his cousin, an Abkhazian slave who became the mother of the famous traveler Evliyā Çelebī;[23] and a Georgian courtier whose son was appointed governor of Baghdad in 1704 and founded the regime of Georgian *mamlūk*s

22 Piterberg, *An Ottoman Tragedy*, 23–29.
23 Evliyā Çelebī, *The Intimate Life of an Ottoman Statesman*, 3, 9, 49.

that would dominate central and southern Iraq until 1831.[24] Palace-trained *mamlūk*s also figured prominently among the "*celālī*" governors who carved out their own bailiwicks in eastern Anatolia and northern Syria during the seventeenth century and occasionally rebelled against the sultan or his grand vizier. Two of the most notorious were Abāza ("Abkhazian") Meḥmed Pasha, governor of the northeastern Anatolian province of Erzurum in the 1620s, who rebelled in 1623 in protest against the *ḳul*s who had killed ᶜO̱smān II,[25] and Abāza Ḥasan Pasha, governor of Aleppo in the 1650s, who spearheaded a massive rebellion of provincial governors in Anatolia and northern Syria against the reforms of the grand vizier Köprülü Meḥmed Pasha (ironically, Melek Aḥmed Pasha took part in crushing their rebellion).[26]

In Egypt, by the same token, the governors and military commanders, themselves often of *devşirme* origin, increasingly purchased Caucasian *mamlūk*s as personal retainers and clients for their households, often promoting them through the officer ranks of the provincial regiments and ultimately to the post of *ṣancaḳ beyi*. Consequently, between the end of Öküz Meḥmed Pasha's tenure as governor (1607–11) and the 1640s, we find a huge increase in *mamlūk*s from the Caucasus—above all Circassia—among Egypt's beys.

EAST–WEST ANTAGONISM AND FACTIONALISM

The presence in the military-administrative elite of both *mamlūk*s from the Caucasus and *devşirme* recruits from the Balkans and western Anatolia led to ethno-regional antagonism between the two groups. More specifically, this antagonism pitted "easterners" from the Caucasus, eastern Anatolia, and other parts of Asia against "westerners" from the Balkans and western Anatolia. As Metin Kunt has pointed out, this ethno-regional antagonism was particularly acute during the seventeenth century, when the two pools of manpower competed for influence in the palace and in provincial administrations.[27] This brand of tension clearly informed the above-mentioned revolt of

24 *EI*², s.v. "Ḥasan Pasha" (H. Longrigg); and Holt, *Egypt and the Fertile Crescent*, 143–44.

25 Piterberg, *An Ottoman Tragedy*, 29, 165–76; and Piterberg, "The Alleged Rebellion of Abāza Meḥmed Pasha," 13–24.

26 Hathaway, *The Arab Lands under Ottoman Rule*, 76.

27 Kunt, "Ethnic-Regional (*Cins*) Solidarity," 233–39.

Erzurum governor Abāza Meḥmed Pasha in 1623. When he marched on Istanbul, Abāza Meḥmed was joined by the governor of Diyarbakır in southeastern Anatolia; both men were Caucasians who had recruited armies of Anatolian mercenaries that they now deployed against the palace *ḳul*s of *devşirme* origin. By the same token, the massive rebellion led by Abāza Ḥasan Pasha in 1658–59 pitted Caucasian provincial governors against an Albanian grand vizier. Significantly, Köprülü Meḥmed Pasha, before sending Melek Aḥmed Pasha to confront the rebels, inquired as to whether he would be willing to undertake the command, given that the rebel was a fellow Abkhazian.[28]

In Egypt, this east–west antagonism informed the emergence in the 1640s of two military–administrative factions, the Faqārīs and Qāsimīs, whose rivalry would divide the province for nearly a century. The first manifestation of this factionalism appeared in the early 1640s, when two of Egypt's *ṣancaḳ beyi*s, Qānṣūh and Memi (or Mamay), attempted to displace two rivals, Rıḍvān and ᶜAlī, from the posts of pilgrimage commander (*emīrü'l-ḥacc*) and governor of the Upper Egyptian sub-province of Jirja, respectively. While Qānṣūh and Memi were ostensibly Qāsimīs, Rıḍvān and ᶜAlī were ostensibly Faqārīs, although these factional labels were applied to them only in later narrative sources.[29] We know that Rıḍvān was Georgian, but the origins of the other three beys are less certain; it seems likely, however, that Qānṣūh and Memi, at least, were Circassian. In other words, all four beys were probably "easterners;" however, they recruited their armies from different ethno-geographical pools. Whereas Rıḍvān's and ᶜAlī's army consisted of what Turcophone provincial chronicles call *Rūm oğlanı* ("sons of Rūm," referring to the Ottoman central lands), Qānṣūh's and Memi's consisted of *evlād-i ᶜArab*. This term referred not so much to ethnic Arabs as to "locals" from Egypt, as well as Asiatic mercenaries of various kinds, including, possibly, deserters from the Safavid and Shaybānid Uzbek armies.[30] Thus, despite the presence of Caucasians in the leadership stratum of both factions, the Faqārīs' rank and file appears to have consisted largely of "westerners," that of the Qāsimīs of "easterners."

28 Kunt, "Ethnic-Regional (*Cins*) Solidarity," 239.
29 Hathaway, *A Tale of Two Factions*, 88–89, 165–67, 181–82.
30 Hathaway, "The *Evlād-i ᶜArab* ('Sons of the Arabs') in Ottoman Egypt," 205, 207, 208, 210–14.

ETHNOGRAPHIC CURIOSITY IN THE MIDST OF ANTAGONISM: EVLIYĀ'S DESCRIPTION OF CIRCASSIANS

Despite the increasing numbers of Circassians, or perhaps because of it, they still seemed exotic and somewhat dangerous to observers. A sort of horrified fascination with Circassians and other Caucasian peoples is easily detectible in the *Seyāḥātnāme*, or Book of Travels, by the famously peripatetic seventeenth-century Ottoman courtier Evliyā Çelebī, who was himself of Abkhazian descent, as noted above. Recounting his travels through Circassia, which would have occurred in the 1650s (although the travelogue was compiled some twenty-five years later), the traveler describes the distinctively Caucasian custom—found among the Circassians and Abkhazians—known in Ottoman Turkish as *atalıḳ* ("fatherhood"), whereby a young boy was sent away to be reared by "strangers," often distant relatives, so as to prevent his being raised a weakling by the women of the family.[31] Evliyā would have been familiar with the practice from his own patron, Melek Aḥmed Pasha, who, as an Abkhazian born in Ottoman territory, had been sent to his ancestral homeland for such an upbringing. Apparently, specific Caucasian tribes maintained agreements with the Ottomans to provide such a service; thus, in describing the tribe of Ḳamış, Evliyā notes that "among these people of Ḳamış, the children of the Abāza are sent from Istanbul and Cairo."[32] This ancient practice can only have helped to maintain native Caucasian languages and customs, even in the midst of powerful forces of assimilation into Ottoman elite society, such as the palace school. It may also have provided the Ottoman administration with a reliable link to the Caucasus, thus helping to ensure a continuing supply of *mamlūk*s.

Despite this regularization of Ottoman contact with Circassians and neighboring Caucasian peoples, these populations still struck Evliyā and other foreign observers as outlandish and even threatening. In describing his travels in the Caucasus, Evliyā repeatedly deploys a set of almost stock negative descriptors for the Circassians; the Abkhazians, who spoke a language related to Circassian; and the Mingrelians, a people

31 Evliyā Çelebī, *The Intimate Life of an Ottoman Statesman*, 272–73; *EI*², s.v. "Čerkes" (C. Quelquejay); *EI*², s.v. "Čerkes: Ottoman Period" (H. İnalcık); and Ditson, *Circassia*, 416.

32 Evliyā Çelebī, *Seyāḥatnāme*, 2:59; 10:53; and Evliyā Çelebī, *The Intimate Life of an Ottoman Statesman*, 49, 273.

related to the Georgians. He consistently depicts all three groups as rebellious, using the term *ᶜāṣī*, which can also connote religious sedition.[33] Correspondingly, all three groups are considered heavily armed and prone to violence (*tüfenk-endāz, pür-sīlāḥ*); they are brave, even terrifying, fighters (*bahādır, āznāvūr*).[34] Their moral values are suspect: they are inveterate thieves who steal each other's children to sell on the slave market.[35] Even those few who profess Islam are untutored Muslims; "they have no knowledge of religion or literacy" (*bir mez̲heb nedir bilmezler ve kitāb nedir bilmezler*).[36] Evliyā's rather appalled reactions to Caucasian customs are strikingly similar to those of his French contemporary Jean de Chardin (1643–1713), who traveled extensively in the Caucasus en route to the Safavid court in Isfahan. "They are a People altogether Savage," Chardin says of the Circassians, "of no Religion, not having so much as the Light of Nature among [them]. . . . The Inhabitants make Slaves one of another, and sell one another to the Turks and Tartars."[37]

Even all this negativity, however, reflects a degree of familiarity. After all, both Evliyā and Chardin are describing indigenous customs in some detail. This is a far cry from dismissing all Circassians with the unexamined label *Çerākise-i nākise*. In other words, ethnographic curiosity, even if it bred fear and loathing in this instance, played a part in normalizing contact between the peoples of the Caucasus and the core populations of the Ottoman Empire.

CIRCASSIAN PREPONDERANCE AND ETHNO-REGIONAL PRIDE: RIḌVĀN BEY'S GENEALOGY

At the same time, however, the critical mass of Circassians in the ranks of the Ottoman military administration could generate a distinctive brand of ethnic pride. A key indicator of this ethnic pride is the appearance in 1632 of the Arabic-language genealogy of the Circassian grandee Rıḍvān Bey Abū'l-Shawārib ("moustachioed"), a leader of Egypt's Qāsimī

33 Evliyā Çelebī, *Seyāḥatnāme*, 2:56, 2:57, 2:59, 2:61.

34 Evliyā Çelebī, *Seyāḥatnāme*, 2:57, 2:59. 2:60.

35 Evliyā Çelebī, *Seyāḥatnāme*, 2:57, 2:59, 2:60.

36 Evliyā Çelebī, *Seyāḥatnāme*, 2:59; see also 2:61: "*Kitābī degiller ve bir mez̲hebde degiller.*"

37 Chardin, *The Travels of Sir John Chardin into Persia and the East-Indies*, 1:76; also see 1:78.

faction.[38] In brief, the genealogy purports to demonstrate that Rıḍvān—like all Circassians—is descended from the Prophet Muḥammad's tribe of Quraysh via a tribesman named Kīsa, who fled from the early Muslim armies spreading north from the Arabian peninsula, eventually migrating to what is now Circassia and settling in a place that he named Basna, presumably the district of Besne in what is now Kabardia. The name "Circassians" (*Sarākisa*, otherwise *Jarākisa*, in Arabic) supposedly derives from the Arabic *sarā Kīsa*, or "Kīsa fled."

This rather fanciful origin myth did not begin with Rıḍvān Bey but was apparently deeply rooted in Circassia itself; it is reported, though in a slightly different form, by Evliyā Çelebī and by various eighteenth- and nineteenth-century European travelers, as well as by the nineteenth-century Circassian historian and folklorist Shora Bekmursin Nogmov.[39] The aim of Rıḍvān's genealogy seems to be to demonstrate that, by virtue of his exalted Qurayshī (though not Prophetic) lineage, as well as his putative ancestors' lengthy tradition of service to Mecca, he deserves the post of pilgrimage commander more than Egypt's other Rıḍvān Bey, the Georgian leader of the Faqārīs, who in fact held the position at the time of the genealogy's composition yet who could claim no such ancestry—and who, moreover, had no sons to carry on his lineage. In contrast, as the genealogy is careful to mention, Rıḍvān Bey Abū'l-Shawārib has seven sons. Three of these, Özbek, Khūshqadam (Ḫoşḳadem), and Maḥmūd, are documented in other provincial narrative sources.[40] The names of the first two, Özbek and Khūshqadam, allude unequivocally to great personages of the late Mamluk Sultanate, which, of course, was dominated by Circassians: namely, Özbek Bey (or Azbak, in its Arabicized form), the general who had scored victories over the Ottomans in the two empires' late fifteenth-century confrontations; and Khūshqadam, Mamluk sultan from 1461 to 1467, who, incidentally, was not Circassian but *Rūmī*, probably meaning a Greek from Anatolia.[41]

38 Anonymous, *Nisba sharīfa wa-risāla munīfa tashtamil ʿala dhikr nasab al-Jarākisa min Quraysh*. P.M. Holt erroneously identified the commissioner of the genealogy as the Faqārī leader Rıḍvan Bey. See Holt, "The Exalted Lineage of Riḍwān Bey," 221–30; Hathaway, *A Tale of Two Factions*, 151–64; and Hathaway, "The Exalted Lineage of Rıḍvān Bey Revisited," 97–111.

39 Evliyā Çelebī, *Seyāḥatnāme*, 7:273–76, 7:281, 7:283, 7:285–7, 10:52; and Nogmov, *Die Sagen und Lieder des Tscherkessen-Volks*, 44–46.

40 Hathaway, "The Exalted Lineage of Rıḍvan Bey Revisited," 99n11.

41 Petry, *Twilight of Majesty*, 46–50, 94–100; and *EI*[2], s.v. "Khūshḳadam" (P. M. Holt).

By 1632, apparently, the ban on Circassian names was in abeyance, and Circassian pride had asserted itself among certain elements of the military–administrative elite of Cairo. Indeed, the Qāsimī faction at the time seems to have included a critical mass of Circassians. In the years after his death in the late 1650s, Abū'l-Shawārib Rıḍvān Bey came to be remembered as a pillar, if not a founder, of the Qāsimī faction, to the extent that a Qāsimī sub-faction that emerged in the 1720s was labeled "Shawāriba"; the leader of this splinter group, the son of a Circassian *mamlūk* distantly connected to Abū'l-Shawārib's household through clientage ties, was buried in his tomb.[42] Abū'l-Shawārib's son Özbek Bey, meanwhile, took over his father's household and became a prominent grandee in late seventeenth-century Egypt. Evliyā Çelebī—who spent the last decade or so of his life as Özbek Bey's guest in Cairo, where he compiled his famous *Book of Travels*—describes the bey as head of a "great household" (*ulu ḫānedān*) with five hundred fighting men.[43] Years later, in the 1740s, Özbek Bey's son sent the *Book of Travels* to Istanbul as a gift for the Ottoman Chief Harem Eunuch Ḥācı Beşīr Agha, who had it copied, thus introducing this critical work to Ottoman high society.[44] Indirectly, then, Circassian entrenchment in seventeenth-century Egypt enabled the Ottoman intelligentsia to read Evliyā's negative depictions of Circassians in their native habitat.

THE POST-CRISIS MULTI-ETHNIC ENVIRONMENT: ÇERKES MEḤMED BEY

By the early eighteenth century, however, Circassians were just one of a number of ethno-regional groups competing for influence in the Ottoman Empire's increasingly diverse administrative ranks, both in the imperial capital and in the provinces. In Egypt, the critical mass of Circassians in the military and administrative ranks had been diluted, first by Bosnians who had entered the province during the 1650s and 1660s, then, in the eighteenth century, by Georgians. With the collapse in 1722 of Iran's Safavid empire, which had made extensive use of Georgian *mamlūks*

42 Hathaway, *A Tale of Two Factions*, 163–64; Aḥmed Çelebī, *Awḍaḥ al-ishārāt*, 397, 476, 477, 486, 504, 523, 535, 569; and al-Damūrdāshī, *Al-Durra al-muṣāna*, 265.

43 Evliyā Çelebī, *Seyāḥatnāme*, 10:282, 10:503.

44 MacKay, "The Manuscripts of the *Seyahatname* of Evliya Çelebi," 278–98, especially 278–79.

(or *ghulāms*, as they were called in Safavid parlance), eastern Georgia became an Ottoman protectorate; consequently, Georgian *mamlūks* began to flood into the Arab provinces. By 1775, the governors of Baghdad, Basra, and Damascus were all former Georgian *mamlūks*, while the leadership of Egypt's dominant Ḳazdağlı household was almost entirely Georgian.[45] Even in semi-autonomous Tunisia, some of the most influential posts in the beylical administration were held by Georgian *mamlūks*.[46] This situation did not mean that Circassian *mamlūks* were no longer employed in the Ottoman Arab provinces, simply that their dominance had been diluted by the availability of this alternative source. In this environment, the animus against them was drastically reduced.

The checkered career of Çerkes Meḥmed Bey, the last Circassian grandee of great renown in Egypt, illustrates both the new multi-ethnic character of Ottoman Egypt's administrative ranks and, in that context, the changing attitude toward Circassians. Çerkes Meḥmed, known in the Arabic sources as Jarkas Muḥammad or Muḥammad Bey Jarkas, was a *mamlūk* of the Bosnian grandee Ibrāhīm Bey Abū Shanab, who in turn seems to have come to Egypt as part of a Bosnian "injection" into the province from the imperial capital in the late 1650s.[47] Abū Shanab had joined the household of Murād Bey (known as "the *defterdār*" for his lengthy tenure as Egypt's chief financial officer), a *mamlūk* of Özbek Bey, the son of Rıḍvān Bey Abū'l-Shawārib, commissioner of the Circassian genealogy. By 1700, the Bosnian Abū Shanab was running the Qāsimī faction in partnership with Murād Bey's Circassian *mamlūk*, Ivāẓ Bey. Ivāẓ was assassinated in 1711, in the course of the infamous "civil war" among Egypt's grandees, while Abū Shanab died of the plague in 1718.[48] After the deaths of the faction's two pillars, a rift opened between Çerkes Meḥmed Bey and Ivāẓ Bey's young son, Ismāᶜīl Bey. It was Ismāᶜīl Bey who led the sub-faction known as "Shawāriba," mentioned above. The rift concerned the typical issues over which Egyptian grandees—indeed, grandees in any Ottoman

45 Hathaway, *The Politics of Households in Ottoman Egypt*, 169n1; and Hathaway, "Mamlūk 'Revivals' and Mamlūk Nostalgia in Ottoman Egypt," 400–401.

46 Oualdi, *Esclaves et maîtres*, 112–14.

47 On this point, see Hathaway, *The Politics of Households in Ottoman Egypt*, 35; and Hathaway, *A Tale of Two Factions*, 182, 191.

48 Al-Damūrdāshī, *Al-Durra al-muṣāna*, 155–56, 225; and al-Jabartī, *ᶜAjaʾib al-āthār*, 1:124. On the 1711 civil war, see Raymond, "Une 'révolution' au Caire sous les Mameloukes."

province—quarreled: rights to the revenue from tax farms, particularly those of key Egyptian villages endowed to the imperial pious foundations for the holy cities of Mecca and Medina, and rights to lucrative and influential offices, such as that of pilgrimage commander. Çerkes Meḥmed went so far as to cross factional lines, joining with the Faqārī chieftain Zülfiḳār Bey, whose ethnic origin is unclear, to assassinate Ismāᶜīl Bey in 1724.[49] With Ismāᶜīl Bey out of the way, however, the same brand of rivalry opened between Çerkes Meḥmed and Zülfiḳār. Clearly, the Circassian solidarity of a century earlier had given way to a multi-ethnic environment dominated by political and pecuniary concerns.

This did not mean that Circassian solidarity had vanished entirely from Ottoman Egypt's political culture. Çerkes Meḥmed Bey seems to have had an interest in achieving a concentration of Circassians within his own household, although the origins of his *mamlūk*s can be difficult to determine. One, however, acquired the nickname "Little Çerkes" (*Jarkas al-Ṣaghīr* in Arabic) when his master promoted him to the rank of *ṣancaḳ beyi*; we can thus hazard the guess that he was Circassian.[50] In addition, Çerkes Meḥmed brought family members to Cairo from what the Arabic chronicles call *diyār al-kufr*, "the realm of unbelief," meaning, in this case, Circassia.[51] His brother became a full-fledged member of Çerkes Meḥmed's household and was killed, along with Çerkes al-Ṣaghīr, during a crackdown on Çerkes Meḥmed's followers in the wake of his death.[52]

Still, Çerkes Meḥmed did not attempt to construct a purely Circassian household. He employed a number of mercenary bodyguards known, in the Arabic singular, as *sarrāj*, literally "saddler." Most of these men were Anatolian. They were widely employed in eighteenth-century Egyptian grandee households, regardless of the ethnicity of the household heads.[53] The Egyptian chronicler al-Damūrdāshī even recounts how Çerkes

49 Al-Damūrdāshī, *Al-Durra al-muṣāna*, 176, 229–33, 262–64; and al-Jabartī, *ᶜAjāʾib al-āthār*, 1:135–39, 1:143.

50 Al-Jabartī, *ᶜAjāʾib al-āthār*, 1:148.

51 Aḥmed Çelebī, *Awḍaḥ al-ishārāt*, 482.

52 Al-Jabartī, *ᶜAjāʾib al-āthār*, 1:163. Al-Damūrdāshī (*al-Durra al-muṣāna*, 319–20) mentions that Çerkes Meḥmed brought his brother from *Rūm*, i.e., Anatolia and/or the Ottoman central lands. It is possible that the brother, on leaving Circassia, spent time in the imperial palace, or in the household of an Ottoman vizier or the governor of an Anatolian province.

53 On *sarrāj*es, see Hathaway, *The Politics of Households in Ottoman Egypt*, 55, 57–58, 63–64.

Meḥmed's arch-rival, Zülfiḳār Bey, hired a *sarrāj* whom he called al-Shatwī ("wintry") to counter Çerkes' notoriously brutal *sarrāj* al-Ṣayfī ("summery").[54] At first blush, the rival beys might appear to be following the household-building strategies that Rıḍvān, ᶜAlī, Qānṣūh, and Memi had employed a century earlier, with Caucasian household heads presiding over contrasting ethnic elements in the rank and file. Çerkes Meḥmed and Zülfiḳār, however, were drawing on the same pool—Anatolian mercenaries—for their rank and file. Moreover, these mercenaries were only one of numerous ethno-regional elements incorporated into eighteenth-century households.

Perhaps the most striking evidence that Çerkes Meḥmed Bey's saga provides of the altered perception of Circassians in the eighteenth century is the complete lack of ethno-regional references in responses to or descriptions of his seditious overtures to the Habsburg emperor in 1730. While sultanic orders are outraged and chroniclers' accounts are incredulous, neither type of source adduces the bey's Circassian identity as a factor in his treasonous adventures.

Çerkes Meḥmed's rebellion resulted from his struggle against Zülfiḳār Bey. In early 1730, he was driven out of Cairo by Zülfiḳār's forces. Rather than head for Istanbul to plead his case at the Ottoman court, he embarked on an odyssey, making his way first to Algiers and then sailing across the Mediterranean to the Adriatic port of Trieste, which at the time served as the Habsburg Empire's chief Mediterranean port. From Trieste, he traveled to Vienna, where he sought the aid of the Habsburg emperor Charles VI (r. 1711–40). Unfortunately for Çerkes Meḥmed, the emperor received a stern letter from Sultan Aḥmed III (r. 1703–30) that prompted him to withdraw his support, and the bey was forced to flee Vienna for Libyan Tripoli, from where he ultimately re-entered Egypt by stealth.[55]

54 Al-Damūrdāshī, *Al-Durra al-muṣāna*, 229–31, 277, 297–303, 311, 375, 380. Aḥmed Çelebī spells al-Ṣayfī's name with a *sīn*, so that it becomes the adjectival form of the Arabic word for "sword," a far more conventional name. See Aḥmed Çelebī, *Awḍaḥ al-ishārāt*, 375.

55 Hathaway, "Ottoman Responses to Çerkes Meḥmed Bey's Rebellion," 108–109. As noted on page 112 of that article, the Ottoman archival documents tell a different story of Çerkes Meḥmed's itinerary from that described in al-Damūrdāshī's chronicle, which has the bey going to Moscow, then Malta. He ultimately drowned in the Nile in April 1730, while fleeing from one of Zülfiḳār's allies. Zülfiḳār himself had been assassinated by a hostile grandee five days earlier.

Throughout his peregrinations, the Ottoman chancery issued a series of strident all-points bulletins branding Çerkes Meḥmed a traitor (*hāʾin*) to the entire Dār al-Islām and urging his immediate execution if he were caught entering any Muslim territory. Yet for all the opprobrium that these imperial orders hurl at this wayward grandee, they never make any mention of his Circassian identity, apart from his sobriquet Çerkes, which they use simply to identify him. Ottoman and Egyptian chronicles likewise make no mention of his ethnicity in describing his rebellion, nor does either type of source suggest that other Circassian grandees might be seduced into joining his rebellion by virtue of their ethno-regional identity alone.

Çerkes Meḥmed's career, instead, highlights the diversity, if not cosmopolitanism, within Egypt's military–administrative hierarchy, and by extension within the administrative hierarchy of the Ottoman Empire as a whole, at this juncture. As noted above, Çerkes Meḥmed Bey's patron, Ibrāhīm Bey Abū Shanab, was a Bosnian. His archenemy, Ismāʿīl Bey ibn Ivāẓ Bey, was the Egyptian-born son of his patron's Circassian comrade-in-arms. His bodyguards were Anatolian. In the somewhat more stable administrative echelons of the post-seventeenth-century crisis, post-*devşirme* Ottoman Empire, the old east–west ethno-regional antagonism was greatly reduced, although it had not disappeared entirely. *Rūmī*s no longer cast aspersions on rivals from the Caucasus, since Caucasian personnel were as likely to be valued colleagues as fierce competitors. In this ethno-regionally transformed atmosphere, the *Çerākise-i nākise* stereotype, as well as that of the treacherous Abkhazian, was laid to rest. The "eastern alternative" that the Circassians represented had been assimilated.

BIBLIOGRAPHY

Sources

Aḥmed Çelebī ibn ʿAbd al-Ghanī. *Awḍaḥ al-ishārāt fī man tawalla Miṣr al-Qāhira min al-wuzarāʾ wa-l-bashat*. Edited by A. A. ʿAbd al-Raḥīm. Cairo: Maktabat al-Khānji, 1978.

Anonymous. *Nisba sharīfa wa-risāla munīfa tashtamil ʿala dhikr nasab al-Jarākisa min Quraysh*. Princeton University Library, Garrett Manuscript Collection, MS 186H.

Barkan, Ömer Lutfi, ed. "Mısır Ḳanūnnāmesi." In *XV ve XVIıncı Asırlarda Osmanlı İmparatorluğu Ziraî Ekonominin Hukukî ve Malî Esasları*, edited by Ömer Lutfi Barkan, vol. 1, chapter 105. Istanbul: İstanbul Üniversitesi Edebiyat Fakültesi Yayınları, 1943.

Celālzāde Muṣṭafā Çelebī. *Selīmnāme*. Edited by Ahmet Uğur and Mustafa Çuhadar. Ankara: Başbakanlık Basımevi, 1990.

Chardin, Jean de. *The Travels of Sir John Chardin into Persia and the East-Indies, through the Black Sea, and the Country of Colchis: Containing the Author's Voyage from Paris to Ispahan, to Which is Added, the Coronation of This Present King of Persia Solyman III*. Published simultaneously in French and English. 2 vols. London: Printed for Christopher Bateman, 1691.

al-Damūrdāshī, Aḥmad Katkhudā ᶜAzabān. *Al-Durra al-muṣāna fī akhbār al-Kināna*. British Museum, MS Or. 1073–74.

Ditson, George Leighton. *Circassia; or, a Tour to the Caucasus*. New York: Stringer and Townsend; London: T.C. Newby, 1850.

Evliyā Çelebī. *Seyāḥatnāme*. Edited by Zekeriya Kurşun, Seyit Ali Kahraman, and Yücel Dağlı as *Evliyâ Çelebi Seyahatnâmesi*. Vol. 2. Istanbul: Yapı Kredi Yayınları, 1999.

Evliyā Çelebī. *Seyāḥatnāme*. Edited by Yücel Dağlı, Seyit Ali Kahraman, and Robert Dankoff as *Evliyâ Çelebi Seyahatnâmesi*. Vol. 7. Istanbul: Yapı Kredi Yayınları, 2003.

Evliyā Çelebī. *Seyāḥatnāme*. Edited by Seyit Ali Kahraman, Yücel Dağlı, and Robert Dankoff as *Evliyâ Çelebi Seyahatnâmesi*. Vol. 10. Istanbul: Yapı Kredi Yayınları, 2007.

Evliyā Çelebī. *The Intimate Life of an Ottoman Statesman: Melek Aḥmed Pasha (1588–1662) as Portrayed in Evliyā Çelebi's Book of Travels*. Translated and published with commentary by Robert Dankoff. Historical introduction by Rhoads Murphey. Albany, NY: State University of New York Press, 1991.

al-Isḥāqī, Muḥammad ᶜAbd al-Muᶜti. *Akhbār al-uwal fī man taṣarrafa fī Miṣr min arbāb al-duwal*. Bulāq: Al-Maṭbaᶜa al-ᶜUthmāniyya, 1304/1887.

Istanbul, Başbakanlık Osmanlı Arşivi. Mühimme Defteri 2, no. 612 (17 Cemāziyülāḫir 963/28 April 1556); no. 905 (21 Receb 963/31 May 1556); no. 955 (6 Şaᶜbān 963/15 June 1556); no. 1042 (20 Şaᶜbān 963/29 June 1556); no. 2038 (7 Cemāziyülevvel 964/8 March 1557).

Istanbul, Başbakanlık Osmanlı Arşivi. Mühimme Defteri 4, no. 380 (26 Receb 967/22 April 1560); no. 644 (4 Şaᶜbān 967/30 April 1560); no. 718 (18 Şaᶜbān 967/14 May 1560); no. 843 (10 Ramaẓān 967/4 June 1560); no. 1214 (27 Zilḳaᶜde 967/19 August 1560).

Istanbul, Başbakanlık Osmanlı Arşivi. Mühimme Defteri 6, no. 487 (Cemāziyülevvel 972/December 1564).

Istanbul, Başbakanlık Osmanlı Arşivi. Mühimme Defteri 25, no. 260 (12 Ramaẓān 981/4 April 1574).

Istanbul, Başbakanlık Osmanlı Arşivi. Mühimme Defteri 29, no. 9 (18 Cemāziyülevvel 984/13 August 1576).

Al-Jabartī, ᶜAbd al-Raḥmān ibn Ḥasan. *ᶜAjaʾib al-āthār fī-l-tarājim wa-l-akhbār*. Edited by Shmuel Moreh. 4 vols. Jerusalem: The Hebrew University of Jerusalem, Faculty of Humanities, Institute of Asian and African Studies, 2013.

Keşfī Meḥmed Çelebī. *Selīmnāme*. Istanbul, Süleymaniye Library, MS Esad Efendi 2147.

Muṣṭafā ᶜĀlī. *Muṣṭafā ᶜĀlī's Description of Cairo of 1599*. Edited by Andreas Tietze. Vienna: Österreichische Akademie der Wissenschaften, 1975.

Nogmov, Shora Bekmursin. *Die Sagen und Lieder des Tscherkessen-Volks*. Translated by Adolf Bergé. Leipzig: Verlag von Otto Wigand, 1866.

Rıḍvān Paşazāde ᶜAbdullāh Çelebī. *Tārīḫ-i Mıṣır*. Istanbul, Süleymaniye Library, MS Fatih 4362.

Ṣafī, Muṣṭafā. *Muṣṭafā Ṣafī'nin Zübdetü't-tevārīh'i*. Edited by İbrahim Hakkı Çuhadar. 2 vols. Ankara: Türk Tarih Kurumu, 2003.

Süheylī Efendi. *Tevārīh-i Mıṣīr* [sic] *ül-ḳadīm*. Istanbul, Süleymaniye Library, MS Fatih 4229.

Studies

Ayalon, David. "The End of the Mamlūk Sultanate (Why Did the Ottomans Spare the Mamlūks of Egypt and Wipe Out the Mamlūks of Syria?)." *Studia Islamica* 65 (1987): 125–48.

Hathaway, Jane. *The Arab Lands under Ottoman Rule, 1516–1800*. With contributions by Karl K. Barbir. Harlow, Essex: Pearson/Longman, 2008.

Hathaway, Jane. "The *Evlād-i ᶜArab* ('Sons of the Arabs') in Ottoman Egypt: A Rereading." In *Frontiers of Ottoman Studies: State, Province, and the West*, edited by Colin Imber and Keiko Kiyotaki, 1:203–16. London: I .B. Tauris, 2005.

Hathaway, Jane. "The Exalted Lineage of Rıḍvān Bey Revisited: A Reinterpretation of the Spurious Genealogy of a Grandee in Ottoman Egypt." *International Journal of Turkish Studies* 13, no. 1–2 (2007): 97–111.

Hathaway, Jane. "The '*Mamlūk* Breaker' Who Was Really a *Ḳul* Breaker: A Fresh Look at *Ḳul Kıran* Meḥmed Pasha, Governor of Egypt 1607–1611." In *The Arab Lands in the Ottoman Era: Essays in Honor of Professor Caesar Farah*, edited by Jane Hathaway, 93–109. Minneapolis: Center for Early Modern History, University of Minnesota, 2009.

Hathaway, Jane. "Mamlūk 'Revivals' and Mamlūk Nostalgia in Ottoman Egypt." In *The Mamlūks in Egyptian and Syrian Politics and Society*, edited by Michael Winter and Amalia Levanoni, 387–406. Leiden: Brill, 2004.

Hathaway, Jane. "Ottoman Responses to Çerkes Meḥmed Bey's Rebellion in Egypt, 1730." In *Mutiny and Rebellion in the Ottoman Empire*, edited by Jane Hathaway, 105–13. Madison: University of Wisconsin Press, 2002.

Hathaway, Jane. *The Politics of Households in Ottoman Egypt: The Rise of the Qāzdāğlıs*. Cambridge: Cambridge University Press, 1997.

Hathaway, Jane. *A Tale of Two Factions: Myth, Memory, and Identity in Ottoman Egypt and Yemen*. Albany, NY: State University of New York Press, 2003.

Holt, P. M. *Egypt and the Fertile Crescent: A Political History, 1516–1922*. Ithaca, NY: Cornell University Press, 1966.

Holt, P. M. "The Exalted Lineage of Riḍwān Bey: Some Observations on a Seventeenth-Century Mamlūk Genealogy." *Bulletin of the School of Oriental and African Studies* 22, no. 2 (1959): 221–30.

Jaimoukha, Amjad. *The Circassians: A Handbook*. New York: Palgrave, 2001.

Kunt, Metin. "Ethnic-Regional (*Cins*) Solidarity in the Seventeenth-Century Ottoman Establishment." *International Journal of Middle East Studies* 5 (1974): 233–39.

MacKay, Pierre A. "The Manuscripts of the *Seyahatname* of Evliya Çelebi—Part I: The Archetype." *Der Islam* 52 (1975): 278–98.

Oualdi, M'hamed. *Esclaves et maîtres: Les mamelouks des beys de Tunis du XVIIe siècle aux années 1880*. Paris: Publications de la Sorbonne, 2011.

Peirce, Leslie. *Morality Tales: Law and Gender in the Ottoman Court of Aintab*. Berkeley: University of California Press, 2003.

Petry, Carl F. *Twilight of Majesty: The Reigns of the Mamlūk Sultans al-Ashraf Qāytbāy and Qānṣūh al-Ghawrī in Egypt*. Seattle: Henry M. Jackson School of International Studies, University of Washington, 1993.

Piterberg, Gabriel. "The Alleged Rebellion of Abāza Meḥmed Pasha: Historiography and the Ottoman State in the Seventeenth Century." In *Mutiny and Rebellion in the Ottoman Empire*, edited by Jane Hathaway, 13–24. Madison: University of Wisconsin Press, 2002.

Piterberg, Gabriel. *An Ottoman Tragedy: History and Historiography at Play*. Berkeley: University of California Press, 2003.

Raymond, André. "Une 'révolution' au Caire sous les Mameloukes: La crise de 1123/1711." *Annales Islamologiques* 1 (1966): 95–120.

Shaw, Stanford J. *The Financial and Administrative Organization and Development of Ottoman Egypt, 1517–1798*. Princeton: Princeton University Press, 1962.

Winter, Michael. *Egyptian Society under Ottoman Rule, 1517–1798*. London: Routledge, 1992.

Dispelling the Darkness of the *Halberdier's Treatise*: A Comparative Look at Black Africans in Ottoman Letters in the Early Modern Period

Baki Tezcan

for Hossein Modarressi

This article presents a comparative study of the *Risāle-i teberdāriyye fī aḥvāl-i aġa-yı dārü's-sa*ᶜ*āde* (Halberdier's Treatise on the Affairs of the Chief Black Eunuch) that was written in 1741 by a former halberdier of the Old Palace, which once occupied what is now the grounds of the central campus of Istanbul University, in the Beyazıt area. The first part of the chapter offers a summary of the image of the black African that emerges from the *Halberdier's Treatise*, which one could have called blatantly racist had it been written today. In the second part, I contrast this image with two works from the early seventeenth century that reflect an entirely different image of black Africans. One of these works, the *Rāfi*ᶜ*ü'l-ġubūş fī fežāy-ili'l-ḥubūş* (Dispelling the Darkness on the Merits of the Ethiopians), by Mollā ᶜAlī,[1] could well have become the Bible of the "black is beautiful"

* I would like to thank Hakan Karateke, Helga Anetshofer, and Erdem Çıpa for organizing "Xenophobia and Alterophobia in Pre-Modern Ottoman Lands," the conference at which this article was first presented and discussed, in October 2015 at the University of Chicago. I should acknowledge a UC Davis Academic Senate Small Grant in Aid of

movement if it had been published in the 1960s. By analyzing and contrasting these two earlier works with the *Halberdier's Treatise*, each within its respective socio-political context, I both underline the impact of the political framework of patron-client relationships on literary works and demonstrate that phobias are amplified in certain socio-political contexts. While the present study warrants some historiographical and theoretical discussion on questions of race and slavery in pre-nineteenth-century Ottoman lands as well as the larger premodern world, the politics of studying these questions historically in majority Muslim societies is so complex that I would prefer to postpone such discussions to the introduction of a longer future study. The goal of this chapter is more pointed. It demonstrates that whereas Islam does not have a given attitude to Africans, race, or slavery, Muslims positioned in different relationships to power interpret the Islamic heritage differently. Through a comparison of the *Halberdier's Treatise* with two other works, I thus argue that the intellectual heritage of Islam could be appropriated for diametrically opposed projects about the ways in which Black Africans were to be perceived.

THE HALBERDIER'S TREATISE

The halberdier in question is a certain Dervīş ᶜAbdullāh. All we know about him comes from the autobiographical remarks found in his treatise, which was introduced by Cengiz Orhonlu in an article published in 1976.[2] Six years ago, a complete edition of the treatise was published

Research in 2015, which helped me finance a research trip to Istanbul in the summer of 2015, and a Faculty Development Award from the Office of Academic Affairs at UC Davis in Winter 2016, which provided me with a course release and thus facilitated the production of the first draft of the present study. I am also grateful to the participants at the Xenophobia conference for their comments and questions, as well as to my UC Davis colleagues Corrie Decker, Lorena Oropeza, and Mairaj Syed, and the anonymous reviewer, who read the first draft and provided critical but encouraging feedback, which led me to cut one third of the draft with a view to treat the subject at greater length later. Finally, I would like to express my gratitude to Hossein Modarressi, Bayard Dodge Professor of Near Eastern Studies at Princeton University, not only for introducing me to Islamic Law more than twenty years ago, but also for continuing to answer my questions over e-mail ever since, as he did, once again, for this article (see note 78 below).

1 See Tezcan, "*Dispelling the Darkness.*"

2 Orhonlu, "Derviş Abdullah'ın Bir Eseri." The second half of the treatise, which is dedicated to the Ottoman period, was transcribed by Hızır Ali Telatar and Reşat Karpuzcu, two seniors in the History Department at Istanbul University, who wrote their senior theses under the direction of Cengiz Orhonlu in 1973–74. See Telatar, "Derviş Abdullah"; and Karpuzcu, "Derviş Abdullah."

by Pınar Saka, who had worked on it for her master's thesis.[3] Thanks to these works, which culled ᶜAbdullāh's text for autobiographical details, it is possible to provide a faint sketch of his life.

ᶜAbdullāh entered the corps of the halberdiers at the Old Palace in 1680 and served for eighteen years. During his service he interacted closely with black eunuchs, some of whom became his students. What exactly he taught them is not quite clear. He calls it *ᶜilm-i şerīf*, or sacred knowledge, which might refer to reading the Koran. His epithet, dervish, suggests that ᶜAbdullāh must have had a connection with a Sufi brotherhood, perhaps the Naqshbandī order, for he does not seem to be fond of whirling ceremonies, which most Naqshbandīs also shunned, and one of the authors he cites as a—very likely fictive—source reminds one of a Naqshbandī personage.[4] In the last years of the seventeenth century, he probably retired to Bursa and yet kept in touch with Istanbul, as he narrates various events of the first part of the eighteenth century, some in great detail. He notes his visits to Istanbul in 1737 and 1739, which seem to have been driven by a desire to secure a sort of appointment. He completed the treatise that came to be known as the *Halberdier's Treatise* in 1741 in Bursa.[5]

Apart from its last page, the first chapter of the treatise is not extant. Yet, based on the second chapter, which focuses on Noah and his sons,[6] it is safe to assume that it was devoted to world history before Noah and offered a certain understanding of it. This understanding, the trajectory of which can be followed in the rest of the work, divides humanity into two groups, the believers and the unbelievers. Whether one belongs to the first group or the second depends, to a large extent, on one's ancestors. Based on the assertions made in the rest of the work, one might assume that the first chapter focused on Adam, Eve, Abel, Cain, and Seth, constructing opposing groups of evil and good, represented, respectively, by the descendants of Cain—Adam's eldest son, who killed his younger brother, Abel—and the descendants of Seth, Adam's youngest son, who was born after the murder of Abel.

---

3 ᶜAbdullāh, *Risāle-i teberdāriyye* (2011); and Saka, "Derviş Abdullah."

4 See note 28 for the Naqshbandī personage. For the author's representation of whirling, see ᶜAbdullāh, *Risāle-i teberdāriyye*, 67a; and ᶜAbdullāh, *Risāle-i teberdāriyye* (2011), 152.

5 The unicum manuscript of the work is wanting at the beginning; thus, the introduction in which the author would have spelled out the title of the work is missing. The title by which the work came to be nown was noted on the flyleaf in a different hand. The completion date of the work is noted on folio 97a. See ᶜAbdullāh, *Risāle-i teberdāriyye* (2011), 207–208.

6 ᶜAbdullāh, *Risāle-i teberdāriyye*, 2a–8b; and ᶜAbdullāh, *Risāle-i teberdāriyye* (2011), 38–49.

This moral contrast, based on biological inheritance between the children of Cain and the children of Seth, is not unheard of in Islamic sources. Al-Thaᶜlabī (d. 1035), for instance, states:

> Adam had ordered the children of Seth not to intermarry with the children of Cain. . . . They intermarried and intermingled until the children of Cain increased so much that they filled the Earth and spread corruption.[7]

ᶜAbdullāh was probably inspired by this understanding when he set out to write his version of the Curse of Ham,[8] which has an antediluvian introduction. At the beginning of the second chapter of his treatise, one reads that Noah married Māṣiye, who was a descendant of Cain, Adam's son who did not believe in God; she did not accept Noah's invitation to faith.[9] Māṣiye gave birth to Ham and Canaan—in this version of Islamic world history, Ham and Canaan are brothers rather than father and son, which is a common assumption in some Islamic sources.[10] According to ᶜAbdullāh, Canaan followed his mother and became an unbeliever. Canaan appears as an unbeliever in other Islamic sources as well, yet his lack of belief is not connected with an inherited trait from his mother, despite the fact that in the Koran his mother, Noah's wife, is also punished by God for unbelief.[11] In ᶜAbdullāh's version, while Ham became

7 Al-Thaᶜlabī, *ᶜArāʾis al-majālis*, 92–93.

8 For the Curse of Ham in the monotheistic tradition, see Goldenberg, *The Curse of Ham*.

9 Saka's reading of her name as "Mâşiye" must be corrected; compare ᶜAbdullāh, *Risāle-i teberdāriyye* (2011), 39, 41, with ᶜAbdullāh, *Risāle-i teberdāriyye*, 2b, 4a. There is a Jewish tradition that also identifies Noah's wife as a descendant of Cain, but her name in that tradition is Naamah. See Rapaport, *Tales and Maxims*, 73. Al-Ṭabarī also identifies Noah's wife as a descendant of Cain, but with a different name: ᶜAmzūrah, who bore Shem, Ham, and Japheth to him. He relates another report according to which "Noah married a woman of the children of Cain and she bore him a son whom he named Būnāẓir." See al-Ṭabarī, *The History*, I:347, II:18. Al-Kisāʾī ascribes two wives to Noah: Amorah and Walia bint Mahwil. See al-Kisāʾī, *The Tales of the Prophets*, 95.

10 Al-Ṭabarī, *The History*, I:368; al-Kisāʾī, *The Tales of the Prophets*, 95, 103; and *DİA*, s.v. "Hâm" (Ş. Kuzgun).

11 "God advances the example of Noah's wife and the wife of Lot for those who do not believe. They were married to Our two pious devotees, but they were unfaithful to them, and even (the apostles) could not avail them in the least against God; and it was said to them: 'Enter Hell with those (who are condemned) to enter it.'" See ᶜAlī, trans., *Qurʾān*, 66:10; see also al-Kisāʾī, *The Tales of the Prophets*, 95.

a believer, he remained susceptible to his mother's influence and insisted on marrying her niece Tehīne, another descendant of Cain, rather than one of the daughters of his father's paternal relatives—presumably descendants of Seth.[12] Noah did not insist, as he was afraid that Ham would run away to his maternal relatives if he did not allow him to marry Tehīne. So, Ham married her. While Tehīne became a believer, their children became unbelievers, as they were led astray by their grandmother Māṣiye and uncle Canaan.[13]

Noah was very upset about this development, and about the fact that the "light of Muhammad" (*nūr-ı Muḥammed*)—which was entrusted to Noah, who carried it on his forehead—did not pass to Ham. This must be a reference to the belief held by many Muslims, especially Sufis, that the eventual coming of Muhammad was known to all previous prophets, including Adam, who carried the "light of Muhammad," God's first creation, on his forehead and passed it on to his chosen descendants.[14] Most probably, ᶜAbdullāh explained the transmission of this "light" from Adam all the way to Muhammad's parents in the first chapter of his work, as the very end of this chapter, which follows the missing folios, refers to the "aforementioned parents of the Prophet and his ancestors."[15] While Noah was so upset, the Angel Gabriel descended to earth and told him that he should marry Maḥmūde, one of the daughters of his paternal relatives, as his auspicious sons would be born to her. Noah followed Gabriel's directions, and when Maḥmūde became pregnant, the light of Muhammad passed on to her forehead, and then to the forehead of her son, Shem. Three years later, Maḥmūde gave birth to Japheth. Noah married both Shem and Japheth to daughters of his paternal relatives.[16] While some Islamic sources do assert that Noah married more than once,

---

12 Saka's reading of "Tehyine" should be corrected; compare ᶜAbdullāh, *Risāle-i teberdāriyye* (2011), 39, with ᶜAbdullāh, *Risāle-i teberdāriyye*, 3a. The name of Noah's paternal ancestor is not spelled out in the second chapter; his paternal relatives are referred to as "paternal uncles." Since Māṣiye's ancestor is specifically referred to as Cain, it would be safe to assume that Noah's ancestor would be Seth, Adam's son who was born after Cain killed his brother Abel. Yet the first chapter of the book, in which this connection would have been spelled out, is missing.

13 ᶜAbdullāh, *Risāle-i teberdāriyye* (2011), 40; and ᶜAbdullāh, *Risāle-i teberdāriyye*, 3a.

14 On the "light of Muhammad," see *DİA*, s.v. "Nûr" (S. Uludağ); *DİA*, s.v. "Hakîkat-ı Muhammediyye" (M. Demirci); al-Kisāʾī, *The Tales of the Prophets*, 92; and Rubin, "Pre-Existence and Light."

15 ᶜAbdullāh, *Risāle-i teberdāriyye* (2011), 38; and ᶜAbdullāh, *Risāle-i teberdāriyye*, 2a.

16 ᶜAbdullāh, *Risāle-i teberdāriyye* (2011), 40; and ᶜAbdullāh, *Risāle-i teberdāriyye*, 3.

the claims that Shem and Japheth had a different mother than Ham, or that they were born to Noah's second wife, are not mentioned in well-known Islamic sources.[17] ᶜAbdullāh's construction of a second wife for Noah—one of Noah's paternal relatives, who carries a name that is etymologically and semantically related to the name Muhammad,[18] and who transfers the light of Muhammad from her husband to her son, Shem—serves his intention of creating a framework of history in which moral traits of good and evil, as represented by belief and unbelief, respectively, are inherited through generations.

According to ᶜAbdullāh, when the Deluge hit the earth, Noah did not take his first wife, Māṣiye, their son, Canaan, and Ham's children to the Ark. When faced with Ham's frustration, Noah explained that he could not take them, as God instructed him to take with him only the believers. ᶜAbdullāh may well have been inspired by other Islamic sources, as the exclusion of Canaan (understood as one of Noah's sons) from the Ark is not uncommon among them.[19] Noah also told every creature that they should not engage in sexual activities, as God forbade sex while on board the Ark. Almost all of the humans and animals obeyed this rule, but Ham and his wife did not. Noah asked God to punish them. That night, while Ham and his wife were asleep, they turned black. When Noah saw them the next morning, he declared that their punishment was meted out: "From now till the last day, all of your descendants will thus be black like you."[20] While this is not the most common version of the Curse of Ham, there are Islamic literary sources that could well have inspired ᶜAbdullāh to construct it. For instance, al-Thaᶜlabī relates that after "Ham had intercourse with his wife on the ark, and Noah prayed to his Lord . . . Ham's sperm became altered, and he brought forth black [offspring]."[21]

After the Deluge, upon leaving the Ark, Noah and all the other Muslims—except Ham—prostrated to give thanks to God. ᶜAbdullāh's use of the term "Muslim" in this pre-Islamic context might sound anachronistic, but it is not so from a Muslim perspective, according to

17 Compare al-Kisāʾī, *The Tales of the Prophets*, 95; al-Thaᶜlabī, *ᶜArāʾis al-majālis*, 92–104; and al-Ṭabarī, *The History*, I:347; II:18.

18 Both *maḥmūd*, the masculine version of *maḥmūde*, and *muḥammad* could be translated as "praiseworthy," and they share the same three Arabic root letters: ḥ-m-d.

19 See, for instance, al-Thaᶜlabī, *ᶜArāʾis al-majālis*, 98; and al-Kisāʾī, *The Tales of the Prophets*, 103.

20 ᶜAbdullāh, *Risāle-i teberdāriyye* (2011), 42; and ᶜAbdullāh, *Risāle-i teberdāriyye*, 4b.

21 Al-Thaᶜlabī, *ᶜArāʾis al-majālis*, 97. Other versions of the Curse of Ham will be discussed in the second part of this article.

which all the previous prophets were carrying the same message, of which Muhammad reminded humankind for a final time. When Noah asked Ham why he was not prostrating, Ham replied: "Should I prostrate [in thanking God] for my body turning black? From now on, I will never prostrate and will not believe in you!"[22] Thus, Ham became an unbeliever. He took his wife with him, settled somewhere near his father, and became a fire-worshipper. His wife gave birth to three boys and three girls. She gave birth to all of them at once, "like a dog," writes ᶜAbdullāh. He adds: "After that, every time she gave birth, she gave birth—like a pig—to six, eight, up to twelve [children]."[23]

Ham's many sons were "lustful and carnal," always engaged in sexual activity, and they did not differentiate among their mothers, daughters, sisters, and other women as partners. They would not cover their genitals, and they would engage in sex in the open—"like dogs," says ᶜAbdullāh. They also would engage in sexual intercourse with any animal they found, including donkeys, mules, horses, buffalo, sheep, goats, dogs, bears, and pigs. Another malice in which they engaged was robbery. Their father, Ham, taught them that the "whites" were their worst enemy and instructed them to rob their goods, drink their blood, and eat their meat. Thus, one day, ten of Ham's sons attacked one of Japheth's sons, killing him, stealing some of his sheep, and eating them all. When Noah summoned Ham, Gabriel once again descended to earth and instructed Noah to send Ham and his descendants to a distant part of the world. Noah told Ham that he "reverted to the veins and natures" of his mother and her ancestor Cain, who were unbelievers, and that he was worse than Cain, who killed his brother, because Cain at least buried him after his murder, whereas Ham and his children ate their victims' flesh. Then, Noah asked Japheth to take Ham and his offspring to North Africa.[24] While some Islamic narratives ascribe to Noah the division of the earth among his three sons—with Ham taking North Africa[25]—other sources postpone this division to a later generation, as will be discussed below. ᶜAbdullāh's narrative about the background to this division, however, is not to be found in mainstream sources.

22 ᶜAbdullāh, *Risāle-i teberdāriyye* (2011), 42–43; and ᶜAbdullāh, *Risāle-i teberdāriye*, 4b.

23 ᶜAbdullāh, *Risāle-i teberdāriyye* (2011), 43; and ᶜAbdullāh, *Risāle-i teberdāriyye*, 5a.

24 ᶜAbdullāh, *Risāle-i teberdāriyye* (2011), 43–46; and ᶜAbdullāh, *Risāle-i teberdāriyye*, 5a–6b.

25 See, for instance, al-Thaᶜlabī, *ᶜArāʾis al-majālis*, 104.

As for the other descendants of Noah, Shem fathered two sons, Arpachshad and Aram, the first of whom inherited the light of Muhammad. Japheth had four sons: Khitā, Khotan, Chīn, and Māchīn. According to Noah's dispensation, while the sons of Shem were to settle in different parts of Arabia, Persia, Anatolia, and Egypt, and produce prophets, the sons of Japheth were to settle to the northeast of India and produce kings. Noah prayed that kingship would never disappear from among Japheth's sons. As will be discussed below, this division of labor between the descendants of Shem (especially those of Arpachshad) and those of Japheth was a feature in other Islamic narratives on Noah's family as well. What is rather unique is ᶜAbdullāh's connection of this division with the Ottomans. He states that Noah's prayer was answered by God, as Gabriel descended to earth and gave the good news of the coming of Muhammad and the Koran, the stipulations of which were to last until the Day of Judgment. Gabriel added that emperors from among the descendants of Japheth would execute the sharia of Muhammad and the commandments of the Koran until the Day of Judgment. ᶜAbdullāh then notes that Noah's prayer was accepted, as the emperors of the Ottoman dynasty, who were descendants of Japheth, were applying the sharia of Muhammad and the commandments of the Koran, and that they would continue doing so until the coming of the Mahdi, the Muslim Messiah.[26]

While some Islamic versions of the biblical Curse of Ham narrative include certain features of the story narrated by ᶜAbdullāh—such as the divine punishment of Ham for sexual transgression aboard the Ark, the division of the earth among the sons of Noah, and the bestowal of prophethood on the descendants of Arpachshad[27]—I have not seen any Islamic narrative that is so elaborate and attentive to establishing categorical genealogies of good and evil that correspond (after the Deluge) to "whites" and "blacks," respectively. While ᶜAbdullāh cites some sources—such as the *Gulshan-i Tavārīkh* by Imām Muḥammad Badakhshānī, and the *Tabyīn Milal* by Khayr al-Dīn al-Ramlī (d. 1671)—for his account of Noah and his sons, these works are either not extant or, most probably, never existed.[28]

---

26 ᶜAbdullāh, *Risāle-i teberdāriyye* (2011), 43, 47–49; and ᶜAbdullāh, *Risāle-i teberdāriyye*, 5a, 7b–8b.

27 See pp. 61–62, 66–67 below. See also Tezcan, "Dispelling the Darkness," 87–88.

28 ᶜAbdullāh, *Risāle-i teberdāriyye* (2011), 49–50; and ᶜAbdullāh, *Risāle-i teberdāriyye*, 8b. Khayr al-Dīn al-Ramlī was a well-known Palestinian scholar whose works on Hanafi law

ᶜAbdullāh's attempts to construct a genealogy of evil among black Africans does not end with the exile of the sons of Ham to North Africa. They continue in the third chapter of his treatise, which is devoted to the malice that Ham and his offspring generated after the Deluge. ᶜAbdullāh asserts that, after settling in North Africa, the Children of Ham multiplied, as their women gave birth, "like pigs," to six or eight babies at a time. Ham claimed divinity by stating to his children that he was their god. His children confirmed this by prostrating before him. After that Ham, the unbeliever, told his children that

> the Whites are our enemies. We do not have any bigger enemy than them. My advice to you is this: wherever you find the Whites, take their goods, kill them, and eat their flesh. And I created women for the man. Your mothers, daughters, sisters, and other relatives, and strangers, whoever they might be—it is permissible to have sex with them all.[29]

ᶜAbdullāh then repeats his earlier assertions about the sexual habits of the Children of Ham, stating that the blacks engaged in sex with all women, whether their mothers, sisters, daughters, other relatives, or complete strangers. They walked around with their genitals exposed and mated like dogs in public.[30]

---

were quite influential in the Ottoman Empire. His known works do not include the titles *Tabyīn Milal* and *Ḥadīqat al-Tawārīkh*, which ᶜAbdullāh ascribes to al-Ramlī. See ᶜAbdullāh, *Risāle-i teberdāriyye* (2011), 72; and ᶜAbdullāh, *Risāle-i teberdāriyye*, 21b. For a short biography of al-Ramlī, see *DİA*, s.v. "Remlî, Hayreddin b. Ahmed" (A. Pekcan). A history work entitled *Gülşen-i Tevārīḫ*, which would have been well known in Ottoman realms, is the one by Cenābī Muṣṭafā Efendi (d. 1590), but its account of Noah is quite different than the one provided by ᶜAbdullāh. See Muṣṭafā Cenābī, *Gülşen-i Tevārīḫ*, 7b–9b. As for "Imām Muḥammad Badakhshānī," there are a few people who could be identified as Muḥammad Badakhshānī in the online catalog of the Süleymaniye Library that is accessible through the Library of the Centre for Islamic Studies in Istanbul. But they appear as copyists or translators of other works. One of these figures is the translator of the letters of al-Sirhindī (d. 1624), the well-known Indian Naqshbandī scholar "who in time would be cast as the very epitome of orthodoxy within the Naqshbandī tradition." See Le Gall, *A Culture of Sufism*, 103. If ᶜAbdullāh meant to invoke this particular Badakhshānī, one might speculate that he belonged to the Naqshbandī order, and perhaps to the Mujaddidī branch of it, which was established by the followers of al-Sirhindī in India and brought to Istanbul by Murād al-Bukhārī (d. 1720) while ᶜAbdullāh was a halberdier in the Old Palace. See Abu-Manneh, "Sheikh Murād al-Bukhārī." Another author ᶜAbdullāh cites (or pretends to cite) is a certain Imām Ṣaffānī, whom I could not identify.

29 ᶜAbdullāh, *Risāle-i teberdāriyye* (2011), 50; and ᶜAbdullāh, *Risāle-i teberdāriyye*, 9a.

30 ᶜAbdullāh, *Risāle-i teberdāriyye* (2011), 51; and ᶜAbdullāh, *Risāle-i teberdāriyye*, 9a.

According to ᶜAbdullāh, before the Deluge, Ham had learned magic from a woman named ᶜAnāḳ, who was one of Cain's children.[31] Ham produced master magicians by teaching what he learned to some of his children after he moved to Africa. They became such great masters of magic that they were able to converse with Satan. After Ham's death, with the help of the magicians, Satan divided the children of Ham into four groups. The first group worshipped an idol that represented their father, Ham. The second one adopted their chief as their god and prostrated before him. The third and the fourth groups worshipped fire and vulva (*ferc*), respectively. Thus the fourth group, for instance, prostrated in front of a vulva in the mornings and evenings. ᶜAbdullāh claims that

> every week on Saturdays they took their chief to their midst, draped a red silk bed sheet over his head, and prostrated before him. And when the sun entered Cancer [June 21], they would take their chief to a plain, seat him on an exalted throne, and likewise drape a red silk bed sheet over his head. Then they would prostrate before him, crying out, and asking in prayer what is in their hearts. Those magicians used to sit on chairs at the foot of the throne and demonstrate acts with the power of their magic. When the Blacks around the magicians saw that act, they used to shout together, each one of them imitating the sound of an animal. And since they were excessively carnal, they used to be close to all animals and know them carnally. They used to [also] eat all types of live animals.[32]

ᶜAbdullāh adds that these "black infidels" have committed infidelity, malice, and brigandage in Africa and are continuing to do so. He announces that, in the rest of the third chapter, he will write about what they did in the surrounding realm of the whites, in three parts. The first part is devoted to the pre-Islamic period, the second covers the Umayyads and the Abbasids, and the third one is devoted to the Ottomans. For the sake of brevity, suffice it to say that ᶜAbdullāh continues to produce a fictive history of evil perpetrated by "black infidels," re-writing such well-known stories of sacred pre-Islamic history as Abraham and

---

31 While Saka read this name as İnâf, I believe that it is spelled ᶜİnāḳ in the text (compare ᶜAbdullāh, *Risāle-i teberdāriyye* [2011], 51, with ᶜAbdullāh, *Risāle-i teberdāriyye*, 9a), which reminds one of ᶜAnāq, a sister of Cain in Islamic mythology. See *DİA*, s.v. "Ûc b. Unuk" (N. Bozkurt).

32 ᶜAbdullāh, *Risāle-i teberdāriyye* (2011), 51; and ᶜAbdullāh, *Risāle-i teberdāriyye*, 9b.

Nimrod, Moses and the Pharaoh, and the People of the Elephant, with black villains of his own creation as they are not found in other sources. The stories he recreates with evil African characters in Islamic history include the murder of Ḥusain at Karbala and the conquest of Baghdad by the Mongols.[33]

Intermittently, ᶜAbdullāh inserts his own voice to set up his harsh criticism of the role of the black eunuchs in Ottoman politics, which becomes the focus of the third part of his text. For instance, after his version of the story of Moses and the Pharaoh, which features evil black eunuchs, he addresses his readers (and listeners) to assert that it was also black eunuchs who were responsible for the murder of Sultan İbrāhīm, in 1648, and of his mother, Kösem Sultan, in 1651. They had seized the state apparatus during the reign of Meḥmed IV (r. 1648–87), who was enthroned at the age of six, and brought about a disturbance in the affairs of the Ottoman Empire that has lasted all the way down to his times. ᶜAbdullāh ends this short excursion to his own times with a prayer, asking God to grant Maḥmūd I, the reigning sultan (r. 1730–54), discernment and zeal to expel the black eunuchs from his palace so that the order of the reign of Süleymān I ("the Magnificent," r. 1520–66) could be reestablished.[34]

After his version of the Koranic story of the People of the Elephant, ᶜAbdullāh again intervenes in his text with his own voice, stating that his intention is to give advice to sultans, administrators, and his believing brethren—a statement that legitimately places this text into the corpus of advice literature, the Ottoman *naṣīḥatnāme*s, especially when taken together with the earlier reference to the order of the reign of Süleymān I.[35] His advice is to keep black eunuchs away from the circles of politics and to appoint them as shepherds for sheep and cattle, as it is better for shepherds to be unmarried. And the blacks who are not eunuchs should be married to black concubines and employed on farms; if they were employed in households, they would ultimately cause disorder in those households.[36]

---

33 I will dwell on these stories in a longer study, tentatively entitled "*Shades of Black*: Perceptions and Self-Perceptions of Africans in the Pre-Modern Islamic *faḍā*ᵓ*il* Genre devoted to Africans."

34 ᶜAbdullāh, *Risāle-i teberdāriyye* (2011), 63–64; and ᶜAbdullāh, *Risāle-i teberdāriyye*, 16b–17a.

35 On Ottoman advice literature, see Howard, "Genre and Myth in the Ottoman Advice for Kings Literature"; Abou-El-Haj, "The Ottoman *nasihatname* as a discourse over 'morality'"; and Tezcan, "From Veysî (d. 1628) to Üveysî (fl. ca. 1630)."

36 ᶜAbdullāh, *Risāle-i teberdāriyye* (2011), 71; and ᶜAbdullāh, *Risāle-i teberdāriyye*, 21a.

It is after all this rewriting of Islamic world history that ᶜAbdullāh begins writing about what he perceives to be the misdeeds of black eunuchs in the Ottoman Empire, starting with the deposition of Muṣṭafā I in 1618 and continuing to his own time, when the office of the chief black eunuch had been occupied by Beşīr Agha (d. 1746) since 1717.[37] I will not provide a summary of this part of his treatise, which amounts to almost half of the extant text, as it has been studied more carefully by both Cengiz Orhonlu and Pınar Saka, who chose not to focus on the pre-Ottoman sections of ᶜAbdullāh's treatise. As should be clear by now, ᶜAbdullāh was not fond of the black eunuchs. Thus, in this section of his text he did his best to show them in the worst possible light over the course of the seventeenth and eighteenth centuries, holding them responsible for almost all the disorders and military defeats that the Ottomans suffered during this period—and I should add that the contemporary chief black eunuch, Beşīr Agha, is at the center of his attacks.

As in the previous sections of his treatise, ᶜAbdullāh did not mind resorting to fiction in this part. For instance, he claims that Aḥmed III executed his chief black eunuch, Süleymān Agha (d. 1715), and intended to expel the black eunuchs from his palace, but his grand vizier İbrāhīm Pasha changed his mind and invited Beşīr Agha back from his exile in Egypt. What really happened was a little different: in 1713, Süleymān Agha was exiled to Cyprus, where he died in 1715. ᶜAlī Pasha, Aḥmed III's grand vizier from 1713 to 1716, did indeed send orders to Egypt to stop the castration of African slaves there, which stood in stark contrast to earlier and later orders requesting black eunuchs for imperial palaces. But Beşīr Agha, after his exile in Cyprus and Egypt, returned as the chief black eunuch in 1717, a year before İbrāhīm Pasha assumed the grand vizierate (in 1718). And in the period between Süleymān Agha and Beşīr Agha, the office of the chief eunuch of the Imperial Palace was occupied by ᶜAmber Meḥmed Agha, another black African.[38]

37 For a biography of Beşīr Agha, see Hathaway, *Beshir Agha*.

38 ᶜAbdullāh, *Risāle-i teberdāriyye* (2011), 151; ᶜAbdullāh, *Risāle-i teberdāriyye*, 66b; Hathaway, *Beshir Agha*, 39; *DİA*, s.v. "Damad İbrâhim Paşa, Nevşehirli" (M. Aktepe); *DİA*, s.v. "Şehid Ali Paşa" (A. Özcan); Junne, *The Black Eunuchs*, 124–25; Turan, "Mahremiyetin Muhafızları," 147; and Aḥmed Resmī, *Ḫamīletü'l-küberā*, 63. According to Ülkü Altındağ, İsmail Agha, who served as the chief eunuch of the Imperial Palace during the second reign of Muṣṭafā I (1622–23), was the last non-African chief eunuch. See *DİA*, s.v. "Dârüssaâde" (Ü. Altındağ), 1. The biography of İsmāᶜīl Agha is not included in Aḥmed Resmī's *Ḫamīletü'l-küberā*. Junne's statement that ᶜAlī Pasha "ordered the governor of Egypt to castrate all Abyssinians

While a detailed summary of this part of ᶜAbdullāh's treatise is outside the scope of this article, one of the targets of ᶜAbdullāh's attacks in this section deserves some attention in order to better situate the author within the political networks of the first half of the eighteenth century. Almost every time that ᶜAbdullāh mentions the name of Beşīr Agha, described as an evil magician who misled Maḥmūd I in several significant decisions during the 1730s, he names him in the company of a certain "Pīrīoġlu," who is supposed to have been a heretic. He is clearly targeting the contemporary imam of Maḥmūd I, Pīrīzāde Meḥmed Ṣāḥib (d. 1749). Pīrīzāde was the son of a janissary agha and had held several positions in the Ottoman hierarchy of legal scholars and judges before he was appointed as the second imam of the sultan and the teacher of the princes in 1140/1727–28, during the reign of Aḥmed III (r. 1703–30). He was appointed to the judgeship of Bursa in 1142/1729–30, and he replaced the first imam when the latter died in 1143/1730–31. He was also made the chief judge of the imperial capital in conjunction with his first imam appointment. In 1733 he was promoted to the chief justiceship of the Asian provinces, and in 1737 he became the chief justice of the European provinces, a position he held until 1739. Besides, Pīrīzāde was the author of an incomplete translation of Ibn Khaldūn's (d. 1406) *Muqaddimah*, which he presented to Maḥmūd I. ᶜAbdullāh claims that it was Beşīr Agha who recommended his appointment to the first imamate and that the two of them were very close allies, acting together throughout the 1730s, which might well have been the case.[39] In the years that followed the completion of ᶜAbdullāh's treatise, Pīrīzāde was to hold the office of the chief justice of the European provinces again, and he was also to become grand mufti (*şeyḫülislām*) for a year (1745–46). He was practically exiled from Istanbul after 1746,[40] the year Beşīr Agha died. The significance of ᶜAbdullāh's attacks against Pīrīzāde becomes apparent in the concluding section of his treatise.

---

living in his country" is erroneous, most probably caused by a mistranslation; compare Akşit, *Osmanlı'nın Gizemi Harem*, 77.

39 ᶜAbdullāh, *Risāle-i teberdāriyye* (2011), 152–58, 162–64, 166, 169–72; and ᶜAbdullāh, *Risāle-i teberdāriyye*, 67a–70a, 72b, 73b–74a, 75a–b, 77a–78b.

40 Pīrīzāde first went to pilgrimage and then lived in Gelibolu and Tekfurdağı (modern Tekirdağ). Finally, in 1748, he was allowed to live in Üsküdar, across the Bosphorus from the Ottoman capital. See *DİA*, s.v. "Pîrîzâde Mehmed Sâhib Efendi" (T. Özcan), 288.

In his treatise's conclusion, ᶜAbdullāh articulates three pieces of advice for the sultan. The first is about individual Islamic practice. The sultan should fulfill his obligations of prayer and fasting. He should select a devout imam to lead his prayers, not a heretic, which is the descriptor ᶜAbdullāh consistently uses for Pīrīzāde.[41] For a treatise that is almost entirely dedicated to the misdeeds of black Africans throughout history, the fact that the primary advice is about whom the sultan should select as his imam at the palace is quite surprising, and it warrants a pause to consider the question of why ᶜAbdullāh might have chosen to target Pīrīzāde to this extent. I would argue that Pīrīzāde might have become a target of attacks in part due to ᶜAbdullāh's aspirations related to his own contemporary vocation. While it is unclear what exactly ᶜAbdullāh was doing in Bursa after his retirement from the corps of the halberdiers, one can speculate that he held a preaching-related post, as his treatise often reads like a sermon, especially when he addresses his readers with frequent statements such as "Oh, my believing brethren (*ey benim müʾmin ḳarındaşlarım*)!"[42] If he were not a preacher at a mosque with an appointment, he may have been the sheikh, or a self-appointed elder brother, at a convent of a Sufi order. Either way, he must have been regarded as someone who belonged to the professional group of imams and preachers, as he notes his presence in the salon (*meclis*) of the royal imam Pīrīzāde, the target of some of his most vicious words, at some point in 1739–40, just a few years before he completed the treatise.[43] Most probably, ᶜAbdullāh was seeking an appointment related to a mosque or convent, over which Pīrīzāde could have some influence. One could further speculate that ᶜAbdullāh's Sufi allegiance, likely to the Naqshbandī order, was at some variance with that of Pīrīzāde, whom ᶜAbdullāh accuses of "dancing at convents." Last but not least, ᶜAbdullāh claims that Pīrīzāde was keeping Kızılbaş

41 ᶜAbdullāh, *Risāle-i teberdāriyye* (2011), 183–87; and ᶜAbdullāh, *Risāle-i teberdāriyye*, 84b–86a.

42 ᶜAbdullāh, *Risāle-i teberdāriyye* (2011), 38; and ᶜAbdullāh, *Risāle-i teberdāriyye*, 2a. See also ᶜAbdullāh, *Risāle-i teberdāriyye* (2011), 63, 71, 77, 78, 84, 88–89, 113, 121, 126, 131, 148, 150, 156, 166, 173, 174, 178, 181, 182, 200, 204; and ᶜAbdullāh, *Risāle-i teberdāriyye*, 16b, 21a, 24a, 25a, 28b, 31a, 45a, 49b, 53a, 55b, 65a, 66a, 68b, 75a, 79a, 80a, 81b, 83a, 84a, 93b, 95b.

43 ᶜAbdullāh, *Risāle-i teberdāriyye* (2011), 166; and ᶜAbdullāh, *Risāle-i teberdāriyye*, 75a. One can date this moment with reference to the tenure of the grand vizier Ḥācı Meḥmed Pasha (1739–40), who is mentioned by Pīrīzāde, in a statement quoted by ᶜAbdullāh, as the contemporary grand vizier.

sympathizers in his company. Clearly, ᶜAbdullāh stood in opposition to the ulema faction headed by Pīrīzāde and supported by Beşīr Agha.[44]

ᶜAbdullāh's second piece of advice is about justice and is quite common to all examples of advice literature: the sultan must be just in all of his affairs. In order to ensure that justice prevails in his realm, the sultan should appoint competent administrators and judges; the administrators, in turn, should carefully select tax collectors, ensuring that the subjects are not oppressed by excessive taxation. The two wings of the sultan are the sharia and the sunna, and the law of the emperor (*ḳānūn-ı pādişāh*) is dependent on them. The sultan should follow the example of past sultans, such as Süleymān I, "the Master of the Law" (*ṣāḥib-i ḳānūn*).[45]

ᶜAbdullāh's final advice is quite predictable: the sultan should expel the black eunuchs from his palace. According to him, this is not simply necessary because of all the evil deeds of black eunuchs in Islamic history but also is required according to sharia, as the protection of the sultan's female servants necessitates the dismissal of eunuchs from palace service. ᶜAbdullāh claims that black eunuchs are not devoid of sexual desire, and he relates an anecdote about two of his comrades from the corps of halberdiers, who were married to two former female slaves from the palace. These comrades apparently divorced their wives one week after marrying them because their wives told them that they could not find with their husbands the pleasure they used to find with the black eunuchs.[46] Moreover, according to ᶜAbdullāh, there is really no difference among young men, old men, and eunuchs in terms of limited access to one's female servants or wives. He even produces several legal opinions on this question that support his assertions—without, however, citing any authors or sources.[47] ᶜAbdullāh also states that black eunuchs should not

44 ᶜAbdullāh, *Risāle-i teberdāriyye* (2011), 152, 166; and ᶜAbdullāh, *Risāle-i teberdāriyye*, 67a, 75a. Because Pīrīzāde's father was a janissary agha, his Sufi allegiance might have been to the Bektaşi order. This possibility, coupled with the fact that Pīrīzāde was one of the scholars consulted about the peace treaty with Persia—which involved the question of accepting Twelver Shiᶜism as the fifth orthodox legal school under the name of the Jaᶜfari school—makes the alleged presence of Kızılbaş sympathizers around him quite interesting and worth investigating further. See *DİA*, s.v. "Pîrîzâde Mehmed Sâhib Efendi" (T. Özcan), 288.

45 ᶜAbdullāh, *Risāle-i teberdāriyye* (2011), 194; and ᶜAbdullāh, *Risāle-i teberdāriyye*, 90a.

46 ᶜAbdullāh, *Risāle-i teberdāriyye* (2011), 196–97; and ᶜAbdullāh, *Risāle-i teberdāriyye*, 91b.

47 ᶜAbdullāh, *Risāle-i teberdāriyye* (2011), 201–2; and ᶜAbdullāh, *Risāle-i teberdāriyye*, 94a–b.

be employed as guardians of the Prophet's tomb in Medina, since they cannot be canonically pure because they do not have complete control over their urination (they use cotton and a sponge for this purpose).[48] Assigning eunuchs to the protection of the Prophet's tomb in Medina is a practice that dates back to the twelfth century.[49] Beşīr Agha had served as the chief of these eunuchs before he became the chief black eunuch at the Ottoman palace.[50]

I do not believe that we could find a better example than ᶜAbdullāh's treatise to demonstrate the heights to which alterophobia directed against black Africans could reach in Ottoman times. However, it is also important to recognize the political context in which the work was produced and the purpose it seems to have had. The empowerment of the black eunuchs in the Ottoman palace dates to the reign of Murad III (r. 1574–95) in the late sixteenth century.[51] The man at the center of ᶜAbdullāh's attacks, Beşīr Agha, was arguably the most powerful chief black eunuch in Ottoman history, as he remained in this office for almost thirty years. ᶜAbdullāh visited Istanbul several times during this period, most probably trying to secure an appointment for himself in the hierarchy of imams and preachers, as he twice notes his visits to Istanbul to see the grand vizier and also mentions his presence in the salon of Pīrīzāde.[52] He must have been quite frustrated at the failure of his attempts. Perhaps he belonged to a faction that lost its influence in the capital,[53] or to one that was aspiring to replace the network of Beşīr Agha and Pīrīzāde. Reminding one of Muṣṭafā ᶜĀlī (d. 1600),[54] who channeled his frustration at the slow pace of his career to writing political advice literature critiquing the corruption he observed at many levels of the Ottoman government, ᶜAbdullāh penned a very unusual piece of political advice literature that essentially targeted the black eunuchs in general and Beşīr

48 ᶜAbdullāh, *Risāle-i teberdāriyye* (2011), 198; and ᶜAbdullāh, *Risāle-i teberdāriyye*, 92b.

49 Marmon, *Eunuchs*.

50 Hathaway, *Beshir Agha*, 45–58.

51 Tezcan, *The Second Ottoman Empire*, 100–104.

52 ᶜAbdullāh, Risāle-i teberdāriyye (2011), 164, 169; and ᶜAbdullāh, Risāle-i teberdāriyye, 74a, 76b–77a. See also p. 56 above. Saka interprets these visits as career-oriented as well. See ᶜAbdullāh, Risāle-i teberdāriyye (2011), 16.

53 Orhonlu suggests this as a possible explanation for ᶜAbdullāh's retirement. See Orhonlu, "Derviş Abdullah'ın Bir Eseri," 229.

54 Fleischer, *Bureaucrat and Intellectual in the Ottoman Empire*.

Agha in particular. Yet the framework according to which he produced his critique of the power of black eunuchs in Ottoman politics was historically fictive, as he constructs an argument about black Africans being inherently evil as a result of (what we would today call) genetic inheritance. Thus, ᶜAbdullāh arguably authored the first racist treatise in Ottoman letters.

ALTERNATIVE VISIONS OF BLACK AFRICANS

ᶜAbdullāh's treatise, however, is not the only Ottoman volume dedicated to black Africans. More than one hundred years before ᶜAbdullāh produced his fictive history of black Africans, two Ottoman scholars had written works in praise of black Africans. I have discussed one of these works, *Dispelling the Darkness*, and its author, Mollā ᶜAlī, in some detail elsewhere.[55] Before returning to *Dispelling the Darkness*, I would like to introduce ᶜAlī Mekkī, or ᶜAlī of Mecca, and his *Mirʾāt al-ḥubūş fī'l-uṣūl* (The Reflection of the Ethiopians in the Sources), or *Ḥabeşler Āyinesi* (The Mirror for Ethiopians).

According to his own statements in *The Mirror for Ethiopians*, ᶜAlī Mekkī had been a professor of law in Bursa during the last quarter of the sixteenth century. In 1587 he moved to Mecca with all of his extended family ("twenty-seven souls"), and he returned to the central lands of the Ottoman Empire in 1599. He had observed Ethiopians in Mecca and had read about them. When he found other Ethiopians in Istanbul, in the service of the sultan, he wanted to write about what he learned, but it took him a while to find a patron who, like Muṣṭafā Agha, would appreciate his work. Muṣṭafā Agha became Aḥmed I's (r. 1603–17) chief black eunuch in 1605 and remained in this position until 1620, serving Muṣṭafā I (r. 1617–18, 1622–23) and Osman II (r. 1618–22) as well. Since ᶜAlī mentions Aḥmed I as the reigning sultan, he must have authored *The Mirror for Ethiopians* between 1605 and 1617.[56] If my assumption about ᶜAlī Mekkī's work preceding that of Mollā ᶜAlī, which I discuss below, is correct, one could further shorten this window to 1605 to 1612. These biographical clues point to ᶜAlī Ḫābī (d. 1612) as the most likely author of *The Mirror for Ethiopians*. Ḫābī was a professor of law from Bursa who

55 Tezcan, "*Dispelling the Darkness*."
56 ᶜAlī Mekkī, *Mirʾāt al-ḥubūş*, 4a–10a.

is known to have held an appointment in Mecca in 1005/1596–97. He returned to Istanbul, awaiting an appointment closer to the capital. He first secured a professorship at a college of law in Bursa in 1602. In 1603 he was assigned to a college in Medina, a position which he declined. Then, in 1604, he was appointed to a college in Istanbul, eventually moving up to the College of Meḥmed II in 1606, the year after Muṣṭafā Agha became chief black eunuch. He apparently acquired his epithet Ḫābī (literally "dreamy") in connection with his efforts to base his claim of being a descendant of the Prophet on a dream. His given name, birthplace, service in Mecca, and return to Istanbul fit well into the biographical details provided by the author of *The Mirror for Ethiopians*. I must add that very few Ottoman professors of law from the central lands of the empire moved to Mecca for extended periods of time, so it is quite unlikely that we could find another ᶜAlī from Bursa who lived in Mecca for twelve years and returned to the imperial capital in 1599. As his epithet seems to have been given to him by others in order to tease him, it is understandable that he might have preferred to be identified as "Mekkī" (that is, of Mecca), the name found on the flyleaf of *The Mirror for Ethiopians*. Keeping this in mind, I will refer to him as ᶜAlī Mekkī.[57]

The Mirror for Ethiopians follows a long tradition of writings in Arabic literature that can be grouped together as a subcategory of the *faḍāʾil* (virtues, sg. *faḍīla*) genre with a focus on Africans.[58] The representation of black Africans in the work of ᶜAlī Mekkī stands in stark contrast to that in the *Halberdier's Treatise*. In *The Mirror for Ethiopians*, black Africans are part and parcel of the foundational narratives of Islam, with references to the Koran, the Prophetic traditions, the Christian king of Ethiopia who converts to Islam, Bilal, the companions of the Prophet, and their descendants.

57 ᶜAtāʾī, *Ḥadāʾiḳu'l-ḥaḳāʾiḳ*, 566–67; and ᶜAlī Mekkī, *Mirʾāt al-ḥubūş*, 1a.

58 For a study that focuses on the origins of this genre, see Gruber, *Verdienst und Rang*; for an early example of the subcategory focusing on Africans, see al-Jāḥiẓ, "The superiority of Blacks to Whites"; for later examples that focused on Africans, see Tezcan, "*Dispelling the Darkness*," 85–86. As noted by Akbar Muhammad, ᶜAlī Mekkī closely follows a late sixteenth-century work in this subcategory, Muḥammad bin ᶜAbd al-Bāqī's *al-Ṭirāz al-manqūsh fī maḥāsin al-Ḥubūsh* (The Colored Brocade on the Good Qualities of the Ethiopians). For a German translation of the preface, introduction, and the first three of the four chapters of this work, see Weisweiler, *Buntes Prachtgewand*. For a brief comparison of its contents with *The Mirror for Ethiopians*, see Muhammad, "The Image of Africans in Arabic Literature," 61–62, 64–65. I will provide a more detailed comparison of the two works in *Shades of Black*.

The work includes sections on praises written for black Africans by Muslim authors. And there is nothing to suggest that black Africans carry the evil inheritance of unbelief. To make this point clearer, I will focus on the fourth section of the first chapter of *The Mirror for Ethiopians*, which tackles the question of the skin color of Africans and is probably the only part of the book that is directly comparable to the *Halberdier's Treatise*.

ᶜAlī Mekkī begins the section on the skin color of Africans with a quotation from the *Tanwīr al-ghabash* (Lightening [or Enlightenment] of the Darkness), by Abū al-Faraj Ibn al-Jawzī (d. 1201):

> As for colors, it is evident that they were created such as they are, without any obvious reason, except what we have already transmitted, namely that the descendants of Noah—Peace be upon him—divided the earth among themselves after his death. The one who did the separation was Faligh bin ᶜAbir. The descendants of Shem settled in the central region of the world. There were dark and light complexioned people among them. The descendants of Japheth settled in the northern [and eastern] regions. A red complexion existed among them. And the descendants of Ham inhabited the southern and western regions. Thus their complexions were changed. . . . But as for what is related about Noah's genitals having been uncovered, [and the explication that] because Ham did not cover them Noah invoked a curse and Ham was darkened, is unproven and incorrect.[59]

Ibn al-Jawzī's narrative, quoted by ᶜAlī Mekkī through Ibn ᶜAbd al-Bāqī, is quite different from ᶜAbdullāh's version of how Ham and his descendants became black. First, ᶜAlī rejects the Curse of Ham story as an explanation for Africans' skin color outright. He later quotes another version of it in a Prophetic tradition, according to which Noah cursed Ham with blackness for looking at him while he was taking a bath, only to add that it was deemed a weak tradition.[60]

---

59 ᶜAlī Mekkī, *Mirʾāt al-ḥubūş*, 35 (in Arabic); compare Ibn ᶜAbd al-Bāqī, *Al-Ṭirāz al-manqūsh*, 30 (Weisweiler, *Buntes Prachtgewand*, 34–35); and Ibn al-Jawzī, *Tanwīr al-ghabash*, 35 (Alawiye, "Ibn al-Jawzī's Apologia," 67). I used Muhammad's translation of this passage by Ibn al-Jawzī, with some modifications; see "The Image of Africans in Arabic Literature," 56, whence "and eastern" comes.

60 ᶜAlī Mekkī, *Mirʾāt al-ḥubūş*, 35b–36a (in Arabic); compare Ibn ᶜAbd al-Bāqī, *Al-Ṭirāz al-manqūsh*, 31 (Weisweiler, *Buntes Prachtgewand*, 35). Ibn ᶜAbd al-Bāqī and,

Moreover, ᶜAlī's version of the dispersal of Noah's descendants to different parts of the world is very different from ᶜAbdullāh's version. Noah does not banish Ham and his descendants to North Africa; his descendants divide the world among themselves. ᶜAlī's reference to Faligh bin ᶜAbir as the one who divided the world places this event in a time that is several generations removed from Noah, as ᶜAlī explains in the Turkish part of his text: "Noah is his third great grandfather (literally, his ancestor in five degrees)."[61] Faligh bin ᶜAbir is the Arabic version of Peleg, son of Eber, at whose time, according to the Old Testament (Gen. 10:25), the world was divided among the descendants of Noah. Al-Ṭabarī relates this tradition as well and notes that his name "means Qasim [one who divides, distributes]" in Arabic. He identifies Peleg as the son of Eber, grandson of Shelah, great-grandson of Qaynan, second great-grandson of Arpachshad, third great-grandson of Shem, and fourth great-grandson of Noah. The reason for al-Ṭabarī's removal of Peleg one generation further from Noah is quite interesting. He states that Qaynan is not mentioned in the Torah:

> He was the one of whom it was said that he was not worthy of being mentioned in the revealed scriptures, because he was a magician and called himself a god.[62]

Thus, ᶜAlī Mekkī's account of how the descendants of Noah were dispersed all around the world places the immigration of Ham's offspring to Africa several generations away from Noah and leads us to an Islamic historical source that identifies a magician who called himself a god among the descendants of Shem. This could not be more different than the image of black Africans depicted in ᶜAbdullāh's version of world history, according to which they received their skin color from Noah's curse; they were banished to Africa by Noah; magic was something in which they excelled; and it was they who either claimed divinity or seduced others to do so.

---

copying him, ᶜAlī cite Ḥākim al-Nīsābūrī (d. 1014), *al-Mustadrak ᶜalā al-Ṣaḥīḥayn fī al-ḥadīth* for the tradition, and al-Dhahabī (d. 1348), *Talkhīṣ al-Mustadrak*, and al-Suyūṭī (d. 1505), *Azhār al-ᶜurūsh fī akhbār al-ḥubūsh* for the assertion that it is a weak one. For the references, see Ibn ᶜAbd al-Bāqī, *Al-Ṭirāz al-manqūsh*, 31n2–3.

61 ᶜAlī Mekkī, *Mirʾāt al-ḥubūş*, 36b.

62 Al-Ṭabarī, *The History*, II, 15, 16n53.

So, how did Ham's descendants become black? Interpreting his quotation from Ibn al-Jawzī—that their move to the southern and western regions of the world led to a change in their skin color—ᶜAlī Mekkī explains in the Turkish part of his text that this change was the result of the influence of "the soil and the air of that area."[63] This is the well-known environmental explanation for the skin color of Africans, which one finds in other (Islamic and non-Islamic) sources, to which I return below in the context of evaluating Mollā ᶜAlī's *Dispelling the Darkness.*

The Mirror for Ethiopians was not the only work that took as its subject black Africans and was dedicated to the chief black eunuch Muṣṭafā Agha. Mollā ᶜAlī, himself an African man, wrote his *Dispelling the Darkness on the Merits of the Ethiopians* while he was a professor of law at the College of Süleymān I, the highest-ranking college of law in the Ottoman Empire, and completed it in 1612.[64] Mollā ᶜAlī most probably had access to ᶜAlī Mekkī's work, as it is possible to identify Turkish statements copied from the latter. Overall, however, *Dispelling the Darkness* represents an expansion of *The Mirror for Ethiopians.*[65]

63 ᶜAlī Mekkī, *Mirʾāt al-ḥubūş*, 37a.

64 His work very much follows the structure of Ibn ᶜAbd al-Bāqī's *The Colored Brocade* as well—although without acknowledging this work, which, as evidenced by ᶜAlī Mekkī and others, was not uncommon in premodern Ottoman practices of authorship. For another example of this practice, see Terzioğlu, "Bir Tercüme ve Bir İntihal Vakası." I must add that Kadızade Meḥmed, who, as Terzioğlu shows, presents someone else's work as his own, was actually the well-known Kadızade after whom the Kadızadeli movement was named. See Tezcan, "The Portrait of the Preacher as a Young Man."

65 Mollā ᶜAlī clearly went back to the source of *The Mirror for Ethiopians* as he translated parts of *The Colored Brocade* that ᶜAlī Mekkī had omitted. I closely compared the sections on Prophetic traditions about the merits of Ethiopians in the three works: Ibn ᶜAbd al-Bāqī, *Al-Ṭirāz al-manqūsh*, 35–38 (Weisweiler, *Buntes Prachtgewand*, 38–40, has some paragraphs missing); ᶜAlī Mekkī, *Mirʾāt al-ḥubūş*, 26a–27a (in Arabic), 27a–29a (in Turkish); and Mollā ᶜAlī, *Rāfiᶜü'l-ġubūş*, 39b–45a. While Mollā ᶜAlī's Turkish translation of Ibn ᶜAbd al-Bāqī's work is not exactly the same as ᶜAlī Mekkī's translation, the latter's technical explanation about the nuance between the Arabic words *daᶜwa* and *duᶜwa* is reproduced almost verbatim by Mollā ᶜAlī; compare ᶜAlī Mekkī, *Mirʾāt al-ḥubūş*, 28a; and Mollā ᶜAlī, *Rāfiᶜü'l-ġubūş*, 40a. Mollā ᶜAlī, however, translated and expanded upon the last part of this section in Ibn ᶜAbd al-Bāqī's work, which ᶜAlī Mekkī omitted. Compare Ibn ᶜAbd al-Bāqī, *Al-Ṭirāz al-manqūsh*, 37–38 (Weisweiler, *Buntes Prachtgewand*, 39–40); ᶜAlī Mekkī, *Mirʾāt al-ḥubūş*, 27a (in Arabic), 29a (in Turkish); and Mollā ᶜAlī, *Rāfiᶜü'l-ġubūş*, 41b–45a. Moreover, Mollā ᶜAlī added to the first chapter of *The Colored Brocade* five new sections, which are specifically dedicated to black eunuchs; see Tezcan, "*Dispelling the Darkness*," 94–95n76. While ᶜAlī Mekkī's work reads like an abridgement of Ibn ᶜAbd

More importantly, Mollā ᶜAlī's work differs from ᶜAlī Mekkī's intellectually.

While ᶜAlī Mekkī rejects the Curse of Ham as an explanation for the skin color of Africans, he does not have a problem with the environmental explanation, to which he also alludes in the preface to his work.[66] Mollā ᶜAlī, however, is keen to reject that explanation as well. In the introduction to his work, he states:

> The arguments of those who claim that the diversity of the colors of humans does not stem from the beginning of the creation but happened afterwards, as a result of an accident, are grounded on two points. One of them is the curse of Noah—Peace be upon our Prophet and upon him—and the second one is the influence of the air of [different] places.[67]

Mollā ᶜAlī was able to see that the environmental explanation had the effect of turning black skin into the result of an accident rather than an inherent feature of humanity. That is why, as I have discussed elsewhere in more detail, he strongly argued that blackness and darkness were equally inherent in the essence of Adam as was whiteness.[68] Thus, in the invocation section of the preface to his work, Mollā ᶜAlī thanks God for "creating the essence of the human from a piece of changeable and putrefied black mud."[69]

Another disagreement between ᶜAlī Mekkī and Mollā ᶜAlī is about Lukmān, a pre-Islamic figure after whom the thirty-first chapter of the Koran was named. According to ᶜAlī Mekkī, there is disagreement on the question of whether Lukmān was a prophet. He states that the overwhelming majority of scholars regards him as a wise man (*ḥakīm*) and a saint (*walī*), and relates a story according to which Lukmān selected wisdom when he was given a choice between wisdom and prophethood.[70]

---

al-Bāqī's (with some additions and a Turkish translation), Mollā ᶜAlī's work represents an expanded version of it in Turkish that is specifically addressed to black eunuchs. This is one of the reasons why I believe that the undated *The Mirror for Ethiopians* preceded *Dispelling the Darkness*; the other reason is that the most likely person to have been the author of the former died the year in which the latter was completed.

66 ᶜAlī Mekkī, *Mirʾāt al-ḥubūş*, 1b (in Arabic), 3a (in Turkish).

67 Mollā ᶜAlī, *Rāfiᶜü'l-ġubūş*, 23a.

68 Tezcan, "*Dispelling the Darkness*," 91–93.

69 Mollā ᶜAlī, *Rāfiᶜü'l-ġubūş*, 1b. For the significance of the invocation for the argument of a text, see Tezcan, "The Multiple Faces of the One."

70 ᶜAlī Mekkī, *Mirʾāt al-ḥubūş*, 22b–23a (in Arabic), 23b–25a (in Turkish); compare Ibn ᶜAbd al-Bāqī, *Al-Ṭirāz al-manqūsh*, 29 (Weisweiler, *Buntes Prachtgewand*, 33–34).

For Mollā ᶜAlī, however, Lukmān is joined by two other prophets of African origin. The first is one of those prophets whose stories were not narrated to Muhammad. Mollā ᶜAlī must have been inspired by his principal source Ibn ᶜAbd al-Bāqī, a sixteenth-century author who, in the section on the Prophetic traditions on Ethiopians in his *The Colored Brocade*, referred to a report, according to which ᶜAlī (d. 661), the young cousin and son-in-law of the Prophet who became the fourth caliph, interpreted the phrase "and among them are those [whose stories] We have not related to you" (Koran, 40:78) as a reference to a prophet who was an Ethiopian slave. He added that some interpreters of the Koranic reference to the believers who were burned by the "People of the Ditch" (Koran, 85:4) believe them to be Ethiopians who had an Ethiopian prophet. Mollā ᶜAlī expands on this paragraph and carries it to his section on notable Ethiopians in the pre-Islamic period, adding a story about why the believers were burned by the "People of the Ditch."[71]

Mollā ᶜAlī's second Ethiopian prophet is Lukmān, to whom he devotes a much longer section in *Dispelling the Darkness* than ᶜAlī Mekkī did in *The Mirror for Ethiopians*.[72] While declaring Lukmān a prophet is not unheard of in the Islamic tradition, Mollā ᶜAlī's next move is less common, as he declares Alexander the "Two-horned" an Ethiopian prophet as well and devotes a long section to his exploits.[73] The "Two-horned One" (*Dhū'l-qarnayn*) is a figure whose story is told in the Koran (18:83–98). Usually he is associated with Alexander the Great (d. 323 BCE) in Islamic literature; and, although generally not regarded as a prophet, he enjoys great popularity throughout the Islamic world.[74] Yet even in Ethiopia, where a local Christian tradition of Alexander romance developed, he was not regarded as Ethiopian.[75] Mollā ᶜAlī's source for Alexander's Ethiopian origins is a report by Ibn al-Kawwāʾ, who asked ᶜAlī about the "Two-Horned One." According to Mollā ᶜAlī, ᶜAlī stated that he was Ethiopian (*Ḥabeşī*).[76] There are slightly different versions of this report, but in none of them is there a reference to Ethiopia. Moreover, according to the

71 Mollā ᶜAlī, *Rāfiᶜü'l-ġubūş*, 45a–50a; compare ᶜAlī Mekkī, *Mirʾāt al-ḥubūş*, 26b (in Arabic), 28 (in Turkish). A version of this story is translated into English by David Cook; see his *Martyrdom in Islam*, 172–73.

72 Mollā ᶜAlī, *Rāfiᶜü'l-ġubūş*, 50a–58a; compare p. 65 above.

73 Mollā ᶜAlī, *Rāfiᶜü'l-ġubūş*, 58a–72a.

74 See, for instance, Stoneman, Erickson, and Netton, *The Alexander Romance in Persia and the East*; Zuwiyya, "The Alexander Romance in the Arabic Tradition"; and Aḥmedī, *İskender-nāme*.

75 Asirvatham, "The *Alexander romance* tradition from Egypt to Ethiopia."

76 Mollā ᶜAlī, *Rāfiᶜü'l-ġubūş*, 58.

extant versions of the report, Ibn al-Kawwāʾ asked whether the "Two-Horned One" was an angel or a prophet. ʿAlī described him as neither, but "a pious slave (or a pious servant of God [*kānᵃ ʿabdᵃⁿ ṣāliḥᵃⁿ*])."[77] It seems that Mollā ʿAlī decided to interpret *ʿabd* in the sense of a slave, rather than a servant of God, and then chose to take it as a synonym for Ethiopian. He might have been inspired in this choice by Ibn al-Jawzī, who also counted the "Two-Horned One" among the black prophets—on the authority of another report that also goes back to ʿAlī, who purportedly said that he was black (*aswad*)—or by al-Bīrūnī (d. 1048), who connected the "Two-Horned One" with the Himyarite Kingdom in ancient Yemen, which at some point in its history controlled parts of Ethiopia; but he cites neither.[78]

Why was Mollā ʿAlī concerned with identifying Ethiopian prophets to the extent that he forced a very unlikely reading onto some of his sources? The answer lies in an implication of the Curse of Ham, with which Mollā ʿAlī had to grapple: the divine predestination of black Africans to slavery. Both Ibn ʿAbd al-Bāqī and, following him, ʿAlī Mekkī relate several traditions on this issue in the introductions to their works. According to the first, which is cited in Ibn ʿAbd al-Ḥakam's (d. 871) *The History of the Conquest of Egypt, North Africa, and Spain*, the Prophet said that Noah asked God to provide his offspring with the means of subsistence for them to become perfect with growth and blessing. God promised that. So Noah called upon his sons, who were sleeping at dawn. He called Shem, who came quickly. Then Shem shouted to his sons, none of whom came, except Arpachshad. Noah put his right hand on Shem and his left hand on Arpachshad, and then asked God to bless Shem with the best blessing and to grant kingship and prophethood to the offspring of Arpachshad. Then Noah called Ham. He turned left and right, but no one responded; neither Ham nor any of his sons came. Thus Noah prayed that God might render Ham's sons servile, turning them into slaves for the sons of Shem and Japheth.[79] Next, Ibn ʿAbd al-Bāqī cites al-Ṭabarī:

---

77 Al-Muttaqī, *Kanz al-ʿummāl*, II:456, no. 4491.

78 Ibn al-Jawzī, *Tanwīr al-ġhabash*, 85 (Alawiye, "Ibn al-Jawzī's Apologia," 104); and al-Bīrūnī/Sachau, *The Chronology of Ancient Nations*, 49–50. I would like to thank Hossein Modarressi, who drew my attention to this passage in al-Bīrūnī and to the fact that the Himyarite Kingdom controlled parts of Ethiopia during some periods of its history.

79 ʿAlī Mekkī, *Mirʾāt al-ḥubūş*, 15b–16a (in Arabic), 18b–19a (in Turkish); compare Ibn ʿAbd al-Bāqī, *Al-Ṭirāz al-manqūsh*, 27 (Weisweiler, *Buntes Prachtgewand*, 31); and Ibn ʿAbd al-Ḥakam, *The History of the Conquest*, 7.

> According to Ibn Humayd—Salamah—Ibn Ishaq: The people of the Torah claim that while Noah slept his genitals were exposed, and Ham saw them but did not cover them. Shem and Japheth, on the other hand, saw them, and the two of them threw a garment over him and concealed his genitals. When he awoke from his sleep he knew what Shem and Japheth had done. Thus he said: "Cursed is Canaan, son of Ham. Slaves will they be to his brothers!" Then he said: "May my Lord bless Shem, and may Ham be a slave of his two brothers." Others besides Ibn Ishaq have said that Noah prayed that prophets and apostles would be descended from Shem and that he prayed that kings would be among the descendants of Japheth. He prayed that Ham's color would be changed and that his descendants would be slaves to the children of Shem and Japheth. It is mentioned in the books that Noah took a milder attitude toward Ham afterwards and prayed that he should be granted compassion by his brothers.[80]

ᶜAlī Mekkī paraphrases Ibn ᶜAbd al-Bāqī's citation of al-Ṭabarī, adding that the part about the change in Ham's skin color is an unfounded opinion. In the Turkish part of his text, he emphasizes once again that the Curse of Ham is limited to them becoming slaves.[81]

Thus, while the Curse of Ham was seen as irrelevant to the skin color of Africans, it still had currency as a way of envisioning Africans as potential slaves. In the invocation section of his preface to *The Colored Brocade*, for instance, Ibn ᶜAbd al-Bāqī describes God as a creator who made some human beings rulers and others servants, who granted prophethood and caliphate to some of the sons of Noah and slavery to others.[82]

Mollā ᶜAlī, too, noted in the invocation section of his preface to *Dispelling the Darkness* that some of the sons of Noah became the fathers of prophets, while others turned out to be the fathers of kings, and the offspring of others became servants to their own kind. But he asserted that God also favored Africans, turning some of the Ethiopians into prophets and others into kings.[83] Destabilizing the notion that all prophets came

80 Al-Ṭabarī, *The History*, II, 11–12, 14. I modified Brinner's translation to reflect the wording of Ibn ᶜAbd al-Bāqī, *Al-Ṭirāz al-manqūsh*, 27–28 (Weisweiler, *Buntes Prachtgewand*, 31–32).

81 ᶜAlī Mekkī, *Mirʾāt al-ḥubūş*, 16a (in Arabic), 19b–20a (in Turkish).

82 Ibn ᶜAbd al-Bāqī, *Al-Ṭirāz al-manqūsh*, 19 (Weisweiler, *Buntes Prachtgewand*, 22).

83 Mollā ᶜAlī, *Rāfiᶜü'l-ġubūş*, 2.

from among the sons of Shem was important for Mollā ᶜAlī, as it opened up the possibility of questioning the assumption that black Africans were destined to be slaves—as he does in his introduction.

After relating the different versions of the Curse of Ham story cited by Ibn ᶜAbd al-Bāqī and ᶜAlī Mekkī, Mollā ᶜAlī asks how it is that a prophet like Noah could curse his son simply because he did not respond when he was called. "It is evident to those who have reason and intelligence," Mollā ᶜAlī states, that if Ham were not forgiven, his punishment had to be a moderate one, suitable for his crime. Otherwise, one would have to ascribe oppression to Noah, a prophet. Finally, even if one assumes that Ham deserved a curse so strong as to render his descendants slaves, one would expect that only Ham's sons would be enslaved. However, the offspring of Noah's other sons, including the European and Semitic peoples, are also enslaved. Thus, the story of Noah's curse on his son is nonsensical.[84]

CONCLUSION

Despite their differences discussed above, ᶜAlī Mekkī and Mollā ᶜAlī have much in common when one compares their work to ᶜAbdullāh's (later) treatise. They both reject the Curse of Ham as an explanation for the skin color of Africans, and they both acknowledge the place of Africans in the very foundation of Islam. So, how should we interpret these three texts? I concluded the article in which I studied Mollā ᶜAlī's text and the socio-political context of his career by stating that racial tensions in early seventeenth-century Istanbul were not simple reflections of prejudice against blacks but rather reproductions of those prejudices with political connotations, just as the African identity that Mollā ᶜAlī embraced was not merely a natural extension of his African origins but a recreation of those origins in connection with the empowerment of the black eunuchs of the imperial palace.[85] I believe the same remarks may be applicable to the works of ᶜAlī Mekkī and ᶜAbdullāh as well.

ᶜAlī Mekkī is quite straightforward about why he wrote his work. In a section of his Turkish preface, which was not included in the Arabic version and thus was specifically meant for his addressee in Istanbul, he states that he wished to find pleasure and enjoyment but could not

84 Mollā ᶜAlī, *Rāfiᶜü'l-ġubūş*, 21a–26a; and Tezcan, "*Dispelling the Darkness*," 89–90.
85 Tezcan, "*Dispelling the Darkness*," 95.

identify a patron who would appreciate his work so that "this praise and eulogy may be useful, the purpose of the book and satisfaction may be obtained, and enjoyment may be reached." That is why he delayed writing for so many years, until God "facilitated his being honored with the honor of conversing with someone who was endowed with the aforementioned qualities." This patron was Aḥmed I's chief black eunuch, Muṣṭafā Agha.[86] That ᶜAlī's career improved after Muṣṭafā Agha came to office, with an appointment to the College of Meḥmed II, was discussed above. Thus, ᶜAlī Mekkī was either asking for such an appointment or thanking the chief black eunuch for it, depending on the exact date of composition, which, unfortunately, is unknown.

Most likely, Muṣṭafā Agha passed *The Mirror for Ethiopians* to Mollā ᶜAlī, who owed the launching of his career to Meḥmed Agha, either the first or the first prominent chief black eunuch of the Ottoman palace. Mollā ᶜAlī seems to have followed ᶜAlī Mekkī's footsteps, with an appointment to the College of Meḥmed II in 1607.[87] With *Dispelling the Darkness*, which includes sections specifically devoted to black eunuchs, he was thanking his patron Muṣṭafā Agha and also demonstrating that ᶜAlī Mekkī's work could be rewritten with sensitivity to such issues as the environmental explanation for the skin color of Africans or the use of the Curse of Ham to justify the enslavement of black Africans.

As I have discussed elsewhere in some detail, the rise of the office of the chief black eunuch to great prominence in the late sixteenth and seventeenth centuries was related to Ottoman monarchs' search for new loci of power within the court that could balance the growing power of vizier households.[88] Muṣṭafā Agha, for instance, witnessed the dismissal of seven grand viziers during his first tenure as the chief black eunuch (1605–20). But none of the chief black eunuchs had served the palace as long as the chief target of ᶜAbdullāh's treatise, Beşīr Agha, who in his almost twenty-nine years of service saw fourteen grand viziers.[89] Like

86 ᶜAlī Mekkī, *Mirʾāt al-ḥubūş*, 4a–10a, at folio 7; compare 3b–4a (Arabic).

87 For the details of Mollā ᶜAlī's career and his relationships with the black eunuchs, see Tezcan, "*Dispelling the Darkness*," 76–82.

88 Tezcan, *The Second Ottoman Empire*, 93–108. Other important factors that need a more detailed discussion are the slave trade between Africa and the Ottoman Empire, which grew in the sixteenth century, and the Ottoman imperial ambitions in East Africa. On the latter, see Orhonlu, *Habeş Eyaleti*.

89 Ḥācı Ḫalīl Pasha (1716–17), Nişāncı Meḥmed Pasha (1717–18), Nevşehirli Dāmād İbrāhīm Pasha (1718–30), Silāḥdār Dāmād Meḥmed Pasha (1730–31), Ḳabaḳulaḳ

Muṣṭafā Agha's support for Mollā ᶜAlī, Beşīr Agha, too, provided patronage for many, including Pīrīzāde, whom ᶜAbdullāh tried to approach at his salon but probably did not impress. Had ᶜAbdullāh found what he sought from Pīrīzāde, he might have written a very different book.[90]

Each one of the works of ᶜAlī Mekkī, Mollā ᶜAlī, and ᶜAbdullāh survived in a single manuscript only. It seems that the specificity of the political context of patronage, in which the first couple of them were produced, limited their circulation beyond the immediate audience they addressed, which might be an indication of the relative insignificance of questions of race and its relationship with slavery to the larger reading public. Since we do not have reliable statistics that could provide us with the ratio of African slaves to the slave population at large, it is difficult to test this hypothesis, but the fact that European and Caucasian slaves continued to be available in Ottoman slave markets during the seventeenth century would, at the least, suggest that Africans were only one group among many whose members were enslaved when ᶜAlī Mekkī and Mollā ᶜAlī were writing their works.

As for ᶜAbdullāh's treatise, it was clearly meant to reach a larger group, as it often reads like a sermon. But since the chief targets of ᶜAbdullāh's critique were palace functionaries in Istanbul, the work could not have meant much to his audience in Bursa, where black eunuchs probably did not constitute a major demographic group or a political power house. The work found its way to Istanbul, and that is where its extant manuscript is today; it is in the collection of the Köprülü Library, which was the first freestanding public library in the empire—as opposed to being connected with a college of law or a mosque.[91] Yet there are not many marginal notes in the manuscript, which could be taken as a sign of circulation; and the existing ones note how preposterous the claims made

İbrāhīm Pasha (1731), Topal ᶜOs̱mān Pasha (1731–32), Hekīmoğlu ᶜAlī Pasha (1732–35, 1742), Gürcü İsmāᶜīl Pasha (1735), Silāḥdār Seyyid Meḥmed Pasha (1736–37), Muḥsinzāde ᶜAbdullāh Pasha (1737), Yeğen Meḥmed Pasha (1737–39), ᶜİvaż Meḥmed Pasha (1739–40), Nişāncı Ḥācı Aḥmed Pasha (1740–42), Seyyid Ḥasan Pasha (1742–46).

90 A very different book was indeed written about black eunuchs within the decade that followed the completion of the *Halberdier's Treatise*: the *Ḫamīletü'l-küberā*ʾ, or *The Thicket of Great Men* by Aḥmed Resmī (or Aḥmed of Rethymno, d. 1783), an Ottoman statesman from Crete. See Aḥmed Resmī, *Ḫamīletü'l-küberā*. For a biography of the author in English, see Aksan, *An Ottoman Statesman*. I will revisit this work in *Shades of Black*.

91 On Ottoman libraries, see Erünsal, *Osmanlılarda Kütüphaneler ve Kütüphanecilik*.

by the author were.[92] So, the *Halberdier's Treatise* most probably did not create the splash that ᶜAbdullāh wished. And that is why I believe his ideas about black Africans, which would well be considered racist today, did not have much resonance among Ottoman readers. It was ᶜAbdullāh's position as an outsider to the circles of patronage centered around the chief black eunuch that prompted him to write what he did—just as it was the position that ᶜAlī Mekkī and Mollā ᶜAlī occupied within those circles that informed their approach to black Africans. Thus, while different forms of alterophobia are to be found in all societies, including Ottoman society, it is specific socio-political contexts that amplify them and bring about their more elaborate articulations.

This is not to say, however, that the *Halberdier's Treatise* should be evaluated simply as the result of ᶜAbdullāh's frustrations, late in his career, with a patronage network that excluded him. As evidenced in the issues on which Mollā ᶜAlī differed from ᶜAlī Mekkī, serious racial prejudices were directed against Africans in Ottoman intellectual heritage, just as others were directed against Christians, Jews, and the Kızılbaş, not to mention the various ethnic groups in Ottoman society, and women in general. While most of ᶜAbdullāh's work is fiction, some of his foundational stories, which allowed him to create many more fictive historical narratives, are rooted in the Curse of Ham that ᶜAlī Mekkī could not completely disavow—perhaps because of the Prophetic traditions associated with it. Mollā ᶜAlī did reject these foundational stories completely, not through a detailed study of the relevant Prophetic traditions, but through simple reason, daring to ask the basic question of how someone who is supposed to be a prophet could curse the offspring of his son just because he did not respond to his call at dawn.

BIBLIOGRAPHY

Sources

[Dervīş] ᶜAbdullāh. *Risāle-i teberdāriyye fī aḥvāl-i aġa-yı dārü's-saᶜāde*. (1) MS Köprülü II/233. Köprülü Yazma Eser Kütüphanesi, Istanbul. (2) Edited by Hızır Ali Telatar as "Derviş ᶜAbdullāh – Risale-i Teberdarriye [*sic*] fi ahvalı ağa-yı darü's-saᶜade (Metin ve Dizin, yp. 53–77)." Senior thesis, Istanbul University, 1973–74. (3) Edited by Reşat Karpuzcu as "Derviş ᶜAbdullāh – Risale-i Teberdarriye [*sic*] fi Ahval-i Ağa-yı Darü's-

92 Orhonlu, "Derviş Abdullah'ın Bir Eseri," 231.

saᶜade (Metin ve Dizin)." Senior Thesis, Istanbul University, 1973–74. (4) Edited by Pınar Saka as "Derviş Abdullah – Risâle-i Teberdâriyye fî Ahvâl-i Darü's-saᶜâde (Değerlendirme-Çeviri Metin)." M.A. thesis, Marmara University, 2007. (5) Edited by Pınar Saka as *Risale-i Teberdariye fi Ahval-i Darüssaade*. Istanbul: İnkılâp, 2011.

Aḥmed Resmī. *Ḫamīletü'l-küberā*. Edited by Ahmet Nezihi Turan as *Hamîletü'l-küberâ: Darüssaade ağaları*. Istanbul: Kitabevi, 2000.

Aḥmedī. *İskender-nāme: İnceleme – Tıpkıbasım*. Edited by İsmail Ünver. Ankara: Türk Tarih Kurumu, 1983.

Alawiye, Imran Hamza, ed. and trans. "Ibn al-Jawzī's Apologia on behalf of the Black People and their Status in Islam: A critical edition and translation of *Kitāb tanwīr al-gh-abash fī faḍl'l-Sūdān wa'l-Ḥabash*." Ph.D. dissertation, University of London, 1985.

ᶜAlī, Aḥmed, trans. *Al-Qur'ān: A Contemporary Translation*. Final revised edition. Princeton: Princeton University Press, 2001.

[Mollā] ᶜAlī. *Rāfiᶜü'l-ġubūş fī feżāᵓili'l-ḥubūş*. Istanbul, Süleymaniye Kütüphanesi, MS Fatih 4360.

ᶜAlī [Mekkī]. *Mirᵓāt al-ḥubūş fī'l-uṣūl*. Istanbul, Süleymaniye Kütüphanesi, MS Esat Efendi 484.

ᶜAtāᵓī, Nevᶜīzāde. *Ḥadāᵓiḳu'l-ḥaḳāᵓiḳ fī tekmīleti'ş-şaḳāᵓiḳ*. 2 vols. in one (Istanbul, 1268/1852), reprinted with indices in Abdülkadir Özcan, ed., *Şakaik-ı Nu'maniye ve Zeyilleri*, vol. 2. Istanbul: Çağrı Yayınları, 1989.

al-Bīrūnī. *The Chronology of Ancient Nations: an English version of the Arabic text of the Athár-ul-Bákiya of Albírúní or 'Vestiges of the past.'* Translated and edited by C. Edward Sachau. London: W. H. Allen & Co., 1879.

Ibn ᶜAbd al-Bāqī, Muḥammad. (1) *Al-Ṭirāz al-manqūsh fī maḥāsin al-Ḥubūsh*. Edited by ᶜAbd Allāh Muḥammad ᶜĪsā al-Ghazālī. Kuwait: Jāmiᶜat al-Kuwayt, 1995. (2) Weisweiler, Max, trans. *Buntes Prachtgewand: über die guten Eigenschaften der Abessinier von Muḥammad ibn ᶜAbdalbâqî al Buḫârî al Makkî*. Hannover: Heinz Lafaire, 1924.

ᶜAbd al-Ḥakam. *The History of the Conquest of Egypt, North Africa and Spain known as Futūḥ Miṣr*. Edited by Charles C. Torrey. New Haven: Yale University Press, 1922.

Ibn al-Jawzī, Abū al-Faraj ᶜAbd al-Raḥmān. *Tanwīr al-ghabash fī faḍl al-Sūdān wa-al-Ḥabash*. Edited by Marzūq ᶜAlī Ibrāhīm. Riyad: Dār al-Sharīf, 1998.

al-Jāḥiẓ. "The Superiority of Blacks to Whites." In *Sobriety and Mirth: A Selection of the Shorter Writings of al-Jahiz*, translated by Jim Colville, 25–51. London: Kegan Paul, 2002.

al-Kisāᵓī. *The Tales of the Prophets of al-Kisāᵓi*. Translated by Wheeler M. Thackston Jr. Boston: Twayne Publishers, 1978.

Muṣṭafā Cenābī. *Gülşen-i Tevārīḫ*. Cairo, Dār al-Kutub al-Qawmiyya, Taᵓrīkh Turkī Ṭalᶜat 170.

al-Muttaqī, ᶜAlī b. ᶜAbd al-Malik. *Kanz al-ᶜummāl fī sunan al-aqwāl wa-al-afᶜāl*. Edited by Bakrī Ḥayyanī and Ṣafwa al-Saqqā. 18 vols. Bayrūt : Muᵓassasat al-Risāla, 1985–86.

Rapaport, Samuel, trans. *Tales and Maxims from the Midrash*. London and New York: G. Routledge and E. P. Dutton, 1907.

al-Ṭabarī. *History of al-Ṭabarī (Taʾrīkh al-rusul wa'l-muluk)*. Edited by Ehsan Yar-Shater et al. Translated by Franz Rosenthal et al. 39 vols. Albany: State University of New York Press, 1989–98.

al-Thaʿlabī, Aḥmad bin Muḥammad. *ʿArāʾis al-majālis fī qiṣaṣ al-anbiyāʾ or "Lives of the Prophets."* Translated by William M. Brinner. Leiden: Brill, 2002.

Studies

Abou-El-Haj, Rifaʾat Ali. "The Ottoman *nasihatname* as a discourse over 'morality.'" In *Mélanges Professeur Robert Mantran*, edited by Abdeljelil Temimi, 17–30. Zaghouan: Publications du Centre d'Etudes et de Recherches Ottomanes, Morisques, de Documentation et d'Information, 1988 [*Revue d'histoire maghrébine* 47–48 (1987)].

Aksan, Virginia H. *An Ottoman Statesman in War and Peace: Ahmed Resmi Efendi, 1700–1783*. Leiden: Brill, 1995.

Akşit, İlhan. *Osmanlı'nın Gizemi Harem*. Istanbul: Akşit Kültür ve Turizm Yayıncılık, 2000.

Asirvatham, Sulochana. "The *Alexander romance* tradition from Egypt to Ethiopia." In *Alexander in Africa*, edited by P. R. Bosman [*Acta Classica: Proceedings of the Classical Association of South Africa – Supplementum 5*], 109–27. Pretoria: Classical Association of South Africa, 2014.

Cook, David. *Martyrdom in Islam*. Cambridge: Cambridge University Press, 2007.

Erünsal, İsmail E. *Osmanlılarda Kütüphaneler ve Kütüphanecilik: Tarihî Gelişimi ve Organizasyonu*. Istanbul: TİMAŞ, 2015.

Fleischer, Cornell. *Bureaucrat and Intellectual in the Ottoman Empire: The Historian Mustafa Âli (1541–1600)*. Princeton: Princeton University Press, 1986.

Goldenberg, David M. *The Curse of Ham: Race and Slavery in Early Judaism, Christianity, and Islam*. Princeton: Princeton University Press, 2003.

Gruber, Ernst August. *Verdienst und Rang: Die* Faḍāʾil *als literarisches und gesellschaftliches Problem im Islam*. Freiburg: Klaus Schwarz, 1975.

Hathaway, Jane. *Beshir Agha: Chief Eunuch of the Ottoman Imperial Harem*. Oxford: One World, 2005.

Howard, Douglas A. "Genre and Myth in the Ottoman Advice for Kings Literature." In *The Early Modern Ottomans: Remapping the Empire*, edited by Virginia H. Aksan and Daniel Goffman, 137–66. Cambridge: Cambridge University Press, 2007.

Junne, George. *The Black Eunuchs of the Ottoman Empire: Networks of Power in the Court of the Sultan*. London: I.B. Tauris, 2016.

Le Gall, Dina. *A Culture of Sufism: Naqshbandīs in the Ottoman World, 1450–1700*. Albany: State University of New York Press, 2005.

Marmon, Shaun. *Eunuchs and Sacred Boundaries in Islamic Society*. New York: Oxford University Press, 1995.

Muhammad, Akbar. "The Image of Africans in Arabic Literature: Some Unpublished Manuscripts." In *Slaves and Slavery in Muslim Africa*, edited by J. R. Willis, 2:47–74. London: Frank Cass & Co., 1985.

Orhonlu, Cengiz. "Derviş Abdullah'ın Darussaade Ağaları Hakkında Bir Eseri: Risale-i Teberdariye Fî Ahvâl-ı Dâru's-saâde." In *Ord. Prof. İsmail Hakkı Uzunçarşılı'ya Armağan*, 225–49. Ankara: Türk Tarih Kurumu Basımevi, 1976.

Rubin, Uri. "Pre-Existence and Light—Aspects of the Concept of Nūr Muḥammad." *Israel Oriental Studies* 5 (1975): 62–119.

Stoneman, Richard, Kyle Erickson, and Ian Netton, eds. *The Alexander Romance in Persia and the East*. Groningen: Barkhuis, 2012.

Terzioğlu, Derin. "Bir Tercüme ve Bir İntihal Vakası: Ya da İbn Teymiyye'nin *Siyasetü'ş-şer*^{c}*iyye*'sini Osmanlıcaya Kim(ler) Nasıl Aktardı?" *Journal of Turkish Studies/ Türklük Bilgisi Araştırmaları Dergisi* 31, no. II (2007): 247–75.

Tezcan, Baki. "*Dispelling the Darkness*: The Politics of 'Race' in the Early Seventeenth Century Ottoman Empire in the Light of the Life and Work of Mullah Ali." In *Identity and Identity Formation in the Ottoman World: A Volume of Essays in Honor of Norman Itzkowitz*, edited by Baki Tezcan and Karl K. Barbir, 73–95. Madison: University of Wisconsin, Center for Turkish Studies, 2007.

Tezcan, Baki. "From Veysî (d. 1628) to Üveysî (fl. ca. 1630): Ottoman Advice Literature and Its Discontents." In *Reforming Early Modern Monarchies: The Castilian* Arbitristas *in Comparative European Perspectives*, edited by Sina Rauschenbach and Christian Windler, 141–55. Wiesbaden: Harrassowitz [Wolfenbütteler Forschungen, 143], 2016.

Tezcan, Baki. "The Multiple Faces of the One: The Invocation Section of Ottoman Literary Introductions as a Locus for the Central Argument of the Text." *Middle Eastern Literatures* 12 (2009): 27–41.

Tezcan, Baki. "The Portrait of the Preacher as a Young Man: Two Autobiographical Letters by Kadızade Mehmed from the Early Seventeenth Century." In *Political Thought and Practice in the Ottoman Empire* [Proceedings of the Halcyon Days in Crete IX Symposium, Rethymno, 9–11 January 2015], edited by Marinos Sariyannis. Rethymno: Crete University Press, forthcoming.

Tezcan, Baki. *The Second Ottoman Empire: Political and Social Transformation in the Early Modern World*. New York: Cambridge University Press, 2010.

Turan, Ahmet Nezihi. "Mahremiyetin Muhafızları: Darüssaade Ağaları." *Osmanlı Araştırmaları / The Journal of Ottoman Studies* 19 (1999): 123–48.

Zuwiyya, Z. David. "The Alexander Romance in the Arabic Tradition." In *A Companion to Alexander Literature in the Middle Ages*, edited by Z. David Zuwiyya, 73–112. Leiden: Brill, 2011.

The Jew, the Orthodox Christian, and the European in Ottoman Eyes, ca. 1550–1700

Bilha Moor

This study examines representations of the Jew, the Orthodox Christian, and the European in illustrated Ottoman cosmographies, and serves as a case study for the reception of the "other" in the capital city of Istanbul and in the Ottoman provinces. It explores continuity and change in illustrated manuscripts of *ᶜAjāʾib al-Makhlūqāt wa Gharāʾib al-Mawjūdāt* (Wonders of Creation and Oddities of Existence) by Zakariyyā al-Qazwīnī (d. 1283),[1] a thirteenth-century cosmographer, geographer, and Qāḍī.[2]

This popular Arabic encyclopedia of the natural and the supernatural worlds,[3] often referred to as a cosmography, was copied and illustrated for six hundred years, from the Ilkhanids to the Ottomans and Qajars, in different parts of the Muslim empires. The text was translated into

---

* I wish to thank Professor Esther Levinger for discussing this paper with me, and for her valuable remarks. I am also grateful to the editors and the two anonymous readers for their suggestions.

1 Hereafter, "Qazwīnī's *ᶜAjāʾib*."

2 For a recent account of his life and works, see Berlekamp, "Qazwīnī Al-, Zakarīya B. Muḥammad B. Maḥmūd."

3 Von Hees, "Al-Qazwīnī's *ᶜAjāʾib al-Makhlūqāt* – An Encyclopaedia."

Persian and Ottoman Turkish in the fifteenth and sixteenth centuries.[4] Over the centuries, the text, the cycle of illustrations, and the iconography of the illustrated manuscripts were subject to change. Some entries were omitted, altered, or added, while others remained constant.[5] The following examination reveals that representations of the Jew as a human-frog hybrid were regularly included in Qazwīnī's manuscripts from the late thirteenth century onward, whereas realistic images of the Orthodox Christian and the European were added to copies of the encyclopedia not before the Ottoman period.

THE JEW

One recurring entry in Qazwīnī's *ᶜAjāᵓib* is that of *al-shaykh al-yahūdī* (the old/wise Jew, hereafter the "Jewish *shaykh*"), a hybrid water creature that is presented with a human head and a frog's body (fig. 1). The entry appears in the treatise as part of the discussion of seas and islands, in which the author surveys their inhabitants and water creatures. The entry is listed in several manuscript catalogues, but it has not yet been studied.[6] Sometimes the creature is referred to as human-frog, omitting its Jewish identity.[7] A brief description of the creature appears in a few studies of specific manuscripts, but without further analysis of the context or the possible meaning of the entry at the time it was written or

4 The Persian translator of Qazwīnī's *ᶜAjāᵓib* is unknown. Karin Rührdanz discusses two Persian versions of the text in "Qazwīnī's *ᶜAjāᵓib al-Makhlūqāt* in illustrated Timurid Manuscripts"; see especially 474. The Ottoman Turkish translations from the fifteenth and sixteenth centuries are mentioned in Berlekamp, *Wonder, Image, and the Cosmos*, 157–58. Most surviving Ottoman Turkish illustrated manuscripts of Qazwīnī's *ᶜAjāᵓib* are copies of Sürūrī's translation (mid-sixteenth century).

5 For some of the changes that occurred in Qazwīnī's manuscripts in the fifteenth and sixteenth centuries, see Rührdanz, "Illustrated Persian *ᶜAjāᵓib al-Makhlūqāt* Manuscripts"; and Moor, "*Shāhnāma* Heroes and Kings in *ᶜAjāᵓib al-Makhlūqāt*."

6 See, for example, Schmitz et al., *Islamic Manuscripts in the New York Public Library*, 83, cat. no. II. 5, Spencer, Pers. Ms. 49, probably Shiraz, ca. 947/1540, 94a; Titley, *Miniatures from Persian Manuscripts*, 112, cat. no. 246, Ms. Or. 12220, Herat 909/1503–4, 79a; Duda, *Islamische Handschriften I*, 1:165, Ms. Mixt. 324, 984/1576–77, 70b; and Schmitz and Desai, *Mughal and Persian Paintings*, 92, Ms. A.4600 (M.K.603), probably Bijapur, 979/1571, 153.

7 Examples are Titley, *Miniatures from Persian Manuscripts*, 87, cat. no. 238, Ms. Add. 23564, Shiraz, 845/1441, 91b; Robinson, *Persian Paintings in the John Rylands Library*, 43, Ms. Ryl Pers 37, Shiraz, ca. 1440, 90b; and Robinson, *A Descriptive Catalogue of the Persian Paintings*, 37, Ms. Laud Or. 132, ca. 1480–90, 87a.

illustrated.[8] Julie Badiee proposes that "many of the animals described by Qazwīnī are fantastic in nature, one need only mention the Old Jew, the Waterman, and the various sea-serpents and dragons."[9] Contrary to this, I argue that the "Jewish *shaykh*" creature signifies the Jew who lived in Islamic lands, not on a fanciful, faraway island.

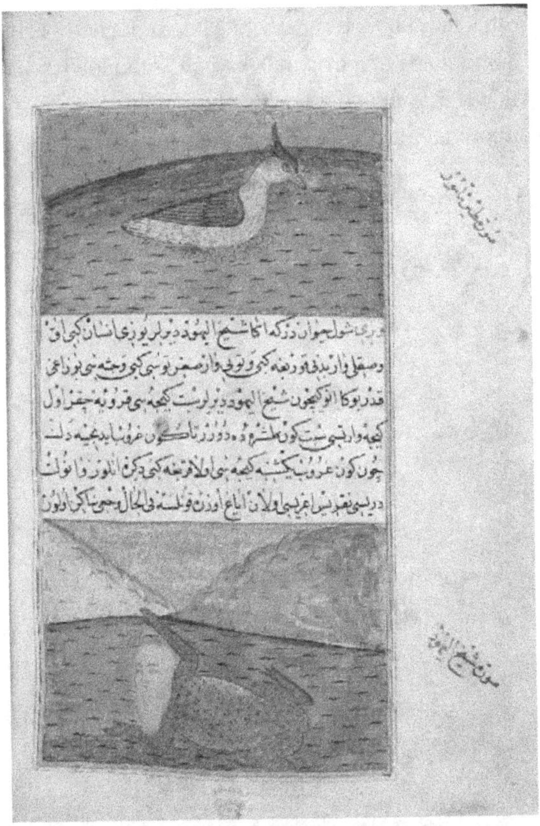

Fig. 1. The "Jewish *shaykh*" (below). Qazwīnī, *'Ajā'ib al-Makhlūqāt*, translated into Ottoman Turkish by Sürurī, Istanbul, ca. 1594–95. London, British Library, Add. 7894, fol. 148b. © The British Library Board, Add. 7894, fol. 148b.

The entry "Jewish *shaykh*" appears in a corpus of about fifteen Ottoman manuscripts of Qazwīnī's *ᶜAjāᵓib* in Arabic, Persian, and Ottoman Turkish, dating roughly from 1550 to 1700. It forms part of

8 Badiee, "Islamic Cosmography," 119, pl. 37; Carboni, "Wonders of Creation and Singularities of Ilkhanid Painting," 1:124; and Moor and Rezvan, "Qazwīnī's *ᶜAjāᵓib al-Makhlūqāt*," 51–52, pl. 3.

9 Badiee, "Islamic Cosmography," 132.

the earliest known illustrated *ʿAjāʾib* manuscript, which was copied in Arabic in Wasit, Iraq, in 1280, during Qazwīnī's lifetime;[10] and its text remains almost unchanged throughout the centuries (fig. 2). It reads:

> And among them [the wondrous water animals of the Western Sea] is *al-shaykh al-yahūdī* [the Jewish *shaykh*]. Abū Ḥāmid said that this is an animal with a human face and a white beard. Its body is in the size of a calf and in the shape of a frog. It is known as the Jewish *shaykh* because it exits the water to the land on the eve of Sabbath until the sun sets on the eve of Sunday. It does not enter the water or eat, nor does it move;

Fig. 2. The "Jewish *shaykh*." Qazwīnī, *ʿAjāʾib al-Makhlūqāt* (Arabic), Wasit, Iraq, 1280. Munich, Bayerische Staatsbibliothek, Cod.arab. 464, fol. 69b. © Bayerische Staatsbibliothek München, Cod. arab. 464, fol. 69b.

10 Munich: Bayerische Staatsbibliothek (hereafter, "BSB"), Cod.arab. 464. This manuscript is the subject of several studies: Ettinghausen, *Arab Painting*, 138–40; Von Bothmer, "Die illustrationen der 'Münchener Qazwīnī' von 1280"; Von Hees, *Enzyklopädie als Spiegel des Weltbilde*; Rebhan, *Die Wunder der Schöpfung*, 62–65; and Berlekamp, *Wonder, Image, and the Cosmos*.

> even if it is beaten up or killed, it does not enter the water. And when the sun sets on the eve of Sunday, it leaps like a frog and enters the sea. And the ships do not catch up with it. It was reported that when its skin is put on a [person suffering from] gout, the pain is immediately relieved.[11]

The entry reflects the perception of the Jew and his religious customs in Islamic lands. It shows that observing the Sabbath was received as a perplexing and obstinate act, one that recalls the behavior of an amphibian. That the skin of this creature allegedly has curing properties coincides with other fauna entries in Qazwīnī's text, where organs of some animals are described as having medicinal uses.

Qazwīnī cites Abū Ḥāmid al-Gharnāṭī (d. 1169–70),[12] a medieval Andalusian traveler who lived in Granada until the age of thirty, when he embarked on his journeys.[13] In Gharnāṭī's treatise, *Tuḥfat al-Albāb wa-Nukhbat al-Aᶜjāb* (Gift of the Hearts and Selected Wonders), there is indeed a similar description of a creature called *al-samak al-yahūdī*, the "Jewish fish."[14] This treatise was written sometime around 1155–60, in Baghdad or Mosul.[15] The text reads:

> And in the sea there is also a type of animal, whose head resembles that of a calf. It has teeth like beasts of prey, and its skin is hairy like a calf. It has a neck, a chest and a stomach, and legs like those of a frog, on which it leaps like a frog. It has no hands. And it is known as *al-samak al-yahūdī* [the Jewish fish] because when the sun sets on the eve of Sabbath it exits the sea and throws itself on the land. It does not move, or eat, even if it is being killed, it does not enter the sea

---

11 My translation is based on the text in manuscript BSB, Cod.arab. 464, 69b–70a.

12 Caiozzo, "L'image de l'Europe," 107.

13 On his biography and travels, see Al-Gharnāṭī, *Tuḥfat al-Albāb*, 7–10.

14 For the Arabic text, see Ferrand, "Le *Tuḥfat al-Albāb*," 99; and Al-Gharnāṭī, *Tuḥfat al-Albāb*, 123–24. For a French translation of Gharnāṭī's text, see Ducatez, "La Tuḥfa al-Albāb," 200; and Caiozzo, "L'image de l'Europe," 107.

15 Gharnāṭī composed his text about a century after the Muslim attack on the Jewish community of Granada in 1066, when Joseph ibn Naghrela and hundreds or thousands (depending on the source) of Jews were murdered. After these riots, Granada was no longer the center of the Jewish community in southern Spain. In 1090, when Gharnāṭī was about ten years old, the Jewish quarter suffered another blow when Granada was sacked by the Almoravids. It is therefore possible that the "Jewish fish" entry echoes local anti-Jewish sentiments expressed in Gharnāṭī's hometown. On the events that occurred in Granada, see Ashtor, *The Jews of Moslem Spain*, 2:187–94; Stillman, *The Jews of Arab Lands*, 59; and Gilbert, *In Ishmael's House*, 49.

> until the sun sets on the eve of Sunday. And when it enters the sea, the ships do not catch up with it because of its lightness and strength. Its skin is used for shoes for those who suffer from gout. And the [person who suffers from] gout feels no pain as long as he wears that shoe. And it [the Jewish fish] is from the wonders of this world.[16]

The description in Qazwīnī's text clearly relies on his twelfth-century predecessor, albeit with a few changes. One change regards the creature's name. Qazwīnī transforms Gharnāṭī's "Jewish fish" to the "Jewish *shaykh*." This shift indicates that Qazwīnī received the entry as a marker for the Jew. He adds that the creature's human head has a white beard, which signifies old age but could also imply elderly wisdom, a duality which is suggested by the very use of the word *shaykh*. Another salient change concerns the creature's organs. Gharnāṭī describes a composite creature, without human features (that is, head of a calf, beast's teeth, and legs of a frog), whereas Qazwīnī describes a human-frog hybrid. The change is significant, as scholars of monsters in medieval European thought have noted that "the combination of human head and animal body is a deforming that preserves reason."[17]

Of all the animals that Gharnāṭī uses to describe the creature, Qazwīnī favors the frog, and he attributes to the "Jewish *shaykh*" its formal and behavioral qualities (leaping). Qazwīnī's *ʿAjāʾib* also includes a lengthy entry on the frog (*ḍafdaʿ*, fig. 3).[18] He describes it as an amphibian (land and water animal, *ḥayawān barrī baḥrī*) with protruding eyes and sharp senses of hearing and seeing. The author draws on several sources that reflect the transmission of knowledge of the natural world from antiquity to Islam. He cites Balīnās (Pliny the Elder, d. 79), al-Jāḥiẓ (d. 869), Ibn Sīnā (whom he refers to as *al-shaykh al-raʾis*, d. 1037), and the *ḥadīth*. According to the latter, one should not kill the frog, as its croaks are praises to God (*tasbīḥ*). Qazwīnī describes the evolution of tadpoles, mentions three types of frogs, and recounts several beliefs about them. For instance, if the number of frogs increases in certain years more than usual, an epidemic will follow; moreover, frogs croak frequently at night, but if they see fire they stop croaking. Much information in this entry, however, refers to the medicinal uses of frogs. For example, if one puts

---

16 My translation is based on the Arabic text in Ferrand, "Le *Tuḥfat al-Albāb*," 99.

17 See especially Williams, *Deformed Discourse*, 137.

18 BSB, Cod.arab. 464, 76a–b. The entry "Frog" was translated into German and discussed in Von Hees, *Enzyklopädie als Spiegel des Weltbilde*, 189–204.

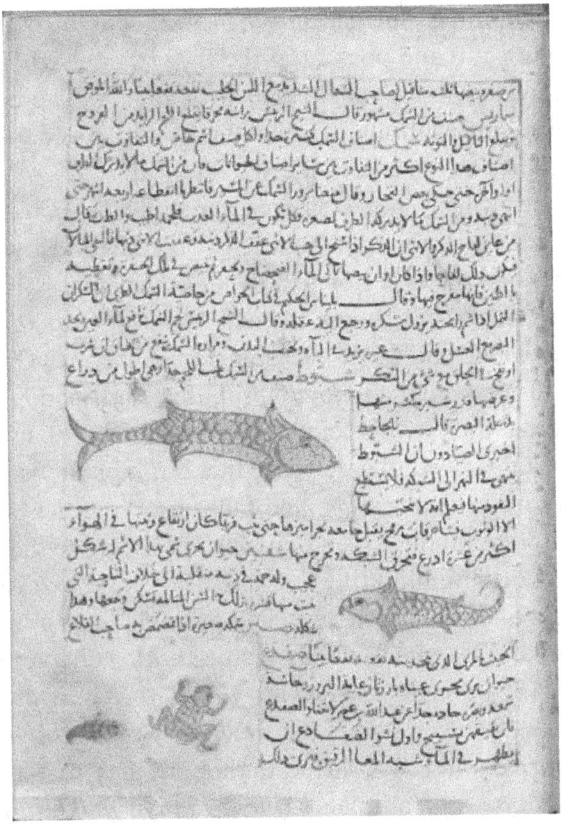

Fig. 3. The "Frog" (below). Qazwīnī, *ʿAjāʾib al-Makhlūqāt* (Arabic), Wasit, Iraq, 1280. Munich, Bayerische Staatsbibliothek, Cod.arab. 464, fol. 76a. © Bayerische Staatsbibliothek München, Cod.arab. 464, fol. 76a.

a frog's tongue on a woman's heart while she is asleep, she will speak about what she has been doing while awake. He who splashes his face with frog's blood will be loved by whomever lays eyes on him. It is also said that the frog's heart and gall bladder are deadly poisons.[19]

But what is the reader of Qazwīnī's *ᶜAjāʾib* to make of this diverse information on the frog in regard to the "Jewish *shaykh*"? Does the hybrid possess both human and frog qualities? Is one to assume that the information given on the frog's head is not valid because the "Jewish *shaykh*" has a human head? The medicinal effects attributed to the frog differ from those associated with the "Jewish *shaykh*," implying that the latter is distinct from the frog. A comparison between the illustration of

19 BSB, Cod.arab. 464, 76a–b.

the frog and that of the "Jewish *shaykh*" shows that the body of the latter is indeed in the form and posture of the frog (figs. 2–3). The difference is that the "Jewish *shaykh*" is covered with an aquatic creature's scales, and its size is significantly larger than the frog's (in accordance with the text that describes the hybrid as the size of a calf).

When discussing water creatures generally (*al-qawl fī ḥayawānāt al-māʾ*), Qazwīnī distinguishes between two categories: water creatures without lungs, like the types of fish (*samak*) that live only in the water, and water creatures with lungs, which, like the frog (*ḍafdaʿ*), "combine between water and air."[20] Keeping in mind that Qazwīnī altered Gharnāṭī's fish into a human-frog hybrid, this clarification seems significant. It indicates that, by associating the frog (rather than the fish) with the Jew, Qazwīnī wished to emphasize that this creature is an amphibian, capable of living in two realms, and that observing the Sabbath means entering a different modus vivendi, which is obscure to the author.

It is also worth highlighting that the "Jewish *shaykh*" is listed under "water animals of the Western Sea," and presented as a hybrid in text and illustration alike. Qazwīnī ends his treatise with a chapter on odd-looking creatures (*khātima fī ḥayawānāt gharībat al-ṣuwar wa'l-ashkāl*), which includes three categories. One category regards hybrids (*al-ḥayawānāt al-murakkaba*), which the author defines as the offspring of "two different types of animals" (*ḥayawānayn mukhtalifay al-nawʿ*), like a man and a bear.[21] The "Jewish *shaykh*" is not mentioned in this chapter, but it is likely that the reader of the encyclopedia could deduce that it falls into the category of odd hybrids.

In medieval and early modern European literature and art, the frog or toad usually bears negative connotations,[22] and is occasionally associated with the Jew, signifying "the usurer, who is swollen with greed."[23] No such association, however, is mentioned in Qazwīnī's text. Also, in European examples the Jew is sometimes presented as having demonic, animal, or monstrous features,[24] but is not shown as a human-frog hybrid. To the best of my knowledge, the entry "Jewish *shaykh*" appears only in

---

20 BSB, Cod.arab. 464, 72a.

21 BSB, Cod.arab. 464, 209a–209b.

22 Robbins, "The Truculent Toad in the Middle Ages"; Rebold Benton, *The Medieval Menagerie*, 111; and Vervoort, "The Pestilent Toad."

23 Lipton, *Images of Intolerance*, 44; and Lipton, *Dark Mirror*, 7, 244.

24 See in particular, Higgs Strickland, *Saracens, Demons, and Jews*, 77–78, 128–30, 133–36, 219–20.

Qazwīnī's *ᶜAjāᵓib* and in two later Islamic encyclopedic treatises that cite him almost word for word: *Nuzhat al-Qulūb* (Pleasure-trip of the Hearts)[25] and *Majmaᶜ al-Gharāᵓib* (Compendium of Oddities).[26] These treatises cannot shed additional light on the association of the Jew with the frog, but they do attest to the relevance of the entry at the times and places in which they were composed, copied, and illustrated.

The *ᶜAjāᵓib* manuscripts are not alone in presenting images of Jews in Islamic lands. Historical and quasi-historical treatises that were also illustrated in the Ilkhanid period, when the earliest *ᶜAjāᵓib* manuscripts were produced, include a few depictions of Jews in negative contexts.[27] One example is a folio from Abū al-Qāsim Ferdowsī's (d. 1019 or 1025) *Shāhnāmeh* (Book of Kings, completed in 1010), which shows the Sassanian king Bahrām Gūr sweeping up his horse's droppings in the presence of a stingy Jew called Barāhām (fig. 4). The verses recount that the Jew made the Persian king sleep outdoors while Barāhām feasted in his comfortable home.[28] In this case, although Ferdowsī describes the Jew in an unflattering manner, he is nonetheless depicted as human. The *Shāhnāmeh* was a highly favored text in the Persianate world, and was lavishly illustrated in hundreds of manuscripts from the fourteenth to the nineteenth century. Interestingly enough, this anti-Jewish iconography was not popular. Among the hundreds of surviving copies of the *Shāhnāmeh* there are only two known illustrations of the scene.[29] This stands in contrast to the abundant number of illustrations of the "Jewish *shaykh*" in Qazwīnī's manuscripts.

During the following centuries, numerous *ᶜAjāᵓib* manuscripts repeated the late thirteenth-century model of the "Jewish *shaykh*." However, in every

25 Ḥamdallāh al-Mustawfī al-Qazwīnī, *Nuzhat al-Qulūb* (composed in the fourteenth century). See, for example, London: British Library (hereafter, "BL"), Ms. Add. 7710, India, seventeenth century, 283b. On this manuscript, see Titley, *Miniatures from Persian Manuscripts*, 115–17, cat. no. 250.

26 Muḥammad al-Muftī, *Majmaᶜ al-Gharāᵓib* (composed in the mid-sixteenth century). See, for example, Dublin: The Chester Beatty Library, Ms. 9, India, ca. 1650–60, 59a. On this manuscript, see York Leach, *Mughal and Other Indian Paintings*, 2:590–604.

27 See the discussion on the illustrations of Muḥammad and the Jewish tribes of Medina in Rashīd al-Dīn's *Jāmiᶜ al-Tawārīkh* (Compendium of Histories) in Soucek, "The Life of the Prophet," especially 201. On negative perceptions of Jews in other medieval texts, see Barry, "Jews, Islamic Mysticism, and the Devil."

28 Ferdowsī, *Shāhnāmeh*, 5:1604–6.

29 According to the Cambridge Shahnama Project's database, one illustration is from ca. 1300 (fig. 4), and the other is from the turn of the fifteenth century. Accessed February 2016, http://shahnama.caret.cam.ac.uk/new/jnama/card/cescene:1679601993.

Fig. 4. Barāhām makes Bahrām Gūr sweep up horse droppings. Ferdowsī, *Shāhnāmeh*, Baghdad?, ca. 1300. New York, The Brooklyn Museum of Art, Gift of the Ernest Erickson Foundation, Inc., 86.227.130., 1a–b. Photo: Brooklyn Museum.

region of the Persianate world, India, and the Ottoman realm, artists produced variations on the entry, depicting a human and aquatic creature hybrid, not necessarily a frog. In a late fifteenth-century Persian manuscript, for example, a line was added to the original text so that the "Jewish *shaykh*" becomes a composite animal with cow hands and feet; in the painting they resemble nippers (fig. 5).[30] From late sixteenth-century India[31] one encounters an intriguing illustration in which a yellow "Jewish *shaykh*" stands on the seashore while in the farther plane two turbaned men watch him in wonder (fig. 6). The creature differs from the fishes that swim in the water but also from the two men, and, accordingly, it is positioned in the middle of the composition, as if to show

30 Oxford: Bodleian Library, Ms. Laud Or. 132, ca. 1480–90, 87a. See Robinson, *A Descriptive Catalogue of the Persian Paintings*, 37, no. 254.

31 Oxford: Bodleian Library, Ms. Ouseley 312, 92b. This manuscript is probably modeled after certain Persian manuscripts from the sixteenth century. It is listed in Sachau and Ethé, *Catalogue of the Persian, Turkish, Hindūstānī*, 400, no. 397.

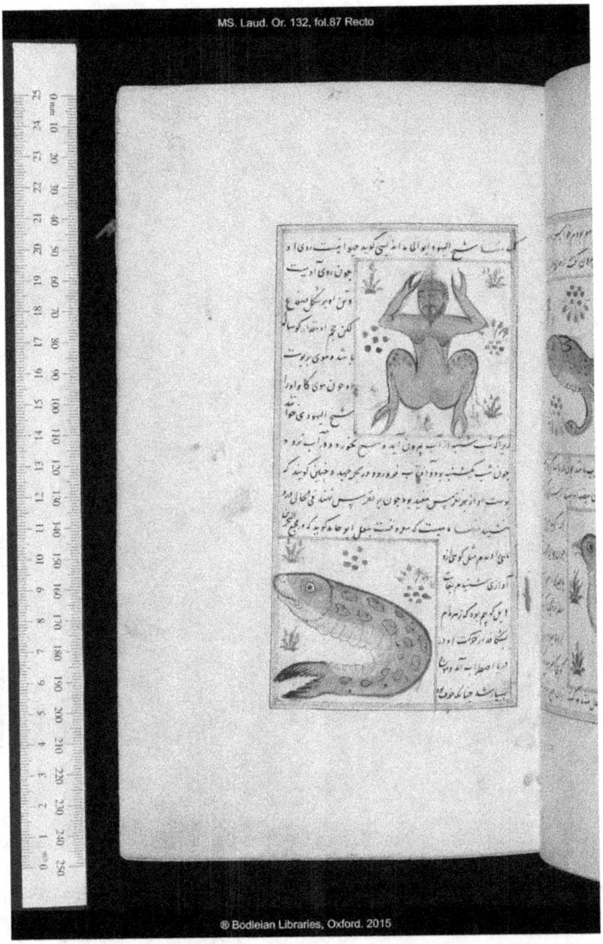

Fig. 5. The "Jewish *shaykh*" (above). Qazwīnī, *'Ajā'ib al-Makhlūqāt* (Persian), Iran, ca. 1480–90. Oxford, The Bodleian Libraries, University of Oxford, Ms. Laud Or. 132, fol. 87a. Photo: The Bodleian Libraries, University of Oxford.

that it is classified somewhere between human and animal. The two Muslims could be interpreted as a reflection of the manuscript's reader, who observes the odd creature just as they do. The two men therefore represent the "self," and the "Jewish *shaykh*" represents the "other." It is as if their astonishment at the sight of the creature instructs the reader on how to perceive the "Jewish *shaykh*" and encourages the process of othering. The artist's choice to depict the creature in yellow is presumably intentional, as it coincides with the dress code for non-Muslims first established by the Abbasid caliph al-Mutawakkil (r. 847–61). According to his ninth-century decree, non-Muslim men

Fig. 6. The "Jewish *shaykh*." Qazwīnī, *ʿAjāʾib al-Makhlūqāt* (Persian), India, late 16th century. Oxford, The Bodleian Libraries, University of Oxford, Ouseley 312, fol. 92b. Photo: The Bodleian Libraries, University of Oxford.

and women, as well as their slaves, should wear certain yellow clothes or headgear.[32]

Perhaps the most noteworthy variant of this entry, however, was introduced in the Ottoman period. Examining the corpus of Qazwīnī's *ʿAjāʾib* from that era, one observes two major variants of the "Jewish *shaykh*." One follows the Istanbul example and presents the hybrid human-frog (see fig. 1).[33] It relies closely on the text but also follows earlier models.

32 On the *ghiyār* (differentiating signs), see Levy-Rubin, *Non-Muslims in the Early Islamic Empire*, especially 60–61, 148–49.

33 London, BL, Add.7894, Istanbul, late sixteenth century, 148b. On this manuscript, see Titley, *Miniatures from Turkish Manuscripts*, 69–71, cat. no. 60.

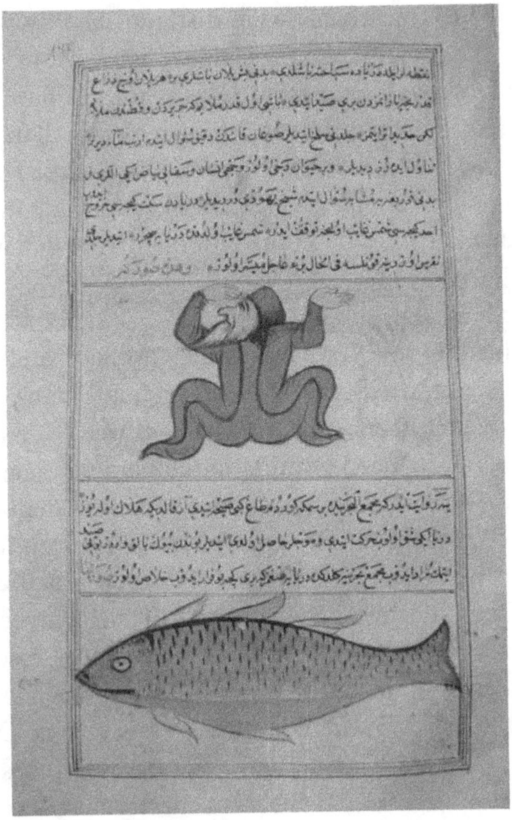

Fig. 7. The "Jewish *shaykh*" (above). Qazwīnī, *ʿAjāʾib al-Makhlūqāt* (Ottoman Turkish), Baghdad, mid-17th century. Jerusalem, The National Library of Israel, Ms. Yah. Ar. 1113, fol. 140a. Photo: Courtesy of the National Library of Israel, Jerusalem.

The second variant, in a manuscript which was likely produced in Baghdad in the mid-seventeenth century,[34] presents the "Jewish *shaykh*" as a human wearing a red hat and blue garb, although the text has remained unchanged (fig. 7). This illustration demonstrates that the "Jewish *shaykh*" creature has indeed been perceived as a Jew. Contemporary European travel accounts and illustrated Ottoman manuscripts of different treatises indicate that in sixteenth-century Istanbul Jewish physicians wore tall

34 Jerusalem: The National Library of Israel, Ms. Yah. Ar. 1113, 140a. The attribution to seventeenth-century Baghdad is noted in Wust, A *Catalogue of the Arabic Manuscripts*. For a similar Ottoman Turkish manuscript with an illustration of a dressed "Jewish *shaykh*," see Baltimore: The Walters Art Museum, Ms. W. 659, Baghdad, 1121/1717, 166a.

red hats, and Jewish merchants were distinguished by yellow turbans.[35] According to other sources, Romaniote Jews wore yellow turbans, while the newly arrived Sephardic Jews wore red hats.[36] In discussing images of "others" in two different Ottoman historical treatises of the late sixteenth century, Lâle Uluç and Emine Fetvacı agree that costumes and headgear are markers for diverse peoples and ethnic identities.[37] Although dressed, the "Jewish *shaykh*" in the Ottoman *ᶜAjāᵓib* manuscripts maintains his frog-like posture.

Stanford Shaw and Bernard Lewis, among other scholars, have discussed the influential role Jews had in the Ottoman lands of the fifteenth and sixteenth centuries. Some were court physicians, financiers, and diplomatic advisers; others were artisans and traders, and it is also well known that Jews introduced printing to the Ottoman lands.[38] It has been argued that few Ottoman families did not have Jewish doctors,[39] and it is generally agreed that the Ottoman Empire was a haven for Jewish exiles from Spain, providing a place where they could practice their religious customs and freely engage in intellectual life. However, there is documentation of restrictions and incidents that reflect resentment toward *dhimmī*s (protected subjects) in general, and Jews in particular.[40] The fact that the "Jewish *shaykh*" continued to feature in Ottoman *ᶜAjāᵓib* manuscripts, both from Istanbul and from the provinces, does not contradict Jews' prominent role in Ottoman society. On the contrary, it indicates that they were continuously relevant, and therefore formed part of a premodern encyclopedia describing the components of the world. They were a minority whom the Ottomans encountered, and with whom they interacted, on a daily basis. Yet, at the same time, Jews were perceived

35 On costumes of Jews in late sixteenth-century Ottoman manuscripts of *Kitāb-i Siyer-i Nebī*, see Uluç, "Images of Jews in Ottoman Court Manuscripts." On the engravings of a dressed Jewish doctor and merchant in Nicolas de Nicolay, *Les quatres premiers livres des navigations et pérégrinations orientales* (Lyon, 1568), see Rubens, *History of Jewish Costume*, 31–42; and Rozen, *History of the Jewish Community in Istanbul*, 284–302.

36 Shaw, *The Jews of the Ottoman Empire*, 80.

37 Fetvacı, "Others and Other Geographies"; and Uluç, "Images of Jews in Ottoman Court Manuscripts."

38 Shaw, *The Jews of the Ottoman Empire*, 86–119; Lewis, *The Jews of Islam*, 129–35; and Levy, "Introduction," 1–84.

39 Shaw, *The Jews of the Ottoman Empire*, 87.

40 Shaw, *The Jews of the Ottoman Empire*, 97–108; Lewis, 135–40; Levy, "Introduction," 14–19, 40–41; Shmuelevitz, *The Jews of the Ottoman Empire*, 30–34; and Masters, *Christians and Jews in the Ottoman Arab World*, 16–40.

as an obscure "other" whose obstinate observance of the Sabbath was not entirely understood.

One might wonder what effects, if any, Jews' strict keeping of the Sabbath had on the Muslim community in premodern times. As some Jews held pivotal duties in the Ottoman court, and many practiced medicine and trade, it is likely that Muslim and other non-Jewish communities were affected by it. We do, in fact, have some reference from Ottoman lands that Muslim law courts were tolerant toward Jews, for they postponed cases between Jews and non-Jews until after the Sabbath.[41] This example shows that Jews' day of full rest was a religious duty that the Ottoman state could not ignore but had to consider in daily routines. Friday, *yawm al-Jumᶜa*, the weekly day of congregational prayer in Islam, is not a day of rest,[42] which could partially explain why the behavior of the "Jewish *shaykh*" on the Sabbath was received as perplexing.

Other hybrids and marvelous beings are depicted in Qazwīnī's *ᶜAjāᵓib*. For example, the dog-headed people, and the people without necks, whose faces are positioned on their chests, were frequently illustrated in manuscripts throughout the centuries, including in Ottoman examples.[43] In a late fifteenth-century illustration (fig. 8),[44] the ship of a Turkman prince reaches the shore of *Jazīrat Sagsar* (Dog-Headed Island). Behind a golden hill, the islanders, who have both human and dog heads, are about to throw stones at the boat. The prince's companions, two turbaned men in the boat, are seen drawing their bows toward the islanders. The reader of the manuscript, who looks at the illustration, is positioned in the sea and could therefore identify with the party in the boat, threatened by the islanders' attack. The dog-headed men and the people without necks also feature regularly in medieval and early modern European books of travel,

41 Shmuelevitz, *The Jews of the Ottoman Empire*, 45–46, cites the *Responsa* of Samuel ben Moses de Medina (Maharashdam), a sixteenth-century rabbi from Salonica, and assumes that the considerate attitude of Muslim law courts toward the Jews during the Sabbath was also the case in other parts of the Ottoman Empire.

42 S. D. Goitein notes that Muḥammad refused to accept the Sabbath's main purpose as a day of rest and retained only its aspect as a day of public assembly and prayer. See his *Jews and Arabs*, 39–40.

43 Badiee, "Islamic Cosmography," 136; Zadeh, "The Wiles of Creation," 44–48; Caiozzo, "Les monstres dans les cosmographies illustrées"; and Berlekamp, *Wonder, Image, and the Cosmos*, 9–11.

44 London: The Royal Asiatic Society, Ms. 178, ca. 1475. On this manuscript, see Robinson, *Persian Paintings in the Collection of the Royal Asiatic Society*, 15–23.

Fig. 8. The dog-headed people and the people without necks. Qazwīnī, *ʿAjāʾib al-Makhlūqāt* (Persian), Iran, ca. 1475. London, The Royal Asiatic Society, Ms. 178, fol. 98b–99a. Photo: Courtesy of the Royal Asiatic Society of Great Britain and Ireland.

bestiaries, and cosmographies, among the "monstrous races," where they are named Cynocephali and Blemmyae, respectively (fig. 9).[45] Referring to the study of mirabilia in European manuscripts, Persis Berlekamp and Anna Caiozzo briefly suggest that many beings in Qazwīnī's *ᶜAjāʾib* could similarly be read as markers of alterity.[46] Taking this assumption a step further, I contend that the continuous inclusion of these creatures in *ᶜAjāʾib* manuscripts indicates a repetition of earlier models, though it could also imply that they were perceived as signifiers of a *changing* "other," of contemporary foes or obstacles that a Muslim patron had to confront in different times and places, as in the illustration just described (see fig. 8). The hybrid human-frog entry, on the other hand, by the mere

45 See, for example, Wittkower, "Marvels of the East"; and Friedman, *The Monstrous Races*, 5–25, 163–77. For a discussion of the monstrous races in Sabastian Münster's *Cosmographia* (fig. 9), see Mclean, *The Cosmographia*, 270–72.

46 Berlekamp, *Wonder, Image, and the Cosmos*, 9–11; and Caiozzo, "Les monstres dans les cosmographies illustrées," especially 63–64.

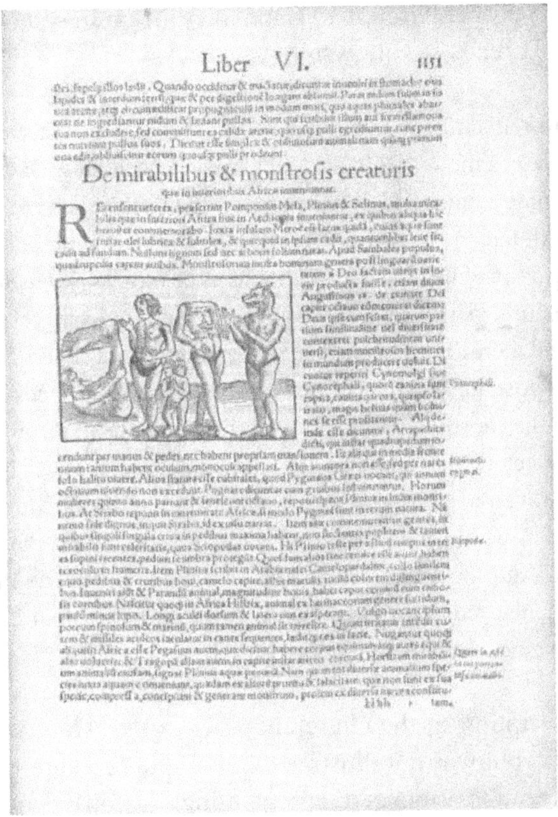
Liber VI. 1151

De mirabilibus & monstrosis creaturis

Fig. 9. "Marvelous and monstrous creatures": Cynocephali and Blemmyae (right). Sebastian Münster, *Cosmographiae Universalis* Lib. VI, Basel, 1554. Munich, Bayerische Staatsbibliothek, Res/2 Geo.u.53, p. 1151. © Bayerische Staatsbibliothek München, Res/2 Geo.u.53, p. 1151.

fact that it is called the "Jewish *shaykh*" and includes a verbal description of Jewish religious customs, *always* signifies the Jew who lived in Islamic lands and not in a faraway terra incognita.

THE ORTHODOX CHRISTIAN

Unlike those of the Jew, illustrations of the Christian were introduced to Qazwīnī's *ʿAjāʾib* manuscripts only in the Ottoman period, in the late sixteenth century. Whereas the depiction of the "Jewish *shaykh*" evinces only minor deviations over three hundred years, the entry on the relationships between Muslims and churchmen reflects continuity in the text but salient changes in iconography. It is called *Jazīrat al-kanīsa* (The Church

Island), and it probably refers to Cape St. Vincent in southern Portugal.[47] Qazwīnī's text reads as follows:

> [The aforementioned Abū Ḥāmid al-Andalusī al-Gharnāṭī] noted that there is a mountain in the black sea near Andalūs. On this mountain there is a church (*kanīsa*) carved into the rock and crowned with a large dome. Atop that dome there is a raven, which always flies around it. Facing this church, there is a mosque (*masjid*), which the Muslims visit, and are blessed in it. And it is said that prayer is answered there. The clergymen, who reside in this church, were obligated to host the Muslims of that mosque. And so, whenever a visitor entered the mosque, the raven would enter its head through a small window set in the dome of the church, and cry out. The number of [the raven's] cries equals the number of visiting Muslims. The clergymen would then bring out enough food for all the [Muslim] visitors. And the church is known as the church of the raven. The clergymen say that they still see a raven on top of that church, but they have no idea where it gets its food.[48]

The description of the church appears in the Arabic manuscripts of Qazwīnī's text but was not illustrated before the fifteenth-century Persian copies. The composition of these paintings is fairly basic: it captures the church and the raven atop the dome (fig. 10).[49] In sixteenth-century Ottoman Turkish manuscripts that were produced in Istanbul, the iconography for the same entry changed almost entirely (fig. 11).[50] At first glance, it seems that the Ottoman painter simply followed the text more closely and depicted the raven, the church, and the mosque, as well as their respective followers, who are engaged in conversation or debate. But the significant change in the painting compared to the Persian copies indicates that something in the text caught the Ottoman patron's or painter's attention, something that agreed with contemporary events and expressed conflict between the Ottomans and the Orthodox Church.

---

47 On the association of the island with Cape St. Vincent, see Al-Gharnāṭī, *Tuḥfat al-Albāb*, 181n284.

48 My translation is based on manuscript BSB, Cod.arab. 464, 69a.

49 Oxford: Bodleian Library, Ms. Laud Or. 132, ca. 1480–90, 85b. See Robinson, *A Descriptive Catalogue of the Persian Paintings*, 37, no. 249.

50 London: BL, Ms. Add. 7894, Istanbul, late sixteenth century, 147a. See Titley, *Miniatures from Turkish Manuscripts*, 71, cat. no. 60.

Fig. 10. The "Church of the Raven." Qazwīnī, 'Ajā'ib al-Makhlūqāt (Persian), Iran, ca. 1480–90. Oxford, The Bodleian Libraries, University of Oxford, Ms. Laud Or. 132, fol. 85b. Photo: The Bodleian Libraries, University of Oxford.

The Ottoman illustration depicts sixteenth-century Istanbul, a city where churches were converted into mosques,[51] like the Kariye Camii and the Fethiye Camii in the late sixteenth century. It is also the city where Miᶜmār Sinān's (d. 1588) major architectural achievement, the Süleymaniye complex, was constructed and completed in 1559,[52] some thirty-five years before the production of this manuscript. It has been argued that, despite the confiscation of churches, the Ottoman state did not interfere in Christians' religious duties, and that Christians could both keep sacred books and icons on their premises and conduct church services and rites unharmed.[53] The illustration under discussion might

51 On the conversion of churches into mosques, see Runciman, *The Great Church in Captivity*, 187–91; Patrinelis, "The Exact Time of the First Attempt," 569–72; Necipoğlu, *The Age of Sinan*, 57–59; and Greene, *The Edinburgh History of the Greeks*, 64–69.

52 Necipoğlu, *The Age of Sinan*, 207–21.

53 Arnakis, "The Greek Church of Constantinople," 242.

reflect that, but it could also convey a sense of Muslim superiority over Christians. A sentiment of authority clearly arises from the text, which mentions that the churchmen ought to serve the Muslim worshipers. The painting tells the same story, as the minaret and the crescent atop the mosque break the upper frame of the illustration and are noticeably higher than the cross that crowns the church.[54]

The tension between the Ottomans and the Orthodox Church notwithstanding, the illustration shows the churchmen realistically, in their typical attire (fig. 11), but the same manuscript, just one folio forward, shows the

Fig. 11. The "Church of the Raven." Qazwīnī, *ʿAjāʾib al-Makhlūqāt.* Translated into Ottoman Turkish by Sürurî. Istanbul, ca. 1594–95. London, British Library, Add. 7894, fol. 147a. © The British Library Board, Add. 7894, fol. 147a.

54 For a similar composition, see Istanbul: Topkapı Sarayı Müzesi Kütüphanesi (hereafter, "TSMK"), A. 3632, 119b. This illustration is reproduced and briefly mentioned in Atıl, "The Art of the Book," 206, 208, ill. 102. In this painting, two Orthodox Christians and a Franciscan friar are depicted in front of the church. Indeed, we know of diverse Christian presence in Istanbul toward the end of the sixteenth century, including Catholic missionaries. However, I contend that the illustrated entry reflects the response to the Orthodox Church as it comprised the majority of Christian subjects in the Ottoman period. On the Jesuits and Capuchins in Istanbul ca. 1583–1600, see Frazee, *Catholics and Sultans*, 72–74; and Greene, *The Edinburgh History of the Greeks*, 140.

"Jewish *shaykh*" in its hybrid form (see fig. 1). Thus, the two consecutive folios prove that at the time this manuscript was illustrated in Istanbul (ca. 1594–95), during the reign of Sulṭān Murād III (r. 1574–1595), Ottoman society perceived the *dhimmī*s as inferiors to varying extents.

THE EUROPEAN

Similar to those of the churchmen, images of Europeans (*al-ifranj*) were also introduced to Qazwīnī's cosmography in the Ottoman period, but not before the late seventeenth century (fig. 12).[55] A unique Arabic manuscript was copied and illustrated, most likely in

Fig. 12. "The Europeans." Qazwīnī, *ʿAjāʾib al-Makhlūqāt* (Arabic). Probably Egypt, 1699. Istanbul, Topkapı Palace Museum Library, Revan 1658, fol. 152b. © Topkapi Palace Museum.

55 Europeans were indeed depicted in Ottoman painting prior to the seventeenth century, but not in the *ʿAjāʾib* manuscripts. Scholars have noted that Europeans often times represent the pagan or the infidel in illustrations of stories of prophets. See Milstein, *Miniature Painting in Ottoman Baghdad*, 13–14; Tezcan, "The Frank in the Ottoman Eye," 272–80; and Fetvacı, *Picturing History in the Ottoman Court*, 168–69.

Egypt, in 1699.[56] Although this copy is entitled *ʿAjāʾib al-Makhlūqāt* and is attributed to Qazwīnī on its title page, it differs greatly from the author's other manuscripts. It includes a new chapter, by an anonymous writer, on the peoples of the lands from China and India to Iran, Iraq, Greater Syria, North Africa, and Europe.

All of the illustrations in this chapter follow a generic type of group portrait, which usually depicts four men and one woman dressed in their traditional, or typical, costumes and headgear. They are seen holding hands, embracing, or waving to the readers or to transient visitors. The text in each entry is rather short; it usually focuses on the people's looks, and sometimes mentions some of their qualities or the natural resources of their lands. The Europeans are said to be of different kinds, such as the English, the Venetians, the French, the Flemish, and the Portuguese. They are described as white or red, and their hair is shown flowing over their shoulders, in accordance with the text. We are also informed that the European women are beautiful, and that adultery is common among them. Their lands are rich in gold and silver, and the weather there is cold.[57] There is no significant criticism of the Europeans in this brief entry, whereas some other people, like the Nubians, are associated with unflattering qualities, such as foolishness or dishonesty.

The Europeans are also depicted in three additional paintings, in entries on Cairo and the pyramids (figs. 13–14).[58] The information provided in these entries accords with other Muslim geographical texts from the medieval and early modern periods. The author discusses the size of the pyramids and recalls that the Abbasid caliph al-Maʾmūn (r. 813–833) was astonished at the sight of these grand structures. He also records an inventory of treasures and mummies hidden inside three of the pyramids. The Europeans are not mentioned in these entries, but in the accompanying paintings they are depicted standing triumphantly atop the pyramids, as if they have just conquered these mountains of stone and their precious objects. Although very small compared to the huge structures, the Europeans are easily recognized by their long hair and cavalier hats. A small inscription near two of the figures, which states "a man traveler" (*shakhs insān mutafarraj*), allows us to contextualize them.

56 Istanbul, TSMK, R. 1658. The manuscript is listed in Karatay, *Topkapı Sarayı Müzesi Kütüphanesi*, 3:794, cat. no. 7171.

57 TSMK, R.1658, 152b.

58 TSMK, R.1658, 17a, 43b–44a.

Fig. 13. "Cairo"—a European atop the pyramid. Qazwīnī, *ʿAjāʾib al-Makhlūqāt* (Arabic), probably Egypt, 1699. Istanbul, Topkapı Palace Museum Library, Revan 1658, fol. 17a. © Topkapi Palace Museum.

During the Renaissance, there occurred a fascination with hieroglyphic writing and a constant attempt to decipher its symbols. Egyptian antiquities were collected in Europe, and mummies were mined extensively. Fragments of mummies and their powdered essence were believed to have medicinal properties, and were included in cabinets of curiosities.[59] The seventeenth century in particular saw the publication of two significant treatises in English that reflect an

59 See Dannenfeldt, "Egypt and Egyptian Antiquities"; Thompson, *Wonderful Things*, especially 60–64; and El-Daly, *Egyptology: The Missing Millennium*, 102–106.

Fig. 14. "The Pyramids"—a European traveler atop the pyramid. Qazwīnī, *'Ajā'ib al-Makhlūqāt* (Arabic), probably Egypt, 1699. Istanbul, Topkapı Palace Museum Library, Revan 1658, fol. 43b. © Topkapi Palace Museum

antiquarian and mensural approach to the pyramids of Giza. First, George Sandys's *A Relation of a Journey* was published in 1615, with adjoining engravings of the pyramids and sphinx.[60] Then, in 1646 appeared the *Pyramidographia*. Its author, the Oxford professor John Greaves, traveled to Egypt to study the pyramids firsthand and wrote what is now considered to be "the first full scholarly treatment of the Giza complex."[61] One of the engravings in Sandys's book shows a delegation of Europeans, presumably Sandys and his companions, on their way to the pyramids and sphinx (fig. 15). The illustrations in the

60 On Sandys's travels in Egypt, see Haynes, *The Humanist as Traveler*, 99–103; and Vine, "'Too Great a Morsell for Time to Devoure,'" 22–26.

61 Shalev, "Measurer of All Things: John Greaves," 557. On English travelers in Egypt during the sixteenth and seventeenth centuries, see Wortham, *The Genesis of British Egyptology*, 12–23; and Vine, "'Too Great a Morsell for Time to Devoure.'"

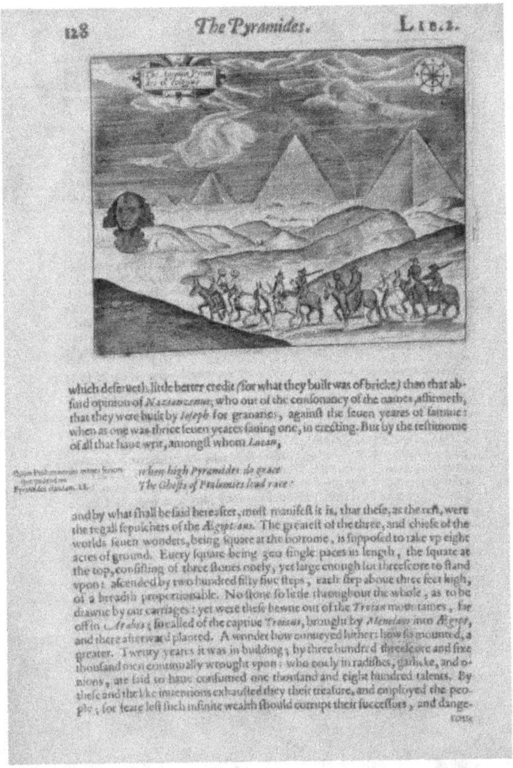

128 *The Pyramides.* LIB. 2.

which deſerueth little better credit (for what they built was of bricke) than that abſurd opinion of *Nazianzenus*, who out of the conſonancy of the names, affirmeth, that they were built by *Ioſeph* for granaries, againſt the ſeuen yeares of famine: when as one was thrice ſeuen yeares ſauing one, in erecting. But by the teſtimonie of all that haue writ, amongſt whom *Lucan*,

when high Pyramides do grace
The Ghoſts of Ptolomies lead race:

and by what ſhall be ſaid hereafter, moſt manifeſt it is, that theſe, as the reſt, were the regall ſepulchers of the *Ægyptians*. The greateſt of the three, and chiefe of the worlds ſeuen wonders, being ſquare at the bottome, is ſuppoſed to take vp eight acres of ground. Euery ſquare being 300 ſingle paces in length, the ſquare at the top, conſiſting of three ſtones onely, yet large enough for threeſcore to ſtand vpon: aſcended by two hundred fifty fiue ſteps, each ſtep aboue three feet high, of a breadth proportionable. No ſtone ſo little throughout the whole, as to be drawne by our carriages: yet were theſe hewne out of the *Troian* mountaines, far off in *Arabia*; ſo called of the captiue *Troians*, brought by *Menelaus* into *Ægypt*, and there afterward planted. A wonder how conueyed hither: how ſo mounted, a greater. Twenty yeares it was in building; by three hundred threeſcore and ſixe thouſand men continually wrought vpon: who onely in radiſhes, garlicke, and onions, are ſaid to haue conſumed one thouſand and eight hundred talents. By theſe and the like inuentions exhauſted they their treaſure, and employed the people; for feare leſt ſuch infinite wealth ſhould corrupt their ſucceſſors, and dangerous

Fig. 15. "The Pyramids." George Sandys, *A Relation of a Journey Begun an Dom. 1610.* London, W. Barrett, 1621, 128.

seventeenth-century Ottoman *ʿAjāʾib* (see figs. 13–14) possibly reflect a similar situation, which the painter might have witnessed.

This is not to say, of course, that the travelers depicted in the Arabic manuscript refer to specific personages, but rather that they represent the phenomenon of European travel and antiquarianism, as well as the presence of foreigners in Egypt. Moreover, the depiction of the personified sphinx, which is seen gazing in horror at the European atop the pyramid, might represent the painter's—and hence the local Egyptian's—dismay toward the growing presence of travelers and the treasures of his land being taken away.

Europeans are described and depicted realistically in this late seventeenth-century manuscript, but the "Jewish *shaykh*" remains in its hybrid form (fig. 16).[62] The recurrence of this entry in numerous

62 TSMK, R.1658, 74b–75a.

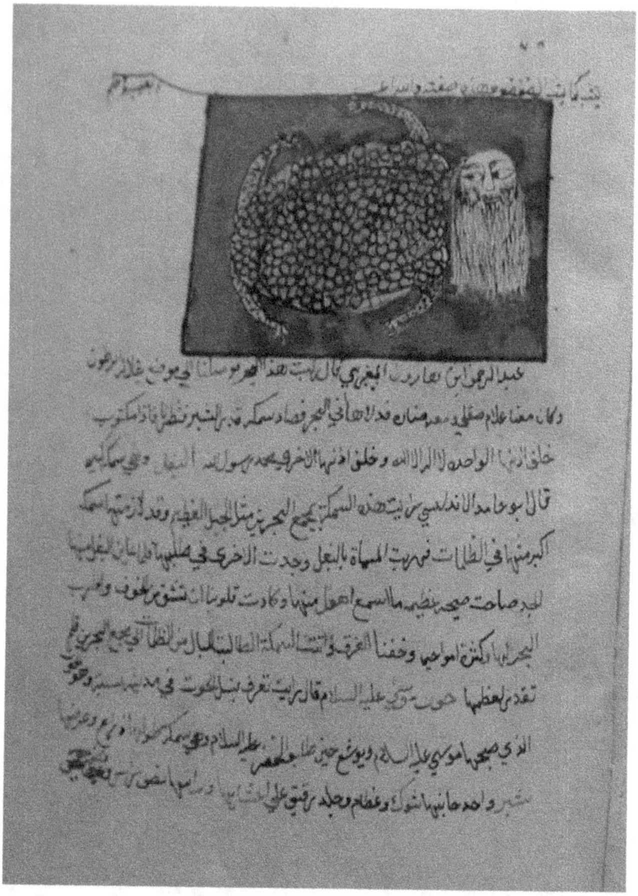

Fig. 16. The "Jewish *shaykh*." Qazwīnī, *ʿAjāʾib al-Makhlūqāt* (Arabic), probably Egypt, 1699. Istanbul, Topkapı Palace Museum Library, Revan 1658, fol. 75a. © Topkapi Palace Museum.

manuscripts could be the result of the continuous copying and canonization of Qazwīnī's *ᶜAjāʾib*. However, as intentional changes are reflected in the Ottoman Qazwīnī manuscripts, one cannot help but wonder why the Jew, although part of Ottoman society, is repeatedly presented in the cosmographies as a hybrid.

CONCLUSION

This study has traced changes in representations of the "other" in illustrated *ᶜAjāʾib* manuscripts from the late thirteenth-century Ilkhanid period to the Ottoman period, with an emphasis on the latter. The examined entries of this popular encyclopedia show that some hybrids and creatures could be perceived as signifiers of a changing "other," whereas the human-frog hybrid always signifies the Jew, who lived in Islamic lands. The Jew was associated with the frog by medieval Muslim authors who envisioned the observance of the Sabbath as an act of an amphibian, capable of living in two realms—the Sabbath (dry land) and the rest of the week (the sea). Keeping the Sabbath was seen as entering a different modus vivendi, which these authors found obscure. Presumably, the Sabbath, Jews' day of full rest, is perceived as perplexing because Friday, the day of congregational prayer in Islam, is not a day of rest. As Jews held pivotal roles at the Ottoman court, and many practiced medicine and trade, it is likely that non-Jewish communities were affected by their strict keeping of the Sabbath. This could partially explain why the perception of the Jew as a hybrid was continuously relevant in premodern Islamic lands.

Contrary to the hybrid Jew, who was included in illustrated encyclopedias for centuries, depictions of the Orthodox Christian and the European were introduced to copies of the *ᶜAjāʾib* not before the Ottoman period. Members of these two groups are portrayed realistically, dressed in their typical attire and headgear. The few paintings in which they appear reflect historical events and conflicts with local Muslim communities, relevant to the time and place in which the specific manuscripts were produced: conversion of churches into mosques in sixteenth-century Istanbul and the reaction to European travelers and antiquarians in seventeenth-century Egypt.

BIBLIOGRAPHY

Sources

Ferdowsī, Abū al-Qāsim. *Shāhnāmeh*. Edited by Jules Mohl. Tehrān: Sharikat Inshārāt ʻIlmī wa Farhangī, 1955.

Ferrand, Gabriel. "Le *Tuḥfat al-Albāb* de Abū Ḥāmid Al-Andalusī al-Ġarnāṭī: Édité d'après les mss. 2167, 2168, 2170 de la Bibliothèque nationale et le ms. D'Alger." *Journal asiatique* 207 (1925): 1–148, 193–304.

Gharnāṭī, Abū Ḥāmid. *Tuḥfat al-Albāb wa-Nukhbat al-Aᶜjāb*. Edited by *Ismāᶜīl al-ᶜArabī*. Bayrūt: Dār al-Jīl, Al-Maghrib: Dār al-Āfāq al-Jadīda, 1993.

Studies

Arnakis, G. Georgiades. "The Greek Church of Constantinople and the Ottoman Empire." *The Journal of Modern History* 24, no. 3 (1952): 235–50.

Ashtor, Eliyahu. *The Jews of Moslem Spain.* Translated by Aaron Klein and Jenny Machlowitz Klein. 3 vols. Philadelphia: The Jewish Publication Society of America, 1979.

Atıl, Esin. "The Art of the Book." In *Turkish Art,* edited by Esin Atıl, 137–238. Washington, D.C.: Smithsonian Institution Press; New York: Abrams, 1980.

Badiee, Julie. "An Islamic Cosmography: The Illustrations of the Sarre Qazwīnī." Ph.D. diss., University of Michigan, 1978.

Barry, Michael. "Jews, Islamic Mysticism, and the Devil." In *A History of Jewish-Muslim Relations from the Origins to the Present Day*, edited by Abdelwahab Meddeb and Benjamin Stora, 869–90. Princeton: Princeton University Press, 2013.

Berlekamp, Persis. "Qazwīnī Al-, Zakarīya B. Muḥammad B. Maḥmūd (d. 1283)." In *Medieval Islamic Civilization: An Encyclopedia*, edited by Josef W. Meri, 651–54. New York: Routledge, 2006.

Berlekamp, Persis. *Wonder, Image, and the Cosmos in Medieval Islam.* New Haven and London: Yale University Press, 2011.

Bothmer, Hans-Caspar G. von. "Die illustrationen der 'Münchener Qazwīnī' von 1280 (cod. Monac. arab. 464): Ein Beitrag zur Kenntnis ihres Stils." Ph.D. diss., Universität München, 1971.

Caiozzo, Anna. "Les monstres dans les cosmographies illustrées de l'Orient médiéval." In *Monstre et imaginaire social: Approches historiques,* edited by Anna Caiozzo and Anne-Emmanuelle Demartini, 47–64. Paris: Creaphis, 2008.

Caiozzo, Anna. "L'image de l'Europe et des Européens dans les représentations de l'Orient médiéval." *Caietele Echinox* 10 (2006): 84–120.

Carboni, Stefano. "The Wonders of Creation and the Singularities of Ilkhanid Painting: A Study of the London Qazwini British Library Ms. Or. 14140." Ph.D. diss., SOAS, University of London, 1992.

Dannenfeldt, Karl H. "Egypt and Egyptian Antiquities in the Renaissance." *Studies in the Renaissance* 6 (1959): 7–27.

Ducatez, Guy. "La Tuḥfa al-Albāb d'Abū Ḥāmid al-Andalusī al-Ġarnāṭī: Traducation annotée." *Revue des études islamiques* 53 (1985): 141–241.

Duda, Dorothea. *Islamische Handschriften I: Persische Handschriften.* 2 vols. Wien: Verlag der Österreichischen Akademie de Wissenschaften, 1983.

El-Daly, Okasha. *Egyptology: The Missing Millennium: Ancient Egypt in Medieval Arabic Writings.* London: UCL Press, 2005.

Ettinghausen, Richard. *Arab Painting.* Geneva: Skira, 1962.

Fetvacı, Emine. "Others and Other Geographies in the Şehnāme-i Selīm Ḫān." *Osmanlı Araştırmaları/The Journal of Ottoman Studies* 40 (2012): 81–100.

Fetvacı, Emine. *Picturing History at the Ottoman Court.* Bloomington and Indianapolis: Indiana University Press, 2013.

Frazee, Charles A. *Catholics and Sultans: The Church and the Ottoman Empire, 1453–1923*. Cambridge: Cambridge University Press, 1983.

Friedman, John Block. *The Monstrous Races in Medieval Art and Thought*. Cambridge and London: Harvard University Press, 1981.

Gilbert, Martin. *In Ishmael's House: A History of Jews in Muslim Lands*. New Haven and London: Yale University Press, 2010.

Goitein, S. D. *Jews and Arabs: Their Contacts through the Ages*. New York: Schocken Books, 1970.

Greene, Molly. *The Edinburgh History of the Greeks, 1453 to 1768: The Ottoman Empire*. Edinburgh: Edinburgh University Press, 2015.

Haynes, Jonathan. *The Humanist as Traveler: George Sandys Relation of a Journey Begun an. Dom. 1610*. Rutherford, Teaneck, Madison: Fairleigh Dickinson University Press; London and Toronto: Associated University Presses, 1986.

Hees, Syrnix von. "Al-Qazwīnī's *ʿAjāʾib al-Makhlūqāt* — An Encyclopaedia of Natural History?." In *Organizing Knowledge: Encyclopaedic Activities in the Pre-Eighteenth-Century Muslim World*, edited by Gerhard Endress, 171–86. Leiden: Brill, 2006.

Hees, Syrinx von. *Enzyklopädie als Spiegel des Weltbildes: Qazwīnīs Wunder der Schöpfung- eine Naturkunde des 13. Jahrhunderts*. Vol. 4: *Diskurse der Arabistik*. Wiesbaden: Harrassowitz Verlag, 2002.

Higgs Strickland, Debra. *Saracens, Demons, and Jews: Making Monsters in Medieval Art*. Princeton: Princeton University Press, 2003.

Karatay, Fehmi E. *Topkapı Sarayı Müzesi Kütüphanesi: Arapça Yazmalar Kataloğu*. Istanbul: Topkapı Sarayı Müzesi, 1966.

Levy, Avigdor. "Introduction." In *The Jews of the Ottoman Empire*, edited by Avigdor Levy, 1–150. Princeton: The Darwin Press; Washington D.C.: The Institute of Turkish Studies, 1994.

Levy-Rubin, Milka. *Non-Muslims in the Early Islamic Empire: From Surrender to Coexistence*. New York: Cambridge University Press, 2011.

Lewis, Bernard. *The Jews of Islam*. Princeton: Princeton University Press, 1984.

Lipton, Sara. *Dark Mirror: The Medieval Origins of Anti-Jewish Iconography*. New York: Metropolitan Books, and Henry Holt and Company, 2014.

Lipton, Sara. *Images of Intolerance: The Representation of Jews and Judaism in the 'Bible moralisée.'* Berkeley: University of California Press, 1999.

Masters, Bruce. *Christians and Jews in the Ottoman Arab World: The Roots of Sectarianism*. Cambridge: Cambridge University Press, 2001.

Mclean, Matthew. *The Cosmographia of Sabastian Münster: Describing the World in the Reformation*. Aldershot, UK, and Burlington, VT: Ashgate, 2007.

Milstein, Rachel. *Miniature Painting in Ottoman Baghdad*. Costa Mesa: Mazda Publishers, 1990.

Moor, Bilha. "*Shāhnāma* Heroes and Kings in *ʿAjāʾib al-Makhlūqāt* Illustrated Manuscripts." In *Shahnama Studies II. The Reception of Firdausi's Shahnama*, edited by Charles Melville and Gabrielle van den Berg, 267–80, figs. 23–26. Leiden: Brill, 2012.

Moor, Bilha, and Efim A. Rezvan. "Al-Qazwīnī's *ʿAjāʾib al-Makhlūqāt wa Gharā'ib al-Mawjūdāt*: Manuscript D370." *Manuscripta Orientalia* 8, no. 4 (2002): 38–68.

Necipoğlu, Gülru. *The Age of Sinan: Architectural Culture in the Ottoman Empire*. Princeton: Princeton University Press, 2005.

Patrinelis, Christos. "The Exact Time of the First Attempt of the Turks to Seize the Churches and Convert the Christian People of Constantinople to Islam." In *Actes du Premier Congrès international des études balkaniques et Sud-Est européennes*, edited by Vladimir I. Georgiev, 567–72. Sofia: Académie bulgare des sciences, 1969.

Rebhan, Helga, ed. *Die Wunder der Schöpfung: Handschriften der Bayerischen Staatsbibliothek aus dem islamischen Kulturkreis*. Wiesbaden: Harrassowitz Verlag, 2010.

Rebold Benton, Janetta. *The Medieval Menagerie: Animals in the Art of the Middle Ages*. New York, London, Paris: Abbeville Press, 1992.

Robbins, Mary E. "The Truculent Toad in the Middle Ages." In *Animals in the Middle Ages: A Book of Essays,* edited by Nona C. Flores, 25–47. New York and London: Garland, 1996.

Robinson, B. W. *A Descriptive Catalogue of the Persian Paintings in the Bodleian Library*. Oxford: Clarendon Press, 1958.

Robinson, B. W. *Persian Paintings in the Collection of the Royal Asiatic Society*. London: The Royal Asiatic Society, 1998.

Robinson, B. W. *Persian Paintings in the John Rylands Library: A Descriptive Catalogue*. London: Sotheby Parke Bernet, 1980.

Rozen, Minna. *A History of the Jewish Community in Istanbul: The Formative Years, 1453–1566*. Leiden: Brill, 2010.

Rubens, Alfred. *A History of Jewish Costume*. New York: Funk and Wagnalls, 1967.

Rührdanz, Karin. "Illustrated Persian ʿAjāʾib al-Makhlūqāt Manuscripts and Their Function in Early Modern Times." In *Society and Culture in the Early Modern Middle East: Studies on Iran in the Safavid Period*, edited by Andrew. J. Newman, 33–47. Leiden: Brill, 2003.

Rührdanz, Karin. "Qazwīnī's *ʿAjāʾib al-Makhlūqāt* in illustrated Timurid Manuscripts." In *Iran, questions et connaissances: Actes du IVe Congrès Européen des Études Iraniennes, Paris 1999. Vol. II: Périodes médiévale et modern*, edited by Maria Szuppe, 473–84. Paris: Association pour l'Avancement des Études Iraniennes, 2002.

Runciman, Steven. *The Great Church in Captivity: A Study of the Patriarchate of Constantinople from the Eve of the Turkish Conquest to the Greek War of Independence*. Cambridge: Cambridge University Press, 1968.

Sachau, Ed., and Hermann Ethé. *Catalogue of the Persian, Turkish, Hindūstānī, and Pushtū Manuscripts in the Bodleian Library*. Oxford: Clarendon, 1889.

Shalev, Zur. "Measurer of All Things: John Greaves (1602–1652), the Great Pyramid, and Early Modern Metrology." *Journal of the History of Ideas* 63, no. 4 (2002): 555–75.

Shaw, Stanford J. *The Jews of the Ottoman Empire and the Turkish Republic*. New York: New York University Press, 1991.

Schmitz, Barbara, with contributions by Latif Khayyat, Svat Soucek, and Massoud Pourfarrokh. *Islamic Manuscripts in the New York Public Library*. New York: The New York Public Library; Oxford: Oxford University Press, 1992.

Schmitz, Barbara, and Ziyaud-Din A. Desai, *Mughal and Persian Paintings and Illustrated Manuscripts in the Raza Library, Rampur*. New Delhi: Indira Gandhi National Centre for the Arts; Rampur: Rampur Raza Library; New Delhi: Aryan Books International, 2006.

Shmuelevitz, Aryeh. *The Jews of the Ottoman Empire in the Late Fifteenth and the Sixteenth Centuries: Administrative, Economic, Legal and Social Relations as Reflected in the Responsa*. Leiden: Brill, 1984.

Soucek, Priscilla P. "The Life of the Prophet: Illustrated Versions." In *Content and Context of Visual Arts in the Islamic World*, edited by Priscilla P. Soucek, 193–218. University Park and London: The Pennsylvania State University Press, 1988.

Stillman, Norman A. *The Jews of Arab Lands: A History and Sourcebook*. Philadelphia: The Jewish Publication Society in America, 1979.

Tezcan, Baki. "The Frank in the Ottoman Eye of 1583." In *The Turk and Islam in the Western Eye, 1450–1750*, edited by James G. Harper, 267–96. Surrey and Burlington: Ashgate, 2011.

Thompson, Jason. *Wonderful Things: A History of Egyptology 1: From Antiquity to 1881*. Cairo and New York: The American University in Cairo Press, 2015.

Titley, Norah M. *Miniatures from Persian Manuscripts: A Catalogue and Subject Index of Paintings from Persia, India and Turkey in the British Library and the British Museum*. London: British Museum Publications, 1977.

Titley, Norah M. *Miniatures from Turkish Manuscripts: A Catalogue and Subject Index of Paintings in the British Library and the British Museum*. London: The British Library, 1981.

Uluç, Lâle. "Images of Jews in Ottoman Court Manuscripts." In *A History of Jewish-Muslim Relations from the Origins to the Present Day*, edited by Abdelwahab Meddeb and Benjamin Stora, 902–10. Princeton: Princeton University Press, 2013.

Vervoort, Renilde. "The Pestilent Toad: The Significance of the Toad in the Works of Bosch." In *Hieronymus Bosch: New Insights into His Life and Work*, edited by Jos Koldeweij, Bernard Vermet, and Barbera van Kooij, 145–52. Rotterdam: Museum Boijmans Van Beuningen, NAi Publishers and Ludion, 2001.

Vine, Angus. "'Too Great a Morsell for Time to Devoure': Seventeenth-Century Surveys of the Pyramids at Giza." *Journeys* 8, nos. 1–2 (2007): 21–40.

Williams, David. *Deformed Discourse: The Function of the Monster in Mediaeval Thought and Literature*. Montreal & Kingston, London, Buffalo: McGill-Queen's University Press, 1996.

Wittkower, Rudolf. "Marvels of the East: A Study in the History of Monsters." *Journal of the Warburg and Courtauld Institutes* 5 (1942): 159–97.

Wortham, John David. *The Genesis of British Egyptology 1549–1906.* Norman: University of Oklahoma Press, 1971.

Wust, Efraim. A *Catalogue of the Arabic Manuscripts in the A. S. Yahuda Collection, Jewish National and University Library, Jerusalem.* Unpublished.

York Leach, Linda. *Mughal and Other Indian Paintings from the Chester Beatty Library.* 2 vols. London: Scorpion Cavendish, 1995.

Zadeh, Travis. "The Wiles of Creation: Philosophy, Fiction, and the *ʿAjāʾib* Tradition." *Middle Eastern Literatures* 13, no. 1 (2010): 21–48.

An Ottoman Anti-Judaism

Hakan T. Karateke

This study is part of a larger research project that explores whether anti-Judaic sentiments in premodern Ottoman society may have been more widespread than historians generally presume. I posit that some Ottoman Muslims nurtured a discernible dislike for Jews that was more directed and elevated than the run-of-the-mill contempt felt toward other religious or ethnic groups. Also of interest to me are related questions, such as how and through which traditions these sentiments were propagated as well as whether they were common among or specific to different demographics.

Scholarship generally has assumed that currents from Christian theology and practice may have influenced the perceptions of Sunni Muslims. That line of received wisdom is contradicted, however, by evidence which suggests that at least some of the hostility was rooted in Islamic and Ottoman traditions. Leaving that topic aside for now, this article approaches the issue from another unexplored angle. It investigates the hostile ideas held, and actions committed, toward Jews by Christian converts. I demonstrate below that Ottoman anti-Judaism was a particular phenomenon insomuch as such sentiments did not spread solely through secondhand influences that occurred on the basis of cross-cultural interactions between Christians and Muslims in that society. Rather, the ideas traveled—along with the people who held them—between cultural spaces; such travel likely was one of the ways in which Christian anti-Judaism made its way into Muslim spheres. This peculiar fluidity of

* Given the complexity of the issue, I plan to expand on the theme of anti-Judaic sentiments that conceivably originated from Islamic Ottoman traditions in a separate study.

boundaries is also what qualifies this strain of anti-Judaism as "Ottoman." Unlike anti-Semitism, which is generally classified as prejudice and hostility rooted in racial categories, I understand anti-Judaism to respond to cultural and theological differences.

A good part of the enmity in Ottoman society was held by people who were recruited as *devşirme*. These boys were collected primarily as a levy imposed on Ottoman Christian populations in the Balkans, but some were taken captive in wars and raids or were trafficked by slave traders. Coerced into converting to Islam and trained to become the *ḳapuḳulu* (or simply *ḳul*), or "slaves of the Porte" (that is, of the sultan), these individuals not only formed the core of the elite military units—the janissaries and palace cavalry—but also sustained manpower for the expanding Ottoman bureaucracy. Therefore, I chronicle several physical assaults committed by janissaries and palace cavalry in large cities and then examine anti-Judaic comments and schemes attributed to bureaucrats who were converts from Christianity. What is important for my interpretation is the fact that these boys were not converted to Islam or indoctrinated at an age at which they would not have remembered the notions with which they were raised. Considering that the median age of the boys collected as Christian levy was mid- to late teens, there can be no doubt that *devşirme* converts carried some of the convictions and traditions from their childhood and adolescent years.

While I use mostly narrative sources and travelers' accounts for the abovementioned sections, my sources and methodology differ in the latter part of the article, in which I scrutinize several instances of blood libel. My presupposition about blood libels is clear-cut: this slander was essentially a Christian phenomenon. In its most widespread version, it accused Jews of sacrificing Christian children (usually) at Passover, to obtain blood for unleavened bread. It is well known that this charge was used frequently by Christians in Europe to incite anger against Jews. In this article, I speculate as to whether accusations of blood libel in Ottoman lands could have been advanced by Christian converts. Sources also mention "proper" Christians as accusers, but I am less interested in that phenomenon. I hold that if a Muslim propagated the slander, there are three options: he had recently converted, he hailed from a converted family in which the idea of such libel may have been cultivated, or he learned such slander from and acted alongside Christians. In this section, the sources also lead me to shift my focus from large cities to the provinces.

Admittedly, in both sections my findings are based not on sweeping studies of the sources but on a random collection of incidents, approached with some degree of speculation. Nevertheless, I wish to submit my views to the scholarly community in order to spark a conversation on new ways of evaluating the experiences of Jews in Ottoman lands. My arguments in the larger research project run to some degree counter to the currently accepted narrative and grapple with the received wisdom, which claims:

1) that strong anti-Judaic sentiment in the Middle East existed mostly among Christians before the nineteenth century; before the spread of intense Judeophobic sensibilities by Christian nationalist groups during the same period, this sentiment did not exist among Muslims in the Middle East
2) if Muslims cultivated (to varying degrees) contempt for Jews prior to the nineteenth century, this aversion must have been due to the influence of Christian theology and practice, learned from Christians living in the Middle East

As must be clear by now, I do not reject these points completely but hope to develop perspectives that identify patterns or currents within anti-Judaic sentiments in Ottoman society.

I was prompted to explore this topic in part by the ways in which the Jewish experience in Ottoman lands is frequently represented. Depending on the type of source consulted, the story of Sephardic migration to the Ottoman Empire is presented as a salvation story of varying degrees of significance: the Ottoman lands may be depicted as a paradise for persecuted Iberian Jews, and the Ottoman government's decision to accept Jews as a generous act of epic proportions. In this telling, the Ottoman lands became a safe haven and a stable home for a sizeable Jewish immigrant community in the early modern period. Here, Sephardic Jews led a peaceful existence and cherished their new home and overlords.

This narrative does bear some truth, particularly if one compares Iberian Jews' experience in Ottoman lands with the concerted state persecution they faced in the Spain of the Catholic Monarchs and in Portugal. The Ottoman state did not systematically persecute Jews—on the contrary, evidence suggests that it protected them as tax-paying subjects. Yet when it comes to anti-Judaic sentiments among different sections of Ottoman society, the realities on the ground may not have been as rosy as described in this widely accepted narrative.

The general tendency of modern scholarship on the status of Jews in Ottoman society may rest on a centuries-old positive feeling cultivated by Ottoman Jews toward the Ottoman government that allowed them to immigrate. Of course, any mass migration creates complications for the migrants and for the recipient societies, inevitably heightening sensitivities between populations. We should leave room for those feelings that may have erupted due to new proximity, but there also appears to be a pattern in which historians may delineate certain deep-rooted sentiments.

JANISSARIES AND PALACE CAVALRY

In a joke presumably dating from Ottoman times, a janissary is sitting in front of his shop when he sees a Jew passing by. Apparently agitated by a piece of information of which he had recently become aware, the janissary walks up to him and strikes him out of the blue. Shocked, the Jew asks, "Did I do something wrong, my agha?" "You people killed Jesus," the janissary responds. The Jew, still more dumbfounded, replies apologetically: "but that happened 1500 years ago?!," upon which the janissary counters, "Doesn't matter. I just learned about it."

It is not a coincidence that the accuser in this joke is a janissary. The accusation of deicide at the hands of the Jewish people was used by Christians during and after the Middle Ages to incite anger and violence against Jews. Because the Islamic tradition does not regard the crucifixion of Jesus as true, the matter was a nonissue for Muslims. It might at first appear illogical that a janissary, who most likely would have been a Christian convert (assuming that the joke is set in the sixteenth century), did not know about such a foundational account of Christianity. Obviously, it would be futile to attempt to put the details of the story to test, but I believe that the joke imparts an important fact, namely, that janissary milieus would have been fertile grounds for anti-Judaic sentiment.

Street violence and lynching, particularly during times of widespread unrest, were not rare in Ottoman Istanbul. Ottoman chronicles are replete with narratives of state grandees being executed at the insistent demand—or the very hands—of unruly military flocks. Examining patterns in these assaults leads us to surmise that Jews were particular victims of prejudice. Indeed, Jewish homes often were among the first targets of the lootings that erupted during periodic power vacuums in Istanbul, and the Jewish quarter continued to be one of the first destinations in almost every *ḳul* revolt.[1] A few striking examples make the case for a broader pattern.

During a series of incidents that started in the spring of 1589, commonly known as "the incident of the governor-general," the cavalry forces (and, according to some sources, the janissaries) attacked and looted Jewish and Christian merchants' shops.[2] A newly introduced tax seems to have incited this first phase of unrest.[3] However, the disturbance became a full-fledged revolt a few days later, when the military units were paid their salaries in debased silver aspers. When the janissaries learned that a Jewish money-changer was reluctant to redeem the coins because they were not pure silver, they turned to the governor-general, who evidently had made the decision to debase the coins. The governor-general once again pointed his finger at the Jewish money-changer, insinuating that he was trying to trick the soldiers. After some back and forth that agitated the soldiers further, the janissary mob plundered several houses in the Jewish quarter. According to Reinhold Lubenau (d. 1631), an eyewitness to the events, the Jews had already buried their valuables in secret vaults underneath their houses. Enraged that they could not find anything, the soldiers set Jewish houses on fire, forcing the occupants to rescue their hidden precious goods—which, apparently, they did. The rebellion ultimately subsided when governor-general Meḥmed Pasha and the head treasurer Maḥmūd Çelebī were executed.[4]

Despite providing a detailed description of the unrest, Ottoman sources are oddly silent about what went down in the Jewish quarter. Selānikī (d. ca. 1600) and Muṣṭafā ᶜĀlī (d. 1600), the two contemporary historians, focus on the turmoil in the imperial palace grounds but do not mention the unrest effecting other parts of the city. One wonders whether

1 Kafadar, "When Coins Turned into Drops of Dew and Bankers Became Robbers of Shadows," 79.

2 The exact dates of the "*beglerbegi* incident" are contested. While Reinhold Lubenau, a pharmacist in the entourage of the Habsburg diplomatic mission and a witness to the events, dates the beginning of the revolts to June 1588, Ottoman sources provide varying dates, several differing by almost a year. İ. H. Danişmend, in his chronology of Ottoman history based on Ottoman sources, also mentions this discrepancy in the dating of the revolt; cf. Danişmend, *İzahlı Osmanlı Tarihi Kronolojisi*, 3:111. Here, I cautiously use the dates from Selānikī and Ḥasan Begzāde.

3 Lubenau, *Beschreibung der Reisen des Reinhold Lubenau*, part 2, 41.

4 Lubenau, *Beschreibung der Reisen des Reinhold Lubenau*, part 2, 43. Cf. Selānikī Muṣṭafā, *Tārīḫ-i Selānikī*, 1:209–12; and Ḥasan Begzāde Aḥmed Paşa, *Tārīḫ*, 2:346ff.

the attacks in the Jewish quarter were such an ordinary occurrence that they were not worth mentioning. Or, were the events transpiring at the palace so consequential that they usurped all the attention? Granted, this was a riot of unprecedented circumstances. According to ᶜĀlī, it was the first attack on the imperial council by the *ḳul* and marked a new low in imperial decline.[5] Furthermore, the head treasurer, Maḥmūd Çelebī, was a dear acquaintance of the historian; devastated by his demise, ᶜĀlī may have concentrated on the circumstances at the imperial palace.

The *beglerbegi* incident may have been the first large, organized *ḳul* rebellion—and one that resulted in an attack on the imperial palace—but it certainly was neither the first nor the last time the janissaries and the cavalry units would plunder the Jewish neighborhood. For example, a century earlier, during a short period of uncertainty following Meḥmed II's (r. 1444–46 and 1451–81) death and prior to Bāyezīd II's (r. 1481–1512) arrival from Manisa in 1481, the janissaries had looted Jewish (and Christian) homes and shops in Istanbul. Upon receiving news of the sultan's death in Maltepe, a township a few hours east of the city, the soldiers in the campaigning army took the trouble to return to Istanbul to do just that. Interestingly, it was not only the regular janissaries who did the pillaging. The "irregulars and brigands" (*levend ve eşḳıyā*) in the city disguised themselves in janissary garb and partook in the looting as well.[6] It appears that the janissary garb provided the necessary disguise for this criminal activity.

The Jewish historian Elijah Capsali, who lived on Crete, in the 1520s reported in some detail about the janissaries' distinct hatred toward Jews and their recurrent plunders of Jewish shops during periods of unrest in the city.[7] Although Capsali may have had increased sensitivity to incidents concerning Jews, his account is corroborated by non-Jewish authors of the time. In fact, contemporary observers report that whenever a sultan died, Jews would bury their valuables in the ground to protect them from the cavalry, janissaries, and members of the novice corps (*ᶜacemī oġlanlar*) in Istanbul, fearing assaults during those uncertain times. Evidently, Jews in town had to be so vigilant that even *rumors* of a sultan's demise would lead them to take precautionary action.[8]

---

5 Fleischer, *Bureaucrat and Intellectual in the Ottoman Empire*, 133.

6 Muṣṭafā ᶜĀlī, *Künhü'l-aḫbār*, 818. Cf. Anonymous, *Tevārīḫ-i Āl-i ᶜOs̱mān* (2013), 116 and Anonymous, *Tevārīḫ-i Āl-i ᶜOs̱mān* (2006), 114.

7 Capsali, *Seder Eliyahu Zuta*, 110–11.

8 Gerlach, *Stephan Gerlachs deß Aeltern Tage-Buch*, 391.

According to an anonymous Jewish chronicler from Istanbul, the cavalry forces once again targeted Jews during the revolt of 1622, which also took the life of the sultan. The chronicler does not provide specifics on the assaults but notes that Jewish subjects of the sultan were fearful of being massacred at the hands of the cavalry units.[9] Examples of Ottoman Jewish subjects who became targets of violence by convert military troops extend to the mid-seventeenth century—and apparently beyond Istanbul. For instance, in a highly dramatic incident, Yasef, the mint director in Cairo, was beaten to death by members of the six regiments, and his body was later burned in a major town square. His successor escaped a similar fate only by converting to Islam.[10]

And then there is, of course, the extraordinarily gruesome murder of Kira Esperanza Malchi, the female Jewish intermediary between the imperial mother Ṣafiyye Sultan (d. 1619) and the outside world. Several sources comment on Malchi's corruption: the accusations levied against her include bribery, control of the customs house, and even meddling with governmental posts and appointments through her influence at the palace. Malchi was murdered by the cavalry units of the palace during an uprising in 1600, a decade after the *beglerbegi* incident.

Despite resistance from the sultan, the grand mufti, and others who proposed banning Malchi from Istanbul, the situation became so tense that several policing forces were ordered to look for the *kira*, who had gone into hiding. The commander of gatekeepers (*ḳapıcılar ketḫudāsı*) and the chief sergeant-at-arms (*çavuşbaşı*), ᶜÖmer Agha, were dispatched to find the Jewish woman. A member of the Civalellis, one of the prominent aristocratic families of Zadar (Zara), a town on the coastline of the Adriatic Sea, ᶜÖmer must have been captured as a prisoner in the early 1570s, and, after turning Turk, taken into service in the palace. A protégée of the powerful Ġazanfer Agha (d. 1603), himself a Venetian convert, ᶜÖmer quickly rose in the hierarchy of the imperial palace, assumed the position of chief sergeant-at-arms, and became a very influential official.[11]

9 Anonymous, *Anonim Bir İbranice Kroniğe Göre 1622–1624 Yıllarında Osmanlı Devleti ve İstanbul*, 41.

10 The events leading up to this incident are described in Hathaway, "The Grand Vizier and the False Messiah," 670. See also Defterdār Ṣarı Meḥmed, *Zübde-i Veḳāyiᶜāt*, 611.

11 Dursteler, *Renegade Women*, 43–44; and Pedani, "Safiye's Household and Venetian Diplomacy," 20.

For my purposes, it is tempting to follow Eric Dursteler and think that the historian Selānikī Muṣṭafā would assign ᶜÖmer Agha a prominent role in the murder of Esperanza Malchi—but he does not.[12] Selānikī does mention that it was ᶜÖmer who "suddenly" located the Jewish woman,[13] but he does not cite him as an agitator or incendiary in the incidents leading up to her murder. He was simply one of the commanding officers of the policing forces who were charged with investigating the issue. In fact, Ġazanfer and ᶜÖmer were close to Ṣafiyye Sultan. Conceivably, ᶜÖmer was taking Malchi to grand vizier's palace, where a solution to the conundrum might have been worked out.

Esperanza Malchi was put on horseback by the palace officers, to be taken to the grand vizier. As the Jewish woman was about to ascend the stairs to the grandee's house, however, the cavalry soldiers charged and captured her. She was stabbed, and her body was cut into pieces and left in the hippodrome for dogs to devour. A later historian, Muṣṭafā Naᶜīmā (d. 1716), claimed shocking details: the cavalry soldiers severed Malchi's hand, "by which she took bribes," and cut out her genitals, then nailed them to the doors of officials known to have worked for her.[14] We can identify at least one commanding officer of the cavalry units that took part in the violent episodes: Frenkbeg-oġlı Meḥmed Agha, né Marcantonio Querini. Son of a Venetian nun and possibly of noble descent, Meḥmed Agha apparently became a passionate Muslim after turning Turk; he also rose in the palace cavalry ranks, holding the position of commander of one of the regular cavalry corps during riots.[15] This piece of information is valuable, as it allows us to put a name to one of the rioters. Otherwise, almost all members of the cavalry forces were, of course, converts from Christianity.

Ṣafiyye Sultan, who was herself Albanian, is quoted as having asked why the Jewish woman's death was carried out in such an obscene fashion, and whether she could not have been killed with a more common punishment for females, such as being thrown into the sea. The imperial mother's astonishment seems to highlight the unusual brutality of Malchi's murder. Based on such evidence, Isabel Lachenauer sought

12 Dursteler, *Renegade Women*, 43.

13 Selānikī Muṣṭafā, *Tārīḫ-i Selānikī*, 2:855.

14 Muṣṭafā Naᶜīmā, *Tārīḫ-i Naᶜīmā*, 162; see further details in Lachenauer, "'One Slice of Hir I Did So See Passe by Our House in Galata.'"

15 Pedani, "Safiye's Household and Venetian Diplomacy," 22.

explanations for this brutality—which shocked not only contemporary observers but also later Ottoman historians—in her gender and/or her Jewishness.[16] In light of the cavalry soldiers' mind-set as described in this article, I believe that Malchi's Jewishness must have been at least an aggravating factor in her particularly cruel murder.

DEVŞİRME BUREAUCRATS

While there seems to have been a pattern of anti-Judaic physical conduct within the *ḳul* in the military regiments, it would be interesting to explore whether such sentiments were also held by the *devşirme* who rose to higher ranks in the bureaucracy. In other words, did such adverse sentiments only surface within the context of mob riots, or can we find other examples of Christian converts lashing out in one way or another? Although the topic requires more systematic research, a few examples may give us an idea.

A curious coincidence relating to the abovementioned head treasurer Maḥmūd Çelebī, who in all likelihood was also of *devşirme* origin, reminds us of the complexity of historical circumstances and the difficulty of reconstructing personal sentiments. We saw above that Maḥmūd was murdered by angry mobs during the infamous *beglerbegi* incident of 1589. Writing some three decades later, Ḥasan Begzāde Aḥmed Pasha (d. 1636 or 1637) shared in his chronicle a detail about the aforementioned bureaucrat's character traits. Praising Maḥmūd Çelebī after describing the circumstances of his unfortunate demise, the historian recounts that the treasurer's piety (*taḳvā*) was so strong that when he received Jewish revenue contractors at his home not only did he take great care not to come physically close to them, he also did not accept the additional gifts and payments conventionally associated with such positions. Apparently, Maḥmūd Çelebī's disgust for Jews was such that he also had the floors in his residence on which the Jewish contractors stepped thoroughly sponge-cleaned after they left.[17]

Then, there are rumors and written evidence about the anti-Judaic sentiments of three powerful grand viziers of the sixteenth century, all

---

16 Lachenauer, "'One Slice of Hir I Did So See Passe by Our House in Galata.'" Two decades later, Bula Rika, yet another Jewish *kira* of the mother of Muṣṭafā I, was severely beaten and later strangled by the *devşirme* troops, on allegations of sorcery and meddling with politics. See Anonymous, *Anonim Bir İbranice Kroniğe Göre 1622–1624 Yıllarında Osmanlı Devleti ve İstanbul*, 64.

17 Ḥasan Begzāde Aḥmed Paşa, *Tārīḫ*, 2:351.

of whom were of *devşirme* origin. Possibly of Slavic or Greek origin and born to Orthodox Christian parents in Parga, today in northwestern Greece, İbrāhīm Pasha (d. 1536) became a favorite of Sultan Süleymān (r. 1520–66), serving as grand vizier for thirteen years. He apparently fell out of grace for several reasons, one of which was his alleged support for Prince Muṣṭafā's cause to the throne. Muṣṭafā would later be executed on his father's orders (1553). Quite curiously, rumors had circulated before Muṣṭafā's demise that, if he had become sultan, he would have killed all of the Jews in Ottoman lands.[18] İbrāhīm Pasha would also be remembered by a Jewish historian—Yosef Sambari (d. ca. 1700s), in his *Sefer Divrei Yosef*—as being anti-Jewish.[19] While Sambari's history, of course, is far from being even near-contemporary to the pasha's lifetime, the historian clearly was quoting from earlier sources.[20] Incidentally, the fact that one of İbrāhīm's nicknames was Frenk—due to rumors that he was a crypto-Christian—is not without relevance to our topic.[21]

At least one contemporary source reported a similar rumor concerning Rüstem Pasha (d. 1561), another grand vizier of Sultan Süleymān. Stephan Gerlach (d. 1612), a priest who was a member of the Habsburg diplomatic mission, related an anecdote about the pasha advising the sultan to drive all Jews from Ottoman lands.[22] While the traveler ties this incident into a lecture given by the sultan about the advantages of a multireligious society, it is important to keep in mind that Rüstem was also a Croatian-born *devşirme*.

These rumors may have been born out of exaggerated anxieties, or based on hearsay and on likely (at least partial) fabrications. Yet the especially insightful reports (*telḫīṣ*) drafted and submitted to the sultan by the five-time grand vizier Ḳoca Sinān Pasha (d. 1596) have reached us in written form. Ḳoca Sinān was a *devşirme* boy taken from a village in Albania. Admittedly, it may be a reach to cherry-pick phrases with which to make pointed suggestions about the convictions and worldview of a man who had converted to Islam some seventy or more years prior. Curiously, though,

18 See, for instance, *Hans Dernschwam's Tagebuch*, 117: "*Wan der Mustaffa, des khaisers son, het sollen kaiser werdn, soll er willens gewesen, alle juden in gancz Turkei vmbzuprengen, das man zw Constantinapol vnd auch Amasia gesagt hot.*"

19 Sambari, *Sefer Divrei Yosef*, 118, 259–61.

20 For Sambari's sources, see Jacobs, *Islamische Geschichte in jüdischen Chroniken*, 122–27.

21 *Hans Dernschwam's Tagebuch*, 100.

22 Gerlach, *Stephan Gerlachs deß Aeltern Tage-Buch*, 61.

in the midst of his insistent requests for a harsh punishment for a Jewish businessman (see below), and his suspicions about the sincerity of two Ottoman pashas in dealings with the Poles, Sinān Pasha felt it necessary to emphasize that it had been seventy years since he converted to Islam.[23] Though he may have uttered the sentence to make a case about his seniority in the religion and to highlight the youth of other convert pashas, his words remind us that his Christian past was not part of a forgotten life or erased from active memory—but instead may have loomed large in his acquired identity. The striking language he uses about Jews in the reports, along with other evidence quoted in this article, designates the topic as a possible area of inquiry for further research and prompts us to ponder the milieu in which such feelings could be nurtured and could live on.

The reports under investigation here—concerning a certain Portuguese Jewish businessman by the name of David Passi (fl. after 1593)—were composed by Sinān Pasha and submitted to Sultan Murād III (r. 1574–95) in 1591. While Sinān Pasha was clearly a passionate adversary of Passi, and his recommendations to the sultan demonstrate a great desire to have himexecuted, the sultan repeatedly denied Sinān Pasha's counsel and spared Passi's life, only to imprison him eventually. Sinān Pasha's tone becomes harsher and his accusations more elaborate over the course of a few letters, as the sultan persistently ignores his wish to see Passi executed.

The reports reveal that Sinān Pasha suspected Passi of spying for the Venetians and Spaniards. Indeed, it is widely accepted in modern scholarship that Passi functioned as an agent with shifting loyalties from 1560 to the 1590s.[24] Of course, Sinān Pasha did not have concrete evidence with which to convince the sultan. We may hail him as a sharp-eyed statesman with good instincts; however, his reasoning as to why the sultan should execute Passi was only partially based on cogent facts. Sinān Pasha did not speak only of this particular individual but built his argument by deducing character traits from

23 "Yet, I do not have a way out: Whenever I raised certain topics [in the past], I have been accused of being prejudiced. Therefore, in order not to appear as holding a grudge, I do not dare submitting many issues [to you]. Thanks be to God, it has been seventy years that I have been Muslim" (*Ammā neyleyelüm, baᶜż-ı umūr ᶜarż eyledügimizde ġarażına ḥaml olunduğın görüp maẓanne-i ġaraż olmayalum dėyü niçe umūr bildürmege cürʾet ėdemezüz. El-ḥamdu li'l-lāhi teᶜālā İslām içinde sinnimiz yetmişi aşdı*). See Ḳoca Sinān Paşa, [*Telḫīṣāt*], 91.

24 Faroqhi, "Ein Günstling des osmanischen Sultans Murad III"; Arbel, *Trading Nations*, 164–68; Arbel, "Passi, David"; and Özgen, "The Connected World of Intrigues."

generalizations about Jews, some based on fundamental Islamic texts. He includes several references to "Jews" in the collective.[25]

"Could a Jew ever be a friend to a Muslim? Aren't Koranic verses and prophetic sayings evident proof against it?," reads a section of the reports. The grand vizier not only cited verses from the Koran stating that Jews were not to be trusted but also gave the Turkish translation of certain passages and interpreted them so as to drive home his point. "To take them as allies is to become one of them," reads the truncated translation of another verse. He continues, using adjectives like "cursed," "mendacious," "deceitful," and "untrustworthy" to describe Passi. Sinān Pasha's main point is built upon a religious foundation.[26]

One could say that these are almost extreme examples of expressions of distrust, born out of ad hominem animosity that may not constitute a pattern. To complicate matters, it is worth noting that Sinān Pasha himself employed a Jewish physician.[27] But dislike nurtured toward a people can take on subtle and complicated forms. The Catholic monarchs, Ferdinand of Aragon (d. 1516) and Isabella of Castile (d. 1504), who in 1492 issued the Alhambra decree to expel practicing Jews from Spain, are also cited as "having Jews as friends, colleagues and councellors." The above condemnations were not uttered with any sort of equivocation or hesitation, which might suggest the sense that they would strike a discordant note. They seem to be delivered as well-known and widely accepted facts. But this is also the type of account that complicates an analysis of the anti-Judaism cultivated by the Ottoman elite. How are we to understand Sinān Pasha's framing his dislike with overtly Koranic references? Should we view such references as evidence of a pragmatic politician who knew how to strike the right chord? Or were some of his sentiments in fact the residue of Christian traditions in the Balkans?

BLOOD LIBELS ADVANCED BY MUSLIMS?

Studies thus far have suggested that prior to the nineteenth century, blood libels in Ottoman lands were exclusively invented by Christians. Yet several Ottoman documents also mention "Muslims" making the

---

25 Fodor, "An Anti-Semite Grand Vizier?," 191–206.

26 In referring to David Passi, the pasha uses such adjectives and nouns as *melᶜūn*, *ṣenāᶜat*, *fesād*, *fāsid* and *ḥabīs̱*; cf. Ḳoca Sinān Paşa, [*Telḫīṣāt*], 12–16, 90–91, 181–84.

27 Baron, *A Social and Religious History of the Jews*, 18:145.

accusation of blood libel. Could such slanders have been appropriated by Ottoman Muslims? Were the Muslims mentioned in the documents perhaps converts from Christianity to Islam?

A handful of imperial orders related to this issue are recorded in registers of important affairs (*mühimme*)—chronologically arranged copies of edicts issued by the sultan after deliberations at the imperial council—that are kept in the Ottoman archives. Admittedly, the following few paragraphs do not constitute a sweeping survey of all cases recorded in the registers but represent only samples. Furthermore, *mühimme* entries in general provide limited information and only a superficial context for the causes and the course of events, thus leaving us with many unanswered questions. Nonetheless, a close look at their wording will reveal some patterns.

An illuminating case about an incident in Foça, a fortress town on the Aegean coast, is recorded in one of the earliest *mühimme* registers, dated 1560. Apparently, whenever there was an unsolved homicide in Foça, the town's Jews were accused of the murder and forced to exonerate themselves. The present case was brought, through an intermediary, as a complaint to the imperial council by a Jewish woman who had recently emigrated from "German lands." "It is your skewed custom to mix Muslim or Christian blood to your bread. Therefore you killed these people," was the accusation that the woman reported to the council. It appears to have been an elaborate setup: some people acted as litigants and others as witnesses to substantiate the cases. Curiously, this edict was issued to request that the local judge repeal the order given to the intermediary, who had come to Istanbul to pursue the case. We do not know the verdict of the original edict given to the Jews or why it was retracted.[28]

The text of an imperial firman with similar content and dated some sixteen years prior was published by Amnon Cohen from the Jerusalem court register. The 1544 firman apparently was dispatched to the governors and judges of the Arab territories (*vilāyet-i ᶜArabistān*), but where exactly the incident took place is not indicated in the document. The accusations against the Jews include not only killing people and mixing their blood into bread but also slandering the accusers' religion and cursing at them. The accusers are referred to as "wicked people" (*eşirrā*),

28 *3 Numaralı Mühimme Defteri (996–968/1558–1560)*, 514, case no. 1169.

but no information on their religious background is provided. The litigants and false witnesses apparently acted in tandem to advance their incrimination, which is clearly defined as extracting cash and profits from Jews. The firman strictly orders the local judges not to listen to such cases advanced against Jews.[29] Almost an identical accusation was recorded in Aydın in 1595. The accusers are similarly referred to as "wicked people," without any information on their religious background. Referring to an earlier edict, the local judge is instructed to forgo pursuing such cases.[30]

The most detailed record on the issue, one that gives us insight into and perspective on blood libels and how they were addressed, was published by Uriel Heyd and is dated 1602.[31] This order was recorded in a manuscript, but the original entry in a *mühimme* register has not yet been discovered. The edict, sent to the judge of Istanbul, lists some of the earlier sultans who had been petitioned about similar slander. The document suggests that Meḥmed II (r. 1444–1446, 1451–1481) issued an edict to the effect that blood libels could not be seen by local judges but were handled exclusively at the imperial council—and only with plaintiffs, defendants, and witnesses present. Süleymān is invoked in the document as having issued an edict in 1553 that essentially dismissed all such accusations (*ḫilāf-ı vāḳiᶜ*) and strongly enforced that blood libel cases be seen only at the imperial council, by the highest officials of the empire. The document states that every sultan since Meḥmed II had ratified earlier decrees, but that the original documents, kept by the petitioners, were destroyed in a fire—and therefore the edict was intended to replace them. For the same reason, historical information on earlier, similar cases is provided in this document.

---

29 Cohen, "Ritual Murder Accusations against the Jews during the Days of Suleiman the Magnificent," 75. I have used the text of the firman as transcribed in Cohen's article. However, I do not share the author's view that the plaintiff and the false witnesses were clearly Muslim. The argument that he advances—that the word for the alleged victim (*ādam*, "man") is not specifically Christian, so he must be Muslim—is not convincing. The term is an idiomatic expression for murder (*ādam ḳatl eyledıŋüz, ādam öldürdüŋüz*) and does not refer to a particular person. Therefore, the religious denomination of the accusers is not identifiable in this incident.

30 Başbakanlık Osmanlı Arşivi, Mühimme Defteri 73, 280, case no. 641; cf. Fodor, "An Anti-Semite Grand Vizier?," 192n3.

31 Heyd, "Ritual Murder Accusations in 15th and 16th Century Turkey," 140ff. I was not able to see the original document and thus have used the complete transcription in Heyd's article. Also see Barnai, "'Blood Libels' in the Ottoman Empire of the Fifteenth to Nineteenth Centuries."

Quoting extensively from Jewish sources and Western travelers' accounts, Heyd provoked a discussion about the 1553 edict, claiming that it must have ratified an earlier firman, which probably was issued after the famous Amasya blood libel incident, commonly dated to the mid- or late 1540s. Supporting Ottoman documents for this particular incident have yet to be unearthed.[32] Based on the information in contemporary sources, Heyd advances the assumption that Süleymān's chief physician, Moses Hamon (d. 1567), was instrumental in convincing him to obtain the firman that blood libel cases could only be seen at the imperial council. Heyd also conjectures that there may have been a connection between Süleymān's edict and his willingness to refute his son Prince Muṣṭafā's supposed anti-Jewish sentiments. As mentioned above, rumors were in circulation that if he had become sultan, he would have killed all of the Jews in Ottoman lands. Muṣṭafā's execution took place only a few months before the 1553 edict. These points are important to understanding the background to Süleymān's firman. According to the 1602 document, however, Meḥmed II had already issued an edict stating that blood libels were only to be seen at the imperial council. If that information is accurate, Süleymān's firman may not have introduced new judicial directives.

Although these decrees allow us to reason that the imperial center viewed blood libels as nothing but ploys that some racketeers used to extort Jews, and acted to dismiss such cases via the highest legal authority, the insistent recurrence of the issue suggests that public opinion in smaller localities allowed such accusations to be advanced comfortably. We can presume that Jews in these towns were in an underprivileged position and thus could not defend themselves, and that the imperial center felt the highest legal authority was the most effective way to deal with such libels justly.

Still, at least one example complicates the matter further: evidently, in 1592 a certain Mīrzā bin Ḥüseyin (an Iranian?) from Bursa accused eight Jews of abducting him, tying him to a pillar in their house, and drawing two containers of blood from his calf. The imperial council ruled to exile the eight men on the Island of Rhodes. The particulars of this

32 The Portuguese Marrano poet Samuel Usque provides some details on the incident in his history from the early 1550s: Usque, *Consolaçam às tribulaçones de Israel*, 210–11.

peculiar case are difficult to determine, but the verdict seems counter to that of the edicts mentioned above. The difference between this case and the ones mentioned above is that the witnesses of the act, as distinctly specified in the document, were also Jews (*birḳaç nefer Yahūdī daḫi daᶜvāların taṣdīḳ eyledüklerin*), which might explain the decision to exile Jews.[33]

As might be expected, it is very difficult to ascertain how these libels disseminated. What we do know is that Meḥmed II's edict, quoted in the 1602 document, explicitly refers to Muslims as the victims (*ṭāᵓife-i Yahūdā vech-i meşrūḥ üzre müslimān ḳatl edüp*) of the allegations. Although the wording of that firman, from the mid-fifteenth century, cannot be confirmed from the original edict definitively, the first document treated above, about the specific case in Foça, explicitly presents "some people from among the Muslims" (*müslimānlardan baᶜżı kimesneler*) as the accusing party. There is no way to determine who these Muslims were. However, it would not be overreaching to suppose that they were recent converts from Christianity to Islam who might have known that Jews were vulnerable to such allegations. Foça (Phokaia), after all, had been a primordial Greek town. If they were freeborn Muslims, did they learn of such libels from their Christian neighbors? Even if they were second-generation converts, it would not be unreasonable to assume that certain strong sentiments might have lived on within their families. While the document is not particularly revealing about the identity of the accusers, other than their being Muslim, blood libel should be considered essentially a Christian phenomenon, and to have spread from there.

CONCLUDING REMARKS

There seems to have been a pattern of outbursts of physical violence against Ottoman Jews, mostly by converts from Christianity. *Devşirme* converts, who probably acquired such hostile ideas as part of their culture growing up in the Balkans, may have naturally continued to nurture them in their new acculturated lives. After all, the soldiers socialized with a group of young men with similar pedigrees, which must have made it easier to

33 Başbakanlık Osmanlı Arşivi, Mühimme Defteri 69, 297, case no. 584–85; also quoted in Heyd, "Ritual Murder Accusations in 15th and 16th Century Turkey," 138–39.

cultivate their views on Jews in general. Furthermore, the *devşirme* soldiers stationed in cities with mixed populations—such as Istanbul—must have come into contact and conversed in their mother tongues with local Christians. While it is very difficult to ascertain whether there was further circulation of ideas between these groups, anti-Judaism appears to have been an ordinary theme at least within some of these Christian communities.[34] Although I have concentrated on cases from the latter half of the sixteenth century, it remains to be seen whether there was a rise in the number of incidents during this time due to particular societal or economic strains.[35]

I admit that this article contains a good deal of speculation. I would like to reiterate that most of these boys were converted to Islam as teenagers and would have remembered the notions with which they grew up. Of course, an inquiry into the psychological implications of being converted to a new cultural milieu, societal dynamic, and, most importantly, a new confessional mobilization—as well as a hypothesis about the perceptions of these teenagers—is bound to be barren, in the absence of any written personal accounts. As historians, however, I think we are well positioned and authorized to speculate about their mind-set.

I am not suggesting that there was a concerted effort or a conspiracy on the part of Christian converts against Jews, or that all *devşirme* converts categorically hated Jews. However, I believe that regarding these attacks merely as the result of ordinary mobsters looting targets for maximum monetary profit would be an oversimplification. Obviously, there is a great deal of danger in essentializing all converts, assigning to them similar feelings of aversion toward Jews. A janissary mobster may well have assaulted Jews while another convert was defending them and yet another was looting Christian shops alongside Jewish ones. A *devşirme* pasha may have despised Jews generally but also employed skilled Jewish physicians in his service. These are expected complexities of human interactions.

34 For example, in 1627 *Κατὰ Ἰουδαίων* (Against the Jews)—written by Kyrillos Loukaris, the Patriarch of Constantinople (in office intermittently between 1620 and 1638)—was the first book published at the Greek Orthodox press in Istanbul. The tract was a theological refutation of Judaism, composed in a genre with a long tradition (*Adversus Judaeos*); cf. Pektas, "The First Greek Printing Press in Constantinople (1625–1628)," 110.

35 Fodor sees rising anti-Jewish sentiment as connected to an economic crisis in the latter part of the sixteenth century. Fodor, "An Anti-Semite Grand Vizier?," 191–206.

Dislike of others is also a complex emotion that is difficult to gauge and substantiate. Depending on several factors, including societal incentives and pressures, the individual's changing approach to life, his or her interests and calculation of benefits, it may take on different forms of expression or may be suppressed altogether. Feelings of aversion may come to be expressed overtly at times of distress and when the opportunity presents itself. I thus am interested in retrieving such instances of personal or group outbursts which may in the end suggest a pattern of motivations.

A related topic that deserves separate study is the obvious aversion and detestation displayed by some of the *devşirme* converts toward all things Christian. The trope that the converts occasionally turned fervent enemies of Christians has been the subject of some studies.[36] I believe that modern theories and findings of psychotherapy can guide historians in our efforts to interpret the motivations and ambivalent worlds of *devşirme* converts. Although the field of psychohistory—the study of psychological motivations for historical events, established by Lloyd deMause (b. 1931) in the 1970s—has been treated cautiously by historians, who prefer to work with incontrovertible evidence, the methods of the field would certainly bring new perspectives to our understanding of the possible motivations of *devşirmes*.[37]

BIBLIOGRAPHY

Sources

3 Numaralı Mühimme Defteri (996–968/1558–1560). Edited by Nezihi Aykut, et al. Ankara: Başbakanlık Devlet Arşivleri Genel Müdürlüğü, 1993.

Anonymous. *Anonim Bir İbranice Kroniğe Göre 1622–1624 Yıllarında Osmanlı Devleti ve İstanbul.* Translated by Nuh Arslantaş and Yaron Ben Naeh. Ankara: Türk Tarih Kurumu, 2013.

Anonymous. *Tevārīḫ-i Āl-i ᶜOs̱mān.* Transliterated by Hüseyin Oğuz as "Arkeoloji Müzesi Kütüphanesi 376 Numarada Kayıtlı Anonim Tevârih-i Âl-i Osman (H.616-929 / M.1219-1519)." MA thesis, Marmara Üniversitesi, 2013.

Anonymous. *Tevārīḫ-i Āl-i ᶜOs̱mān.* Transliterated by Şamil Can as "XVI. Yüzyıla Ait Anonim bir Tevârih-i Âl-i Osman." MA thesis, Dumlupınar Üniversitesi, 2006.

36 See the references in Graf's recent *The Sultan's Renegades.*

37 I would like to mention a term paper written by one of my students, from which I drew my initial ideas on the topic: Kirschbaum, "Psychological Implications of the *Devşirme* System."

Capsali, Elijah. *Seder Eliyahu Zuta*. Partial translations by Nuh Arslantaş in *Yahudiler ve Türkler: Yahudi Tarihçi Eliyahu Kapsali'nin (1483–1555)* Seder Eliyahu Zuta *İsimli Kroniği Bağlamında Bir İnceleme*. Istanbul: İz Yayıncılık, 2013.

Defterdār Ṣarı Meḥmed. *Zübde-i Veḳāyiᶜāt*. Edited by Abdülkadir Özcan as *Zübde-i Vekayiât: Tahlil ve Metin (1066-1116/1656-1704)*. Ankara: Türk Tarih Kurumu, 1995.

Gerlach, Stephan. *Stephan Gerlachs deß Aeltern Tage-Buch . . . an die Ottomannische Pforte zu Constantinopel*. Frankfurt am Main: In Verlegung Johann-David Zunners, 1674.

Hans Dernschwam's Tagebuch einer Reise nach Konstantinopel und Kleinasien (1553/55). Edited by Franz Babinger. Munich, Leipzig: Duncker & Humblot, 1923.

Ḥasan Begzāde Aḥmed Paşa. *Tārīḫ*. Vol. 2. Edited by Şevki Nezihi Aykut as *Hasan Bey-zâde târîhi*. Ankara: Türk Tarih Kurumu Basımevi, 2004.

Ḳoca Sinān Paşa. [*Telḫīṣāt*]. Edited by Halil Sahillioğlu as *Koca Sinan Paşa'nın Telhisleri*. Istanbul: İslam Tarih, Sanat ve Kültür Araştırma Merkezi, IRCICA, 2004.

Lubenau, Reinhold. *Beschreibung der Reisen des Reinhold Lubenau*. Edited by W. Sahm Königsberg: F. Beyer (Thomas & Oppermann), 1915.

Muṣṭafā ᶜĀlī. *Künhü'l-aḫbār*. Vol. 1, part 2. Edited by Ahmet Uğur. Kayseri: Erciyes Üniversitesi Yayınları, 1997.

Muṣṭafā Naᶜīmā. *Tārīḫ-i Naᶜīmā*. Edited by Mehmet İpşirli as *Târih-i Naᶜîmâ: Ravzatü'l-Hüseyn fî hulâsati ahbâri'l-hâfikayn*. Ankara: Türk Tarih Kurumu, 2007.

Petz, Bartholomäus. *Petzsche Gesandtschaftsberichten*. K. K. Haus-, Hof- und Staatsarchiv in Wien, Turcica 1587 Fascikel 38. Convolut I u. II.

Sambari, Yosef. *Sefer Divrei Yosef*. Published as *Mısır'da Türkler, Araplar ve Yahudiler: Yahudi Tarihçi Yosef Sambari'nin (1640–1703)* Sefer Divrey Yosef *isimli İbranice Kroniği Bağlamında Bir İnceleme*. Partial translations by Nuh Arslantaş. Istanbul: İz Yayıncılık, 2015.

Sanderson, John. *The Travels of John Sanderson in the Levant, 1584–1602; with his Autobiography and Selections from his Correspondence*. Edited by Sir William Foster. London: Printed for the Hakluyt Society, 1931.

Selānikī [Muṣṭafā Efendi]. *Tārīḫ-i Selānikī*. Edited by Mehmed İpşirli as *Tarih-i Selânikî*. 2 vols. Istanbul: İstanbul Üniversitesi Edebiyat Fakültesi Basımevi, 1989.

Sevgen, Nazmi. "'İğneli Fıçı' Hikâyesinin Sırrı." *Hayat Tarih Mecmuası* 5 (1974): 63–64.

Silāḥdār Meḥmed Aġa [Fındıḳlılı]. *Silāḥdār Tārīḫi*. Istanbul: Devlet Matbaası, 1928.

Topkapı Palace Museum Archives, E.12321. Edited by Halil Sahillioğlu as *Topkapı Sarayı Arşivi, H. 951–952 Tarihli ve E–12321 Numaralı Mühimme Defteri*. Istanbul: IRCICA, 2002.

Usque, Samuel. *Consolaçam às tribulaçones de Israel*. Translated from the Portuguese and edited by Martin A. Cohen as *Samuel Usque's Consolation for the Tribulations of Israel*. Philadelphia: Jewish Publication Society of America, 1964. Reprint, Skokie, IL: Varda Books, 2002.

Studies

Arbel, Benjamin. "Passi, David." In *Encyclopedia of Jews in the Islamic World*, edited by Norman A. Stillman, accessed July 5, 2016.

Arbel, Benjamin. *Trading Nations: Jews and Venetians in the Early Modern Eastern Mediterranean*. Leiden: Brill, 1995.

Baer, Marc. "Death in the Hippodrome: Sexual Politics and Legal Culture in the Reign of Mehmet IV." *Past and Present* 210, no. 1 (2011): 61–91.

Baer, Marc. "The Great Fire of 1660 and the Islamization of Christian and Jewish Space in Istanbul." *The International Journal of Middle East Studies* 36 (2004): 159–81.

Baer, Marc. *Honored by the Glory of Islam: Conversion and Conquest in Ottoman Europe*. New York: Oxford University Press, 2008.

Barnai, Jacob. "'Blood Libels' in the Ottoman Empire of the Fifteenth to Nineteenth Centuries." In *Antisemitism through the Ages*, edited by Shmuel Almog, translated by Nathan H. Reisner, 189–94. Oxford: Pergamon Press, 1988.

Baron, Salo Wittmayer. *A Social and Religious History of the Jews: Late Middle Ages and Era of European Expansion, 1200–1650*. Vol. 18: *The Ottoman Empire, Persia, Ethiopia, India and China*. 2nd ed. New York: Columbia University Press, 1983.

Benbassa, Esther, and Aron Rodrigue. *Sephardi Jewry: A History of the Judeo-Spanish Community, 14th–20th Centuries*. Berkeley: University of California Press, 2000.

Bulliet, Richard. *Conversion to Islam in the Medieval Period: An Essay in Quantitative History*. Cambridge, MA: Harvard University Press, 1979.

Cohen, Amnon. *Jewish Life under Islam: Jerusalem in the Sixteenth Century*. Cambridge: Harvard University Press, 1984.

Cohen, Amnon. "Ritual Murder Accusations against the Jews during the Days of Suleiman the Magnificent." *Journal of Turkish Studies* 10 (1986): 73–78.

Cohen, Jeremy. "Christian Theology and Anti-Jewish Violence in the Middle Ages: Connections and Disjunctions." In *Religious Violence between Christians and Jews: Medieval Roots, Modern Perceptions*, edited by Anna Sapir Abulafia, 44–60. New York: Palgrave, 2002.

Danişmend, İsmail Hâmi. *İzahlı Osmanlı Tarihi Kronolojisi*. Vol. 3. Istanbul: Türkiye Yayınevi, 1972.

Dursteler, Eric. *Renegade Women: Gender, Identity, and Boundaries in the Early Modern Mediterranean*. Baltimore: The John Hopkins University Press, 2011.

Epstein, Mark Alan. *The Ottoman Jewish Communities and Their Role in the Fifteenth and Sixteenth Centuries*. Freiburg i. Br.: Klaus Schwarz, 1980.

Faroqhi, Suraiya. "Ein Günstling des osmanischen Sultans Murad III: David Passi." *Der Islam* 47 (1971): 290–97.

Fleischer, Cornell H. *Bureaucrat and Intellectual in the Ottoman Empire: The Historian Mustafa Âlî (1541–1600)*. Princeton, N.J.: Princeton University Press, 1986.

Fodor, Pal. "An Anti-Semite Grand Vizier?: The Crisis in Ottoman-Jewish Relations in 1589–91 and Its Consequences." In *In Quest of the Golden Apple: Imperial Ideology,*

Politics, and Military Administration in the Ottoman Empire, edited by Pal Fodor, 191–206. Istanbul: ISIS Press, 2000.

Galante, Avram. *Histoire des Juifs de Turquie*. Istanbul: ISIS, [1986?].

Graf, Tobias P. *The Sultan's Renegades: Christian-European Converts to Islam and the Making of the Ottoman Elite*. Corby: Oxford University Press, 2017.

Hacker, Joseph. "Ottoman Policy toward the Jews and Jewish Attitudes toward the Ottomans during the Fifteenth Century." In *Christians and Jews in the Ottoman Empire*, edited by Benjamin Braude and Bernard Lewis, 117–26. New York: Holmes & Meier Publishers, 1982.

Hathaway, Jane. "The Grand Vizier and the False Messiah: The Sabbatai Sevi Controversy and the Ottoman Reform in Egypt." *Journal of the American Oriental Society* 117, no. 4 (1997): 665–71.

Heyd, Uriel. "Ritual Murder Accusations in 15th and 16th Century Turkey." *Sefunot: Studies and Sources on the History of the Jewish Communities in the East* 5 (1961): 135–50.

Jacobs, Martin. *Islamische Geschichte in jüdischen Chroniken: hebräische Historiographie des 16. und 17. Jahrhunderts*. Tübingen: Mohr Siebeck, 2004.

Kafadar, Cemal. "When Coins Turned into Drops of Dew and Bankers Became Robbers of Shadows: The Boundaries of Ottoman Economic Imagination at the End of the Sixteenth Century." PhD diss., McGill University, 1986.

Kirschbaum, Abigail. "Psychological Implications of the *Devşirme* System: A Psychohistorical Approach." Unpublished term paper, The University of Chicago, 2016.

Lachenauer, Isabel. "'One Slice of Hir I Did So See Passe by Our House in Galata': The Extraordinary Murder of the Kirā Esperanza Malchi." Unpublished term paper, The University of Chicago, 2016.

Lewis, Bernard. *The Jews of Islam*. Princeton: Princeton University Press, 1984.

Lewis, Bernard. "The New Anti-Semitism." *The New York Review of Books*, April 10, 1986.

Nirenberg, David. *Anti-Judaism: The Western Tradition*. New York: Norton, 2013.

Özgen, Elif. "The Connected World of Intrigues: The Disgrace of Murad III's Favourite David Passi in 1591." *Leidschrift* 27, no. 1 (2012): 75–100.

Pedani, Maria Pia. "Safiye's Household and Venetian Diplomacy." *Turcica* 32 (2000): 9–32.

Pedani, Maria Pia. "Venetians in Constantinople at the End of the Sixteenth Century." *Arab Studies Notebooks*. Supplement 15: "Venetians in the Levant. Muslims in Venice" (1997): 67–84.

Pektas, Nil Ozlem. "The First Greek Printing Press in Constantinople (1625–1628)." PhD diss., University of London, 2014.

Rozen, Minna. "The Ottoman Jews." In *The Cambridge History of Turkey*, vol. 3, edited by Suraiya Faroqhi, 256–71. Cambridge: Cambridge University Press, 2008.

Ruether, Rosemary Radford. *Faith and Fratricide: The Theological Roots of Anti-Semitism*. New York: Seabury Press, [1974].

Shaw, Stanford J. "Christian Anti-Semitism in the Ottoman Empire." *Belleten* 54 (1991): 1073–1149.

Evliyā Çelebī's Perception of Jews

Hakan T. Karateke

Evliyā Çelebī's seventeenth-century travel account (*Seyāḥatnāme*) has served as an extraordinary resource for historians seeking to reconstruct the social, economic, architectural, and cultural realities of the Ottoman lands for more than a century. Fortunately, scholars recently have become interested in studying the worldview of the author himself, as Robert Dankoff did in his marvelous exploration of the "mentality" of this elite Ottoman man.[1] This article follows that lead as it seeks to track down the clues in the ten-volume travel account that reveal Evliyā's perception of Jews.

My goal in tracing Evliyā's perception of Jews stems from a fascination with "perception studies," which seeks to reconstruct a person or a group's perceptions of a given phenomenon. The object of these perceptions can be a single notable person, a group of people, a trend, or an idea—essentially, an issue or topic of enough import that an individual or a group of people formed an opinion about it. The difficulty inherent in reconstructing perceptions is obvious: they are deeply personal, difficult to quantify, and often ephemeral and unstable. My mode of inquiry seeks

* Versions of this paper were delivered at a conference titled "Evliya Çelebi, Voyageur ottoman du XVIIe siecle et l'Europe de son temps," on November 14–15, 2011, at l'Institut national des langues et civilisations orientales (INALCO), Paris; on January 13, 2012, as part of the Friday Lecture Series of the Center for Middle Eastern Studies at the University of Chicago; and on November 29, 2012, at Şehir University, Istanbul.

1 Dankoff, *An Ottoman Mentality*.

to define those perceptions that can be construed as "plausible" based on certain indicators, including actions, utterances, or records left by the agents under investigation.

In one of my previous inquiries, I examined Evliyā's perception of the New World.[2] Subsequently, I became intrigued by his perceptions of ethnic and religious groups living in Ottoman lands—particularly Jews. The current article developed from my interest in reconstructing Evliyā's perceptions of the Jews of his time, and of Judaism in general. Can the modern historian, by studying Evliyā's narrative, penetrate the author's mind and make plausible suggestions about his personal stance toward "Jews" as a category? Certainly, authors of any era exercise self-censorship, consciously or unconsciously, when considering precarious topics. Nevertheless, Evliyā's personal and nonchalantly opinionated style—and his minimal concern with what we now think of as political correctness with regards to ethnic, religious, and racial differences—makes the narrative a particularly useful source for understanding his views on ethnic and religious groups. Moreover, the author's well-known penchant for relating amusing anecdotes arguably allows sardonic language more easily.

Several questions that we can pose to the text come to mind. How did Evliyā express his opinions on Jews when he interacted with them generally? How did he portray Jewish individuals he knew, or their actions? What were the elements of his stereotyping? In what ways did he generalize and essentialize certain historic features, or ascribe common clichés to Jews as a whole? The anecdotes or stories need not be specifically about Jews. He may have used a Jewish character, or a trait associated in his mind with "Jewishness," in contrast to a non-Jewish person. Even so, the way in which Evliyā situates such a character in his story may contain valuable details for analysis. While the elements used to reconstruct perceptions are difficult to quantify and often subtle, a careful examination of Evliyā's throwaway remarks, laden with overt or hidden value judgments, his choice of words, and even his general mood of narration will provide us with data to plausibly reconstruct his perceptions.

To state the obvious, I am not interested in the veracity of his stories, and I have not attempted to contrast them with other sources in order to reconstruct historical "realities"—some are clearly legends, with elements that are illogical, anachronistic, or beyond the laws of nature.

2 Karateke, "Evliyâ Çelebi's Perception of the New World."

The rhetoric surrounding these incidents is more important for my purposes than the realities on the ground. I have, however, compared relevant sections throughout the entirety of the travel account in order to understand his remarks on particular matters under consideration, noting whether he used the same kind of language regarding, or took similar stances on, comparable topics.

A wealth of data is recorded about where and how densely Jews lived, the kinds of professions they practiced in different towns, and the characteristics of several famed Jewish individuals. However, I deliberately have not included in this article *all* the information that Evliyā relates about Jews. I am interested specifically in those narrative sections that include judgmental comments or subtext, particulars that I conclude to be reflective of his perception of Jews. Therefore, this is not an article about "Jews in Evliyā Çelebī's travel account" but an attempt to understand the author's perceptions.

Evliyā's stories concerning Jews and Judaism are related to three time periods: first, the ancient history of Jews is retold in different versions on several occasions. While Evliyā's versions of most of these stories are aligned with the Islamicized biblical lore carried over from early historical works, he emphasizes and embellishes some features of those stories in peculiar ways. Furthermore, he explores Jews of the early Islamic era, and, finally, accounts of the Jews of his own time form the bulk of his narrative on Jews. Most of these remarks are based on his own observations, but they also include anecdotes and rumors that apparently were in common circulation in Ottoman society.

PROPHET KILLING

While relating the founding legends of the city of Constantinople, Evliyā mentions a priest in Jerusalem by the name of Makarios, who supposedly informed the Jews about Christ; afterward, they arrested and crucified him.[3] As the story goes, the priest lived through the time of Helena,

3 Evliyā Çelebī, *Seyāḥatnāme*, 1:13b: "*Meger Yahūd ṭāʾifeleri ḥażret-i ʿĪsāyı bu papas üzre ṣalb etmişlerdi.*" Because a definitive critical edition of the *Seyāḥatnāme* is yet to be produced, my references are to the manuscripts. However, I would like to acknowledge the Yapı Kredi Edition (1996–2007), without which I could not have written this article. That edition was carried out by Yücel Dağlı, Robert Dankoff, Orhan Şaik Gökyay, and Seyit Ali Kahraman.

mother of Emperor Constantine, the first Christian ruler of the Roman Empire. The emperor dispatched his mother to Jerusalem after Jesus had appeared in his dreams and instructed him to build a temple in that city. Helena found a few artifacts belonging to Christ and later located Makarios, who led her to the place where Christ's cross was buried. They dug, and, sure enough, found not one but three crosses in the grave. In order to verify the authenticity of the cross, the party laid it on a grave, upon which the buried body was resurrected. Evliyā dates this encounter to 328.[4]

The legend of the True Cross became exceedingly popular in Christian mythology during the Middle Ages. Makarios is remembered in these traditions as the bishop of Jerusalem, and the person who was forced to help Helena and Makarios find the cross is believed to be a Jewish wise man named Judas (Cyriacus).[5] The similarity of his name to that of Christ's disciple Judas Iscariot must have caused Evliyā to confuse the Judas who committed the act of betrayal and the Judas with knowledge of the cross's whereabouts. However, the legend of the unearthing of the cross is of little concern for this article. I am more interested in Evliyā's casual reference to Jews as the crucifiers of Christ. To be sure, the narrative does not take an overtly accusatory tone toward Jews—the accusation is made only in passing. As will be evident below, however, this casual reference fits into a larger framework of Jews' alleged habit of murdering prophets. The accusation of deicide (that is, the killing of Jesus Christ) was essentially a Christian phenomenon, one of the frequent libels faced by European Jews in the Middle Ages. The common assumption has been that if the Muslim Turks in Anatolia also spread the canard, they must have learned it from the Christians of Anatolia. There is no doubt that Evliyā recounts the legend after Christian sources or informants. As a matter of fact, he declares that the tale was narrated in Greek histories (*tevārīḫ-i Yūnān*).

An incident related to the ancient Jewish history repeatedly quoted by the traveler is Nebuchadnezzar's expulsion and murder of Jews in Palestine, Syria, and as far away as Baghdad. In Evliyā's version, the king of the Babylonian Empire killed at least two hundred thousand Jews in an act of revenge for their murder of John (Yaḥyā), a prophet in the

4 Evliyā Çelebī, *Seyāḥatnāme*, 1:13b.
5 Baert, *A Heritage of Holy Wood*, 42ff.

Islamic tradition to whom the king had pledged fealty. Upon slaughtering the Jews, the king proclaimed, "Thanks be to God, I have now taken the revenge of venerable John from the Jewish people (*ḳavm-i Yahūd*)."[6] In Safed alone, some 170,000 Jews of all ages were slaughtered, and, according to Evliyā, the rocks over which their blood flowed could still be observed when he visited the town.[7] The surviving Jews fled to cities near and far. Evliyā quotes this episode to make a case about the origins of the Jewish populations in Isfahan, Salonika, and other cities, and he argues that immigration to these cities took place at that time.[8]

In another tale, Zechariah (Zekeriyyā), father of John and, again, a prophet in the Islamic tradition, was falsely framed and subsequently gruesomely slain—sliced from top to bottom with a saw—by Jews. Upon hearing the news, Ptolemeus, whom Evliyā identifies as the ruler of Macedonia and a follower of Zechariah, set out for Aleppo from Kavala, the seat of his throne, with an armada of 1,700 ships. Docking at the port of İskenderiyye (İskenderun), the army marched to Aleppo and executed 160,000 Jews in one day, an act of revenge for the slain prophet. He then built a mosque in Aleppo—which is known today as the Great Mosque (Jāmiᶜ Ḥalab al-Kabīr) and is still believed to house Zechariah's remains—and took the Jews' wealth back to Kavala.[9]

As the aforementioned tale of deicide was replicated from Christian traditions, so too does the story of John eventually lead back to Christian sources. In the town of Sabastia, Evliyā chats with a monk who shows him the corpse of John and explains that blood oozes from the corpse every year on the Ḫıḍrellez—that is, May 6—because Jews murdered him near Jerusalem on that day.[10] On one occasion, when relating the martyrdom of John and the fate of his corpse, Evliyā explicitly states that Arabic and Turkish histories take their information on the ancient world from Coptic and Greek histories, especially the Greek history of Yanvān.[11]

6 Evliyā Çelebī, *Seyāḥatnāme*, 4:314a.
7 Evliyā Çelebī, *Seyāḥatnāme*, 8:223a.
8 Evliyā Çelebī, *Seyāḥatnāme*, 3:25a, 3:44b–45a, 4:314a, 4:324b, 4:407a, 9Y:118a ff., 9Y:198b, 10Y:9b, 10Y:282b.
9 Evliyā Çelebī, *Seyāḥatnāme*, 8:215b.
10 Evliyā Çelebī, *Seyāḥatnāme*, 9Y:205a.
11 Evliyā Çelebī, *Seyāḥatnāme*, 9Y:118a. For Yanvān's *History*, see Yerasimos, "Enquête sur un héros."

That said, other tales that the traveler relates about prophets murdered by Jews could not have been influenced by Christian traditions. In fact, Evliyā seems convinced that the Jews of yore were repeatedly involved in the killing of prophets. He reports that Jews murdered most of the seventy prophets (*nebī*) who were active in Tiberias and imprisoned forty prophets in a cave near Damascus. The so-called Cave of Starvation takes its name from this alleged incident, and the disturbing wails of these prophets are said to have been heard coming from the cave—in which they eventually died of hunger—for seven years.[12] In the town of Nablus, Evliyā visits a dungeon where Jesus Christ was reportedly imprisoned for forty days by Jews who denied him water.[13] (It is worth keeping in mind that Jesus Christ is considered a prophet in the Islamic tradition, and so all of these incidents are thematically linked.) Notably, Evliyā declares, substantiating his knowledge on works of exegesis and chronicles (*cemīᶜ-i tefāsir ve tevārīḫlerde*), some 4,000 of the 124,000 prophets were martyred by Jews.[14] The pattern of Jews murdering prophets is more or less explicitly mentioned in the Koran (2:61; 3:112), and the exegesis literature uniformly interprets the pronouns in the related verses as referring to Jews. Having memorized the Koran, Evliyā was of course aware of this—but also of the verse which clarifies that Jesus was not killed, thereby clearing Jews from the accusation of having murdered him (4:157). Because Evliyā does not explicitly invoke any of these verses, there is no reason to superimpose the teachings of fundamental texts on him.

In sum, Evliyā's repetition of the accusations of deicide leveled against Jews seems to indicate a convergence of widespread Christian and Islamic traditions.[15] The Ottomans commonly consulted—and reproduced biblical stories and pre-Islamic history from—earlier Arab histories, like those of al-Ṭabarī (d. 923) or Ibn al-Athīr (d. 1233), who in turn appropriated biblical tales from Jewish and Christian traditions. It is well

---

12 Evliyā Çelebī, *Seyāḥatnāme*, 9Y:252a, 9Y:235b.

13 Evliyā Çelebī, *Seyāḥatnāme*, 9Y:207a.

14 Evliyā Çelebī, *Seyāḥatnāme*, 3:44b.

15 Although I have not systematically expanded my research to other Ottoman authors in order to discern whether Evliyā's stories were in wider circulation, I would like to mention an example. Naᶜīmā, writing a few decades after Evliyā, quotes Abaza Pasha's (d. 1634) angry letter to the janissary agha's deputy, in which he uses Nebuchadnezzar's murder of seventy thousand Jews, to avenge John, as a metaphor for his intent to kill so many janissaries as revenge for their murder of Sultan Ahmed I (d. 1617). Naᶜīmā, *Tārīḫ*, 2:549.

known that the theme of Jews murdering prophets developed in early Christian traditions and was explicated by the Church Fathers,[16] but it is difficult to locate the origins of these popular tales in the mélange of Middle Eastern traditions. Evliyā held certain ideas about Jews' involvement in the murder of a number of prophets, and we can reasonably suppose that these ideas influenced his general stance on Jews.

CANARDS

A gripping story begins with the question of why there are no Jews to be found in the city of Trabzon. Evliyā claims that the people of this town are authorized by imperial rescripts to murder Jews who wander into the city. This elevated animosity apparently originated with an incident that transpired during the governorship of Selīm I (1481–1510).

According to legend, two Muslim youngsters go missing in the city. When the inhabitants and administrators of the region fail to find them, the search is called off. Twenty years later, a dervish notices barely legible writing on a piece of leather he is contemplating at the market. It turns out to be a message from the missing boys, who write that they have been held captive in an underground location by Jewish tanners. The dervish hastens to the governor, who swiftly orders raids on Jewish tanneries. The boys are indeed discovered alive in a cave-like workshop. However, the search party is shocked to find that the boys' backs are flayed, and the two are fastened to each other at their rears. While one worked, that is, the other waited on top of his brother for his turn. They had been working and suffering thus in the tannery for two decades. Furthermore, it is discovered that hundreds of boys named Meḥmed had been killed, locked up, or made servants by the tanners. Enraged, the people of Trabzon sealed the gates of the citadel, massacred all the Jews in the city, including women, children, and babies, and obtained imperial permission to kill them from then on.[17]

Blood libels were common accusations against Jews in Christian Europe, and evidence suggests that similar incidents were not unheard of in Ottoman lands. Although the Trabzon incident is not technically a

16 See, for example, Ruether, *Faith and Fratricide*. Apparently the theme also found its way, for different purposes, to Jewish midrashic traditions; for an analysis, see Amaru, "The Killing of the Prophets."

17 Evliyā Çelebī, *Seyāḥatnāme*, 2:253b.

blood libel, as the youths were not kidnapped in order for their blood to be used in a ritual ceremony, it is clearly a story in a similar vein. Because blood libel was essentially a Christian phenomenon, and because the city of Trabzon had always been home to a rather large Greek population, we might have assumed that the report would fit well with local Christian notions. Yet, in a separate reference to the incident, Evliyā explicitly mentions that it was the Muslim "Laz" population of Trabzon who slaughtered the Jews.[18] The author's views on the Laz are confusing: he thinks that the Laz (and the Jews) are wicked people (*şerīr*), but he also finds the formers' religious devotion praiseworthy, particularly with regard to their aversion toward Jews. The paragraph about the episode ends with high praise of Trabzon's Laz population: "The people of Trabzon do not like Jews at all. The reason for this is because they are zealous believers, monotheists and Sunnis. They are gentle and good-tempered too. May God be pleased with them all."[19]

To be sure, the author himself introduces the anecdote as a "strange story" (*ḥikāye-i ʿacībe*), which should make us think that he took its bizarre details with a proverbial grain of salt.[20] But apart from questions regarding the veracity of any part of the above-mentioned tale, how widely it circulated, and even which form it took, important for my purposes is that Evliyā chose to portray the murderers as Muslim Laz who committed the act out of piety. As Evliyā builds his narrative, Jews are depicted as devious and cunning, and he suggests a link between the kidnapped boys' identity as Muslim and the Jewish tanners' preference for them as victims. Furthermore, the trope that Jews killed people named Meḥmed recurs as an anecdote elsewhere in the *Seyāḥatnāme*. In what seems to be recirculated version of a story that was at least a century old, Meḥmed Pasha, the governor of Buda (d. 1551), is poisoned by a Jewish physician. Upon his arrest and interrogation, the doctor allegedly admits to killing forty people with the name Meḥmed.[21] In addition to

18 Evliyā Çelebī, *Seyāḥatnāme*, 3:124b.

19 Evliyā Çelebī, *Seyāḥatnāme*, 2:253b: "*ġāyet müʾmin ve muvaḥḥid ve ehl-i sünnet veʾl-cemāʿat . . .*"

20 Dankoff is also of the opinion that Evliyā himself did not believe the story; cf. Dankoff, *An Ottoman Mentality*, 69.

21 The story was told by Muṣṭafā ʿĀlī (d. 1600) in the sixteenth century; see Schmidt, *Pure Water for Thirsty Muslims*, 260. For Evliyā's version, see Evliyā Çelebī, *Seyāḥatnāme*, 1:47b.

these anecdotes, Evliyā clearly expresses his own belief in the veracity of this allegation.[22] The name Meḥmed, as is well known, is a Turkified version of the Prophet Muḥammad's name. Therefore, we may suppose that these tales insinuate an anti-Islamic motivation for alleged acts of this type, and they may also be seen as linked to the theme of prophet killings mentioned above.

ANTAGONISMS

Evliyā appears to have been aware of the antipathy toward Jews expressed by other ethnic and religious groups. He frequently claims that Jews do not live in this or that town because the townspeople would kill them.[23] Notably, Evliyā presents this explanation concerning several towns inhabited mostly by Greeks. Writing of Athens and of the monks of Penteli Monastery, on the outskirts of the city, the author praises their extraordinary hospitality to strangers—but notes that if a Jew stopped by he would be discovered in the morning, burned and charred.[24] He reports that Jews are afraid of Christians in Galata; that the Laz and Greeks (*Rūm*) do not like Jews and do not allow them to live in Yeniköy; that the Christians of Bucharest hate Jews; and that if the Jews left their quarter in Muğla, in the citadel, Greeks would murder them with pleasure.[25] Evliyā occasionally uses the same explanation for the absence of other groups from certain towns. While this seems to be a trope, it must reflect certain antagonisms toward Jews (and others) in those towns. This narration in and of itself does not say much about Jews themselves, though it does reflect Evliyā's removed stance, as a member of the dominant culture, toward enmities among minorities. The situation becomes more complicated when Evliyā begins comparing ethnic and religious groups.

The traveler quotes a curious poem in the context of presenting an anecdote that, he claims, transpired in the 1550s, during the construction

22 Evliyā Çelebī, *Seyāḥatnāme*, 1:215a–b: "Her şeyleri ümmet[-i] Muḥammede, ḫuṣūṣan Meḥemmed isimli bir müslime ḳatl etme ihānetleri muḳarrerdir." Also see my article "An Ottoman Anti-Judaism," in this volume, for an imperial order mentioning this libel.

23 For example, Evliyā Çelebī, *Seyāḥatnāme*, 2:286b (Erzurum), 2:368a (Türbeli Gönlek).

24 Evliyā Çelebī, *Seyāḥatnāme*, 8:255a.

25 Evliyā Çelebī, *Seyāḥatnāme*, 1:129b, 1:137b, 7:102a, 9:Y61a.

of the Süleymaniye Mosque. When the Safavid Shah Tāhmāsb I (r. 1524–1576) hears that construction has halted for a year due to financial constraints, he sends a large sum of money and a case of valuable jewels, along with a letter asking the Ottoman sultan to consider the gifts a contribution toward financing the mosque. Sultan Süleymān (r. 1520–1566), humiliated, becomes furious, distributes the gifts to Istanbul's Jews, and, summoning the envoy who brought the gifts, quotes the following line (in Persian) to him: "*Rāfiżī*s will be donkeys underneath the Jews on the Day of Judgment." "Since," Süleymān further declares to the Persian envoy, "Jews will be your masters on that day, and having given your money to them now, they shall not whip you or spur you then."[26] "*Rāfiżī*," or heretic, as is well known, is a pejorative term that the Ottomans used to describe the Shiʿi Safavids. The premise behind the episode is clearly meant to insult the Safavid envoy by stating that the Safavids will fare worse on the Day of Judgment than will Jews, who, if we are to make sense of the story, must have been regarded as the lowest of nations.[27]

In fact, Evliyā quotes the same Persian line at least twice more—once while discussing Crimean Jews, and another time when reporting on Hemedan. He states that Crimean Jews live in extremely filthy conditions, and that most work in the leather business; an additional few are meat vendors and *boza* sellers. Other Jews do not like these Karaite Jews, he states. They are "real" Jews, according to his account—they read the Torah but do not speak the "Jewish language"; critically, they do not observe Jewish dietary restrictions. The Karaites are therefore considered "redheads" by other Jews, and, quoting the above-mentioned line, he writes that these "heretic" Jews will not "ride" the "redheads"—that is, the Safavids—on the Day of Judgment. "*Ḳızılbaş*," or "redhead," is another pejorative designation that the Ottomans used to describe Shiʿa Safavids, mocking the red headgear that the latter wore. The word, then, simply means "heretic" in the first instance in the sentence ("*bunlar* [Karaites] *Yahūdīleriŋ ḳızılbaşlarıdır*") but would refer to a Safavid person in the second ("*rūz-ı maḥşer günü bunlar* [Karaites] *ḳızılbaşa binmezler*"), echoing the same meaning as in the above anecdote.[28]

26 Evliyā Çelebī, *Seyāḥatnāme*, 1:44bff.

27 The same line of poetry is quoted in at least one other eighteenth-century Ottoman source; therefore, it must have been widespread; cf. *Risāle-i ġarībe*, 41.

28 Evliyā Çelebī, *Seyāḥatnāme*, 7:122a; for Hemedan, see 4:310b.

On the other hand, Karaites elsewhere are depicted in derogatory terms, according to the "false Jewish tradition." Writing of the holiness of the city of Safed for Jews, Evliyā reports that if a Jew does not make a pilgrimage to this town he or she will be considered a Karaite, not a Jew. Clearly, his impression is that Karaites are heretics within the Jewish tradition.[29]

CHARACTER TRAITS AND DEROGATORY ATTRIBUTES

The characteristics that Evliyā attributes to Jews and Jewish spaces provide a fairly good picture of his set of stereotypes concerning Jews. In one tale, because the Jews do not follow a prophet sent to them, God orders Gabriel to take their lives as punishment. Several centuries later, the prophet Ezra chances upon a large mass of bones around Ashkelon and is instructed by God to pray for the bodies' resurrection. He does so, and the bones are gradually covered with flesh and nerves again; the Jewish tribe is raised from death.[30] The trope of resurrecting people from bones is no doubt an ancient theme, which found its way into Islamic traditions—at least, the Koran records a version.[31] Importantly, Evliyā uses this episode as an etiological explanation for some of the unfavorable physical qualities he attributes to Jews. Evliyā writes that the reason why Jews are weak and have pale complexions and bad breath is that they were resurrected by the prophet Ezra's prayer after having been dead for a long time.[32]

Evliyā also ascribes cowardice to Jews. He declares that "Austrians are like Jews compared to Hungarians, they do not have the guts [lit. "heart"] [to fight]."[33] The castle of Gevher-Kirman on the Crimea is known as Çufud Fortress (*Çufud ḳal*^{c}*e*), or Jews' Fortress, as some 1,500 houses in the fortress are inhabited exclusively by Jews; the officers of the fortress are likewise Jewish. Evliyā states that some non-firearm weapons are kept at the fortress gate, but that Jews do not have the courage to use them. Furthermore, he mentions that there are no firearms present in the

29 Evliyā Çelebī, *Seyāḥatnāme*, 3:44b.
30 Evliyā Çelebī, *Seyāḥatnāme*, 3:45b.
31 Koran 2:259.
32 Evliyā Çelebī, *Seyāḥatnāme*, 3:45b.
33 Evliyā Çelebī, *Seyāḥatnāme*, 7:49b.

fortress, because Jews not only do not have the pluck to use these guns, they cannot stand hearing the roar of a cannon or a rifle.[34]

In a peculiar anecdote, a madman known as Ḳoca Dīvāne chances upon a cortege of about three hundred people carrying a coffin. Not realizing that it is a Jewish funeral, he swaps headgear with someone in the party and starts walking in front of the group, reciting Muslim prayers. As he is rebuked and told that it is not a Muslim funeral, he begins acting up, spitting phlegm and mucus and causing an altercation. Finally, as he attempts to pass underneath the coffin, the Jewish party becomes extremely upset and drops the coffin to the ground. Evliyā explains that Jews believe that if a Muslim passes under a coffin or jumps over it, the deceased becomes a witch and is sent to hell. Unable to cope with the situation, the funeral attendees at first abandon the coffin in the middle of the street, but, through the mediation of others, they eventually shake hands with Dīvāne. Yet the madman then urinates on the corpse of the dead Jew and flees with the cap on his head.

Evliyā relays this story as a funny anecdote. In fact, he thinks that Dīvāne is not an ordinary mad person, but as a humorous character. He states that if one were to compile his jokes, they would compose a sizable collection, similar to that of Naṣreddīn Ḫoca. Moreover, we are given an important detail about the circulation of such jokes: jokes by and about Dīvāne are told by comedians at elite gatherings. We should then take a moment to understand what is being ridiculed here, and in what way. Of course, Evliyā would never present a Muslim funeral or deceased person in such a denigrating context and with such desacralizing vocabulary. Someone urinating on a corpse, even in a joke, is vilification of the highest degree. Evliyā furthermore uses the highly derogatory words "*lāşe*" and "*leş*" ("corpse" and "carcass") for the deceased. In fact, in the *Seyāḥatnāme* he describes deceased Jews with these words a few times, sometimes with the added adjective "*murdār*" ("unclean").[35] The respectful words for Muslims are "*naᶜş-ı şerīf*" and "*cesed-i şerīf*" ("noble corpse") as well as the rather neutral "*meyyit*" ("deceased"). In this case, the variety of words available to describe a dead person's body allows us a peek into the intricacies of jokes from a bygone culture, which

34 Evliyā Çelebī, *Seyāḥatnāme*, 7:122b–123a.

35 He sometimes uses the same word for Christians and, rarely, for Muslim Ottomans who fell from grace before they died.

are generally difficult to grasp without the relevant linguistic and cultural references.

"No blacksmith's shop is without a chicken, no mill without a pig, and no mansion without a Jew" is an axiom Evliyā quotes within the context of an anecdotal incident that, he claims, took place in a Bulgarian village.[36] Even if not intended as a direct insult, the saying reflects the perceived lowly status of Jews, who are depicted as efficient assistant providers, or servants, in large mansions. In a similar vein, Evliyā comments on the fact that Jewish tavern-keepers walk at the very back of the line in the processions of guilds at imperial festivities. The traveler clarifies that their being at the end of the procession was due not to their detestable profession but so as to "denigrate them (*taḥḳīren*) because they were Jews." According to Evliyā, Jewish tavern-keepers are commanded by an imperial order to march at the very back of the line because they are the most dispensable—in fact, a breed of vermin (*ḥaşerāt*)—and because the sultan wants to keep track of their numbers. Still, three fully armed janissary colonels were appointed to the Jewish party in order to prevent spectators from throwing rocks, hitting them with wooden sticks, or committing other acts of physical assault.[37]

Jewish neighborhoods and homes are frequently referred to as "dirty," "filthy," "nasty," and "cursed."[38] In Salonika, for example, the Jewish neighborhood's filthiness is contrasted with the clean cobblestone roads in the rest of the city. Even the garbage superintendent cannot make the inhabitants clean the streets. Evliyā writes that the unclean streets and the Jewish homes, with their tiny doors, make the neighborhood a corner of hell.

One potentially surprising observation is that Evliyā does not replicate a widespread slander that Jews had an aptitude for money-forging, or that Jewish money-changers were exploitative. The anecdote that comes closest to describing Jews as greedy follows: after a blaze in Unkapanı that left many shops in ruins, a Jew named Küpeli ("the earringed") rented the

36 Evliyā Çelebī, *Seyāḥatnāme*, 3:130b: "*naᶜlbend dükkānı ṭavuḳsuz ve degirmenleri ḫınzīrsız ve ekābir ḫāneleri Yahūdīsiz olmaz.*"

37 Evliyā Çelebī, *Seyāḥatnāme*, 1:215a: "*herkes ṭaş atup taḥta ḳaḳup vażᶜ-ı yed etmemeleri–yçün*"; cf. Dankoff, *An Ottoman Mentality*, 85.

38 For example, Evliyā Çelebī, *Seyāḥatnāme*, 1:124a: "*Yahūdīleriŋ ḫāne-i telvīs̱leri*" (Istanbul); 8:228a: "*Ammā çufud maḥallātlarınıŋ soḳaḳları hem daracıḳ dār-ı menḥūsḫānelerdir ve hem cümle zoḳaḳları pis ve mülevves̱dir*" (Salonika).

only shop that remained intact. The former tenant, Ḥüseyin Çelebī, a clog-maker, resisted leaving his shop during the fire, saying that the shop had been in existence since his grandfather's time. Ḥüseyin remained in the shop and continued to work on his clogs; miraculously, he and the shop-keeper survived the fire unharmed. Once rent prices increased, Küpeli took over the shop by paying a few more aspers to the administrator of the foundation that owned the block of shops. People in the neighborhood did not like the fact that "a Jew rented the place instead of Ḥüseyin Çelebī," remarks Evliyā. The story ends with a troubling incident: on his first day at the shop, Küpeli's head was smashed by the shop's pull-down shutter while he was trying to open it. The shop was then returned to Ḥüseyin Çelebī after the "unclean corpse" (*lāşe-i murdār*) was removed. Evliyā relates the story of Ḥüseyin Çelebī within the context of his enumeration of the holy men of Istanbul. The fact that a Jewish merchant was seeking a profit is not its focus, but common prejudices and perceptions concerning Jews are recognizable in these anecdotes.

MASTERS OF SECRET KNOWLEDGE

Evliyā refers to Jews a few times in a neutral, if not positive, light. One episode worth mentioning relates Jews' alleged insights into the secret art of alchemy. He describes the party of the nitric acid (*tīz-āb*, *aqua fortis*) makers—that is, alchemists—among the procession of guilds of 1638 in Istanbul. Nitric acid is used to separate gold and silver or to obtain pure silver, Evliyā explains. Even its fragrance turns Jewish alchemists' beards green or red, and their fingernails black. In the anecdote that follows, the author writes about a fire that breaks out in a Jewish neighborhood in Istanbul. When the commander of the imperial gardeners (*bōstāncıbaşı*) and the janissary agha, hastening to inspect the site, walk into the workshop of a Jewish alchemist, they are amazed to find hundreds of bottles on shelves. A party of thirteen people guzzles the bottles of liquid, which they take to be wine; they vomit up their insides and then burn to death spectacularly. To Evliyā, nitric acid is a cursed substance, but it is necessary for alchemists. He finally declares that some Jews have successfully attained this secret knowledge.[39]

39 Evliyā Çelebī, *Seyāḥatnāme*, 1:187b.

This is only one of Evliyā's several stories about alchemy, and it does not necessarily distinguish Jews as the sole masters of occult knowledge. The sheikhs of Sufi brotherhoods sometimes are depicted as having access to alchemical knowledge as well. When, for instance, a few people try to warn the sultan about the possibility of a revolt by Sheikh Rūmī, financed by the enormous fortune of gold that he obtained through alchemy, the sheikh admits to his grasp of this secret knowledge. "It is among the doings of sheikhs," he declares, adding that they do not practice alchemy for the purposes of acquiring wealth but use small pieces of gold to resist hunger.[40] The corpses of sufis who swallow these golden bits do not decay.[41] Alchemy and alchemists are not depicted in a negative light; it becomes clear from the totality of stories that Evliyā presents men with such secret knowledge as existing within a mystical aura.

In another story, set in the time of Prophet Muḥammad and supposedly paraphrased from "historical works," Evliyā introduces a Jew by the name of İzāᵓīl as a sorcerer with innovative ideas. İzāᵓīl builds a waterwheel in Ḥama during a period of drought. When astonished townspeople inquire as to what use a waterwheel might be when there is no water, he tells them about his idea to bring water from the Nile to town. Subsequently, he travels to the town of Mansura, Egypt, obtains four bottles of water from the river, and casts a spell on them. One branch of the Nile follows him as he walks to the north, and water springs from wherever "that sorcerer" hurls a bottle on the ground. These springs become the sources for larger lakes, including the Dead Sea. As İzāᵓīl reaches the foot of the Gülbin Mountain (Jabal Ansariya), the Prophet is alarmed by the likelihood of the Nile leaving the Holy Land, and calls out to his cousin ᶜAlī bin Abī Ṭālib, who hastens to kill İzāᵓīl. When the Jewish sorcerer drops dead, the final bottle also falls to the ground, causing another stream to spring from the mountain. Unlike other streams, which flow southward, this one flows westward. Evliyā finds the etymology of the name of the Asi River (Orontes), which means "rebel" in Arabic, in its decision, without warning, to flow initially to the west, then to the north, passing through Homs and Hama, and then to the south, passing through Antakiye before flowing into the Mediterranean.[42] Evliyā refers

40 Evliyā Çelebī, *Seyāḥatnāme*, 4:209a.
41 Evliyā Çelebī, *Seyāḥatnāme*, 5:133b.
42 Evliyā Çelebī, *Seyāḥatnāme*, 3:23b, 3:48b.

to a certain book, which he calls *Tuḥfe,* as a source for this story, and he mentions that the Jews consider İzā°īl a prophet.

A few pages later, Evliyā returns to this tale. Though the Asi River passes through Hama, as per the events related above, it does not have the surge to rotate the waterwheel. An "impure" (*nā-pāk*) son of the murdered Jewish sorcerer takes it upon himself to operate the wheel by praying in the name of prophets. The wheel rotates only when the name of Prophet Muḥammad is invoked. Thus, the son decides to become Muslim.[43]

Evliyā's keen interest in explaining the formation of lakes, inner seas, or straits is evident throughout the travel account. Of course, accounts laden with wonders and miracles, hypothesizing about the origins of the physical material of the earth, were no rarity before the development of modern geology in the eighteenth century. Evliyā occasionally attributes such wonders to great men like Alexander the Great or to the legendary figure Ḫıżr, who found the water of life. Notably, these two feature in a legend about the formation of the Bosphorus Strait. Unlike the legend of the Nile, however, the opening of the Strait is explained more or less within the boundaries of logical physical possibility: Alexander puts hundreds of thousands of professional diggers to work for three years, digging out the Bosphorus; no sorcery or magic was involved.[44] This contrast provides us with a context for Evliyā's attribution of sorcery to İzā°īl as a Jewish magician.

OMISSIONS

It will not escape the careful reader's attention that Evliyā's narrative lacks two rather important themes, which could have brought interesting perspectives to his views on Jews in general. First, he does not seem to have considered the mass Jewish immigration from Spain and Portugal to Ottoman lands during the late fifteenth and sixteenth centuries an event worth reporting in detail. He certainly was aware of Jews who immigrated during Ottoman times, as he mentions, for instance, that the Jews of Muğla arrived in this town after the Ottoman conquest, and that there were no Jews there during the Genoese era.[45] Even if the Sephardic

43 Evliyā Çelebī, *Seyāḥatnāme*, 3:26a.
44 Evliyā Çelebī, *Seyāḥatnāme*, 1:9aff.
45 Evliyā Çelebī, *Seyāḥatnāme*, 9:Y61a.

immigration were not an acute situation during Evliyā's lifetime, the lack of any substantial information in the travel account is especially intriguing in light of his general interest in the movements of peoples and their origins. For the pedigree of Salonika Jews, for instance, his explanation includes a substantial migration from ancient Judea and Israel to the Balkan town after Nebuchadnezzar's expulsion, as mentioned above. Apparently, the Jews arrived in Salonika at night, snuck into the walled city, and massacred the resident Greeks. A Karaite Jew, who, Evliyā says, was the lord of the flock, forged an agreement with the Genoese, promising mutual aid in subsequent battles with the Greeks. Eventually, the two nations reconciled, and Jews have lived in the city since.[46]

Evliyā's omission of Jewish immigration becomes especially intriguing in light of his mention of a mass emigration from Spain, but his knowledge seems to be confined to the expulsion of Moriscos. While enumerating the ethnic and religious groups living in Galaṭa, the traveler remarks that the anguished community of Moriscos, whom Evliyā calls *mübtecel* Muslims, does not like Christians at all. He leads us to believe that this animosity is rooted in their suffering under Christian rule in Spain, as a consequence of which they immigrated to Istanbul during the reign of Sultan Aḥmed I (r. 1603–1617).[47] This date coincides with the main expulsion of Moriscos from Spain in 1609 but again leaves us with questions as to why Evliyā would not have known or reported about the even larger Jewish immigration to Ottoman lands.

The other curious omission from the *Seyāḥatnāme* is any information on or commentary concerning Sabbatai Zvi (d. 1676) and the messianic movement associated with him. As is well known, Zvi was quite active and had a growing number of followers in the 1650s–60s, until he was imprisoned by the Ottoman government in 1666. It would be utterly surprising if such a well-connected person as Evliyā, who also had a liking for all sorts of rumors, did not hear anything about a movement which was a point of some concern for the Ottoman central government. Even if the theological intricacies of this messianic movement were outside the bounds of his interests, the social implications would have been worth discussing. Yet Evliyā never mentions Zvi or the movement, for reasons that remain obscure.

---

46 Evliyā Çelebī, *Seyāḥatnāme*, 8:223a.
47 Evliyā Çelebī, *Seyāḥatnāme*, 1:129a.

CONCLUSION

Looking closely at his references to Jews and Jewish history, it is evident that Evliyā Çelebī nurtured unmistakably negative feelings toward Jews on the whole. However, scrutinizing instances of the traveler's portrayal of Jews was only the first step of an inquiry that led to this conclusion.

Evliyā was educated partially at the palace and had strong connections to court society. It is obvious that, as a representative of imperial ideology, he cultivated a superior imperial gaze toward many groups of people who were not part of that social and cultural milieu. I therefore undertook a careful examination of what he had to say about other, potentially comparable, communities–for example, Christians, gypsies, Safavids, Kurds, or Yezidis.

Evliyā also describes Christians with some contempt. He repeatedly revels in illustrations of Ottoman soldiers slaughtering Christians, or reveals his detestation of them. However, these sentiments must be considered within a particular context; the Christians to whom he refers with derision are those enemies the Ottoman army is actively fighting, not those living in Ottoman lands, or Christians in general. Evliyā has a few good things to say about gypsies; some gypsies never lie, for example, and the Balat gypsies are the pride of their neighborhood. Moreover, he points out, gypsies are described in a positive way in some of the Prophet's traditions. Yezidis are perhaps the only other group that Evliyā discusses in such a distinctly denigrating manner. A detailed catalog of his views on these groups exceeds the scope of this paper; a comparison between his views on other groups and his views on Jews, however, reveals that his dislike of Jews was more direct and elevated than the run-of-the-mill contempt he displayed toward other religious or ethnic groups within this society.

The information discussed in this article aside, Evliyā's knowledge of Ottoman Jews and their customs is disappointingly limited. He was an otherwise inquisitive man who took pride in his ethnographic approach to people's customs. During his travels, Evliyā routinely took the trouble to veer off course in order to witness an unusual natural occurrence, chat with an out-of-the-ordinary person, or learn about a given population's customs. We are, then, justified in asking whether he ever visited a synagogue, for instance. If he did, he says almost nothing about his visits. He mentions existing synagogues (*ṣınaġo*) in a few towns yet gives little or no description of them.[1] But because he reports that the Book of Psalms is read by rabbis with "straps" (conceivably *tefillin*) in synagogues, we can presume that he witnessed this.[2] Did he have any substantial contact with the Jewish subjects of the empire? None that he reports in detail. He did have sustained interactions with other "infidels," as he calls them; for example, he studied Greek histories with a certain Simeon/Simyon.[3]

This scenario arguably fits well with the widely held understanding of an Ottoman society in which different religious communities shared a common public space but lived rather segregated lives within their own cultural milieus. Most common people probably did not have access to the innermost spheres of other religious communities and, accordingly, knew little more about their customs and worldviews than what was visible in the public domain (colored, of course, by the stereotypes and prejudices in circulation at the time).

Evliyā's views, outlined in this article, can certainly be taken as a starting point for understanding perceptions about Jews held by elite Sunni Ottomans of the seventeenth century. It is perhaps surprising that the perceptions of this individual, otherwise known as a moderate and nonchalant person, display coherently and unequivocally negative feelings about Jews. As mentioned above, Evliyā heard some of the tales from his Christian sources or informants, but evidence suggests that Islamic/Ottoman traditions were also at play. Although confirming this hypothesis requires further study, the analysis of Evliyā's views concerning Jews in this article certainly challenges the received wisdom that Jews had a perfectly sanguine experience in Ottoman lands.

BIBLIOGRAPHY

Sources

Anonymous. *Risāle-i ġarībe*. Edited by Hayati Develi as *XVIII. Yüzyıl İstanbul Hayatına Dair Risâle-i Garîbe*. Istanbul: Kitabevi, 1998.

Evliyā Çelebī. *Seyāḥatnāme*. Vols. 1 and 2: Bağdat 304, Topkapı Sarayı Müzesi Library, Istanbul; vols. 3 and 4: Bağdat 305, Topkapı Sarayı Müzesi Library, Istanbul; vol. 5: Bağdat 307, Topkapı Sarayı Müzesi Library, Istanbul; vol. 6: Revan 1457, Topkapı Sarayı Müzesi Library, Istanbul; vols. 7 and 8: Bağdat 308, Topkapı Sarayı Müzesi

1 Evliyā Çelebī, *Seyāḥatnāme*, 4:341a, 5:131a, 7:128a, 7:141b, 8:229a, 8:248b.
2 Evliyā Çelebī, *Seyāḥatnāme*, 3:44b.
3 Cf. Dankoff, *An Ottoman Mentality*, 27.

Library, Istanbul; vol. 9Y: Bağdat 306, Topkapı Sarayı Müzesi Library, Istanbul; vol. 10Y: TY 5973, Istanbul University Library.

Muṣṭafā Na[c]īmā. *Tārīḫ-i Na[c]īmā*. Edited by Mehmet İpşirli as *Târih-i Na[c]îmâ: Ravzatü'l-Hüseyn fî hulâsati ahbâri'l-hâfikayn*. Ankara: Türk Tarih Kurumu, 2007.

Studies

Amaru, Betsy Halpern. "The Killing of the Prophets: Unraveling a Midrash." In *Hebrew Union College Annual* 54 (1983): 153–80.

Baert, Barbara. *A Heritage of Holy Wood: The Legend of the True Cross in Text and Image*. Translated from the Dutch by Lee Preedy. Leiden and Boston: Brill, 2004.

Dankoff, Robert. *An Ottoman Mentality: The World of Evliya Çelebi*. Leiden and Boston: Brill, 2004.

Karateke, Hakan. "Evliyâ Çelebi's Perception of the New World." In *Evliyâ Çelebi: Studies and Essays Commemorating the 400th Anniversary of His Birth*, edited by Nuran Tezcan, Semih Tezcan, and Robert Dankoff, 183–89. Istanbul: Ministry of Culture and Tourism, The Bank Association of Turkey, 2012.

Ruether, Rosemary. *Faith and Fratricide: The Theological Roots of Anti-Semitism*. New York: Seabury Press, [1974].

Schmidt, Jan. *Pure Water for Thirsty Muslims: A Study of Muṣṭafā [c]Ālī of Gallipoli's* Künhü l-Aḫbār. Leiden: Het Oosters Instituut, 1991.

Yerasimos, Stephane. "Enquête sur un héros: Yanko bin Madyan, le fondateur mythique de Constantinople." *Mélanges offerts à Louis Bazin par ses disciples, collègues et amis*, edited by Jean-Louis Bacqué-Grammont and Rémy Dor, 213–17. Paris: L'Harmattan, 1992.

Ambiguous Subjects and Uneasy Neighbors: Bosnian Franciscans' Attitudes toward the Ottoman State, "Turks," and Vlachs

Vjeran Kursar

This study focuses on eighteenth-century Franciscan chronicles and other writings as narrative sources rich in individual and collective attitudes toward the ruling Muslims and the rival Orthodox Christian Serbs-Vlachs. These works were created in the wartime and postwar atmosphere of religious and ethnic tensions that marked the turbulent border province of Bosnia. Franciscan attitudes, stereotypes, and prejudices against various others are compared with relevant information from Ottoman documents preserved in the archives of Franciscan monasteries. While one would expect the use of cautious language and self-censorship when referring to Muslims, the authors of these documents openly expressed dislike, loathing, or hatred—in addition to the prevailing indifference, mistrust, anxiety, and fear—toward individual "Turks" who caused them harm or injustice. On the other hand, they occasionally praised virtuous Muslim friends and righteous dignitaries who provided them assistance in various endeavors. A special category was created for Catholics who "crossed to the other side" and "became Turk," occasionally including former Franciscans. Such "deserters" and "traitors" were, unsurprisingly, refuted as "damned" and "doomed souls," and often accused of hatred toward former coreligionists, seemingly in accordance with the old chauvinistic Serbian saying that "a Turkified person is worse than a Turk."[1] This unforgiving attitude might stem from the Catholic Church's weakness of authority when faced with the real danger of loss of its members via assimilation into the Muslim community. Religious leaders of the Orthodox Christians, pejoratively called "Vlachs," "schismatics," or "old believers," were harshly scourged as archenemies, evil-doers, and slanderers of Catholics in front of the authorities. They were portrayed as dirty, unholy, and betraying errants. In this respect, the Franciscan Christian nemeses received worse treatment than the "infidel Turks." This animosity was further increased by competition among Christian elites, both ecclesiastical and lay.

INTRODUCTION: THE STATE OF CATHOLICISM IN OTTOMAN BOSNIA

If we were to take the conventional narrative at face value, at the time of the final Ottoman assault and quick conquest of the kingdom of Bosnia (1463), Fr. Anđeo Zvizdović (d. 1498), the remaining representative of the Roman Catholic Church in the country and the custodian of the Franciscan *vicaria* Bosna Argentina,[2] chose a different, conciliatory approach. On May 28, he appeared in front of the victorious Sultan Meḥmed II ("the Conqueror," r. 1444–46, 1451–81) in Milodraž, central Bosnia, one of the main political centers of the collapsed kingdom, and begged for mercy for the Catholics.[3] The sultan readily responded to the monk's plea and issued him a letter of security (*ᶜahdnāme*). Although it did not regulate the position of the

* This project has been fully supported by the Croatian Science Foundation (project no: 9215).

1 This saying was coined in the first half of the nineteenth century by the Serbian nationalist author Georgije Magarašević, the founder of the first Serbian literary journal, *Letopis Matice srpske*, and later transmitted and further elaborated in Serbian nationalist circles, including by the famous Montenegrin *vladika* and poet Petar II Petrović Njegoš, the author of *Gorski vijenac*. See Aleksov, "Poturica gori od Turčina," 225–58; and Aleksov, "Adamant and Treacherous," 158–90.

2 Also referred to as Bosna Srebrena, the region was elevated to the rank of province in 1517.

3 Matasović, "Fojnička regesta," 89–95; [Šabanović], "Turski dokumenti," 207–8; Boškov, "Pitanje autentičnosti Fojničke ahd-name"; Mandić, "Autentičnost Ahd-name"; and Džaja, "Fojnička ahdnama." On Anđeo Zvizdović, see Vrgoč, "Fra Anđeo Zvizdović."

Catholic Church in Bosnia extensively, it guaranteed security and protection (*emn-ü-amān*) to the Franciscans and their churches. The *ᶜahdnāme* in question was later understood as the founding document of Catholicism in Ottoman Bosnia and as such served as the basis for future imperial edicts, which further regulated the issue.[4]

In later periods, central and provincial authorities regulated the status and the rights of Franciscans and Catholics via *fermāns*, *buyruldus*, *iᶜlāms*, *ḥüccets*, and the like, which were issued on the request of the Franciscans, their patrons, their intermediaries, and the diplomatic representatives of Catholic states, such as France, Austria, Venice, and the Republic of Dubrovnik. These documents and edicts represent sultanic interpretation and implementation of sharia-based legislation concerning non-Muslims and cover topics including religious practices, freedom of movement of clerics (which was particularly important for Franciscan missions), rights of possession and renovation of churches and monasteries, collection of church taxes and donations, tax exemptions, the duty of hosting travelers in the monasteries, and the like.[5] Although many of these regulations were restrictive and discriminatory in nature, the Franciscans were granted certain privileges, including significant tax exemptions. For instance, the monks of the monasteries of Fojnica, Kreševo, and Kraljeva Sutjeska were exempted from major non-Muslims taxes like *ḫarāc* and *ispence*, as well as other sharia and non-sharia taxes. The friars of Fojnica managed to preserve these tax exemptions until the end of the seventeenth century.[6]

In addition to the *ᶜahdnāme*, Zvizdović was cloaked by Meḥmed II with a ceremonial robe of honor (*ḳaftān*, or *ḫilᶜat*), a luxurious object made of silk interwoven with golden threads, still preserved in the museum of the Franciscan Monastery of the Holy Spirit in Fojnica.[7] This garment further implicated a newly established official relation between the Ottoman state and the head of the Franciscans, as the bestowing of

4 Cf. Matasović, "Fojnička regesta," 62, 91; Jelenić, *Kultura i bosanski franjevci*, 1:140; Džaja, *Konfesionalnost i nacionalnost*, 153–55; and Mandić, "Autentičnost Ahd-name," 61, 74.

5 Cf. Džaja, *Konfesionalnost i nacionalnost* (1990), 154–55.

6 Hadžibegić, *Glavarina*, 17–18.

7 Matasović, "Fojnička regesta," 89–91; and Boškov, "Pitanje autentičnosti Fojničke ahd-name," 92. On *ḳaftān*, see *EI*², s.v. "Libās" (T. Majda); and Pakalın, *Osmanlı Tarih Deyimleri*, 2:134 ("*kaftan*").

robes of honor symbolized acceptance into state service or promotion.[8] In addition to state officials, *ḫilᶜat*s as insignia were also bestowed on foreign diplomats, vassals, and other foreign dignitaries.[9]

Generally speaking, the Roman Catholic Church in the Ottoman realm did not receive full recognition, being an institution based in Rome—in the "Abode of War" (*dār al-ḥarb*, the non-Muslim enemy territory outside the "Abode of Islam," *dār al-Islām*)—and an organization whose head, the Pope, was the principal instigator of anti-Ottoman crusader propaganda and occasional wars during the late Middle Ages and the beginning of the early modern era (and thus the arch-enemy of the sultan). The Catholic identity of other great adversaries of the sultan, the mighty emperors of the Holy Roman Empire (that is, members of the House of Habsburg), who dared to question the sultan's domination in the Balkans and Central Europe, seems to have been equally important in this respect. Nevertheless, the Catholics eventually came to terms with the sultan. Their contracts with the state were not made at the imperial level but individually and separately, including smaller Catholic communities in different parts of the Ottoman realm. Groups of Catholics were given *ᶜahdnāme*s as imperial guarantee letters, which granted them the status of protected non-Muslim subjects—that is, *ẓimmī*s.[10] Thanks to Meḥmed II's *ᶜahdnāme*, Bosnian Franciscans became the only representatives of the Catholic Church with officially recognized status, not only in Bosnia but in all European territories of the Ottoman Empire.

Although scores of churches and monasteries were destroyed, abandoned, or converted to mosques and other public buildings during and after the conquest, as well as in later wars (especially between 1526 and 1566), the Franciscan Province of Bosna Argentina managed to recover by the end of the sixteenth century. According to the report of Bishop Franjo Baličević (1588–1615) from 1591, Bosna Argentina (including

---

8 Pakalın, *Osmanlı Tarih Deyimleri*, 2:134 ("*Kaftan giydirmek*"); and Phillips, "Ottoman *Hilᶜat*," 111–38.

9 These included, but were not limited to, Ragusan diplomats (see Miović, *Dubrovačka diplomacija*, 71, 77), the princes and senators of Transylvania, the khans of the Crimea—since the time of Süleymān I (r. 1520–66)—and the Moldavian *voivode*s (see Szabó and Erdősi, "Ceremonies Marking the Transfer of Power").

10 İnalcık, "Ottoman Galata," 279–80, 284–87; *EI*², s.v. "ᶜAhd" (J. Schacht); *EI*², s.v. "Amān" (J. Schacht); Pakalın, *Osmanlı Tarih Deyimleri*, 1:29–30; Boškov, "Ahd-nama Murata III," 279n2; Fotić, "Institucija amana," 241–48; and Biegman, *The Turco-Ragusan Relationship*, 46.

neighboring Slavonia) had sixteen monasteries; by 1678, that number rose to eighteen.[11] Moreover, it soon extended its borders following the Ottoman expansion north, into Slavonia, Hungary, Transylvania, Moldavia, Banat (*eyālet* of Temişvar), Serbia, and Bulgaria.[12] The general absence of Catholic clergy in those areas further stimulated its missionary activities, as it remained the only licensed Catholic institution in the Ottoman Balkans.

The Franciscans often followed, even led, migrations of Catholic populations from Bosnia to the north, where they established new parishes. Apart from missionary work, the Franciscans must have been attracted by economic motives as well: the increase of the number of parishes brought higher income to the mother monasteries in Bosnia. The new territorial magnitude of the Franciscan Province of Bosnia was self-confidently highlighted by the Franciscans themselves. Bishop Balićević wrote that Bosna Argentina, which he calls Il Regno di Bosnia (Bosnian Kingdom), is situated between Macedonia, Carinthia, Styria, and the Adriatic Sea.[13] In a letter to the Pope in 1693, Gabrijel Stanić of Baška, the minister of the Province, stated that the borders of Franciscan Bosnia spread from the Adriatic Sea to "Tartaria."[14]

Nevertheless, the Franciscans' conciliatory and submissive attitude toward the Ottomans may have been the result of pragmatic considerations. Although they were seemingly loyal to the sultan as the political head of the state, their true loyalty and sympathies were bound to the Pope in Rome (as the head of the Catholic Church). Unsurprisingly, the Franciscans had a general inclination toward Catholic states neighboring Bosnia, such as the Republic of Venice (in Dalmatia), and the Habsburg Empire (in Croatia), and to the House of Habsburg, whose head had the right to appoint the Bosnian bishop. Occasionally, at times when their armies managed to penetrate Bosnia, some Franciscan sympathies toward fellow Catholics turned to collaboration with the enemy army. Especially

---

11 Jelenić, *Kultura i bosanski franjevci*, 1:151–54.

12 Hoško, "Djelovanje franjevaca Bosne Srebrne"; Tóth, "Franjevci Bosne Srebrene"; Tóth, "Between Islam and Catholicism"; Molnár, "Relations between the Holy See and Hungary"; Hrabak, "Katoličko stanovništvo Srbije"; and Tóth, "Between Islam and Orthodoxy."

13 Jelenić, *Kultura i bosanski franjevci*, 1:182; cf. 1:150–53.

14 *Pisma fra Luke Ibrišimovića*, 273.

critical were periods of wars with Hungary, between 1520 and 1540, and the Long War with Austria (1593–1606).[15]

Collaboration with the enemy provoked Ottoman retaliation. Franciscan chronicles report that the Ottomans demolished Franciscan monasteries in Konjic, Visoko, Sutjeska, Kreševo, and Fojnica, whose *guardians* were arrested.[16] In 1538 the authorities confiscated the monastery in Zvornik,[17] while in 1563 the monasteries in Mostar and Ljubuški, Herzegovina, were demolished because their Franciscans aided the escape of Daniel Vocensis, the bishop of Duvno, who was accused of espionage and treason.[18] The authorities' resolution to prevent the clergy's collaboration with the enemy is stressed in the provisions of the *ḳānūnnāmes* of the *sancaḳ* of Bosnia from 1516, 1530, and 1542, which prescribe heavy penalties for those "infidels and priests in the churches who are asking questions about the situation and providing information to the land of infidels."[19] The real crisis followed in the second half of the seventeenth century. After significant devastation caused by local military actions during the war of Candia (1645–69) between Venice and the Ottoman Empire, the war with the Holy League following the Ottoman siege of Vienna (1683–99) brought general destruction and resulted in the almost complete disappearance of the Franciscans, amid a large-scale exodus of Catholics, from Bosnia. In the eighteenth century the number of functioning Franciscan monasteries decreased to only three: Kreševo, Fojnica, and Kraljeva Sutjeska.[20] Some of the monasteries were destroyed by the Ottomans as retaliation for betrayal and siding with the enemy; others were abandoned and eventually fell into ruin. Still other monasteries were destroyed by Christian armies for strategic reasons: Venetian soldiers burned down the monastery in Rama (1687) while the Habsburgs burned down the monasteries in Srebrenica (1688–89), Visoko (1697),[21] and Velika, Slavonia (1691).[22] The Catholic Church in Sarajevo was burned

15 Cf. Slijepčević, *Istorija Srpske pravoslavne crkve*, 1:348–50.
16 Truhelka, "Fojnička kronika," 449, f. 6; and Lašvanin, *Ljetopis*, 267.
17 Truhelka, "Fojnička kronika," 449, f. 6; and Lašvanin, *Ljetopis*, 267.
18 Lastrić, *Pregled starina*, 122. Cf. Jurišić, *Katolička crkva*, 34–35.
19 Akgündüz, *Osmanlı Kanunnâmeleri*, 3:377–78, 380; and Đurđev et al., *Kanuni i kanun-name*, 24, 31, 37, 43, 60, 66.
20 Džaja, *Konfesionalnost i nacionalnost* (1990), 186.
21 Džaja, *Konfesionalnost i nacionalnost* (1990), 140.
22 Buturac, *Katolička crkva*, 153.

during the sack of the city by the Austrian army of Prince Eugene de Savoy in 1697.[23]

Those Franciscans who collaborated with the enemy, or who were suspected of having done so, were forced to flee after the Ottoman recovery, taking with them masses of the Catholic population to Venetian and Habsburg territories, which often was arranged in advance with agents and authorities in those locations. Those who stayed, on the other hand, might have suffered the consequences of Catholic betrayal—whether guilty or not. When discussing the questions of Franciscan loyalty and treason, it must be stressed that the Franciscans lived and conducted their activities under discriminatory sharia-based regulations that significantly limited or impeded religious freedoms, such as public worship, display of religious symbols, and the building and renovation of churches. Yet, even under these circumstances, eighteenth-century Franciscans did their best to compensate for the loss with alternative approaches: the general absence of churches in Bosnia had driven the Franciscans to make use of unorthodox places of worship, such as private homes, graveyards, open spaces like meadows, clearings in forests, and the like, usually with the help of so-called "portable altars" (*altare portatile*), which helped them transform lay spaces into consecrated areas.[24]

FRANCISCAN CHRONICLES OF THE EIGHTEENTH CENTURY

Interestingly, despite these harsh conditions and grim perspectives, the eighteenth century witnessed a blossoming of Franciscan chronicles and literature.[25] This flourishing might be ascribed to general global trends—such as an increase in literacy—that were to a great degree sparked by the Counter Reformation. Although the Catholic Church's project of restoration and renewal was primarily geared toward the evangelization and Christianization of the common people—the firm establishment of religious dogmas, beliefs, and practices—efforts in fact focused on the creation of confessional boundaries in public and private life.[26] This process gave rise to confessionalization, through which attempts were made

23 Skarić, *Sarajevo*, 131.

24 See Jelenić, *Kultura i bosanski franjevci*, 1:177, 185–86; and Džaja, *Konfesionalnost i nacionalnost* (1990), 130.

25 Beljan, *Pripovijedanje povijesti*, 15–16.

26 Birely, *Refashioning of Catholicism*, 96 passim; and Schilling, "Confessionalisation," 25.

to establish distinct confessional and cultural identities, primarily aimed at, as Schilling puts it, "internal coherence and external exclusion."[27] Thus, confessionalization closely connected religion with social and political conflicts, and, at least in the western European experience, was linked with formation of the early modern state.[28] By the beginning of the eighteenth century, this process ended successfully in Western and Central Europe.[29]

In Ottoman Bosnia, the Franciscans were not only members of the Catholic Church but also key bearers of reform. The role of the Bosnian Franciscans in the evangelization of Bosnia—as well as Catholicism in Ottoman Europe (via missions in the Ottoman Balkans and in Hungary)—was crucial for the project of Rome. The Franciscans' activity was particularly important for Bosnian Catholics because confessionalization played an important role in the formation of minority identities, which were "often, but by no means always, in fundamental opposition to a particular state."[30] In the Bosnian Franciscan case, the need for affirmation of a clear-cut identity was amplified by fears of Catholic extinction, through amalgamation with other confessions and syncretism or via direct conversion, be it to Orthodox Christianity or to Islam. In the case of the latter, conversion seems to have been fueled by pressure incited by the Islamic fundamentalist Ḳāḍīzādeli movement, which was, interestingly, roughly simultaneous with confessionalization in Europe. Whether or not one fully accepts Tijana Krstić's theory that the Ottoman Empire experienced the same phenomenon as Christian Europe—that is, confessionalization as confessional polarization and Sunnitization—certain analogies, especially concerning the process of integration of politico-religious spheres, seem to be accurate.[31]

On the other hand, the very harshness of the conditions and the seriousness of the situation appear to have been among the main factors that incited the Franciscans to write chronicles. By their own admission, Franciscan authors penned these works to leave testimony of their time for new generations and to serve as examples and

27 Schilling, "Confessionalisation," 33.
28 Birely, *Refashioning of Catholicism*, 71; and Schilling, "Confessionalisation," 25.
29 Birely, *Refashioning of Catholicism*, 96.
30 Schilling, "Confessionalisation," 26.
31 See Krstić, *Contested Conversions*, 12–18 passim.

lessons for the future.[32] The chronicles in question were penned by Fr. Nikola Lašvanin (ca. 1703–50) for the monastery of Fojnica, by Fr. Bono Benić (1708–85) for the monastery of Kraljeva Sutjeska, and by Fr. Marijan Bogdanović for the monastery of Kreševo (1720–72).[33] These three major chronicles are important not only for the history of Bosnian Franciscans and Catholics but also because they provide valuable material for the history of Bosnia in general. While each chronicle focuses primarily on its own monastery, each within its own wide district, the works differ in their authors' specific approaches.

The earliest such chronicle, that of the monastery of Fojnica written by Nikola Lašvanin, seems to be closest to the medieval tradition in the sense that its author left less personal imprint on the text than the other two chroniclers did.[34] Nonetheless, his influence on other chroniclers, especially Bono Benić, was substantial. Benić's chronicle of the monastery of Kraljeva Sutjeska is considered the richest and best-written eighteenth-century Franciscan chronicle. Unlike Lašvanin, Benić left a significant personal imprint on the text both as a judge and as a critic—not to mention as a protagonist of many of the events depicted therein.[35] Marijan Bogdanović, the author of the chronicle of the monastery of Kreševo, on the other hand, was more narrowly focused on his own monastery and its district, as well as its everyday life, which is depicted in detail. Bogdanović, however, abstained from commenting on the wider context and general situation in the province of Bosnia.[36]

The Franciscan chroniclers received a contemporary western European education outside of Ottoman Bosnia. Like many Bosnian Franciscan students since the late sixteenth century,[37] Benić and Bogdanović were educated in Italy; after finishing their studies, they taught philosophy and theology in Dalmatia before returning to Bosnia. Lašvanin was most probably educated in Italy as well. Upon returning to Bosnia, all three held various high offices in their monasteries and in the Franciscan province, from head of the monastery (*guardian*) to the top offices of the deputy (*custodian*) and the head of

32 Beljan, *Pripovijedanje povijesti*, 25–26.
33 Lašvanin, *Ljetopis*; Benić, *Ljetopis*; and Bogdanović, *Ljetopis*.
34 Cf. Beljan, *Pripovijedanje povijesti*, 156–66.
35 Cf. Beljan, *Pripovijedanje povijesti*, 166–96.
36 Cf. Beljan, *Pripovijedanje povijesti*, 196–216.
37 See Molnár, Le Saint-Siège, 114.

the province (*provincial*; Benić) as well as the bishop and apostolic vicar (Bogdanović).[38] Therefore, it seems possible that their chronicles represent the prevailing sentiment of the Franciscan community in Bosnia, if not the official stance of the Catholic Church.

In addition to the proper chronicles, the analysis here will also focus on a text of historiographical character titled *Epitome vetustatum Bosnensis Provinciae seu brevissimum compendium historico-chronologicum* (Survey of Antiquities of the Bosnian Province or the Very Short Historical-Chronological Compendium). Written by Filip Lastrić (Philippo ab Occhevia) and first published in 1765 in Venice,[39] *Epitome* often is praised as the first historiographical work in Bosnia and contains various historical documents that were intended to guarantee the rights of the Province against contenders from the Dalmatian and Slavonian Franciscan provinces.[40] Additionally, the work provides lists and descriptions of demolished monasteries and churches, Franciscan high officials, and the like. Like the authors of the three chronicles, Lastrić was educated in Italy and later served in high offices of the Bosnian Franciscan Province, including the highest one, that of *provincial*.[41]

"WICKED" TURKS

Given the Ottomans' suspicion of the Franciscans, one would expect cautious language and self-censorship in Franciscan writings. Benić, citing Lašvanin, warns in the introduction to his chronicle that

> in the year of Our Lord 1681, the Turks caught certain books [documents] belonging to Fr. Luka Ibrišimović from Požega. And they caught the guardian of [the monastery of] Velika, and he and Fr. Martin Selaković, the cook from Fojnica, spent six months in custody at Funduk Paşa's. And the aforementioned Franciscans were

38 See Gavran, "Uvod," in Benić, *Ljetopis*, 10–19; Gavran, "Uvod," in Lašvanin, *Ljetopis*, 5–12; Gavran, "Uvod," in Bogdanović, *Ljetopis*, 16–28; and Kursar, "Nikola Lašvanin."

39 Lastrić, *Pregled starina*.

40 Following the Peace of Karlowitz (1699), the Franciscan provinces of Dalmatia and Slavonia came under Venetian and Habsburg rule, respectively. Newly separated from the Bosnian Province, the Dalmatian Province was established in 1735 and the Slavonian Province in 1757.

41 Zirdum, "Uvod," 16–45. See also Zirdum, *Filip Lastrić – Očevac*.

> forced to pay five loads of money. And the guardian died after he was released from prison, because he was beaten and tortured in prison. *Oh brother, be careful, it is so dangerous to write about all kinds of misery*; hence look, how some have paid with their heads for the nonsense of others.[42]

In general, however, the Franciscan authors followed the Church's medieval tradition, which was highly polemical toward Islam and Muslims.[43] The chroniclers themselves often could not or did not want to abandon long-established patterns. Following the convention of the time, all Ottoman Muslims were labeled "Turks," regardless of their ethnic origin. Furthermore, this label was used to denote all Muslims in the pre-Ottoman period as well. According to Lašvanin, for example, the Prophet Muḥammad was a "Turkish saint"; the Arab conquerors of Jerusalem in 638 were also "Turks."[44] Following this logic, a Christian who had converted to Islam was considered to have turned Turk.[45] In this respect, the chroniclers accepted the dichotomy of "us" versus "Turks" when discussing contact between Christians and Muslims, or clashes between Christian states and the Ottomans. In a description of events that followed the Habsburg conquest of Lika and Krbava, Croatia, in 1689, Lašvanin mentions a grave with a holy body, which "Turks claim to be theirs, while it is [actually] ours."[46] Similarly, on the occasion of the beginning of the siege of Buda, in 1684, Benić referred to the Austrian army as "ours" besieging the "Turks."[47]

In general, the atmosphere of the chronicles is quite grim. The history of Catholicism in Bosnia is represented as the history of suffering for faith, illustrated with lists of destroyed churches and monasteries, Franciscan martyrs, and various kinds of oppression, injustice, and humiliation. As Lastrić pointed out in this regard,

---

42 Benić, *Ljetopis*, 49. Cf. Lašvanin, *Ljetopis*, 259. Emphasis mine.

43 See Daniel, *Islam and the West*; Kursar, "Srednjovjekovne percepcije islama"; Kursar, "Anti-muslimanski karakter"; and Dukić, *Sultanova djeca*.

44 Lašvanin, *Ljetopis*, 79.

45 See, for example, Benić, *Ljetopis*, 173.

46 Lašvanin, *Ljetopis*, 191. The confessional affiliation of the holy body could not be determined, however. When "a not very clever priest" started to dig, believing that treasure was buried alongside it, a sudden thunderstorm prevented him from finishing the sacrilege.

47 Benić, *Ljetopis*, 51.

> poor Franciscans suffered and are still suffering these things and others, sometimes much more bitter, in this enslaved kingdom of Bosnia, from day to day cultivating the vineyard of the Lord of Armies. Who could say that was not out of hatred towards the faith?[48]

Among the harsh practices of the Ottomans, the worst seems to have been the collection of Christian boys for state services and janissaries, called *devşirme*, and known in the Slavonic Balkans under the ominous name "tribute in blood" (*danak u krvi*).[49] According to Lašvanin, in 1666 the *aġa* of *ᶜacemī oġlan*s (that is, the head of conscripts) came to Bosnia to collect Christian boys for *devşirme*.[50] However, "the Christians proved to be solid in faith: no one went by his own will, nor gave his child, and some [even] jumped into the water [instead]."[51] This practice obviously caused significant distress and trauma in the Christian community. Parents tried almost everything to save their children from collection: boys were married at a very early age (as recruits were required to be unmarried), they were hidden from the *devşirme* collector, parents tried to bribe the collector to omit their sons, the boys had crosses tattooed on their foreheads, and the like.[52] On occasion, *devşirme* might have incited the population to leave its village or rebel, as was the case in Prijepolje.[53]

On the other hand, some saw in *devşirme* an opportunity to elevate their social status. A certain Mihajlo, son of Kirin, from the village of Krstofor in the judgeship of Monastır (Bitola) was one such person. He applied for *devşirme* in exchange for 3,100 *aḳçe*s (collected by the villages of Milovišta and Vlahče), converted to Islam, and changed his name to Meḥmed in 1646–47.[54] In 1574, a Christian (*ẕimmī*) voluntarily converted to Islam to be recruited to the *ᶜacemī oġlan*s corpus.[55] There

48 Lastrić, *Pregled starina*, 147.

49 See Ménage, "Sidelights on the *devshirme*"; *EI*², s.v. "Devshirme" (V. L. Ménage); *EI*², s.v. "Ghulām" (H. İnalcık); and Matkovski, "Prilog pitanju devširme," 275–79.

50 Lašvanin's story is based on the anonymous chronicle of Fojnica and repeated by Benić. Both Lašvanin and Benić dated it 1667.

51 Lašvanin, *Ljetopis*, 101. Cf. Truhelka, "Fojnička kronika," 455, f. 14; and Benić, *Ljetopis*, 47.

52 Matkovski, "Prilog pitanju devširme," 282–85.

53 Matkovski, "Prilog pitanju devširme," 285.

54 Matkovski, "Prilog pitanju devširme," 306–7, doc. no. 10.

55 Başbakanlık Osmanlı Arşivi, Istanbul (hereafter, "BOA"), Mühimme Defteri, vol. 25, 347, no. 3167.

are six other cases of conversion to Islam by brothers of janissaries and *bostāncıs*, troops recruited via *devşirme*, whose members were then granted similar positions, as recorded in the register of important affairs (*mühimme defteri*) of the same year.[56] These cases indicate that *devşirme* was sometimes used as a vehicle for the social elevation of a family. The best-known example of this approach is that of the *devşirme* recruit Meḥmed Pasha Sokolović (Ṣoḳollu, d. 1579), one of the most powerful grand viziers in Ottoman history, who was notorious for promoting members of his family into important state services. He also played an important role in the reestablishment of the Patriarchy of Peć (Serbian Orthodox Church)—and the appointment of his cousin Makarije as Patriarch.[57]

Lašvanin emphasized that in 1666 "the *agha* of *ᶜacemī oğlan*s did not want to collect Turkish children, but Christian" in Bosnia.[58] This might seem surprising, as the general rules governing the *devşirme* required the recruits to be non-Muslim. The Bosnian Muslims, however, enjoyed the privilege that their children were eligible for *devşirme*, enabling them direct entry to various state and court services. According to an order sent to the *ḳāḍī* of the *sancaḳ*s of Bosnia, Herzegovina, and Klis in 1564, the practice was that the majority of the boys collected were to be circumcised.[59] The order sent to the *beglerbegi* of Bosnia in 1595 prescribed that sons of *Potur*s and, additionally, sons of unbelievers (*kefere*) were to be collected, as had been done earlier.[60] The *Potur*s in question were Bosnian Muslim peasants, whose sons were eligible for *devşirme*.[61] This might explain the discontent and opposition of the Catholics in 1666, as in that year their sons were the only recruits. While the Muslims in Bosnia perceived *devşirme* as a privilege and a way to a better life for their sons, for most Christians it must have represented a heavy burden that they would have preferred to avoid. For the Franciscans, as the spiritual heads of the Catholics, any loss of their flock represented an alarming situation that was heavily lamented and condemned.

---

56 BOA, Mühimme Defteri, vol. 25, 158, no. 1578, 172, no. 1727, 284, no. 2626, 341, no. 3108.

57 *EI*[2], s.v. "Ṣoḳollu Mehmed Pasha" (G. Veinstein).

58 Lašvanin, *Ljetopis*, 101.

59 Kovačević, "Jedan dokument o devširmi," 206.

60 BOA, Mühimme Defteri, vol. 73, 371, no. 815.

61 Pakalın, *Osmanlı Tarih Deyimleri*, 2:780.

Generally speaking, Franciscan chroniclers expressed feelings of prejudice, fear, anxiety, and mistrust toward the Ottoman ruling class—and, to a lesser degree, toward Muslims as a privileged community. As Lastrić remarked, sometimes the main cause of the fear was the supposed "Turkish" hatred toward the Christian faith. According to Bogdanović, for example, in 1767 a preacher (*vāʿiẓ*) from Sarajevo by the name of Emīr was preaching against the Franciscans of the monastery of Kreševo. Most likely incited by a desire to obstruct the renovation of the burned monastery and the church, and "out of excessive zeal," Emir "started his sermons with these words: 'he who is of Muḥammad's faith, let's destroy those shits in Kreševo!'"[62] The overzealous preacher in question was probably "the leader of the fanatics, preacher *Emīr*" (*reʾīs-i mutaʿaṣṣıb vāʿiẓ Emīr*) mentioned by Muslim chronicler Mollā Muṣṭafā Başeski, who was the *müderris* of the *medrese* at Bendbaša in Sarajevo in 1766–67.[63] According to Başeski,

> since the *medrese* was in a deserted and faraway place, in order to attract attention, he took the pulpit and held the sermon in Turkish language, crying out and shouting loudly. In each sermon he cursed sheikhs, dervishes, dervish lodges, *külāh*s, *ḳāḍī*s, and dervish orders, and was skillful at it.[64]

This preacher, who came to Sarajevo in 1760 from the Anatolian town of Amasya, was the leader of a puritanical Islamic fundamentalist movement in Sarajevo, which Başeski—a dervish—opposed, labeling them "fanatics," "deniers" (*münkir*), "*Ḳāḍīzādeli*," and "follower of the *emīr*" (*emīrovaç*; Bosnian: *emirovac*). It seems that they were influenced by the puritanical teachings of the seventeenth-century Ḳāḍīzādeli movement, which insisted on a return to "genuine" Islamic principles and a rejection of all "novelties" and non-Islamic elements adopted by later Muslims.[65] As was the case in seventeenth-century Istanbul, this movement created a rift in the Muslim community of Sarajevo in the eighteenth century, dividing it into the supporters of Ḳāḍīzādelis and the backers of the dervishes. According to Başeski, *vāʿiẓ Emīr* was so zealous and self-righteous that he

62 Bogdanović, *Ljetopis*, 89.
63 Mollā Muṣṭafā, *Mecmūʿa*, 78; and Filan, "Religious Puritans," 44.
64 Mollā Muṣṭafā, *Mecmūʿa*, 145–46. Cf. Filan, "Religious Puritans," 45.
65 See Zilfi, *The Politics of Piety*.

cursed many Muslim religious figures and persons of authority.[66] In this regard, his negative attitude toward the Franciscans should not be surprising. It was also in line with the original harsh stance of the Ḳāḍīzādelis toward non-Muslims, their absolute opposition to newly erected churches, and the ideal of bringing "unbelievers" to the "real" faith.[67] The actions of such a man and his followers must have contributed to an atmosphere of fear and distrust. Thus, Bogdanović commented in a note from 1768, the monastery of Kreševo, which had been renovated the previous year, suffered the most and "against it the whole hell was growling."[68] Although the preacher initially received such recognition that he was appointed *müftī*, he later was dismissed from service due to his incompetence and left for Istanbul, where he entered the orthodox, Sunni-bound order of Naḳşbendī dervishes. Upon his return, Başeski relates (not without pleasure), the former preacher did not play any significant role in the life of Sarajevo, was ashamed, and hid from the people.[69] In another note from 1775, however, Başeski writes that the preacher eventually was exiled from Sarajevo by the authorities. This banishment was the result of his fourteen-years-long agitation and attacks on dervishes, state officials, and other moderate Muslims of the city, which caused rifts among the citizens.[70] Yet, even with their leader gone, Ḳāḍīzādelis and *emīrovaç*s continued to play a significant role in the city's social life, while the preacher's teachings remained alive and influential.[71]

According to Benić, the appeal of "Turks of Fojnica" for the 1746 removal of the cross erected on the grave of the Franciscan Mijo Kunić at Ruknovac, near the monastery of Fojnica, was motivated by the same kind of hatred—that is, animosity toward the symbol of the Christian faith. Incited by the Krivići *ḳāḍī*s, the "Turks" falsely claimed, in front of the authorities, that there had been no cross there previously and that their horses were afraid of the cross at night, because it was close to the road. The accusation resulted in the demolition of the cross, a fine of 1,100 *aḳçe*s, and the imprisonment of many Franciscans, up to fifteen days in

66 Mollā Muṣṭafā, *Mecmūʿa*, 120. Cf. Filan, "Religious Puritans," 49.
67 Zilfi, *The Politics of Piety*, 150–59; and Baer, "The Great Fire of 1660."
68 Bogdanović, *Ljetopis*, 115.
69 Mollā Muṣṭafā, *Mecmūʿa*, 146.
70 Mollā Muṣṭafā, *Mecmūʿa*, 120.
71 Filan, "Religious Puritans," 56–58.

individual cases.[72] According to Lašvanin, the person who was the main protagonist of this affair, "Mustafa Čelebić, called Bego, a wicked man, *muzuvir* (Ott. *müzevvir*, "mischief-maker"), *telbiz* (Ott. *telbīs*, "cheating")," was miraculously punished by destiny in a very painful way three years later. He fell prey to a strange illness, could not find a remedy, and "rotted alive." Eventually, he asked the Franciscans for forgiveness. Nevertheless, "it was said that he was thrown out by the soil three times. And this is not surprising, because he was a man worse than all perversities."[73] The fate of the principal culprit of the Franciscan trouble—and a form of justice unachievable for the Franciscans other than by divine means—obviously amused the chronicler.

In some cases, when particular "Turks" caused the Franciscans harm or inflicted injustice, Franciscan chroniclers openly displayed dislike—and sometimes loathing and hate. On such occasions "Turks" were most often condemned due to their unjust, insincere, and deceitful behavior, which was depicted as an inherent characteristic and fault. According to Benić, reliance on the Ottomans was a mistake, as was shown in the example of John Zápolya, the Ottoman-backed pretender to the throne of the Hungarian king: in 1541, after the sultan had sent his army to help Zápolya and had conquered Buda, he sent Zápolya's son and successor with his mother to Transylvania. Benić's final comment was a warning: "Poor is he who relies on Turkish help."[74] In his depiction of the long-lasting and expensive procedure to rebuild the monastery of Kreševo after the fatal fire in 1765, Bogdanović seems to be the harshest critic of this "Turkish fault." His criticism, however, must be understood in light of the urgency that the repair of the monastery represented for its monks, who were left literally without a roof above their heads in bitter winter. When a "lying" envoy who was sent to the sultan to obtain a *fermān* for the repair of the monastery returned to Bosnia without even meeting the sultan or the vizier, let alone submitting the petition, Bogdanović angrily commented, "Let the unfaithful Turks, who tricked us, suffer the destiny of Greeks!"[75]

72 Benić, *Ljetopis*, 169–70.
73 Lašvanin, *Ljetopis*, 231.
74 Benić, *Ljetopis*, 43.
75 Bogdanović, *Ljetopis*, 63. Here, the author probably refers to the collapse of the Byzantine Empire.

"Turkish" deceitfulness often was connected with their perceived rapacity and greed. In 1768, the "perfidious *mollā*" of Sarajevo deceitfully extorted three hundred *ḳuruş* from the city's Franciscans by threatening to demolish the newly erected building of the monastery of Kreševo. Bogdanović condemned "Lucifer's way to extort the money," concluding that "that was, hence, thief and bandit."[76] In order to protect their rights and ensure their security, the Franciscans had to bribe the whole group of officials. As Bogdanović said, "we were shutting the lion's jaws with money, so they would not harm us."[77]

"Turkish" peasants were not immune to the vices of greed and deceit either. The peasants of the villages of Smuske and Korče "proved to be unfaithful" because they did not respect their contract with the Franciscans about an order of planks: "They did not adhere to any of that, as *balija*s."[78] The word "*balija*" is a derogatory term for Muslim peasants that denotes crudeness and roughness. Bogdanović used another derogatory term, "green," for Muslims when he depicted Muslim "sorrow" and "confusion" caused by Russian defeats in 1770.[79]

Yet another proof of "Turkish" immorality seems to be their abuse of alcohol. In 1771, Bogdanović condemned an attack on the monastery of Kreševo carried out by three drunk "Turkish" youngsters from the neighborhood; they even fired gunshots into the door, which the Franciscans refused to open: "In our time such a thing never happened, especially coming from our neighbors. The Turks are, hence, becoming worse and worse; or, is this because the fall becomes faster as you go further towards the end?"[80]

The worst treatment was reserved for the real bullies, the perpetrators of perpetual mischief and violence throughout the eighteenth century in Bosnia, namely the local janissaries, also known as *başa*s. The need for troops triggered a quick rise in the number of janissaries, resulting in the recruitment of individuals who traditionally had been considered outside the pool of *devşirme*: first, brothers and cousins of janissaries, later, townsmen, and, finally, peasants. New janissaries readily resorted

76 Bogdanović, *Ljetopis*, 115.
77 Bogdanović, *Ljetopis*, 89.
78 Bogdanović, *Ljetopis*, 91.
79 Bogdanović, *Ljetopis*, 151–52. Both of these pejoratives sometimes are used in the modern Croatian and Serbian languages. The word "*balija*" conveys an especially negative meaning.
80 Bogdanović, *Ljetopis*, 171.

to violence and rebellion, and the Franciscans often happened to be their target for extortion.[81]

Bogdanović portrayed the *başa*s in a particularly negative light—quite possibly because of the killing in 1769 of Fr. Luka Mikulić, a monk from Bogdanović's monastery, by a janissary called Nuhan. According to Bogdanović, Nuhan had come from Foča and grew up alongside the people of Kreševo, who "had picked him up from dung."[82] Because he was a janissary, he was briefly imprisoned by the deputy head of the janissaries, while the Franciscans were compelled to pay ninety *ḳuruş* for the process that followed the murder. Frustrated, Bogdanović commented: "Oh, what a wonderful justice! The culprit is released while innocents are punished by fine and scared with threats! If God does not take revenge, it is pointless to rely on justice."[83]

Nuhan later went to the Russian campaign but soon afterward returned to Kreševo, where he threatened the Franciscans who had not forgotten his crime. In 1772, he disappeared. This was not the end of problems for the Franciscans, however; they were accused of arranging Nuhan's disappearance and forced to pay not only fees for various documents that proved their innocence but also reparations to Nuhan's cousin.[84] It was in this context that Bogdanović cried out on the occasion of the departure of the janissaries for the Russian campaign in 1769: "God forbid they return, because they were excrements of Bosnia."[85]

The chroniclers' negative attitude toward the "Turks" might have been, at least partially, a product of their fear and personal trauma. As senior members of their monasteries and the Franciscan Province, they were involved in several litigations with the Ottoman authorities. In 1743, Lašvanin was imprisoned for several days along with six other Franciscans—including the guardians of Fojnica, Sutjeska, and Kreševo—on the suspicion that the monastery of Fojnica had been rebuilt higher and larger than its previous iteration, thus violating an imperial *fermān*.[86] The pasha threatened them, stating that "if a single nail was found nailed over the *fermān* [prescribes], it should

81 See Sućeska, "Seljačke bune u Bosni."
82 Bogdanović, *Ljetopis*, 120.
83 Bogdanović, *Ljetopis*, 121.
84 Bogdanović, *Ljetopis*, 123, 129, 130, 134, 194–96.
85 Bogdanović, *Ljetopis*, 122.
86 Lašvanin, *Ljetopis*, 219–21.

be demolished!"[87] Fortunately for the Franciscans, no transgression was found and they were set free, although they were compelled to pay the expenses and fees for the procedure.

In 1741, Benić experienced a dramatic turn of events. Several Franciscans were imprisoned in Visoko due to "slander" and to a petition to the pasha written by a certain Ḥasan, who was incited by the townsmen of Visoko. The petition alleged that Ḥasan was sold by the Franciscans to the "infidels" (*kauri*; Ott. sg. *kāfir*, vulg. *gavur*). Therefore, the guardian of Sutjeska entrusted Benić to submit a petition to the pasha in Travnik. While waiting for the petition-writer to awake the following morning, Benić was imprisoned by Izan Ugla, the brother of the *voyvoda* of Visoko. During his transfer from prison, Benić was beaten several times by the *mübāşir* of the pasha, and was imprisoned again once they were in Travnik, where he waited for a verdict in fear of his life. While he was walked to the audience with the pasha, Benić was verbally assaulted by Muslim onlookers with the words "Hey, you faithless dog, how can you sell the Turks to the infidels?"[88] Eventually, Benić's fears did not materialize. Although the charges were dropped, the Franciscans were fined no less than five hundred *ḳuruş*.[89]

To sum up, personal insecurity and a permanent feeling of danger must have influenced the chroniclers' anxious tone, contributing to a more critical and suspicious stance toward the "Turks." The general situation in the country, on the other hand, was marked by several incursions of the Austrian army, a rebellion in Montenegro, Ottoman fear of spies and treason, as well as inner insecurity, rebellions among the Muslim population, and brigandage. The war with Russia in 1769 was marked by defeats and large-scale desertion by Bosnian Muslim soldiers, creating in Bosnia a situation so unsafe that the Franciscans of Kreševo decided to celebrate the day of the patron of their monastery, St. Catherine (November 25), quietly and modestly. In order to prevent any provocation, the people of the nearby parishes were forbidden from attending the celebration. Although some believers from Fojnica and Sutjeska eventually participated, the Franciscans from those monasteries did not

87 Lašvanin, *Ljetopis*, 220.

88 Benić, *Ljetopis*, 155.

89 The affair did not end without a fatal outcome. Fr. Andrija Čatić, the guardian of the monastery of Sutjeska, was hit with a rifle by one of the pasha's men on the road from Visoko to Travnik, causing the unfortunate guardian's death soon thereafter.

come.[90] The anxiety in the country caused by the Russo-Ottoman war only increased the following year, when, due to security considerations, the feast of the Pentecost in June once again was celebrated quietly and modestly in Kreševo. Furthermore, its Franciscans forbade their flock attending the feast in Fojnica, where the central celebration took place, as its monastery was consecrated to the Holy Spirit. Nonetheless, the feast in Fojnica was also modest: only three monks from Sutjeska participated, and none of the brethren from Kreševo came.[91]

THOSE WHO TURNED TURK

On the other end of the spectrum, an especially condemnable category was created for the Catholics who "became Turk." Such "deserters" and "traitors" were, unsurprisingly, refuted as "damned" and "doomed souls" and often were charged with hatred of their former coreligionists. The prospect of the diminution of the Catholic flock via Islamization may have provoked such a harsh, unforgiving response. It is usually thought that the pace of Islamization had significantly diminished (if not completely stopped) in the sixteenth century, along with the halt of the Ottoman conquest, at least in the western Balkans. Recent studies, however, show that although Islamization was not as substantial as it had been in the sixteenth century, it continued to be a remarkable process in the centuries that followed.[92] Although we do not possess precise numbers and statistics for the seventeenth and eighteenth centuries, the sheer number of cases noted in the chronicles—not to mention the chroniclers' condemning and alarming remarks—seems to testify that the process of conversion to Islam during this period was far from over in Bosnia as well. Contra Minkov, who maintains that the process ended in the first quarter of the eighteenth century,[93] I argue that the process of Islamization actually continued in Bosnia, albeit perhaps at a slower pace. Admittedly, my argument is based on individual cases from the Franciscan chronicles. Yet, in my opinion, the social status of the converts—including a significant number of former Franciscans—reveals the ongoing vitality of the process of Islamization. Mollā Muṣṭafā Başeski, the Muslim chronicler of

90 Bogdanović, *Ljetopis*, 133.
91 Bogdanović, *Ljetopis*, 145.
92 Cf. Baer, *Honored by the Glory of Islam*; and Krstić, *Contested Conversions*.
93 Minkov, *Conversion to Islam*, 60, 152.

Sarajevo, notes that in 1199/1784–85 many non-Muslims accepted Islam, which confirms this impression:[94] the relatively large number of "those who turned Turk" (*poturčenjak*) mentioned in the chronicle suggests that in the second half of the eighteenth century Islamization remained an active and stable process. Pressure on non-Muslims to convert to Islam and to accept it as the true faith was especially strong in the Ottoman Empire in the seventeenth century, predominantly due to the activities of the Ḳāḍīzādeli movement, which also influenced the attitude of the Ottoman state.[95] Bosnian chronicles suggest that pressure on Christians was strong in eighteenth-century Bosnia as well. Lašvanin wrote that in 1736,

> for many days not one Christian person could come out of the house, because a large crowd of Turkish idlers with drums and pipes would follow them [that is, the Christians] not only in the streets of the town, but even below the monastery. And when they meet someone of the Christian faith, they curse, scold, bang at the houses, and say: "Would you like to turn Turk (*hoćeš li se poturčit*)?"[96]

The crowd in 1736 (mentioned by Lašvanin) and the followers of the preacher *Emīr* who threatened the monastery of Kreševo and terrorized the people of Sarajevo in the 1760s (mentioned by Bogdanović and Başeski) seem to have acted like seventeenth-century Ḳāḍīzādelis. Başeski criticized the pressure, violence, and injustice toward non-Muslims several times in his chronicle. In conclusion, he wrote that "a lot of people in our town [Sarajevo] are senseless and crazy when they think that their duty is to cause grief to *re^{c}āyā*. . . . As far as I know, such actions are against the book I know [that is, the Koran]."[97]

The chroniclers noted a surprisingly high number of ex-Franciscan converts. It seems that the conversion of a priest, as the representative of an adversarial confession, was an especially desired goal for zealous Muslims.[98] Converts to Islam from the ranks of the Christian priesthood were particularly encouraged by rich stipends and gifts from the

94 Bašeskija, *Ljetopis*, 238.
95 Cf. Baer, *Honored by the Glory of Islam*; and Krstić; *Contested Conversions*.
96 Lašvanin, *Ljetopis*, 208.
97 Mollā Muṣṭafā, *Mecmū^{c}a*, 134; and Bašeskija, *Ljetopis*, 156.
98 See Krstić, *Contested Conversions*, 68–69.

authorities. The chroniclers were especially troubled by the conversion of their own brethren. In addition to personal wickedness, the ex-Franciscan converts were primarily condemned on moral grounds, such as infatuation with Muslim women and alcoholism. "Turkish" women seem to have been an irresistible temptation for a few "weak" Franciscans. As Benić explained in the case of the guardian of the monastery of Srebrenica in 1611, the main reason for enamored Catholic men to convert to Islam was the stipulation of Islamic law that Muslim women could marry only Muslim men (although Muslim men could marry non-Muslim women): the guardian "fell madly in love with a Turkish girl, [and] came after her into her faith, because he could not have married her otherwise; and thus, because of a temporary pleasure, he lost the eternal one."[99] In 1752 the vicar of Sutjeska, Fr. Jozip Vukadinović from Velika, who decided to convert to Islam, was also bewitched by *bula*—that is, a Muslim woman.[100] As a new Muslim name he chose ᶜAlī, and henceforth he was known as Deli ᶜAlī (Del' Alija). Later, Deli ᶜAlī obtained two *fetvā*s and started a case in court (*mešćema*, Ott. *maḥkeme*) against the Franciscans. The Franciscans won the case but nevertheless paid 120 *ḳuruş* for various fees. Eventually, however, Deli ᶜAlī came to his senses, which for Benić must have meant reconversion to Catholicism, and ran across the River Sava to Habsburg territory.[101]

The fall from the Catholic faith by a Franciscan named Petar Bukaraš, on the other hand, was caused by drunkenness. In 1672 he was drinking with janissaries in a tavern in Tuzla. Once drunk, he denounced the Catholic faith and accepted Islam. When, later, in Zvornik, he wrongly predicted the "Turkish" victory in the war, he was hanged by the "Turks." Benić's point is moralistic: "Hence, this is how drunkenness is rewarded."[102]

On several occasions, however, Franciscans were accused by the authorities or by local Muslims of reconverting new Muslims back to Christianity. Lašvanin notes that in 1635 the monastery of Fojnica paid a high fine for the allegedly false accusation of reconverting a "Turkified child" to "the faith."[103] Interestingly, this case had a precedent: an

99 Benić, *Ljetopis*, 45. Cf. Lašvanin, *Ljetopis*, 245.
100 Ott. "elder sister." Non-Muslims in Bosnia use the term as a pejorative for Muslim women in general.
101 Benić, *Ljetopis*, 181–84.
102 Benić, *Ljetopis*, 48.
103 Lašvanin, *Ljetopis*, 268.

Ottoman document from 1626, from the archive of the monastery of Sutjeska, states that the Franciscans did not reconvert to Christianity a boy (*oġlancıḳ*) who had converted to Islam.[104]

The Franciscans were careful to deny such accusations in front of the authorities; such acts could have represented a grave danger. Yet several sources suggest that the reality was in accordance with the very character of the fundamental Franciscan missionary vocation. A letter of Pope Urban VIII (d. 1644) dated to 1626 gave the Franciscans permission to "baptize all children of Christian parents, as well as Turks and other unbelievers."[105] The most iconic figure of Bosnian Catholicism under the Ottomans, Fr. Anđeo Zvizdović, was said to have converted "many thousands of unbelievers to Christ."[106] The number of converts must have been inflated to serve the image of Zvizdović as a holy person who fulfilled many miracles after his death. Similarly, in 1700, Fr. Jako Tvrtkovčanin is reported to have converted to Christianity and baptized 337 Muslims during his tenure as the guardian of Sutjeska.[107] This impressive number, which appears to be more or less acceptable, testifies that the Franciscans were not merely "Turkish victims" and passive observers but active agents ready to take risks in the battle for souls with their mighty adversary.

GOOD TURKS

Generalizations should be avoided, however. In fact, chroniclers occasionally recognized as virtuous and righteous "Turkish" dignitaries who acted justly or "Turkish" friends who provided them assistance in various endeavors, echoing portrayals of collaboration with the Ottomans from the seventeenth century, the golden age of Bosnian Catholicism. For instance, in the immediate aftermath of the death of Avdulah-paša

---

104 The boy had returned to his Christian father and spent some time with him, which aroused the suspicion of some zealous Muslims that the Franciscans made him abandon Islam and return to Christianity. See Archive of the Monastery of Kraljeva Sutjeska. Tursko-arapski spisi 1, II/58, r. & v.

105 Lastrić published this letter alongside other important documents concerning the Bosnian Franciscans. See Lastrić, *Pregled starina*, 95.

106 Lastrić, *Pregled starina*, 128.

107 Jelenić, *Kultura i bosanski franjevci*, 1:179. The information is based on the testimony of Ivan Sekula, the captain of Slavonia, and the Bosnian bishop Fr. Nikola Olovčić.

(Muḥsinzāde ᶜAbdullāh Pasha, d. 1749),[108] Lašvanin wrote that he "was four times pasha in Bosnia and every time he acted properly. And during his reign the poor did not know what evil was."[109] Benić and Bogdanović also praised the pasha as good and righteous. Benić basically repeated what Lašvanin wrote, adding that the situation in Bosnia was very peaceful during the pasha's tenure.[110] Bogdanović, on the other hand, praised in particular his son Meḥmed Pasha (d. 1774) as "a truly good man" and a "really noble and genuine duke."[111] The reason for the chronicler's praise of this pasha was an inexpensive permission ("only two hundreds *ḳuruş*") for the renovation of the recently burned monastery of Kreševo. In a similar fashion, Bogdanović commented upon the new *mollā* of Sarajevo, whom a Franciscan delegation of the three guardians visited in 1771. According to the chronicler, "the *mollā* received them properly, and even said: 'The Emperor does not want injustice (*ẓulüm*). However, if it happens to you, complain to me immediately, and I will take care of it. . . .' In these stormy wartimes, this was not a little thing to say."[112]

Although otherwise the harshest critic of the "Turks" among the chroniclers, Bogdanović expressed appreciation toward individuals who were just toward the Franciscans. Despite his ostensible prejudices toward Muslims, he readily recognized the honesty and fairness of the few among them who, in his opinion, differed from the majority. Ḥüseyin Gušter from Sarajevo was one such ordinary "good Turk," with whom the Franciscans did business: "This Turk, leather-worker, buys leather from this monastery for years . . . he is gentle, and he is not violent, neither does he act perfidiously toward the Franciscans—according to the Turkish custom; therefore they work with him, because they are satisfied with the fair price."[113] In a similar manner he remarked on the *emīn* of

108 Muḥsinzāde ᶜAbdullāh Pasha was four times governor of Bosnia (1720–27, 1733–35, 1740–41, 1748–49) and briefly the grand vizier (1737).

109 Lašvanin, *Ljetopis*, 231. On the pasha's career, see Hickok, *Ottoman Military Administration*, 12–14; and Muvekkit, *Povijest Bosne*, 1:470–72, 480–81, 509, 515.

110 Benić, *Ljetopis*, 178.

111 Bogdanović, *Ljetopis*, 57, 62. On the pasha, see *DİA*, s.v. "Muhsinzâde Mehmed Paşa" (Y. Nagata); and Muvekkit, *Povijest Bosne*, 1:531–33, 554–57. Meḥmed Pasha was twice governor of Bosnia (1760–64, 1770–71) and twice grand vizier (1765–68, 1771–74).

112 Bogdanović, *Ljetopis*, 175.

113 Bogdanović, *Ljetopis*, 133.

Kreševo, who was ready to help the Franciscans in a certain court case in Travnik: "a man really good, because I have not seen such a Turk."[114]

SCHISMATIC VLACHS

The chroniclers appear to have reserved their worst treatment for fellow Christians of the Eastern rite—that is, members of the Orthodox Church, particularly the Serbian Orthodox Church and its representatives. The roots of this mistrust and enmity were historical and dogmatic. In their depictions of the Ottoman conquest of Constantinople in 1453, Lašvanin and Benić highlighted the dogmatic error of the "Greek" Church, arguing that "the conquest was God's punishment of the Greeks, who do not believe that the Holy Ghost originates both from the Son and the Father [*filioque*]."[115] The Bosnian Franciscan enmity toward Orthodox Christianity had its local particularities as well. While Orthodox Christians were called "Greeks" and "schismatics" in accordance with the Catholic European tradition, the Franciscans also used a local denomination, "Vlach" (originally meaning "Roman"), to denote Serbian Orthodox Christians.[116] Alongside the Slavicization of ethnic Vlachs and the administrative "Vlachisation" of the Slavs in the western Balkans, "Vlach" eventually came to mean (predominantly) Orthodox Slav, that is, Serbian. Thus, Ottoman official documents labeled the Serbian Orthodox Church—the Patriarchate of Peć (İpek)—as "Greek, Serbian, and Vlach" (*Rūm ve Ṣırf ve Eflāḳ*).[117] The Franciscans appear to have used the term "Vlach" in a pejorative way, which the ethnonym "Serb" could not express.

In the Bosnian context, the clash between the Catholic and the Orthodox Churches was aggravated by the worldly rivalry between competing Christian elites—namely, the attempt of the Orthodox Church to subdue the Catholics in fiscal terms. As fiscal submission was perceived as a first step toward religious submission and the eventual loss of a separate Catholic identity, the Franciscan response was intense. Furthermore, linguistic and other close ties between Bosnian and Croatian Catholics

114 Bogdanović, *Ljetopis*, 157.

115 Lašvanin, *Ljetopis*, 261; and Benić, *Ljetopis*, 38.

116 This was originally the name of the nomadic and semi-nomadic pastoral autochthonous populations of the western Balkans. Over time, however, the Ottomans began to use "*Eflāḳ*" as an administrative term for all pastoral clan groups in the region.

117 See Kursar, "Being an Ottoman Vlach."

and Orthodox Christian Serbs/Vlachs must have posed a great danger of syncretism and acculturation.

The first conflicts between the two Christian denominations in front of the Ottoman authorities began in 1498.[118] In 1575, the Catholics brought a case to the attention of the *ḳāḍī* of Mostar. They accused the Serbian Orthodox Metropolitan Savatije, who was riding through the region in the company of twelve horsemen, of illegal and unprecedented extortion of taxes from Catholic villagers as well as violence toward a representative of the Catholic Church, the Franciscan Ivan from the *nāḥiye* of Imotski.[119]

Despite the otherwise-acknowledged independence of the Catholic community, Ottoman authorities often included the right to tax Catholics in the *berāt*s issued to the members of the Orthodox Church, thus triggering numerous litigations.[120] In the Ottoman register (*defter*) of the "metropolitanates and episcopacies of Rumelia and Anatolia" (*pisḳopos muḳāṭaᶜası*), dated 1655, the Franciscan Province of Bosna Argentina was included under the name "Dioceses of the Church of the Latin Monks in the *sancaḳ*s of Bosnia, Klis, and Herzegovina" and obliged to pay fifty golden coins as the *pīşkeş* tax.[121] It seems that this subjugation was only of a fiscal nature, while the Franciscans retained autonomy in all other spheres.[122] The conflict that broke out in 1661 initially was recorded in the *Anonymous Chronicle* of Fojnica, although the account of the dispute was transmitted and embellished by later chroniclers.[123] According to the conventional narrative, the "schismatic Greek patriarch" not only attempted to force Catholics and their priests to pay an annual tax but also tried to subdue them to the "Greek rite and schism." Catholics managed to prevent the Patriarchate's attempt in Livno with the help of "Turkish grandees, their patrons, and lords," which cost them a significant sum of money. In 1662, however, "the monster schismatic patriarch" (*belva Schismaticus Patriarca*), as Lastrić called him, came again to Bosnia

118 Boškov, "Turski dokumenti," 9.
119 Boškov, "Turski dokumenti," 20–21, doc. 8.
120 Boškov, "Turski dokumenti," 9.
121 Tričković, "Srpska crkva," 149.
122 Tričković, "Srpska crkva," 136.
123 Lašvanin transformed it into a poem, and Benić and Lastrić wrote prose versions of the story. See Trhuhelka, "Fojnička kronika," 453; Lašvanin, *Ljetopis*, 269–70; Benić, *Ljetopis*, 46; and Lastrić, *Pregled starina*, 146.

from Constantinople, with permission to collect taxes from the Catholics. The litigation took place in Banjaluka and Temişvar, but the Patriarch once again failed in subduing the Catholics. Lastrić wrote that "with the mercy of God, they achieved the victory in the case and freed Catholics from the jaws of the dragon."[124] In 1669, the Patriarch attempted to subdue the Catholics once more, this time in front of the judge in Sarajevo. The Catholics again managed to win the case but incurred high expenses, amounting to seven carts of money, which, according to Lastrić, was more than three thousand *real*, or *ḳuruş*. As Lastrić graphically explained, however, this time the Orthodox Christian side paid an exceptionally high price:

> However, it is well said: *where there is no human help, there will come a divine one*. And here it is! During the case that dragon [the Patriarch] got a stroke, so he was carried away from there crippled and lame. His ally, layman-litigant, suddenly died after eight days. And the third one received three hundred strikes with the stick and was fined three hundred *thaler*s for another reason which is not related to this case.[125]

Lašvanin's description of the events of 1661 was his most creative and most offensive account, in which the author targeted the mother of the "Orthodox Christian bishop" (*vladika*).[126] Lašvanin depicted her as a beautiful Vlach woman, slightly blind in one eye and Albanian by tribe, who raised the future Patriarch while begging. The beard of the Patriarch's Vlach secretary resembled that of a male goat. The Croats and their young wives, who attacked "Vlachs" with sticks and stones during the litigation, called the Patriarch names such as "pig" and "swine" (*krmak*, *svinja*).[127]

Lašvanin composed a lengthy versified text in which he described another litigation with the Patriarch that took place in Sarajevo in 1697.[128] This long "poem" is even fuller with invectives and prejudice. Therein, the "infidel" Patriarch's attempt "to subdue the Latins to his rite" is

124 Lastrić, *Pregled starina*, 146, Latin facsimile, 91.

125 Lastrić, *Pregled starina*, 146. Emphasis in original.

126 Following the example of the *Anonymous Chronicle* of Fojnica, the term is used here as a synonym for "Patriarch."

127 Lašvanin, *Ljetopis*, 270.

128 Lašvanin, *Ljetopis*, 275–79. Interestingly enough, this event is not mentioned in other chronicles.

confronted by the Franciscans and the Catholics, who took an oath to sacrifice their lives rather than their faith, because "the Vlachs are schismatics, and defectors from the Church." Lašvanin warns that "the Patriarch is of Greek faith, and worse than all Lutherans; monks and priests are all slaves of the Devil."[129] Furthermore, the Patriarch is cursed once again as worse than Luther and Calvin and called an "apostate" (*murtat*).[130] These reference are in accordance with the fact Lutheranism and Calvinism, that is, protestantism, seized to represent the major threat to Catholicism by the end of the sixteenth century, when the focus of the attention of the Church was shifted to the inner problems such as "magic" and various deviations in the core Catholic lands.[131] In the periphery of the Catholic world, however, an enemy was rediscovered in the Orthodox Church, even as references to Protestantism echoed the Counter Reformation. In addition to the aforementioned curses directed at the Patriarch ("swine," "schismatic dog," and the like), Lašvanin introduced another Ottoman Turkish word, stating that Catholics cursed the Patriarch as *pačavra* (Ott. *paçavra*), "meaning rag (*sudoper*),"[132] and as a "worthless" or "shameless person." This loan word may have been introduced because it sounded similar to the Franciscan pejorative for the Patriarch, *paćara*. In addition to these vulgar insults, the Patriarch was ridiculed due to his appearance: his black beard (which he was said to dye), his white hair, and his dark face. Although all of his teeth were rotten, and he stank strongly, the Vlachs liked him because he was their saint.[133] He also was attacked on moral grounds by the celibate Franciscan, who deemed it improper for a Christian priest to have relations with women: "Although he sleeps all night with a Vlach woman, he gives the Communion to the Vlachs; [he] who touches a woman's 'clothes' (*espap*) should not touch holy things."[134]

Benić and Lastrić recorded a new litigation with the Orthodox Christians in 1760, which they may have witnessed when the Serbian

129 Lašvanin, *Ljetopis*, 276.

130 The term appears as "*mürted*" in Ottoman Turkish, which is an interesting inter-religious loan word for an apostate. See Lašvanin, *Ljetopis*, 279.

131 Birely, *Refashioning of Catholicism*, 68.

132 Lašvanin, *Ljetopis*, 278–79.

133 Lašvanin, *Ljetopis*, 277.

134 Lašvanin, *Ljetopis*, 279.

Patriarch of Peć and the Bishop of Ohrid (Ohri)[135] came to Travnik. To refute the claims of the Orthodox Church and to obtain confirmation of their privileges from the new sultan, the Franciscans sent a certain Anto Dobretić to Istanbul. Once again, they managed to win the case, albeit at the huge expense of 1,300 Venetian gold coins.[136] In 1761 or 1764, the Patriarch went to Istanbul as well. Assuming the name Ahmetaga (Aḥmed Agha), he "completely renounced and became Turk, and with this unbelief went to hell."[137] After describing the 1761 dispute between the two Orthodox Christian *vladika*s concerning the seat of the bishop in Sarajevo, which eventually involved Ottoman intervention, Benić comments that the way the Orthodox clergy administers its Church is sad, because "they do not see their blindness, but rely more on the justice of Süleymān (*iustitiae sulimanae*) than that of Rome."[138] It is noteworthy that Benić made this point despite the fact that the Franciscans themselves appealed to the Ottoman authorities many times in inter-Catholic disputes, the best known being the quarrel about the chapel of Belgrade in the first half of the seventeenth century.[139]

The animosity that at times turned into open hatred toward Orthodox Christians significantly surpassed the antipathy the Franciscan chroniclers expressed toward genuine "unbelievers," that is, the "Turks." In my opinion, the antagonism between the Franciscans and Orthodox Christians must be understood not only in light of religious and dogmatic differences but also within the context of a more worldly rivalry between competing Christian elites. Such extremely negative attitudes toward "Christian brethren" could be explained by the real danger of being subdued in fiscal terms by the Serbian Orthodox Church. The process that Lašvanin called "Vlachisation" probably was rightly understood as a first step toward the "Orthodoxisation" of Bosnian Catholics and the gradual loss of their distinct ethno-confessional identity. The closeness of the two South Slavic communities in this respect must have increased the danger, while the need to draw firm boundaries between them might have

135 Lastrić refers to this figure as the bishop of Rumelia, whereas Benić calls him the bishop (*vladika*) of Sarajevo.
136 Lastrić, *Pregled starina*, 146; and Benić, *Ljetopis*, 207–17.
137 Lastrić, *Pregled starina*, 146; and Benić, *Ljetopis*, 233.
138 Benić, *Ljetopis*, 226–27.
139 Molnár, "Struggle for the Chapel."

urged the chroniclers to an uncompromising stance toward the Orthodox Church.

As for the role of the Ottoman authorities in the conflict between the representatives of the two Christian churches, it must be noted that the Catholics won the majority of the cases, thereby securing their autonomy. Out of thirty-five Ottoman documents that pertain to conflicts between Orthodox and Catholic Churches in the western Balkans between 1498 and 1698, the Orthodox Church managed to win only two cases.[140] According to Pál Fodor, who studied Ottoman attitudes toward Christians in Ottoman Hungary, the Ottomans were mainly interested in maintaining the status quo without interfering in the conflict between denominations.[141] The Ottoman authorities handled conflicts between Christian denominations in Hungary—Catholic, Orthodox, and various Protestant churches—in a similar manner, and often inconsistently.[142] It is difficult to determine whether or not the Ottoman state wanted to keep Christians divided and in conflict, which would have eased Ottoman supremacy.[143] Numerous and seemingly never-ending litigations, on the other hand, obviously raised significant amounts of money via fees to the state treasury and to the Ottoman institutions and individuals involved.[144] Despite their indifference toward disputes between non-Muslims, the authorities did not want—but could not prevent—their non-Muslim subjects using state courts and admitting their own feuds to the supposedly disliked system of "Turkish justice."

The feud between the two communities appears to have had an economic dimension as well. In the eighteenth century, the economic rise of "conquering Orthodox merchants" coincided with the downfall of the once-successful Catholic Bosnian and Ragusan merchants, who had dominated trade in the region until the end of the seventeenth century. Reports of disputes between Orthodox Christian and Catholic merchants throughout the Balkans confirm the more mundane, economic dimension of this

140 These documents were collected by Vančo Boškov. See Boškov, "Turski dokumenti," 9.

141 Fodor, "The Ottomans and Their Christians," 144, 146–47.

142 Tóth, "Between Islam and Orthodoxy," 539–40.

143 Džaja, *Konfesionalnost i nacionalnost* (1990), 176–77; and Tóth, "Between Islam and Orthodoxy," 539–40.

144 Boškov, "Turski dokumenti," 11; Nilević, *Srpska pravoslavna crkva*, 208; Hadrovics, *Srpski narod i njegova crkva*, 80; and Fodor, "The Ottomans and Their Christians," 146–47.

intercommunal conflict.[145] In this respect, Lašvanin's description of an event in 1697 involving two members of the powerful Bosnian Catholic merchant family Brnjaković in litigation with the Orthodox Christian Patriarch in Sarajevo appears to reveal the intersection of confessional interests with lay, mercantile ones.[146]

Conflicts between the Orthodox and the Catholic Churches were not specific to the Balkans. While the first confrontations started as early as the late fifteenth century, the attitude of the Patriarchate of Constantinople toward the more aggressive Catholic infiltration into the Ottoman realm began to worsen in the first half of the seventeenth century—when the papal office of the Congregation for the Propagation of Faith started its activities.[147] Conflicts ensued in the second half of the seventeenth century, in areas where Catholic missionary presence and activities were perceived as intrusions into the domain of the Orthodox Church, such as the territory of the Eastern Patriarchates of Antioch, Jerusalem, and Alexandria, as well as the Aegean islands.[148] In the eighteenth century, enmities escalated due to the increasingly aggressive attitude of the Patriarchate of Constantinople.[149] The Patriarchate's anti-Western stance was supported by the Ottomans not only due to political and diplomatic calculations but also as a result of the rising influence of the Phanariot Greeks.[150] In Bosnia, the conflict between the two competing Christian denominations was aggravated by the unbearable economic pressure that any further levying of taxes could represent. Vast fiscal obligations of the Orthodox Church to the Ottoman state—such as taxes like *pīşkeş* and *paṭriḳliḳ rüsūmu*—pressured the Orthodox clergy to attempt to extract taxes from any potential revenue source, including the Catholics.[151] The Franciscans themselves were obliged to pay the *cülūs* tax, which became a great burden in the eighteenth century. To enable its payment,

145 See Stoianovich, "The Conquering Balkan Orthodox Merchant"; Köse, "Osmanlı Balkanı'nda Kara Ticareti," 51; and Vinaver, *Dubrovnik i Turska*, 39.

146 Lašvanin, *Ljetopis*, 277. About the family, see Džaja, *Konfesionalnost i nacionalnost* (1999), 173–74.

147 Molnár, Le Saint-Siège, 270–71.

148 Çolak, "Catholic Infiltration in the Ottoman Levant"; and Bayraktar Tellan, "The Clash of '*Rum*' and '*Frenk*.'"

149 See Bayraktar Tellan, "The Clash of '*Rum*' and '*Frenk*.'"

150 Bayraktar Tellan, "The Clash of '*Rum*' and '*Frenk*,'" 72–73.

151 See Papademetriou, *Render unto the Sultan*, 175, 216–18 passim; and Hadrovics, *Srpski narod i njegova crkva*, 61–67, 76–80.

the Franciscans introduced a tax of the same name, imposed on the Catholics. Upon the intervention of Rome in 1755, however, they were forced to discontinue this unpopular practice despite protestations and warnings that this decision might jeopardize the solvency of Franciscan monasteries.[152] Under these circumstances, any attempt of one church to introduce a new fiscal burden could trigger a fierce and uncompromising reaction from the other.

Their otherwise unforgiving attitude toward the Orthodox Church and its clergy notwithstanding, Franciscan chroniclers do not seem to have judged common Orthodox Christian folk in such a harsh manner. Bogdanović, for example, praises "schismatic" masons from Mostar, who worked on the renovation of the monastery of Kreševo, as good workers and excellent masons.[153] Although the Franciscans wanted to hire exclusively Catholics for carpentry work, the lack of skilled carpenters forced them to also hire a significant number of "schismatics," who proved to be good workers.[154] Confidential work, such as the gilding of the stylized sultanic monogram (*ṭuġra*) of the *fermān*, was also given to a "shismatic, who was very skillful in this business."[155]

Intercommunal collaborations did not always bear positive results, however. The employment of a "Greek schismatic" carpenter in the renovation of the monastery of Rama in 1695, for example, resulted in catastrophe for the Franciscans. When the carpenter found a bone in his meal, he decided to take revenge, believing that it was planted purposefully by the Franciscans who served the meal on the day of the Orthodox Christian fast. One night after all work on the monastery was finished, "the damned hypocrite" set the building ablaze, burning it to the ground.[156] Still, it can be concluded that the Franciscans' animosity toward the Orthodox Church and its clergy did not necessarily result in segregation and discrimination toward all Orthodox Christian believers. On the contrary, when necessary, the Franciscans hired Orthodox Christians, used their services, and treated them according to their merits.

---

152 Benić, *Ljetopis*, 190–94.
153 Bogdanović, *Ljetopis*, 85.
154 Bogdanović, *Ljetopis*, 87. Special mention is made of Marko Vukaljević from Tešanj, who is described as "a true expert and excellent young man."
155 Bogdanović, *Ljetopis*, 78.
156 Benić, *Ljetopis*, 116.

CONCLUSION

Franciscan attitudes toward members of other communities were by and large influenced by the spirit of the time, above all by confessionalization, which involved the affirmation of one's own religious identity through insistence on internal coherence and external exclusion. Local circumstances further radicalized those tendencies. While the proximity of three South Slavic ethno-confessional communities in Bosnia must have represented an obstacle to the establishment of clear-cut boundaries, the atmosphere of fear and anxiety created by war and unrest further aggravated inter-confessional relations. In such circumstances, the Catholics, as the smallest and most vulnerable community, seem to have fully adopted the postulates of confessionalization to build and secure their own separate identity at any cost. Thus, uncompromising attitudes present in the Franciscan chronicles seem to have been necessary for the affirmation and protection of the fragile Bosnian Catholic community. In this project, negative emotions, including hatred, played important social and political roles. The power of hatred, as the antithesis of kinship or friendship,[157] seems to have been used occasionally to further strengthen the walls of besieged Catholicism both externally (against Muslims and Orthodox Christians) and internally (against potential renegades). Negative emotions seem to have risen in accordance with the social and cultural proximity of the contender.[158] Thus, the condemnation of the Orthodox Church and its representatives as natural rivals of the Franciscans was much stronger and harsher than that of "the enemy of the Christ," that is, the Muslims.

According to the Franciscan chroniclers, the framework of the so-called *Pax Ottomanica* did not offer the Catholics, a non-Muslim minority in a Muslim state, sufficient equality or satisfying prospects. Sharia-based legislation introduced discriminatory regulations that limited or banned the public performance of Catholic rites, demanded that symbols of the Catholic faith be invisible, and imposed various obstacles on the renovation of churches. Local authorities and the ordinary Muslim populace often suspected the Franciscans, as well as the Catholics in general, to be potential traitors and collaborators with the sultan's

157 Cf. Smail, "Hatred as Social Institution," 94.
158 Cf. Smail, "Hatred as Social Institution," 105 passim.

Catholic enemies. Furthermore, fiscal pressure exerted by both central and local authorities—as well as the Serbian Orthodox Christian clergy—worsened the position of the Catholic Church in eighteenth-century Bosnia. The proselytizing activities of Muslim puritans that sometimes received the support of the state further aggravated the situation. As a result, in the eyes of Franciscan authors, the Ottoman state always remained a foreign power to be feared and mistrusted, while interactions across confessional borders, especially with the dominant Muslims, were to be avoided whenever possible.

BIBLIOGRAPHY

Sources

Unpublished Sources

Archive of the Monastery of Kraljeva Sutjeska. Tursko-arapski spisi 1.

Başbakanlık Osmanlı Arşivi (BOA), Istanbul. Mühimme Defteri, vols. 25, 73.

Published Sources

Akgündüz, Ahmed. *Osmanlı Kanunnâmeleri ve Hukukî Tahlilleri*. Vol. 3. Istanbul: Osmanlı Araştırmaları Vakfı, 1991.

Başeskija, Mula Mustafa Ševki. *Ljetopis (1746–1804)*. Translated by Mehmed Mujezinović. 2nd ed. Sarajevo: Veselin Masleša, 1987.

Benić, Bono. *Ljetopis sutješkoga samostana*. Edited and with Latin and Italian sections translated by Ignacije Gavran. Sarajevo and Zagreb: Synopsis, 2003.

Bogdanović, Marijan. *Ljetopis kreševskog samostana*. Translated by Ignacije Gavran. Sarajevo and Zagreb: Synopsis, 2003.

Boškov, Vančo. "Ahd-nama Murata III stanovnicima Bara iz 1557. godine." *Godišnjak Društva istoričara Bosne i Hercegovine* 28–30 (1977–79): 279–83.

Boškov, Vančo. 'Turski dokumenti o odnosu katoličke i pravoslavne crkve u Bosni, Hercegovini i Dalmaciji (XV–XVII vek)." *Spomenik Srpske akademije nauka i umetnosti* 131, *Odeljenje istorijskih nauka* 7 (1992): 7–95.

Đurđev, Branislav, et al., eds. *Kanuni i kanun-name za Bosanski, Hercegovački, Zvornički, Kliški, Crnogorski i Skadarski Sandžak*. Sarajevo: Orijentalni institut, 1957.

Lastrić, Filip. *Pregled starina Bosanske provincije*. Bilingual edition by Andrija Zirdum, with Italian and Latin translated by Ignacije Gavran and Šimun Šimić. Sarajevo and Zagreb: Synopsis, 2003.

Lašvanin, Nikola. *Ljetopis*. Edited and with Latin and Italian sections translated by Ignacije Gavran. Sarajevo and Zagreb: Synopsis, 2003.

Matasović, Josip. "Fojnička regesta." *Spomenik Srpske kraljevske akademije* 67, drugi razred 53 (1930): 61–431.

Mollā Muṣṭafā [Başeski]. [*Mecmūᶜa*]. Edited by Kerima Filan as *XVIII. Yüzyıl Günlük Hayatına Dair Saraybosnalı Molla Mustafa'nın Mecmuası*. Sarajevo: Connectum, 2011.

Muvekkit, Salih Sidki Hadžihuseinović. *Povijest Bosne*. Vol. 1, translated by Abdulah Polimac, Lamija Hadžiosmanović, Fehim Nametak, Salih Trako. Sarajevo: El-Kalem, 1999.

Pisma fra Luke Ibrišimovića zagrebačkim biskupima (1672.–1697.), edited by Josip Barbarić and Miljenko Holzleitner. Jastrebarsko: Naklada Slap, 2000.

[Šabanović, Hazim]. "Turski dokumetni u Bosni iz druge polovine XV stoljeća." *Istorisko-pravni zbornik* 2 (1949): 177–208.

Tričković, Radmila. "Srpska crkva sredinom XVII veka." *Glas Srpske akademije nauka i umetnosti* 120, no. 2 (1980): 61–164.

Truhelka, Ćiro, ed. "Fojnička kronika." *Glasnik Zemaljskog muzeja u Sarajevu* 21 (1909): 443–59 and 15 facsimiles.

Studies

Aleksov, Bojan. "Adamant and Treacherous: Serbian Historians on Religious Conversions." In *Myths and Boundaries in South-Eastern Europe*, edited by Pål Kolstø, 158–90. London: Hurst & Co., 2005.

Aleksov, Bojan. "Poturica gori od Turčina. Srpski istoričari o verskim preobraćanjima." In *Historijski mitovi na Balkanu*, 225–58. Sarajevo: Institut za istoriju Sarajevo, 2003.

Baer, Marc David. *Honored by the Glory of Islam: Conversion and Conquest in Ottoman Empire*. Oxford: Oxford University Press, 2008.

Baer, Marc David. "The Great Fire of 1660 and the Islamization of Christian and Jewish Spaces in Istanbul." *International Journal of Middle East Studies* 36, no. 2 (2004): 159–81.

Bayraktar Tellan, Elif. "The Clash of '*Rum*' and '*Frenk*': Orthodox-Catholic Interactions on the Aegean Islands in the Mid-Seventeenth to Mid-Eighteenth Centuries and Their Impact in the Ottoman Capital." In *Islands of the Eastern Mediterranean. A History of Cross-Cultural Encounters*, edited by Özlem Çaykent and Luca Zavagno, 64–78. London & New York: I. B. Tauris, 2014.

Bejtić, Alija. "Bosanski namjesnik Mehmed paša Kukavica i njegove zadužbine u Bosni (1752–1756 i 1757–1760)." *Prilozi za orijentalnu filologiju* 6–7 (1956–57): 77–114.

Beljan, Iva. *Pripovijedanje povijesti. Ljetopisi bosanskih franjevaca iz 18. stoljeća*. Sarajevo and Zagreb: Synopsis, 2011.

Biegman, N. H. *The Turco-Ragusan Relationship according to the Firmâns of Murâd III (1575–1595) Extant in the State Archives of Dubrovnik*. The Hague and Paris: Mouton, 1967.

Birely, Robert. *Refashioning of Catholicism, 1450–1700: A Reassessment of the Counter Reformation*. Washington, DC: The Catholic University of America Press, 1999.

Boškov, Vančo. "Pitanje autentičnosti Fojničke ahd-name Mehmeda II iz 1463. godine." *Godišnjak Društva istoričara Bosne i Hercegovine* 28–30 (1977–79): 87–105.

Buturac, Josip. *Katolička crkva u Slavoniji za turskog vladanja*. Zagreb: Kršćanska sadašnjost, 1970.

Çolak, Hasan. "Catholic Infiltration in the Ottoman Levant and Responses of the Greek Orthodox Patriarchates during the late 17th and early 18th centuries." *Aram* 25, nos. 1–2 (2013): 85–95.

Daniel, Norman. *Islam and the West—The Making of an Image*. Oxford: Oneworld, 1993.

Dukić, Davor. *Sultanova djeca: predodžbe Turaka u hrvatskoj književnosti 16. do 18. stoljeća*. Zadar: Thema, 2004.

Džaja, Srećko M. "Fojnička ahdnama u zrcalu paleografije, pravne povijesti i politike." *Bosna Franciscana* 17, no. 31 (2009): 103–28.

Džaja, Srećko M. *Konfesionalnost i nacionalnost Bosne i Hercegovine. Predemancipacijski period 1463–1804*. Translated by Ladislav Z. Fišić. Sarajevo: Svjetlost, 1990.

Džaja, Srećko M. *Konfesionalnost i nacionalnost Bosne i Hercegovine. Predemancipacijski period 1463–1804*. Translated by Ladislav Z. Fišić. 2nd ed. Mostar: Ziral, 1999.

Filan, Kerima. "Religious Puritans in Sarajevo in the 18th Century." *Osmanlı Tarihi Araştırma ve Uygulama Merkezi Dergisi* 24, no. 33 (2013): 43–62.

Fodor, Pál. "The Ottomans and Their Christians in Hungary." In *Frontiers of Faith. Religious Exchange and the Constitution of Religious Identities 1400–1750*, edited by Eszter Andor and István György Tóth, 137–54. Budapest: Central European University and European Science Foundation, 2001.

Fotić, Aleksandar. "Institucija amana i primanje podaništva u Osmanskom Carstvu: primer sremskih manastira." *Istorijski časopis* 52 (2005): 225–56.

Gavran, Ignacije. "Uvod." In Bono Benić, *Ljetopis sutješkoga samostana*, edited and with Latin and Italian sections translated by Ignacije Gavran, 5–31. Sarajevo and Zagreb: Synopsis, 2003.

Gavran, Ignacije. "Uvod." In Marijan Bogdanović, *Ljetopis kreševskog samostana*, translated by Ignacije Gavran, 5–39. Sarajevo and Zagreb: Synopsis, 2003.

Gavran, Ignacije. "Uvod." In Nikola Lašvanin, *Ljetopis*, edited and with Latin and Italian sections translated by Ignacije Gavran, 5–32. Sarajevo and Zagreb: Synopsis, 2003.

Hadrovics, Laszlo. *Srpski narod i njegova crkva pod turskom vlašću*. Translated by Marko Kovačević. Zagreb: Nakladni zavod Globus, 2000.

Hadžibegić, Hamid. *Glavarina u Osmanskoj Državi*. Sarajevo: Orijentalni institut u Sarajevu, 1966.

Hickok, Michael Robert. *Ottoman Military Administration in Eighteenth-Century Bosnia*. Leiden, New York, and Cologne: Brill, 1997.

Hoško, Franjo Emanuel. "Biskup Nikola Ogramić-Olovčić." *Bosna Franciscana* 23, no. 42 (2015): 73–94.

Hoško, Franjo Emanuel. "Djelovanje franjevaca Bosne Srebrne u Slavoniji, Srijemu, Ugarskoj i Transilvaniji tijekom XVI. i XVII. stoljeća." In *Povijesno-teološki simpozij u povodu 500. obljetnice smrti bosanske kraljice Katarine (Sarajevo 24. i 25. listopada 1978.)*, 103–15. Sarajevo: Kršćanska sadašnjost, 1979.

Hrabak, Bogumil. "Katoličko stanovništvo Srbije 1460–1700." *Naša prošlost* 2 (1987): 77–125.

İnalcık, Halil. "Ottoman Galata, 1453–1553." In *Essays in Ottoman History*, 271–376. Istanbul: Eren, 1998.

Jelenić, Julijan. *Kultura i bosanski franjevci*. Vol. 1. 1912. Reprint, Sarajevo: Svjetlost 1990.

Jurišić, Karlo. *Katolička crkva na Biokovsko-neretvanskom području u doba turske vladavine*. Zagreb: Kršćanska sadašnjost, 1972.

Köse, Metin Ziya. "Osmanlı Balkanı'nda Kara Ticareti ve Rekabet: Rumeli'de Dubrovnik Tüccarları (1600–1630)." *Pamukkale Üniversitesi Sosyal Bilimler Enstitüsü Dergisi* 16 (2013): 41–58.

Kovačević, Ešref. "Jedan document o devširmi." *Prilozi za orijentalnu filologiju* 22–23 (1972–73): 203–9.

Krstić, Tijana. *Contested Conversions to Islam: Narratives of Religious Change in the Early Modern Ottoman Empire*. Stanford: Stanford University Press, 2011.

Kursar, Vjeran. "Anti-muslimanski karakter protuturskih govora." *Radovi Zavoda za hrvatsku povijest Filozofskog fakulteta Sveučilišta u Zagrebu* 34–36 (2004): 29–46.

Kursar, Vjeran. "Being an Ottoman Vlach. On Vlach Identity(ies), Role and Status in Western Parts of the Ottoman Balkans (15th–18th Centuries)." *Osmanlı Tarihi Araştırma ve Uygulama Merkezi Dergisi* 24, no. 34 (2013): 115–61.

Kursar, Vjeran. "Nikola Lašvanin." In *Historians of the Ottoman Empire*, edited by Cemal Kafadar, Hakan Karateke, and Cornell Fleischer, published May 2006, accessed March 17, 2016, https://ottomanhistorians.uchicago.edu/en/historian/nikola-lasvanin.

Kursar, Vjeran. "Srednjovjekovne percepcije islama." Povijesni prilozi 22 (2003): 133–48.

Mandić, Dominik. "Autentičnost Ahd-name Mehmeda II B.H. franjevcima." *Radovi Hrvatskog Povijesnog Instituta u Rimu* 3–4 (1971): 61–90.

Matkovski, Aleksandar. "Prilog pitanju devširme." *Prilozi za orijentalnu filologiju* 14–15 (1964–65): 273–309.

Ménage, V. L. "Sidelights on the devshirme from Idrîs and Sa'duddîn." *Bulletin of the School of Oriental and African Studies* 18, no. 1 (1956): 181–82.

Minkov, Anton. *Conversion to Islam in the Balkans*: Kisve Bahası *Petitions and Ottoman Social Life, 1670–1730*. Leiden and Boston: Brill, 2004.

Miović, Vesna. *Dubrovačka diplomacija u Istambulu*. Zagreb and Dubrovnik: Hrvatska akademija znanosti i umjetnosti, Zavod za povijesne znanosti u Dubrovniku, 2003.

Molnár, Antal. *Le Saint-Siège, Raguse et les missions catholiques de la Hongrie ottomane 1572–1647*. Rome: Accademia d'Ungheria; Budapest: Bibliothèque nationale de Hongrie, Société pour l'Encyclopédie de l'Histoire de l'Église en Hongrie, 2007.

Molnár, Antal. "Relations between the Holy See and Hungary during the Ottoman Domination of the Country." In *Fight against the Turk in Central Europe in the First Half of the 16th Century*, edited by István Zombori, 191–226. Budapest: METEM, 2004.

Molnár, Antal. "Struggle for the Chapel of Belgrade (1612–1643): Trade and Catholic Church in Ottoman Hungary." *Acta Orientalia Academiae Scientarium Hung* 60, no. 1 (2007): 73–143.

Nilević, Boris. *Srpska pravoslavna crkva u Bosni i Hercegovini do obnove Pećke patrijaršije 1557. godine.* Sarajevo: Veselin Masleša, 1990.

Pakalın, Mehmet Zeki. *Osmanlı Tarih Deyimleri ve Terimleri Sözlüğü.* Vols. 1–2. Istanbul: Millî Eğitim Basımevi, 1971.

Papademetriou, Tom. *Render unto the Sultan: Power, Authority, and the Greek Orthodox Church in the Early Ottoman Centuries.* Oxford: Oxford University Press, 2015.

Phillips, Amanda. "Ottoman Hil^cat: Between Commodity and Charisma." In *Frontiers of the Ottoman Imagination. Studies in Honour of Rhoads Murphey*, edited by Marios Hadjianastasis, 111–38. Leiden & Boston: Brill, 2015.

Schilling, Heinz. "Confessionalisation and Religious Frontiers." In *Frontiers of Faith: Religious Exchange and the Constitution of Religious Identities*, 1400–1750, edited by Eszter Andor and István György Tóth, 21–35. Budapest: Central European University, European Science Foundation, 2001.

Skarić, Vladimir. *Sarajevo i njegova okolina od najstarijih vremena do austro-ugarske okupacije. Izabrana djela.* Vol. 1. Sarajevo: Veselin Masleša, 1985.

Slijepčević, Đoko. *Istorija Srpske pravoslavne crkve.* Vol. 1. Munich: Iskra, 1962.

Smail, Daniel Lord. "Hatred as Social Institution in Late-Medieval Society." *Speculum* 76, no. 1 (2001): 90–126.

Stoianovich, Traian. "The Conquering Balkan Orthodox Merchant." *The Journal of Economic History* 20, no. 2 (1960): 234–313.

Sućeska, Avdo. "Seljačke bune u Bosni u XVII i XVIII stoljeću." *Godišnjak Istorijskog društva Bosne i Hercegovine* 17 (1966–67): 163–207.

Szabó, János B., and Péter Erdősi. "Ceremonies Marking the Transfer of Power in the Principality of Transylvania in East European Context." *Majestas* 11 (2003): 111–60.

Tóth, István György. "Between Islam and Catholicism: Bosnian Franciscan Missionaries in Turkish Hungary, 1584–1716." *The Catholic Historical Review* 89, no. 3 (2003): 409–33.

Tóth, István György. "Between Islam and Orthodoxy: Protestants and Catholics in Southeastern Europe." In *Reform and Expansion 1500–1600*, The Cambridge History of Christianity 6, edited by R. Po-Chia Hsia, 542–55. Cambridge and New York: Cambridge University Press, 2007.

Tóth, István György. "Franjevci Bosne Srebrene u osmanskoj Mađarskoj i Transilvaniji od 16. do 18. stoljeća." *Bosna Franciscana* 13, no. 22 (2005): 16–41.

Vinaver, Vuk. *Dubrovnik i Turska u XVIII veku.* Srpska akademija nauka, posebna izdanja CCCXXXI, Istoriski institut knj. 11. Belgrade: Naučno delo, 1960.

Vrgoč, Miro. "Fra Anđeo Zvizdović (1420./?/–1498.)." In Miro Vrgoč, *Duhovni stupovi Bosne Srebrene*, 7–40. Sarajevo and Zagreb: Svjetlo riječi, 2007. Originally published in *Bosna Franciscana* 5, no. 7 (1997): 167–98.

Zilfi, Madeline C. *The Politics of Piety: The Ottoman Ulema in the Postclassical Age (1600–1800)*. Minneapolis: Bibliotheca Islamica, 1988.

Zirdum, Andrija. *Filip Lastrić – Oćevac, 1700–1783. Prilog kulturnoj povijesti Bosne i Hercegovine*. Zagreb: Kršćanska sadašnjost, 1982.

Zirdum, Andrija. "Uvod. Filip Lastrić Oćevac, začetnik kritičke historiografije Bosne i Hercegovine." In Filip Lastrić, *Pregled starina Bosanske provincije*, bilingual edition, edited by Andrija Zirdum, with Italian and Latin translated by Ignacije Gavran and Šimun Šimić, 7–45. Sarajevo and Zagreb: Synopsis, 2003.

"Those Violating the Good, Old Customs of our Land": Forms and Functions of Graecophobia in the Danubian Principalities, 16th–18th Centuries

Konrad Petrovszky

To anyone acquainted with the study of Ottoman history from a Southeast European perspective, focusing on alterophobia may appear as just another way of reproducing a well-established narrative of enmities and hatred. For it is true that for a remarkably long time the research on intercommunal relationships in the Ottoman period was fueled by the idea of opposing alterities and reciprocal phobias. Accordingly, the complexity of Ottoman history seemed reducible to episodes of religious conflict, most notably between Muslims and Christians, between Turks and Greeks (and others), or between the barbarians and the civilized, etc. Fortunately, this overtly biased view has been challenged and critically revised in many ways by a series of historical works from the 1980s onward.[1] On the other hand, what looks

* An earlier draft of this article was translated by John Heath, with financial support from the Austrian Science Fund (SFB VISCOM-FWF F42).

1 See Kiel, *Art and Society of Bulgaria in the Turkish Period*; and Greene, *A Shared World* as examples of important studies that have contributed significantly to nuanced understandings of intercommunal life and of Ottoman rule as a whole.

like a salutary adjustment of nationalist zeal has given way to equally problematic (and politicized) approaches, which—for various reasons impossible to elaborate here—tend to downplay intercommunal conflicts to a mere myth of post-Ottoman nationalism(s).[2]

What has passed unnoticed in these similarly biased takes on Ottoman history is the fact that xenophobia and alterophobia were phenomena that existed *within* the respective religious communities of the Empire; such enmities occurred amid fellow Muslims or Christians or Jews, no less than *among* the various groups. In reality, the exploitation of difference did not coincide with major religious boundaries, although this is largely claimed by the corresponding rhetorics from all sides, but adopted many forms that cut across the respective communities.[3] Pushing this argument a little further, one might even argue that various forms of *infra-communal* alterophobia coexisted with and rivaled—and, at times, even superposed—*interreligious* resentments, as I will demonstrate by focusing on anti-graecism in the tributary principalities of Moldavia and Walachia.

Questioning the reasons for and mechanisms of early modern graecophobia in what are nowadays the southern and eastern parts of Romania cannot forego historiography altogether, simply because historical writing is closely tied to the phenomenon itself, as I will show. An important, yet still hardly studied, aspect of Ottoman Hellenism, graecophobia was one of the most persistent negative stereotypes in the region throughout early modernity, with significant repercussions in modern Romanian scholarship to the present day.

In the context of Romanian intellectual history, it was particularly in the mind of the zealots of an independent nation-state in the middle of the nineteenth century that the term "Greek" became associated with the so-called Phanariot regime and, by implication, with all the evils of the "Turkish yoke."[4] Against this image, which proved remarkably resistant to the successive stages and changes of public memory over the course of the nineteenth and twentieth centuries, an opposite opinion has been

2 For a very pertinent critique of these views, see Reinkowski, "The Ottoman Empire and South Eastern Europe from a Turkish Perspective."

3 For a judicious discussion of the uses and fallacies of the concept of confessionalization (*Konfessionalisierung*), see Krstić, *Contested Conversions to Islam*.

4 See the highly influential essay by Zallony, *Traité sur les princes de la Vallachie et de la Moldavie,* published in Paris in 1830, as well as Obedeanu, *Greciĭ în Țara-Românească*, from 1900, which remains valuable for the wealth of material included.

advocated, including by some of the leading figures of Romanian historiography.[5] According to them, Greek influence on Romanian society and culture must be acknowledged—beyond mentions of occasional mischief and abuse of power (for which Phanariot Greeks were deemed responsible)—by underscoring the beneficial aspects, especially for religious, artistic, and intellectual life, of the bitter "centuries of Turkish oppression."[6] Despite the stark differences between these two readings of Greek influence north of the Danube, there is a shared sense of "we" and "them," a strong projection of obviously modern identity concepts onto early modern realities.[7]

Against the background of a still-controversial scholarly field, the purpose of this article is neither to examine the variety of views situated between those two poles of interpretation (the dark "Phanariot regime" and the bright "Byzance après Byzance" model) nor to engage in the critical discussion regarding the role of "the Greek" and everything associated with it in the Romanian national narrative.[8] Suffice it to say that the negative stereotyping of Greekness is not an exclusive trace of Romanian history but, along with many other phenomena, belongs to the shared legacy of Balkan societies, traceable to the various social changes brought by Ottoman rule.[9] In order to advocate a more dispassionate reading of an issue that is charged both emotionally and intellectually, I should finally emphasize that foregrounding "phobia" by no means covers the multitude of forms that linked the two tributary principalities to the Ottoman core

---

5 For a historiographical account, see Rados, "Societatea Junimea şi interesul pentru studiile bizantine"; and Rados, "Influenţa greacă în disputele istoriografice din spaţiul românesc."

6 In this reading, exemplified by the very numerous works of Nicolae Iorga, the nationalist approach to Romanian history is mitigated by the extolment of Orthodox solidarity. On the political and identity debates surrounding the establishment of modern historical disciplines, most notably Byzantine studies, in Southeastern Europe, see the comprehensive study by Mishovka, "The Afterlife of a Commonwealth."

7 Convincingly pointed out by Iordachi, "From Imperial Entanglements," 69, 72.

8 On the role of the Phanariots in the emerging national self-understanding, see Lemny, "La critique du regime phanariote"; and Iordachi, "From Imperial Entanglements," especially 127–31. Apparently, Petrescu, *Οι Έλληνες ως "άλλοι"*, provides a new and comprehensive take on this issue. However, his study was unfortunately not available to me when I was writing this article.

9 It should be added, of course, that although anti-Greek attitudes differ considerably in place, time, and institutional context, certain characteristic attributions recur. For the Bulgarian case, see, for instance, Kitromilides and Tabaki, *Greek-Bulgarian Relations*; and Daskalov, "Bulgarian-Greek Dis/Entanglements."

region of the Balkans and Asia Minor. It does, however, cast light on the ways in which complex social and political processes were registered, translated, and endowed with meaning.

Although the two principalities of Wallachia and Moldavia had never been administrative parts of the Ottoman Empire, the constant growth of Greek influence in these territories proves to be particularly revelatory of their gradual integration into the Ottoman world.[10] This entanglement—or, rather, its reflection in elite discourse—will be at the center of my paper, with a special focus on the seventeenth century, when anti-Greek discourse surfaced most prominently in historical and legal literature. Only occasionally will I throw a side glance into the eighteenth and early nineteenth centuries, as this period (better known as the Phanariot period, the pinnacle of Greek cultural hegemony in the Danubian principalities and in Southeastern Europe in general) is extensively covered in the literature.[11] Rather than trying to give a full account of the "Greek question" with all its ramifications and modern repercussions,[12] I will content myself to show the various meanings that "Greek" and "Greekness" could adopt under particular historical circumstances, and, eventually, to expose the profound ambivalence and corollaries of anti-Greek rhetoric within the Ottoman imperial setting to which the two principalities clearly belonged.

While there is no substantial difference between Wallachia and Moldavia as far as the evolution and intensity of anti-Greek sentiments are concerned, documentary evidence is earlier and more consistent in Wallachia, probably due to its geographical position and economic importance, which resulted in increased exposure to Ottoman influence.

THE "FOREIGN GREEK": NARRATIVE EVIDENCE AND LEGAL ACTION IN THE EARLY SEVENTEENTH CENTURY

The first individual to record the atmosphere of hostility and violence facing Greeks in the Danubian principalities was himself a Greek: Matthew

10 In order to capture the interplay of political, economic, and cultural aspects, I proposed, on a different occasion, the term "Ottoman-Orthodox space of communication." See Petrovszky, *Geschichte schreiben im osmanischen Südosteuropa*.

11 Overviews are offered by *Symposium l'époque phanariote*; and Kitromilides and Tabaki, *Relations gréco-roumaines*. For a recent study with a special focus on the nineteenth century, see Petrescu, *Migrație și ortodoxie*.

12 An extensive study is provided by Iordachi, "From Imperial Entanglements to National Disentanglement."

of Myra (ca.1550–1624), the abbot of Dealu monastery in Wallachia and honorary Metropolitan of Myra (today Demre) in Asia Minor. In his highly interesting *History of the Events in Wallachia*, which covers the events between 1602 and 1618 and was printed posthumously in 1638 in Venice, [13] Matthew combines a sometimes quite personal account of political turmoil and military violence with fatherly advice to the ruling prince, Alexandru Iliaş.[14] Among the most remarkable passages of his *History* are repeated descriptions of atrocities against Greek merchants or dignitaries, committed by factions of the local nobility or by anonymous crowds. Thus, he writes about the plot against Radu Mihnea,[15] a favorer of "the Greeks":

> They [his opponents] suddenly wanted to kill Prince Radu . . . and then haste straight to the merchants, and slaughter them, and confiscate their merchandise. They intended to exterminate the Greek community, so that all Greeks living in their land would vanish, nobles and subordinates and the poor alike, the very people who provide their households with wares and goods. But God did not want what they wanted, and He judged them according to their crime.[16]

As is to be expected from a man of his origin and position, Matthew strongly condemns these outrages, which obviously found wide popular

---

13 The full title is Matthaios Myreōn, *Ἑτέρα ἱστορία τῶν κατὰ τὴν Οὐγγροβλαχίαν τελεσθέντων, ἀρξαμένη ἀπὸ Σερμπάνου βοηβόνδα μέχρι Γαβριὴλ βοηβόνδα, τοῦ ἐνεστῶτος δουκός, ποιειθεῖσα παρὰ τοῦ ἐν ἀρχιερεῦσι πανιερωτάτου μητροπολίτου Μυρέων κυροῦ Ματθαίου, τοῦ ἐκ Πωγονιανῆς, καὶ ἀφιερωθεῖσα τῷ ἐνδοξοτάτῳ ἄρχοντι κυρίῳ Ἰωάννῃ τῷ Κατριτζῇ*, according to Legrand, *Bibliothèque grecque vulgaire*, 231–333, based on the edition Venice, 1672. On Matthew's life and work, see Vincent, "Byzantium Regained? The History, Advice and Lament by Matthew of Myra." For the Wallachian context, see Panou, "Greek-Romanian Symbiotic Patterns."

14 After his first reign, from 1616 to 1618, which is covered by Matthew's chronicle, he reigned again in Wallachia, from 1628 to 1629.

15 Radu Mihnea was prince of Wallachia four times between 1601 and 1623.

16 Legrand, *Bibliothèque grecque vulgaire*, 245, lines 393–402: "Τὸν Ῥάδουλ βόδα ἤθελαν ἔξαφνα νὰ σκοτώσουν, … καὶ παρευθύς νὰ δράμουσιν εἰς τοὺς πραγματευτάδαις,/ ἐικείνους νὰ σκοτώσουι, νὰ πάρουν τοὺς ταφτάδαις·/ καὶ νὰ ἐξολοθεύσουσι τὸ γένος τῶν Ῥωμαίων,/ ὅσ' εἶναι εἰς τὴν τζάρα τους νὰ μὴ φανοῦσι πλέον,/ ἄρχοντας καὶ ἀρχόμενους καὶ τὴν πτωχολογίαν,/ ποῦ θρέφουσι τὰ σπίτια τους ὅλοι μὲ πγραγματείαν·/ ἀλλ' ὁ θέος δὲν ἤθελε σὰν ἤθελαν ἐκεῖνοι, / ἀμμὴ μὲ τὴν αἰτίαν τους ἤθελε νὰ τοὺς κρίνῃ"; translation according to Panou, "Greek-Romanian Symbiotic Patterns," part I, 78.

support. While insisting on the nobleness of the Greeks ("a holy people, blessed people, a people most Christian in its Orthodoxy, and widely honored"[17]), Matthew also engages in reprimanding his Greek compatriots, switching characteristically from second to first person in plural:

> But you too, Greek lords! You should also be careful, both the courtiers among you, and those who deal in business; be on guard and do not succumb to injustice: you should not allow your greed to burden the people of Wallachia, nor should you be excessively demanding upon the poor. . . . It seems to me that you behave like tyrants to the poor Wallachians, and your greed has turned them into Greek-haters, to the extent that they abhor even the mere sight of you; you look down on them as if they were dogs, and, after all, if they were not mistreated they would not be complaining. But it does seem that they have good reasons to whine. Stop, then, and refrain from injustice, or God will inflict an eternal punishment upon you. These poor devils provide for us, and they take good care of us, and, willy-nilly, they even call us "masters,"[18] so we must feel for them and love them; and we must honor them, for they are our brothers.[19]

Matthew's testimony is quite unique for his time, not only due to the general lack of narrative sources of local origin from this period but also because he pays unusual regard to the peasants' grievances. The list of

---

17 Legrand, *Bibliothèque grecque vulgaire*, 245, lines 415–16: "εἶναι γένος ἅγιον, γένος εὐλογημένον,/ γένος ὀρθοδοξάτατον, ἀπ' ὅλους τιμημένον·"

18 Note that *ζουπούνουλε* transliterates the Romanian vocative *jupânule* ("oh master!," "oh lord!"), thus producing a very vivid picture of the encounter.

19 Legrand, *Bibliothèque grecque vulgaire*, 246, lines 423–44: "ἀλλὰ καὶ σεῖς πορσέχεσθε, ὦ ἄρχοντες Ῥωμαῖοι, / ὅσοι 'ς τὴν κούρτην βρίσκετε καὶ ὅσοι ἀγοραῖοι· / ἰδέτε καὶ προσέχετε ἀπὸ τὴν ἀδικίαν, / τοὺς Βλάχους μὴ πειράζετε μὲ τὴν πλεονεξίαν· / μηδὲ νὰ ἦστ'ἀχόρταγοι 'ς τοὺς ἐπτωχοὺς ἀπάνω, . . . θαρρῶ καὶ δυναστεύετε τοὺς ἐπτωχοὺς τοὺς Βλάχους, / καί ἡ πλεονεξία σας τοὺς κάμνει ῥωμαιομάχους, / καί δὲν μποροῦν νὰ σᾶς ἰδοῦν μηδὲ ζωγραφισμένους· / ὡσὰν σκύλους τοὺς ἔχετε πολλὰ ὠνειδισμένους, / ἄὰν δὲν εἴχασιν ἄδικον δὲν ἤθελαν φωνάζῃ, / ἀμμὴ διατὶ κλαίγουνται ἔχουσιν ὁμοιάζῃ· / καὶ παύσετε καὶ λείψετε ἀπὸ τὴν ἀδικίαν, / μὴν σᾶς κολάσῃ ὁ θεὸς κόλασιν αἰωνίαν. / Αὐτ' οἱ πτωχοὶ μᾶς θρέφουσι καὶ μᾶς ἀποκυττάζουν, / θέλοντες καὶ μὴ θέλοντες «ζουπούνουλε» μᾶς κράζουν, / καὶ πρέπει νὰ τοὺς ἔχωμεν καὶ νὰ τοὺς ἀγαποῦμε, / ὅτι μᾶς εἶναι ἀδελφοὶ, πρέπει νὰ τοὺς τιμοῦμε." Translation according to Panou, "Greek-Romanian Symbiotic Patterns," part II, 82–83, with minor amendments (K. P.). For this episode, the first in which the Greeks are mentioned as conspirators, see Iordachi, "From Imperial Entanglements to National Disentanglement," 67.

negative characteristics attributed to the Greeks—such as greed, conceit, slyness, deviousness, maliciousness, etc.—comprises a repertoire which would remain strikingly unaltered over the following decades, if not centuries. Moreover, we learn from his vivid description that popular discontent, however justified, could very easily be mobilized—and turned into a powerful political instrument—by the slightest mention of the "Greeks." Thus, the longest, final episode in Matthew's chronicle dedicated to the reign of Alexandru Iliaş is particularly revealing in that it demonstrates that Greekness could be very effectively brought into play as a negative category in order to contest the prince's legitimacy. In explicit language, he writes about repeated attempts by his enemies "to flock together in order to kill the Greeks, whom they hated like dogs and Jews."[20]

Given his own background and privileged position as a member of the country's social elite, Matthew could, of course, be suspected of producing a highly distorted image while at the same time obscuring other, more decisive reasons for the prince's failure—if there were no comparable description in other narrative sources.[21] Thus, it seems that Alexandru Iliaş's regime was confronted with similar resistance in Moldova, where he also held the throne for two periods,[22] as we learn from the chronicle of the Moldovan aristocrat Miron Costin, written several decades later. When finally the prince was forced to step down and to leave the country, he and his entourage were held back by an infuriated crowd shouting:

> "Give us the Greeks, our Lord!" Some of them lampooned, other cursed and plundered. There, they called for Batişte's extradition who always stood close to Alexandru as he noticed that he was shouted for. Yet the prince did not care for him but only for himself

20 Legrand, *Bibliothèque grecque vulgaire*, 261, lines 855–56: "συμβούλιον ἐποίησαν, νὰ κόψουν τοὺς Ῥωμαίους, / ὅτι τοὺς ἐσυχάθηκαν σὰν σκύλους, σὰν Ἑβραίους·."

21 See, for instance, the passage dedicated to Alexandru in the early eighteenth-century chronicle by Radu Popescu, "And when Alexandu-vodă arrived after having been appointed by the Porte, he brought with him numerous Greeks who, in addition to those who had already been here, added up to quite a bunch of people [*grămadă*]. Since they could not tolerate the Romanian boyars, they had them all killed." (Popescu, *Istoriile*, 87: "Viind Alixandru vodă domn de la Poartă, adusease mulţi greci cu dînsul, şi cu ce mai era nainte aicea, să făcusă o grămadă, carii nesuferind boiarii rumîni, au făcut sfat să-i tae.") A similar portrayal is provided by the anonymous chronicle of Wallachia written at the turn of the century. See *Istoria Ţării Romîneşti*, 91.

22 Between 1620–1621 and 1631–1633.

> and hence commanded him to stay away. And so they caught him and handed him over to the peasants' hands. Oh, unheard-of wrath of the mob! And so with no mercy, alive, they chopped him into pieces alive, with hatchets.[23]

Constantin Batişte (Battista) Vevelli, the prince's protégé of Cretan origin, was one of many Ottoman Greeks whose abrupt rise to power and wealth was sparking local outrage.[24] Therefore, it comes as no surprise that, only about a decade after these events, Leon Tomşa (1629–1632), Alexandru Iliaş's successor to the throne of Wallachia, issued a charter of liberties pressured by the powerful members of the country's nobility. The preamble states:

> In view of the omnipresent poverty and desolation of the land My Splendidness and the Boyars' Council sought the reasons for the ruin that has descended upon the land. And it transpired and proved that all the ruin and misery in the land comes from the foreign Greeks, who interfere in the ruling relations, sell the land without compassion and speculate with it at usurious rates of interest. For when they come to the territory they do not attempt to act according to the customs of the land, but to spoil the good things and to introduce bad and oppressing laws.[25]

This register of evils is repeated almost verbatim in another charter, issued just a week later and aimed at exempting parish priests from taxes. Highly

---

23 Costin, *Opere*, 99: "Striga: 'Dă-ne, doamne, pre greci.' Unii hăicăia, alții suduia şi jecuiia. Şi acolo au strigatŭ pre Batişte, să le dea, carele era tot aproape de Alexandru vodă, văzdândŭ [sic] strigarea pre sine. Ce, nu sta domniia de grijea lui, ce de grijea sa şi numai ce i-au dzis să să depărtédză de la dînsul. Şi aşe l-au apucat şi l-au dat pre mîna țăranilor. Nespusă vrăjmăşiia a prostimei! Şi aşea, fără de nice o milă, de viu, cu topoară l-au făcut fărîme."

24 On Vevelli, see Stoicescu, *Dicționar al marilor dregători*, 346–47.

25 Charter issued on July 15, 1631, in Bucharest, edited in *Documenta Romaniae historica. B.*, vol. 23, doc. no. 255, 406–7: "Deci văzînd toți atîta sărăcie şi pustiire țerîi, căutam domnia mea, cu tot sfatul țerîi, să se afle de unde cad acéle nevoi pre țeară. Aflatu-se-au şi se-au adevărat cum toate nevoile şi sărăcia țerăi se începe de la greci striini, carii ameastecă domniile şi vînd țeara fără milă şi o precupescu pre camete asuprite. Şi deaca vin aici în țeară, eu nu socotescu să umble după obicéiul țerîi, ei nu socotescu să umble după obicéiul țerîi, ce strică toate lucrurile bune şi adaogă legi réle şi asuprite . . ."

indignant about the "bad things and customs introduced in the country under my rule," the prince again praises himself for having "together with the Country's Council eradicated and stamped out the bad customs; and my Lordship removed those foreign Greeks out of the country, for they are to be considered enemies of the country."[26]

What made the ruling prince, Leon Tomşa, pass this judgement in the preamble to both charters, meant to order the departure of all non-naturalized Greeks from the principality (without effect, I should add), when only a year prior he had relied precisely on those "Greeks" to uphold his power, offering them tax exemption in exchange? And how is it that for the following decades there was almost no ruler who was not confronted—either as victim, instigator, or beneficiary—with anti-Greek resentments?[27]

THE TRANSFORMATION OF THE TRADITIONAL POWER PLAY AND THE "GREEK TAKEOVER"

For the moment, we may assume that the striking image of the Greek, as revealed in the narrative and legal sources cited above, points to an intricate nexus of social and political motives (and motifs) that seems to have reached a new level of escalation in the first decades of the seventeenth century. In order to develop a better understanding of the reasons for the outbreak of anti-Greek resentment, and for the adoption of anti-Greek measures precisely in this period, we must take a closer look at the evolution of the two principalities of Wallachia and Moldavia, with special regard to the composition of the social elite and the distribution of power.

In both cases, the belated emergence of the polity on the political map of Europe in the second half of the fourteenth century more or less coincided with the disintegration of medieval statehood in the Balkans, accelerated by the expansion of the Ottoman Empire into

26 Charter issued on July 23, 1631, in Bucharest, edited in *Documenta Romaniae historica. B.*, vol. 23, doc. no. 258, 412: ". . . nişte lucrure şi obicéiure réle ce au fost adaos de oamnei streini în ţeara domnii méle," and 413: ". . . cu tot sfatul ţerîi, călcat-am acéle obicée réle şi le-am pus domnia mea toate jos şi am scos acei grecu streini den ţeară afară, ca pre nişte nepriateni ţerîi fiindu."

27 The most exhaustive, although very biased, survey is still offered in Obedeanu, *Greciĭ în Ţara-Românească.*

Central Europe.[28] Wallachia and Moldavia's location in a religious and political border area—between the Kingdom of Hungary, the Polish-Lithuanian Commonwealth, and the Ottoman Empire, and between Catholicism, rivaling Protestantisms, Orthodoxy, and Islam—had a large impact on their internal political workings. These were characterized by ceaseless struggles between the prince (*voivod* or *gospodar*) and the nobility (*boyars*), who themselves were split into rival factions constantly looking for support in the neighboring countries. One might claim, of course, that this kind of power relation—a weak ruler, on the one hand, and a powerful nobility on the other—was a constellation far from unique in early modern Europe. Yet, unlike comparable cases such as in Hungary or in Poland, this tense relationship did not result in a constitutional system of estate-based shared rule. Instead, it evolved into a highly contradictory system of aristocratic clientelism centered on autocratic lordship—a process exacerbated by progressive integration into the Ottoman economic and governance system.[29]

Although, as is well known, neither principality was ever an administrative entity of the Ottoman Empire, the tributary status held by both implied a number of financial, material, and military obligations toward the Sublime Porte.[30] The rapid increase of Ottoman demands in the second half of the sixteenth century led, among many other consequences, to the further weakening of the prince's internal position and, at the same time, to the strengthening of the politically and economically potent boyar class.[31] In order to meet rising financial pressure, the ruling princes in both principalities (who had to be approved by—and, later, nominated by—the Porte) increasingly were forced to rely on the financial support of those from non-domestic circles within the Ottoman Empire, primarily Greeks but also Albanians, Aromanians, and Italians from Istanbul, the Aegean Islands, or Macedonia, who were lured to the principalities by the

---

28 Pilat, "Between Ottoman Empire and Latin Christendom." For the general political context, see Fine, *The Late Medieval Balkans*.

29 On the history and function of the estate assemblies, see Stoicescu, *Sfatul domnesc şi marii dregători*; and Brătianu, *Sfatul domnesc şi adunarea stărilor*. For an incisive study of this peculiar system, its virtues, and its shortcomings, see Barbu, *Bizanţ contra Bizanţ*, 47–88.

30 Maxim, *L'Empire ottoman au nord du Danube*; and Panaite, *The Ottoman Law of War and Peace*.

31 For the development of various payments in money and in kind to the Sublime Port, see Murgescu, *Circulaţia monetară în Ţările Române*, 214–20.

prospect of advancement in political or military positions that they could not obtain within the Ottoman Empire.[32] Designated under the generic name of "Greeks,"[33] these individuals married into local families and purchased landed estates. Thus, through diverse strategies of social promotion, "Greeks" became part of the landed gentry that the boyar class essentially was.[34]

To be sure, migration from south of the Danube was by no means a new phenomenon; it had begun with the Ottoman conquests of the Balkans, which led members of the Christian aristocracy, as well as a significant number of clerics, into the principalities.[35] They were followed by merchants and tradesmen, who resided either temporarily or permanently in the two principalities and were largely involved in both the long-distance trade linking the Levant and the Central Balkans with east-central Europe and—most decisively—the provisioning of Istanbul itself.[36] Although it is impossible to quantify, documentary evidence from rural and urban settlements alike clearly indicates that immigration from the core Ottoman regions reached a hitherto-unknown degree at the turn of the seventeenth century. While the influx of Levantines was not confined to the upper strata of society, but also effected the urban and even village population,[37] it was particularly at the level of the ruling establishment and of the higher church hierarchy that the Greek presence became most notable. According to estimates for Moldova, for instance, the average

---

32 Păun, "La circulation de pouvoir."

33 For the social and intellectual history of the ethnonym, see Roudometof, "From 'rum millet' to Greek Nation"; and Anagnostopoulou, "L'historicité des termes: les Grecs et la domination ottomane."

34 In addition to Păun, "La circulation de pouvoir," see Lazăr, "'De la boutique à la terre.'"

35 Curiously enough, despite a large number of studies dedicated to individuals and specific periods, there is no comprehensive study of migration from Ottoman core territories in Southeastern Europe to the Danubian Principalities regarding its phases, extent, reasons, social and regional impact. For an overview, see Georgescu, *Bizanțul și instituțiile românești*; and Cotovanu, "L'émigration sud-danubienne vers la Valachie et la Moldavie."

36 Lazăr, *Les marchands en Valachie*; Apetrei, "Marele negustor grec din Moldova"; and Luca, "The Rise of the Greek 'Conquering Merchant'." For the general context of the takeoff of Christian merchants and their networks, see the classical study by Stoianovich, "The Conquering Balkan Orthodox Merchant"; and Faroqhi, "Crisis and Change, 1590–1699."

37 Apetrei, "Fome de integrare socială." For an in-depth study of four cases of social advancement in Moldova around 1600, also see Franck, "Grecii din Moldova."

number of foreigners holding the highest positions of state office admitted to the Princely Council (*sfatul domnesc*) stood at twenty-five per cent, and under some princes even reached more than forty per cent.[38] Moreover, beyond the highest political body, this new ascendant class was particularly well represented in the key positions of diplomacy, finance, and higher offices of the court, adding up to what the legal historian Valentin Georgescu suggestively dubbed the "Greek takeover."[39] However, due to the mixing of locals and immigrants over the course of time, as well as the shifting awareness of group affiliation, it should be noted that these numbers must be considered carefully.

Because the monocratic system of rule was never questioned in principle, the staffing of state offices, taxation policy, the granting of privileges, and a host of other matters depended largely on the prince, whose room for maneuver was, however, de facto restricted by the demands of imperial policy and by his circle of supporters inside and outside the country.[40] Under these circumstances, the Greek *homines novi* were, in a way, in an advantageous position: faced with a chronically unstable situation within the principality, in which power was more efficiently secured through clientelist relationships than via promotion procedures (which were never clearly established), many of those elevated to positions of power brought with them a great deal of economic capital and adeptness at making social connections, often acquired within the Ottoman economic and administrative system.[41] Their growing representation in the most important state and church institutions also shows that their appointment to official positions in the principalities did not depend on ethnic affiliation. The minimum criteria was, of course, an Orthodox Christian identity, which is at the core of the

---

38 See Păun, "Les grands officiers d'origine gréco-levantine," from which these figures are taken, covering the period 1574–1710. For Wallachia, average numbers are supposedly even higher for the same period. See Neagoe, "Mari dregători şi negustori greci în Ţara Românească"; and Cicanci, "Dregători greci." For the eighteenth century, see Ionaşcu, "Le degré de l'influence"; and Cernovodeanu, "Mobility and Traditionalism."

39 "Greek takeover" (*acaparea grecească*) constitutes a key notion in Georgescu's study of the Byzantine afterlife in Romanian institutions and culture. See Georgescu, *Bizanţul şi instituţiile româneşti*.

40 For the sake of clarity, it should be added that the far-flung network of creditors whom the princes had to entertain included not only Christians but also Muslims and Jews. For the case study on Constantin Brâncoveanu, see Murgescu, "Romanian Information regarding the Ottoman Capital Market."

41 Păun, "Les grands officiers d'origine gréco-levantine."

notion of "Greek," although there were several cases of Catholics who made a career in the princely entourage.

THE POLITICAL USES OF GREEKNESS

All evidence suggests that it was in the first decades of the seventeenth century that the princes' practices of selling positions of state office, creating new ones, and appointing their favorites compounded the animosity that the established boyar families (Romanian or not) felt toward their parvenu rivals. Against this background of the escalating, often violent rivalry within the oligarchy, it is interesting to see that recourse to the so-called "old customs" became rampant in public discourse. While a feeling of contempt for the "Greeks" was probably quite widespread even before the turn of the century, Leon Tomşa's charter, cited above, marked a decisive step toward the politicization of what was considered "ours" and what was considered "foreign."[42] As we can learn from the document, the qualities of the "native" (*pământean*, literally "from the soil") were opposed to the unlawfulness of the invading "foreigner" (*striin* or *străin*), or, more commonly, the "Greek" (*grec*). While this terminology is used repeatedly in other official documents from about the same period—all of which aim in one way or another to restrict access for or expel "Greeks" from positions in state administration or church institutions—a positive definition is conspicuously lacking, which indicates that it "was defined only in opposition with intruders and had to be adjusted in order to be efficient in excluding these intruders."[43]

A more elaborate take on the issue of foreignness can be observed in the contemporary chronicles written by members of the boyar class.[44] In a very characteristic way, while deploring the absence of orderliness in troubled times (the standard trope usually invoked), Moldavian and Wallachian chronicles enlarge upon the patriotic theme already manifest

42 Incisively analyzed in Murgescu, "'Phanariots' and 'Pămînteni'"; Nicoară, "Le discours antigrecque et antiphanariote; Nicoară, "Anti-Greek and anti-Phanariot Discourse"; and Stănescu, "Préphanariotes et phanariotes." For political language used by rivaling boyar factions in the seventeenth century, see Rezachevici, "Fenomene de criză," especially part II, 105–16.

43 Murgescu, "'Phanariots' and 'Pămînteni,'" 199. On the legal status of foreigners, see Cicanci, "Statutul social-juridic al grecilor 'împământeniţi.'"

44 I have expanded on this topic elsewhere. See Petrovszky, "Die Entdeckung der historischen Tiefe."

in legal documents by placing great stress on notions of custom, habit, and tradition. Correspondingly, caricaturing and scornful descriptions of foreign parvenus abound; their growing presence obviously was perceived as a threat to the traditional rules of the political game.[45] Thus, Gaspar Grazziani (r. 1619–1620), a Dalmatian who managed to seize the throne of Moldova while being dragoman to the Porte, is depicted by Miron Costin in the following way:

> Gaspar-voda was a man of Italian descent, or, as we use to say in our country, Frankish, a man with no knowledge of the ways and customs of the land; which is the worst thing there can be, when the ruler does not know the language of the country he rules.[46]

His violent death at the hand of two boyars was not completely unjustified because: "This prince, Gaspar-voda never respected fasting, instead he ate in secrecy at all fasting periods."[47] Indeed, in their wording, these listings of misdemeanors against the "good and old ways of the land" (*obiceaiele céle bune, bătrâne ale țărâi*) contain striking parallels to the decrees that were issued by the Wallachian princes Matei Basarab (r. 1632–1654),[48] Constantin Şerban (r. 1654–1658, 1660),[49] and Radu Leon (r. 1665–1669),[50] all of which were aimed at limiting "Greek" presence in ecclesiastical and secular politics.

45 A plentitude of such portrayals is offered in the anonymous *Istoria Țării Romînești*, 90–93, 100, 104–5, 146, 155–60.

46 Costin, *Opere*, 66: "Gaşpar vodă era omŭ de neamul său italianŭ, cum dzicemŭ la noi în țară, frîncŭ, omŭ neştiutoriŭ rîndul şi a obiceaiurilor țărîi, fără limbă de țară, care lucru mai greu nu poate hi, cîndŭ nu ştie domnul limba țărîi unde stăpînéşte."

47 Costin, *Opere*, 72: "Acestŭ domnŭ, Gaşpar vodă, niceodată post n-au avut, ce pre ascunsŭ în tote posturile mîncă carne."

48 For Matei Basarab's church policy aimed at releasing the country's monasteries from subordination to Athos monasteries, and hence from Greek influence, see Lazăr, Barbu, and Olar, "Reforma monastică a domnului Matei Basarab," especially page 44 for the above formula. The edition of the two charters from November 27 and December 8, 1640, is annexed to this study. For an earlier charter from 1639 (with unspecified date), see the edition by Barbu, *O arheologie constituțională*, no. XII, 97–102.

49 To my knowledge the full text is yet unpublished. For the regesta of the charter from May 14, 1657, see *Catalogul documentelor*, no. 138, 98–100.

50 For the charter from December 9, 1669, see the hitherto only edition, by Bălcescu, *Magazin istoric*, no. 3, 131–34.

On both levels—that of legal procedures and that of learned writing—we can thus observe that the influx of Greeks and other foreigners was perceived by long-established boyars as a threat to their political position and self-understanding. In addition to the fact that all of this obviously did not have the effect of reversing the development, it should be noticed that many of the princes and boyars who distanced themselves from the "Greeks," and promoted a discourse of indigenousness, were themselves of non-Moldavian (or non-Wallachian) origin. Radu Leon's wavering policy is a case in point here.The self-acclaimed son of the former prince Leon Tomşa was considered by many of his contemporaries to be Greek, which is reflected in his nickname, "*stridia*" ("the oyster-seller," from the Greek στρείδι, which, in a pejorative sense, also means a clingy person). What is certain is that he grew up in the Greek milieu of Istanbul, and some of his closest allies were of Greek origin. As Radu was facing an ever-growing boyar opposition that threatened to corrode his support in Istanbul, he gave in to their claims in exchange for their support—and thus issued a charter in 1669 establishing the Greeks' principal guilt for all of the maladies that hit the country. Radu followed Leon Tomşa's example; "the foreign Greeks" were accused of "estranging the people of this land from my Lordship with grudge and slander."[51] Despite this professed allegiance to the "domestic party," he did not manage to satisfy their wishes and was deposed by sultanic decree only shortly afterward.[52]

Arguably the most prominent example of the political charge of "Greek" outweighing the ethnic meaning of the term is given by Constantin Cantacuzino (ca. 1640–1716), a leading scholar and cunning statesman whose chronicle very actively promoted the Wallachian self-assertion against Levantine intrudes. Originating from a branch of the famous Constantinopolite family with alleged roots in the Byzantine imperial dynasty, whose members had settled north of the Danube already by the sixteenth century, Cantacuzino considered himself—with the greatest nonchalance—as "*împănântenit*," that is, "naturalized." As such, while extolling the greatness of the Hellenes ("*elini*," not "*greci*") he joins in the lament concerning mischievous newcomers from Istanbul:

51 Bălcescu, *Magazin istoric*, no. 3, 132: " . . . străinând oamenii ţărei de către domnia mea cu pizme şi cu năpăşti."

52 See the lengthy description in the anonymous *Istoria Ţării Romîneşti*, 155–60, which rather reflects the view of the opposing party.

> As long as anyone can remember them being here, there was never a time when there were not some of them standing side by side with the prince when he wished to perpetrate some cruel or tyrannical deed in this country or other evil action against the boyars or against other people, and he chose from among these people [the Greeks] his advisors and executors.[53]

Still, Cantacuzino insists on establishing a clear difference, because "some of them prove to be useful to these lands, while others only come to pillage and plunder."[54] It goes without saying that he considered his own family as belonging to the first category.[55]

Cantacuzino's treatment of the Greek issue, dating from the beginning of the eighteenth century, shows that "Greek" and "foreigner" had become contentious words in the political arena, used to denounce the disloyalty of one's rival by reference to his descent—or, more precisely, his non-indigenousness.[56] At the same time, given the high percentage of noble families of Greek or Levantine origin in the countries' key positions, some of which were already well integrated in the local establishment, the patriotic saber-rattling also called for a more cautious approach. Against this background, emphasizing "foreign Greeks" or "Constantinopolite Greeks" (*greci străini, greci Țarigrădeni*), rather than simply "Greeks," as the common source of evil clearly indicates an awareness of the difference between those that are identified, or identify themselves, with the country (*pământean*) and those very recently arrived, lacking knowledge of local customs and suspected

53 Cantacuzino, *Istoria Țărîi Rumăneşti*, 90: "Şi nici odata nu să ţine minte, de cîtăva suma de ai încoace, de cînd s-au cunoscut de aceia într-acéste părţi mai bine, cum să nu fie fost lîngă domni din ei, cu care domnii, de cîte ori au vrut să facă vreo tirănie sau vreo crudătate sau altă răotate într-această ţară, au în neamurile boereşti au altor cuivaşi, carii să nu fie fost şi ei au sfétnici, au lucrători." Translation according to Nicoară, "Anti-Greek and anti-Phanariot Discourse," 131, with minor amendments (K. P.). For praise of the Hellenes and lament at their demise, see Cantacuzino, *Istoria Țărîi Rumăneşti*, 88 et seq.

54 Cantacuzino, *Istoria Țărîi Rumăneşti*, 90: "Ci de la unii să véde şi rămîne şi folos în pămînturile acéstea; iară alţii ca să jăfuiască şi ca să răpească numai ce vin . . ."

55 His father, with the same name, was among the signatories of Leon Tomsa's decree.

56 Modern historiography continued to use these terms, and thus followed the paths laid by early modern chronicle writing. See the critical remarks by Pippidi, *Tradiția politică*, 164–84; and Rezachevici, "Fenomene de criză," 98–117.

of being driven exclusively by exploitative interests.[57] As far as chronology is concerned, it is quite significant that this specification within the xenophobic discourse gained momentum toward the end of seventeenth century, that is, exactly when Ottoman control over the northern tributaries was significantly tightening following the Cretan War and in the context of continuous warfare against the Habsburg dynasty, Poland, and Russia.

The high degree of grecization within the political and cultural life of the Danubian principalities in this period[58] was a fact also registered by foreigners, who were keenly observing changing power relations in the Ottoman orbit, but at the same time were not free from replicating the stereotypes encountered in situ. For both attitudes we find fascinating evidence in Antonio del Chiaro's *Istoria delle Moderne Rivoluzioni della Valachia*, printed in Venice in 1718. During his time as secretary to the Wallachian prince Constantin Brâncoveanu (1688–1714), the Florentine Del Chiaro could have witnessed the dominance of Greek culture, which, although strongly promoted by the prince himself, could not escape the Italian's sardonic comments:

> As for the use of the Greek language in some churches, I do not find another explanation than this: once Turkish dominance was imposed, Greek monks and priests have shown up, which have been coming into this rich country not only to introduce their language, but also, as is notorious, to dodge the tribute and the taxes to which this nation is subjected in Turkey.[59]

Despite his recognition of their individual motives, he considered the Greeks a "nation perpetually fatal to Wallachia . . . especially those from

57 Stănescu, "Préphanariotes et phanariotes." For other cases, see also Rezachevici, "Prefanariotismul."

58 Thus, for example, the princely academies founded in Bucharest and Iaşi at the turn of the century were run by Greeks scholars exclusively. See Camariano, *Les Académies princières*. It was also in this era that the two principalities became centers of Greek literacy and learning; see Karathanasis, *Οι Έλληνες λόγιοι*.

59 Del Chiaro, *Istoria delle Moderne Rivoluzioni della Valachia*, 83: "Quanto poi all' uso della Lingua Greca nelle Sagre Funzioni in Valachia , non vedo esservi ragione fondamentale che possa indurci a credere, esser ciò seguito, se non dacchè l'Ottomano Impero si rese padrone di quella fertile, e ricca Provincia; dove poi cominciarono a concorrere diversi Monaci, e Prelati Greci, non solo per ricavarne qualche emolumento nell'insegnare la Lingua Greca in Valachia; ma eziandio per esimersi da' Tributi, e da altre angherìe, alle quali soggiace quella Nazione' nella Turchìa , come è ben noto ad ognuno."

Constantinople, whenever they were in charge. In some of them, ambition and conceit have never diminished."[60] In the same vein, nunciatory reports to the Holy See decry the malice of the Greeks' "schismatics" on every possible occasion, which, of course, attests to the Catholic envoys' acute feeling of confessional rivalry rather than to their awareness of the Greeks' social and political role in the Ottoman framework.[61] Yet, these are aspects that point to different contexts and therefore lie beyond the scope of this study.

THE MANY FACES OF ANTI-GREEK DISCOURSE

In order to delineate graecophobia more precisely, we must consider the political role played by Orthodox Christianity in the Ottoman Empire as well as other competing or concurring stereotypes.

Viewed against the complex background of Ottoman Orthodoxy, attitudes toward Greeks and Greekness appear, of course, far more multifaceted than the derogatory language of the cited evidence prima facie suggests. Thus, already the example of Constantin Cantacuzino points to a particular ambivalence within anti-Greek discourse. Apparently, there was no contradiction in the fact that this discourse was embraced by numerous members of the social elite who themselves belonged to the group of polyglot Levantines with family ties that reached far beyond the small principalities and with an intimate knowledge of Greek culture and language.[62] This cultural intimacy betrays the absence of certain ingredients that were usually necessary for the construction of a more or less coherent "Feindbild" comparable to other enemy stereotypes known from medieval and early modern times, such as those directed against Armenians, Tatars, Poles, Hungarians, or Germans. Yet, in contrast to all

---

60 Del Chiaro, *Istoria delle Moderne Rivoluzioni della Valachia*, 123: "Nazione sempre fatale alla Valachia," 208: "I Greci, spezialmente Costantinopolitani, sono stati sempre fatali per la Valachia, ogni qualvolta ne hanno avuto il comando. La orgogliosa ambizione in alcuni di loro non si è punto diminuita."

61 Providing an exhaustive list of these cases is beyond the scope of this study. For statements found in the corpus of early modern travel accounts concerning the Principalities, see *Călători străini*, VII, 178, 274, 297, 314 et seq., 395 et seq., 458.

62 Despite a certain convergence of political or economic interests, a sense of solidarity based on a common heritage, language, or vision cannot be attested for the Greek-Phanariot elite. See Zervos, "Recherches sur les Phanariotes," based on his unpublished dissertation, "Recherches sur les phanariotes et leur idéologie politique: 1666–1821" (Ph.D. diss, L'École des Hautes Études en Sciences Sociales, 1990).

these cases, anti-Greek sentiments could not draw on the most common resource of cultural differentiation: religious difference.[63] This was all the more true as the highest religious authorities of Eastern Christianity were inseparably linked with Greek culture and language. Thus, the underlying tension can be formulated as such: not only was "the Greek" not sufficiently different from oneself in terms of religion, but also Greekness virtually encapsulated all of the spiritual references at the center of Orthodox self-understanding: the prestige of a biblical language, the legacy of the last Roman Empire, the aura of the Ecumenical Patriarchate, and the spiritual supremacy of Eastern monasticism.[64] Finally, there was the sophisticated lifestyle of the Christian elite of Constantinople-Istanbul that proved just as attractive as it was repelling—and unattainable to the Christian population of the empire.

But obviously the high prestige of Greekness as a cultural model, and the absence of religious difference, did not significantly attenuate anti-Greek resentments. Quite to the contrary, precisely because of this affinity, the depiction of scandalous behavior had to resort again to the register of religion to reveal the Greek monstrosity, by evoking "the heretic" and "the Turk." Very often these elements are combined, as in the following case of an anonymous Moldavian chronicle from the early eighteenth century, which intends to defame the Moldavian prince Dumitraşco (Dimitrie) Cantacuzino (r. 1673–75, 1684–85), a "Greek from Istanbul":

> In order to be in favor of the Turks he was eating meat every day both in and outside fasting time, together with the Turks that came as his guests, and he sullied the [religious] law and the holy Lent. And this he did not only to please the Turks, but because he despised to fast, since several Greeks behave heretically by cursing the law and the ones that instituted fasting time.[65]

63 See especially Crăciun, *Protestantism şi ortodoxie în Moldova*, as well as the collective volumes Crăciun and Ghitta, *Church and Society in Central and Eastern Europe*; and Toderaşcu, *Etnie şi confesiune în Moldova medievală*.

64 For this vast topic, see especially Pippidi, *Tradiția politică*.

65 *Letopisețul Țării Moldovei dela Eustratie Dabija*, 69: "Acesta, pentru să intre în voia Turcilor, în fiece zi mânca carne, şi în post şi în căşlegi, cu Turcii ce-i venia oaspeți, şi defăima legea şi sfintele posturi; dar nu doară pentru voia Turcilor, ci pentru că-i era urât a posti, precum o seamă de Greci au acest eres, de ocărăsc legea şi pre cei ce au aşezat posturile."

Thus, in order for the Greek to be depicted as utterly despicable, he must be made into a heretic or even "turkified," that is, metaphorically placed outside the religious community. In other instances, he is depicted as even worse than the Turk, as is underlined by Ion Neculce, a Moldavian chronicler from the middle of the eighteenth century, in very drastic formulations:

> Now, this is how I see it in my humble opinion; when, by God's will, there will be no more rust on iron and Turks in Constantinople and wolves do not eat sheep anymore, maybe then there will be no Greeks in Moldavia and Wallachia, no Greek boyars to gnaw at these two countries like they do. . . . One can put down fire, one can collect water and change its course, one can find shelter and rest when the wind blows, the sun can hide behind clouds and come out again, night follows day and light follows darkness; but Greeks have no mercy or kindness, justice or goodness or fear of God. Only when he can do no harm does the Greek show kindness, but his mind and his heart push him to do all kind of evil things. If one reads the Greek chronography, one can see quite clearly what the Greeks did and worked at the time when they were strong and powerful in their kingdom [the Byzantine Empire].[66]

If we are to believe Neculce's harsh verdict, there are ways of coming to terms with the Antichrist, whose identity is unquestionable; the real problem is his henchmen.

Indeed, over the course of the seventeenth century the negative stereo typing of the "Turk" became toned down. Rather than being

66 Neculce, *Letopisețul Țării Moldovei*, 171: "Aşè socotescu eu cu firea mè această proastă: cînd a vrè Dumnedzeu să facă să nu fie rugină pe fier, şi turci în Țarigrad să nu fie, şi lupii să nu mînînce oile în lume, atunce poate nu vor fi nici greci în Moldova şi în Țara Muntenească, nici or fi boieri, nici or putè mînca aceste doao țări, cum le mînîncă … Focul îl stîngi, apa o iezăşti şi o abați pe altă parte, vîntul cînd bate, te dai în laturi, într-un adăpost şi te odihneşti, soarele intră în nuor, noaptea cu întunerecul trece şi să face iar lumină, iar la grec milă, sau omenie, sau dreptate, sau nevicleşug, nici unele de aceste nu sunt, sau frica lui Dumnedzău. Numai cîndu nu poate să facă rău să arată cu blîndețe, iar inima şi firea, tot cît arŭ putè, este să facă răutate. Căutați de cetiți la hronograful grecescu, de vă încredințați şi mai bine, pe cînd au fost grecii puternici şi împărăția era a lor, ce făcè pre atunce şi ce lucra!" Translation according to Nicoară, "Anti-Greek and anti-Phanariot Discourse," 135, with minor amendments (K. P.).

targeted themselves, "Turks" are addressed via proxy, as it were, by the defaming of the Greek.[67] This becomes particularly clear when compared to the early sixteenth century, when continuous "warfare" (in religious and diplomatic writing) with the expanding Empire was accompanied by tropes of Christian bravery and anti-Islamic invectives.[68] With the ongoing integration of the principalities into the Ottoman Empire, and the de facto acquiescence of Ottoman hegemony, the image of the Turk lost its prominence on the scale of negative others, due to the detriment of the Greek. Of course, well-established rhetorical figures targeting "the enemy of Christianity" were not dismissed; however, despite the phraseology of religious enmity, the Turk appeared as a clearly detectable—and therefore less evil—figure of alterity, compared to the Greek, who turned out to be more ambiguous and therefore more perilous to the "traditional customs" and "old practices."

In addition to the existence of a positive counter-image of Greekness, and the interaction with the stereotype of the Turk, there is a third dimension of the anti-Greek discourse that must be mentioned: its catalyzing function for historiographical debates in the Danubian Principalities. Thus, it is not surprising that, precisely at the height of anti-Greek sentiments and politics, from the 1620s to the 1670s, the theory of the Latin descent of the Romanian people surfaced in learned writing, and rapidly established itself as the founding narrative of history in the region.[69] This, of course, is a huge topic in itself, on which I cannot elaborate here, but I wish to point to the emergence of this narrative, as it reveals the process by which the need to position oneself within uncertain circumstances, perceived as a menace to one's own identity, gave way to a new identity discourse that drew on historical and linguistic evidence. In this sense, one could claim, the "Greek foreigner," more than any other

---

67 The differing emphasis regarding the two figures of alterity is recapitulated in nineteenth-century Romanian schoolbooks; see Murgescu, *Între "bunul crestin" si "bravul român,"* 210–12, 214–16.

68 See Berza, "Turcs, Empire Ottoman"; and Vlad, "Turcul." For related figures of alterity, see Ciobanu, "Imagini ale străinului"; and Ioncioaia, "Veneticul."

69 While a number of humanist historians, such as Enea Silvio Piccolomini and Antonio Bonfini, had already referred to the Roman colonization of Dacia and the Latinity of its inhabitants, it was not until the seventeenth century that the theme was taken up in Romanian scholarship. For a comprehensive inventory of the various medieval and early modern theories on languages and nations, see Armbruster, *Romanitatea românilor.*

figure of alterity, served as a foil for the emerging Romanian patriotic discourse of the seventeenth century.[70]

CONCLUSION

As I have argued, the negative stereotype of the Greek was a central figure in the political and social fabric of early modern Wallachia and Moldova. It was not by chance that the most radical emotions directed toward the Christian *homines novi* of the Ottoman Empire manifested themselves in those two border principalities, where arguably the best opportunities for rapid social advancement were offered. The emergence of a vociferous anti-Graecism at the turn of the seventeenth century, consistently documented in narrative and legal sources, cannot be traced to older forms of xenophobia that were directed against Armenians, Catholics, Protestants, or other groups. The negative stereotype of the Greek had no prehistory grounded in religious alterity or rivalry, and therefore must be interpreted as a genuine reaction to elite immigration to the principalities throughout the Ottoman period and to the rivalries this immigration produced. Significantly, the principal agents of this process of transformation were (not without reason) identified as "Greeks," who in political discourse figured as the main target of contempt, even as Greek culture and language continued to be highly appreciated. This way, graecophobia and graecophilia were tightly bound up with each other, equally produced by the gradual integration of the two principalities into the Ottoman framework.

BIBLIOGRAPHY

Sources

Bălcescu, Nicolae. *Magazin istoric pentru Dacia.* Vol. 1. Bucharest: Colegiul Național, 1845.

Barbu, Daniel. *O arheologie constuțională românească. Studii și documente.* Bucharest: Editura Universității din București, 2000.

Călători străini despre Țările Române. Vol. VII, edited by Maria Holban, Maria Mathilda Alexandresu-Dersca Bulgaru, and Paul Cernovodeanu. Bucharest: Editura Științică și Enciclopedică, 1980.

Cantacuzino, Constantin Stolnicul. *Istoria Țării Rumînești*, edited by Damaschin Mioc. Bucharest: Editura Academiei Române, 1991.

70 Petrovszky, "Die Entdeckung der historischen Tiefe."

Catalogul documentelor Țării Româneşti din Arhivele Naționale. Vol IX: 1657–1659, edited by Mirela Comănescu, Laura Niculescu, and Ileana Dincă. Bucharest: Arhivele Naționale ale României, 2012.

Costin, Miron. *Opere. Ediție critică.* Edited by Petre P. Panaitescu. Bucharest: Editura de stat pentru literatură şi artă, 1958.

Del Chiaro, Antonmaria. *Istoria delle Moderne Rivoluzioni della Valachia, Con la Descrizione del Paese; Natura, Costumi, Riti, e Religione degli Abitanti; Annessavi la Tavola Topografica di quella Provincia, dove si Vede ciò, che Èrstato nella Valachia agli Austriaci nel Congresso di Passarovitza.* Venice: Antonio Bortoli, 1718.

Documenta Romaniae historica: B. Tara Românească. Vol. 23 (1630–1632), edited by Damaschin Mioc. Bucharest: Editura Academiei RSR, 1966.

Istoria Țării Romîneşti 1290–1690. Letopisețul cantacuzinesc, edited by Constantin Grecescu and Dan Simonescu. Bucharest: Editura Academiei Republicii Populare Romîne, 1960.

Legrand, Émile, ed. *Bibliothèque grecque vulgaire.* Vol. 2. Paris: Maisonneuve et Cie, 1881.

Letopisețul Țărîi Moldovei dela Eustratie Dabija până la domnia a doua a lui Antioh Cantemir: 1661–1705. Edited by Constantin Giurescu. Bucharest: Socec, 1913.

Neculce, Ion. *Letopisețul Țării Moldovei şi O samă de cuvinte*, edited by Iorgu Iordan, Bucharest: Editura de stat pentru literatură şi artă, 1955.

Obedeanu, Constantin V. *Grecii în Țara-Românească cu o privire generală asupra stăreĭ culturale până la 1717.* Bucharest: Socec, 1900.

Zallony, Marc-Philippe. *Traité sur les princes de la Vallachie et de la Moldavie sortis de Constantinople, connus sous le nom Fanariotes.* Paris: Arthus Bertrand, 1830.

Studies

Anagnostopoulou, Sia. "L'historicité des termes: les Grecs et la domination ottomane XVIe–XIXe s." In *Méditerranée: Ruptures et Continuités. Actes du colloque tenu à Nicosie les 20–22 octobre 2001, Université Lumière-Lyon 2, Université de Chypre*, edited by May Chehab, Yannis Ioannou, and Françoise Métral, 187–96. Lyon: Maison de l'Orient et de la Méditerranée-Jean Pouilloux, 2003.

Apetrei, Cristian N. "Forme de integrare socială a grecilor din Țara Românească şi Moldova în a doua jumătate a sec. al XVI-lea. Câteva observații generale." In *Arheologie şi istorie în spațiul carpato-balcanic*, edited by Denis Căprăroiu, 303–8. Târgovişte: Editura Cetatea de Scaun, 2011.

Apetrei, Cristian N. "Marele negustor grec din Moldova (cca 1570–1620). Un profil colectiv din perspectivă braudeliană." *Revista Istorică* 23, nos. 1–2 (2012): 65–84.

Armbruster, Adolf. *Romanitatea românilor: istoria unei idei.* Revised edition. Bucharest: Editura Enciclopedică, 1993.

Barbu, Daniel. *Bizanț contra Bizanț. Explorări în cultura politică românească.* Bucharest: Nemira, 2001.

Berza, Mihai, "Turcs, Empire Ottoman et relations roumano turques dans l'historiographie moldave des XVe–XVIIe siècles." *Revue des études sud-est européennes*, 10, no. 3 (1972): 595–627.

Brătianu, Gheorghe I. *Sfatul domnesc şi adunarea stărilor în principatele române*. Bucharest: Editura Enciclopedică, 1995.

Camariano, Ariadna. *Les Académies princières de Bucarest et de Jassy et leurs professeurs*. Institute for Balkan Studies 142. Thessaloniki: Institute for Balkan Studies, 1974.

Cernovodeanu, Paul. "Mobility and Traditionalism: The Evolution of the Boyar Class in the Romanian Principalities in the 18th Century." *Revue des études sud-est européennes* 24, no. 3 (1986): 249–57.

Cicanci, Olga. "Dregători greci în Ţările Române în veacul al XVII-lea." In *Faţetele istoriei. Existenţe, identităţi, dinamici. Omagiu Academicianului Ştefan Ştefănescu*, edited by Teoteoi, Tudor, Bogdan Murgescu, and Şarolta Solcan, 199–210. Bucharest: Editura Universităţii din Bucureşti, 2000.

Cicanci, Olga. "Statutul social-juridic al grecilor 'împământeniţi' (secolele XVI–XVII)." *Cercetări de istorie şi civilizaţie sud-est europeană* 3 (1987): 114–23.

Ciobanu, Veniamin. "Imagini ale străinului în cronici din Moldova şi Ţara Româneascăă (secolul XVIII)." In *Identitate, alteritate în spaţiul cultural românesc*, edited by Alexandru Zub, 115–57. Iaşi: Editura Universităţii "Alexandru Ioan Cuza," 1996.

Cotovanu, Lidia. "L'émigration sud-danubienne vers la Valachie et la Moldavie et sa géographie (XVe–XVIIe siècles): la potentialité heuristique d'un sujet peu connu." *Cahiers balkaniques* 42 (2014). Accessed January 23, 2016. doi: 10.4000/ceb.4772.

Crăciun, Maria. *Protestantism si ortodoxie în Moldova secolului al XVI-lea*. Cluj Napoca: Presa universitară clujeana/ Fundaţia culturală "Cele trei Crişuri," 1996.

Crăciun, Maria, and Ovidiu Ghitta, eds. *Church and Society in Central and Eastern Europe*. Cluj-Napoca: European Studies Foundation Publication House, 1998.

Daskalov, Roumen. "Bulgarian-Greek Dis/Entanglements." In *Entangled Histories of the Balkans. Vol. I: National Ideologies and Language Policies*, edited by Roumen Daskalov and Tchavdar Marinov, 149–239. Leiden: Brill, 2013.

Faroqhi, Suraiya. "Crisis and Change, 1590–1699." In *An Economic and Social History of the Ottoman Empire 1300–1914*, edited by Halil İnalcik and Donald Quataert, 411–636. Cambridge: Cambridge University Press, 1994.

Fine, Jr., John V. *The Late Medieval Balkans: A Critical Survey from the Late Twelfth Century to the Ottoman Conquest*. Ann Arbor: The University of Michigan Press, 1987.

Franck, Gerd. "Grecii din Moldova – între integrare şi asimilare (sfârşitul secolului XVI – prima jumătate a secolului XVII). Modele de ascensiune socială." In *Etnie şi confesiune în Moldova medievală*, edited by Ion Toderaşu, 179–265. Iaşi: Editura Universităţii "Alexandru Ioan Cuza," 2006.

Georgescu, Valentin Al. *Bizanţul şi instituţiile româneşti pînă la mijlocul secolului al XVIII-lea*. Bucharest: Editura Academiei RSR, 1980.

Greene, Molly. *A Shared World: Christians and Muslims in the Early Modern Mediterranean*. Princeton: Princeton University Press, 2000.

Ionaşcu, Ion. "Le degré de l'influence des Grecs des Principautes Roumaines dans la vie politique de ces pays." In *Symposium l'époque phanariote, 21–25 octobre 1970. A la mémoire de Cléobule Tsourkas*, 217–28. Thessaloniki: Institute for Balkan Studies, 1974.

Ioncioaia, Florea. "Veneticul, păgînul şi apostatul. Reprezentarea străinului în Principatele române (secolele XVIII–XIX)." In *Identitate, alteritate în spaţiul cultural românesc*, edited by Alexandru Zub, 159–77. Iaşi: Editura Universităţii "Alexandru Ioan Cuza," 1996.

Iordachi, Constantin. "From Imperial Entanglements to National Disentanglement: The 'Greek Question' in Moldavia and Wallachia, 1611–1863." In *Entangled Histories of the Balkans. Vol. I: National Ideologies and Language Policies*, edited by Roumen Daskalov and Tchavdar Marinov, 67–148. Leiden: Brill, 2013.

Karathanasis, Athanasios. Οι Έλληνες λόγιοι στη Βλαχία: (1670–1714). Συμβολή στη μελέτη της Ελληνικής πνευματικής κίνησης στις παραδουνάβιες ηγεμονίες κατά την προφαναριωτική περίοδο. Thessaloniki: Institute for Balkan Studies, 1982.

Kármán, Gábor, and Lovro Kunčević, eds. *The European Tributary States of the Ottoman Empire in the Sixteenth and Seventeenth Centuries*. Leiden: Brill, 2013.

Kiel, Machiel. *Art and Society of Bulgaria in the Turkish Period. A Sketch of the Economic, Juridical and Artistic Preconditions of Bulgarian Post-Byzantine and its Place in the Development of the Art of the Christian Balkans, 1360/70–1700. A New Interpretation.* Assen, Maastricht: Van Gorcum, 1985.

Kitromilides, Paschalis M., and Anna Tabaki, eds. *Greek-Bulgarian Relations in the Age of National Identity Formation*. Athens: Institute for Neohellenic Research, 2010.

Kitromilides, Paschalis M. and Anna Tabaki, eds. *Relations gréco-roumaines: interculturalité et identité nationale*. Athens: Institut de recherches néohelléniques, 2004.

Krstić, Tijana. *Contested Conversions to Islam: Narratives of Religious Change in the Early Modern Ottoman Empire*. Stanford: Stanford University Press, 2011.

Lazăr, Gheorghe. "'De la boutique à la terre.' Les marchands 'grecs' et leurs stratégies d'insertion sociale (Valachie, XVIIe siècle)." *Studii şi Materiale de Istorie Medie* 26 (2008): 51–67.

Lazăr, Gheorghe. *Les marchands en Valachie (XVIIe–XVIIIe siècles)*. Bucureşti : Institutul Cultural Român, 2006.

Lazăr, Gheorghe, Violeta Barbu, and Ovidiu Olar. "Reforma monastică a domnului Matei Basarab." *Studii şi Materiale de Istorie Medie* 30 (2012): 9–54.

Lemny, Ştefan. "La critique du regime phanariote: cliches mentaux et perspectives historiographiques." In *Culture and Society: Structures, Interferences, Analogies in the Modern Romanian History*, edited by Alexandru Zub, 17–30. Iaşi: Editura Academiei Republicii Socialiste România, 1985.

Luca, Cristian. "The Rise of the Greek 'Conquering Merchant' in the Trade between the Eastern Mediterranean and the Romanian Principalities in Sixteenth and Seventeenth Centuries." *Journal of Mediterranean Studies* 19, no. 2 (2010): 311–34.

Maxim, Mihai. *L'Empire ottoman au nord du Danube et l'autonomie des Principautés Roumains au XVIe siècle. Études et documents.* Istanbul: Isis, 1999.

Mishovka, Diana. "The Afterlife of a Commonwealth: Narratives of Byzantium in the National Historiographies of Greece, Bulgaria, Serbia and Romania." In *Entangled Histories of the Balkans. Vol. II: Shared Pasts, Disputed Legacies*, edited by Roumen Daskalov and Alexander Vezenkov, 118–273. Leiden: Brill, 2015.

Murgescu, Bogdan. *Circulația monetară în Țările Române în secolul al XVI-lea.* Bucharest: Editura Enciclopedică, 1996.

Murgescu, Bogdan. "'Phanariots' and 'Pămînteni': Religion and Ethnicity in Shaping Identities in the Romanian Principalities and the Ottoman Empire." In *Ethnicity and Religion in Central and Eastern Europe*, edited by Maria Crăciun and Ovidiu Ghitta, 196–204. Cluj-Napoca: Cluj University Press, 1995.

Murgescu, Bogdan. "Romanian Information regarding the Ottoman Capital Market. Prince Constantin Brâncoveanu's Debt-Repayments 1694–1703." *Dünü ve Bugünüyle Toplum ve Ekonomi* 10 (1997): 39–51.

Murgescu, Mirela-Luminița. *Între "bunul crestin" si "bravul român". Rolul scolii primare în construirea identității naționale românesti (1831–1878).* Iași: Editura A '92, 1999.

Neagoe, Claudiu. "Mari dregători și negustori greci în Țara Românească în a doua-jumătate a veacului al XVI-ea." *Istros* 13 (2006): 215–23.

Nicoară, Toader. "Anti-Greek and anti-Phanariot Discourse in Romanian Society at the Dawn of the Modern Age (17th and 18th Centuries)." In *Tolerance and Intolerance in Historical Perspective*, edited by Csaba Lévai and Vasile Vese, 125–40. Pisa: Università di Pisa Edizioni Plus, 2003.

Nicoară, Toader. "Le discours antigrecque et antiphanariote dans la société roumaine (XVIIe et XVIIIe siècles." In *Ethnicity and Religion in Central and Eastern Europe*, edited by Maria Crăciun and Ovidiu Ghitta, 205–11. Cluj-Napoca: Cluj University Press, 1995.

Panaite, Viorel. *The Ottoman Law of War and Peace: The Ottoman Empire and Tribute Payers.* Boulder: East European Monographs, 2000.

Panou, Nikos. "Greek-Romanian Symbiotic Patterns in the Early Modern Period: History, Mentalities, Institutions." *The Historical Review/La Revue Historique* 3 (2006): 71–110, and 4 (2007): 59–104.

Păun, Radu. "La circulation de pouvoir dans les Pays Roumain au XVIIe siècle. Repères pour un modèle théorétique." *New Europe College Yearbook* (1998/99): 265–310.

Păun, Radu G. "Les grands officiers d'origine gréco-levantine en Moldavie au XVIIe siècle. Offices, carrières et stratégies de pouvoir." *Revue d'Études Sud-Est Européennes* 45 (2007): 153–95.

Petrescu, Ștefan. *Migrație și ortodoxie în Europa de Sud-Est de la "destrămarea" societății fanariote la constituirea comunităților grecești în prima jumătate a secolului al XIX-lea.* Bucharest: Editura Muzeului Național al Literaturii Române, 2013.

Petrescu, Ştefan. *Οι έλληνες ως "άλλοι" στη Ρουμανία. Η εσωτερική οικοδόμηση του ρουμανικού έθνους-κράτους κατά τον δέκατο ένατο αιώνα και οι έλληνες*. Thessaloniki: Επίκεντρο, 2014.

Petrovszky, Konrad. "Die Entdeckung der historischen Tiefe als Strategie der Krisenverarbeitung: die moldauische Chronistik des 17. Jahrhunderts." In *Krise in der Frühen Neuzeit*, edited by Rudolf Schlögl, Philip R. Hoffmann-Rehnitz, and Eva Wiebel, 295–309. Göttingen: Vandenhoeck & Ruprecht, 2016.

Petrovszky, Konrad. *Geschichte schreiben im osmanischen Südosteuropa. Eine Kulturgeschichte orthodoxer Historiographie des 16. und 17. Jahrhunderts*. Wiesbaden: Harrassowitz, 2014.

Pilat, Liviu. "Between Ottoman Empire and Latin Christendom: Moldavia as Frontier Society in the Late Middle Ages." In *Europe and the 'Ottoman World': Exchanges and Conflicts (Sixteenth to Seventeenth Centuries)*, edited by Gábor Kármán and Radu G. Păun, 171–93. Istanbul: Isis Press, 2013.

Pippidi, Andrei. *Tradiția politică bizantină în Țările române în secolele XVI–XVIII*. 2nd rev. ed. Bucharest: Corint, 2001.

Popescu, Radu. *Istoriile domnilor Țării Româneşti*. Edited by Constantin Greceanu. Bucharest: Editura Acadademiei RPR, 1963.

Rados, Leonidas. "Influența greacă in disputele istoriografice din spațiul romanesc în a doua jumătate a secolului XIX." *Anuarul Institutului de Istorie "G. Barițiu, Cluj-Napoca"* 47 (2008): 123–42.

Rados, Leonidas. "Societatea Junimea şi interesul pentru studiile bizantine." *Anuarul Institutului de Istorie "A. D. Xenopol"* 41 (2004): 513–28.

Reinkowski, Maurus. "The Ottoman Empire and South Eastern Europe from a Turkish Perspective." In *Images of Imperial Legacy. Modern Discourses on the Social and Cultural Impact of Ottoman and Habsburg Rule in Southeast Europe*, edited by Tea Sindbaek and Maximilian Hartmuth, 21–36. Münster: LIT, 2011.

Rezachevici, Constantin. "Fenomene de criză socialpolitică în Țara Românească în veacul al XVII." *Studii şi materiale de istorie medie* 9 (1978): 58–84, and 14 (1996): 85–117.

Rezachevici, Constantin. "Prefanariotismul. Raportul dintre grecii 'împământeniți' şi cei 'țarigrădeni'." *Studii bizantine* 3 (2012), 27–39. Accessed January 23, 2016. http://www.uniunea-elena.ro/Storage/ART639/Magazine.htm.

Roudometof, Victor. "From 'rum millet' to Greek Nation: Enlightenment, Secularization and National Identity in Ottoman Balkan Society 1453–1821." *Journal of Modern Greek Studies* 16 (1998): 11–48.

Stănescu, "Préphanariotes et phanariotes dans la vision de la société Roumaine des XVIIe–XVIIIe siècles." *In Symposium l'époque phanariote, 21–25 octobre 1970. A la mémoire de Cléobule Tsourkas*, 347–58. Thessaloniki: Institute for Balkan Studies, 1974.

Stoianovich, Traian. "The Conquering Balkan Orthodox Merchant." *The Journal of Economic History* 20, no. 2 (1960): 234–313.

Stoicescu, Nicolae. *Dicționar al marilor dregători din Țara Românească și Moldova (sec. XIV–XVII)*. Bucharest: Editura Enciclopedică Română, 1971.

Stoicescu, Nicolae. *Sfatul domnesc și Marii Dregători din Țara Românească și Moldova (sec. XIV–XVII)*. Bucharest: Editura Academiei RSR, 1968.

Symposium l'époque phanariote, 21–25 octobre 1970. A la mémoire de Cléobule Tsourkas. Thessaloniki: Institute for Balkan Studies, 1974.

Toderașu, Ion, ed. *Etnie și confesiune în Moldova medievală*. Iași: Editura Universității "Alexandru Ioan Cuza," 2006.

Vincent, Alfred. "Byzantium Regained? The History, Advice and Lament by Matthew of Myra." *Θησαυρίσματα* 28 (1998): 275–347.

Vlad, Laurenţiu. "Turcul un personaj al imaginarului popular." *Caietele Laboratorului de Studii otomane* 2 (1993): 144–63.

Zervos, Socrate. "Recherches sur les Phanariotes: À propos de leur sentiments d'appartenance au même group sociale." *Revue des études sud-est européennes* 27, no. 4 (1989): 305–11.

The Many Faces of the "Gypsy" in Early Modern Ottoman Discourse

Faika Çelik

As related by his biographer, when the chief imperial architect Sedefkār Meḥmed Agha (d. 1617) first arrived at the imperial gardens, as a young janissary recruit to be trained for imperial service, he was mesmerized by a musician performing in the garden. He was so captivated by the art of music that he wanted to excel at it, and he asked the musician to help him master it. Under the musician's guidance, he progressed rapidly, applying himself to his studies with such passion that he deprived himself of sleep for many nights in order to rehearse. Finally, one night, he was overcome by sleep and dreamed:

> A group of musicians rise up and appear in the form of a band of gypsies. In their hands, some of them hold tambourines, some harps and zithers, some violins and some *pandpre*, some organs, some panpipes, some lutes, some castanets, some dulcimers. In short, when the men and musicians, preparing all the instruments which they had among them, began to play in union, all the *saz* [instruments] which they had in their hands, the sound of the party threw the universe in tumult and resulted in trembling of the earth and the heavens. And saying to the above-mentioned Agha, "if you have a liking for our art, if you want to learn it, God bless you!," all treated him with respect and showed deference to him in a variety of ways.[1]

1 Ca^{c}fer Efendi, *Risāle-i mi^{c}māriyye*, 26. Please note that this quotation is a modified

Waking from the dream, he went to his teacher and asked for an explanation of the dream's meaning. The musician said:

> In truth this art is a Gypsy art (*çingān ṣanᶜatı*). But they are an ignorant tribe. What is a note? What is time? What is harmony? What is dissonance? What is melody? What is interval? What is tone? What is song? They know not.[2]

The master explained these terms to him in detail, taught him the twelve basic notes, and asked him to practice what he had been taught. However, the Agha did not practice but found an excuse to return to his residence. When he arrived and went inside, he plunged again into the sea of thought. In short, the master's advice and words, far from putting his heart to rest, caused him distress, and, addressing himself, he said:

> O unfortunate wretch! As soon as you saw that art you immediately turned and ran toward it like water. Had that art been acceptable and desirable and esteemed and beloved in the sight of the Lord God the all-bounteous, that abject tribe and loathsome [band of gypsies] (*cemāᶜat-i maḳhūrān ve gürūh-ı menfūrān*) which I saw in my dream would not have shown interest in the aforementioned art. They would have turned away from it as Satan—curses upon him—turned away from Adam's form. The best, most necessary, excellent and appropriate [thing to do] is this: not to act on the musician's words but to go to one of the righteous ulema and advice-giving sheikhs and have him interpret the dream. Whatever he says, it will be necessary to act in accord with his noble command. Let the musician's great happiness, eminence and good fortune be entirely his own! I do not need them.[3]

For advice, the Agha turned to the great Ḫalvetī sheikh of the period of Sultan Murād III (r. 1574–95), Vişne Meḥmed Efendi, who told him:

> My son, it is necessary for you to renounce that art. If that art were good, it would be practiced by the righteous and virtuous people. It

---

version provided by Crane. I have deleted Ottoman-Turkish terms for these various musical instruments, which Crane indicated in brackets. I would like to thank my colleague Gül Kale for bringing this source to my attention.

2 Caᶜfer Efendi, *Risāle-i miᶜmāriyye*, 26.

3 Caᶜfer Efendi, *Risāle-i miᶜmāriyye*, 27.

> would not have fallen like this into the hands of the tribe of Satan (*ḳavm-i vesvās*), who are evil men (*erzel-i nās*). Since your desire is [to learn that] art, the appropriate thing to do is this: tarry a few days. If your nature inclines toward another art, consult with us again. If one is encountered by that which is useful in this world and the other world, let us give you blessing and permission [to follow it]. Then, with our blessing and permission, may you master that art! To see gypsies (*cingān*) in a dream is just like seeing the tribe of spirits and demons. And [the word] Gypsy (*cingān*) means jinn (*cinler*) because the suffix *-gān* is a plural [ending]. Originally [the world jinn] was *cinne*, like *zinne*. When the plural form was used in the Persian language, it became *cinnegān*, like *zindegān*. Later, lightening and softening the *nūn*, they said *cingān*. From the point of view of words, *cin* is *cinne* in exactly the same way. And in the Arabic language, *jinn* is a common noun. It refers to both of these groups [gypsies and jinns]. When both types are being referred to, the plural is used. And one of these two types can be seen, the other is invisible. In short, it is necessary that you turn back from this art and ask for God's forgiveness and repent to the fullest degree.[4]

As a result of this advice, Caᶜfer tells us, Meḥmed Agha turned away from music with sorrow and regret. As recent research on dreams demonstrates, this dream of Meḥmed Agha is but one among many that can be found in the biographical dictionaries written (especially after the second half the sixteenth century) to explain significant junctures in the lives of their subjects.[5] My aim here is not to explore the complexities or multiplicities of the dream stories found in different genres of textual sources in the Ottoman world. Nor can I provide a detailed analysis of the questions that may arise in readers' minds: whether this dream was in fact dreamt, why Meḥmed Agha's biographer narrated this dream while describing his

4 Caᶜfer Efendi, *Risāle-i miᶜmāriyye*, 28.

5 On dreams in the early modern Ottoman context, see Niyazioğlu, "How to Read an Ottoman Poet's Dream?"; Niyazioğlu, "Dreams, Ottoman Biography Writing, and the Halveti-Sünbüli Sheikhs of Sixteenth Century Istanbul"; and Niyazioğlu, "Dreams of the Very Special Dead."

subject's "career path," or why Meḥmed Agha wanted to call on the opinion of one of the most influential Ḫalvetī sheikhs of sixteenth-century Istanbul in making his career choices.[6] My engagement with this dream story is limited to reading the image of the *çingāne* (Gypsy)[7] constructed in the text by three males, who belong to different strata of the learned hierarchy, and questioning whether the image that they drew corresponds to or diverges from the image found in court records and registers of important affairs (*mühimme*).

---

6 These and many other questions are elaborated in Niyazioğlu's various articles, mentioned in note 5.

7 Today, "Gypsy" is a contested identification, with modern communities favoring alternatives, such as "Roma," "Romani," "Roma people," and "Sinti." Because "Gypsy" has often been applied as a pejorative term, in 1971 the First Romani Congress rejected the term (and its equivalents in other languages), favoring the term "Roma." Nonetheless, among many Roma and traveling communities "Gypsy" remains a common form of self-identification. See, for instance, Barany, *The East European Gypsies*, 1; Crowe, "Roma: The Gypsies"; and Marsh and Strand, *Gypsies and the Problem of Identities*. Although the Indian origin of the Gypsies is now generally accepted, when they first arrived to Europe in the fifteenth century, "Their place of origin was thought to be either Egypt (hence the Greek name *Gyftos*, the Spanish *Gitano*, the sixteenth-century German *Aegypter*, the English *Gipsy* or *Gypsy*, and the various terms meaning 'Pharaoh's people', such as Romanian *Faraon* and Hungarian *Pharao Nephka*) or Byzantium, where they were assumed to be associated with a Judaizing sect known as the Athinganoi, meaning 'untouchables' (hence Byzantine Greek *Adsincanoi*, German *Zigeuner*, French *Tsigane*, Hungarian *Cigány*, Italian *Zingari* and *Acingani*, Slav (Bulgarian, Polish, Serbian) *Cigan*, Romanian *Tigan*, and the English *tinker*); terms such as *Walachi, Saraceni, Agareni, Nubiani*, French *Bohémiens*, and German *Tartars* also refer to assumed origins." See Campbell, *The Oxford Dictionary of the Renaissance*, s.v. "Gipsies." In Ottoman texts, the terms used for "Gypsy" are *Ḳıbṭī* (in the case of a female, *Ḳıbṭiye*), *Ḳıbṭiyān, Çingene, Çingāne, Cingene, Çingān, Cingān, Çingen, Cingen*, and *Çingeniyān*. Gypsies' communal identity was embodied by terms such as *tāʾife-i çingāne* or *çingāne zümresi* and *tāʾife-i ḳıbṭiyān* or *ḳıbṭiyān zümresi*. On the etymology of *Ḳıbṭī* and *Çingene*, see Tietze, *Tarihi ve Etimolojik Türkiye Türkçesi Lugatı*; and Yıldız, "Türkçede Çingeneler İçin Kullanılan Kelimeler ve Bunların Etimolojileri." In modern Turkey, "Roman" is the name favored by the majority of Roma for self-identification, although some insist on calling themselves *Çingene* (Gypsy), despite the word's pejorative implications. See, for instance, Alpman, *Başka Dünyanın İnsanları Çingeneler*, 53–56; and Aksu, *Türkiye'de Çingene Olmak*. In this study, in accordance with my sources, I generally use "Gypsies" rather than "Roma."

ORIGIN OF GYPSIES: AN OTTOMAN LAYER

Returning to the dream of Meḥmed Agha, music is deemed to be the art of Gypsies. This interpretation is made not only by Gypsies themselves (in the dream) and by the master musician, but also, subconsciously, by Meḥmed Agha, who, while learning the rules of music, dreamed of the Gypsy band and of nothing else. In the dream itself, we find nomadic Gypsies able to play various musical instruments, and their mastery of music is so profound that the sound of the music shakes the earth and the heavens. They are also represented as very welcoming to a stranger, showing him respect in various ways and wishing him God's help in learning *their* art. Until the interpretations of the dream inserted into the text, we do not find any defamation or contempt of the Gypsies; on the contrary, what we see is an appreciation and a romanticization of the Gypsies' performance. Nevertheless, the ways in which the "Gypsy" image within the dream was interpreted discloses abiding stereotypes: Gypsies are represented as talented musicians, but ignorant of formal musical rules, objectified as morally deficient and religiously shallow evil-doers.

Yet another significant issue that must be addressed pertains to Vişne Meḥmed Efendi's explanation of the etymology of the word *cingān*, perhaps one of the earliest examples of such in the Ottoman-Turkish context. In Vişne Meḥmed Efendi's reading, Gypsies are associated (or, rather, equated) with the tribe of spirits and demons. This equation is substantiated by constructing an etymology in which wordplay and the sounds of words give a deeper meaning to a simple understanding of the word *cingān*. The basis of this equation is not only the similarity between the sound of *jinn* and the syllable "cin" in *cingān* but also—and perhaps more so—the similarity between the traits attributed to spirits/demons and those given to Gypsies. Modern etymology would consider "unscientific" what I call a morally and theologically appropriated construction by Vişne Meḥmed Efendi. Nevertheless, this folk etymology, or associative etymology, though unsound according to the parameters of modern etymology, remains significant and cannot be overlooked. It demonstrates not only a certain mode of thought but also one of the many ways to use etymology.[8] By constructing this etymology, I would

---

8 As demonstrated by Derek Attridge, etymology can be used in many ways, "to confirm a dominant ideology, to deny the possibility of purposeful change, to reinforce the myth of objective and transcendent truth; but it can also be used to unsettle

suggest, Vişne Meḥmed Efendi was perhaps attempting to confirm a "truth" of his time—that Gypsies and *jinns* belonged to the same family.

Almost five decades after Vişne Meḥmed Efendi's interpretation of "Gypsy," the well-known seventeenth-century Ottoman traveler Evliyā Çelebī tackled the origins and perceptions of Gypsies in Ottoman society when recording his observations on the town of Gümülcine (Komotini, in modern Greece). According to Evliyā Çelebī,

> the Gypsies (*çingāneler*) in this region and throughout the Ottoman domains originated in Egypt, when Moses battled with the Pharaoh on the shore of the Red Sea near the Sinai desert and 600,000 of Pharaoh's soldiers—along with his magicians and diviners and the tools of their trade—drowned in the whirlpool at the place known as the Straight of Qolundur. Moses put a curse on the people of the Pharaoh who were not present at that battle. As a result of the curse, they could not remain in Egypt but were scattered abroad, condemned to wander from clime to clime and from town to town, hungry and homeless, dwelling in the mountains and the valleys, and raiding and thieving.[9]

As the above excerpt demonstrates, while Vişne Meḥmed Efendi's "origin" story is morally and theologically grounded, Evliyā Çelebī adds yet another spatial dimension to it. But from where did Evliyā procure the idea that Gypsies originated in Egypt? It should be stressed that in Evliyā's account, as well as in other state-generated documents, along with the term *çingāne* and its derivatives, *ḳıpṭī* constituted one of the most pervasive designations for "Gypsy." In Arabic, "qibṭī" denotes native Egyptians ("Coptic"). Yet "Gypsy" in Arabic is identified with terms such as *Ġajar*, *Ḥalab*, *Nawar*, and *Zuṭṭ*.[10] So, why did the Ottomans, including Evliyā Çelebī, adopt the term *ḳıpṭī* to denote "Gypsy," rather than one of the various designations found in Arabic or in other Islamic languages? According to Eyal Ginio, "the Gypsies were named by the Ottoman

---

ideology, to uncover opportunities for change, to undermine absolutes and authority—and to do so without setting up an alternative truth claim." See Attridge, "Language as History/History as Language," 202.

9 Friedman and Dankoff, "The Earliest Known Text in Balkan (Roumelian) Romani," 156.

10 Hanna, *Ghagar of Sett Guiranha*.

administration as kıptî, 'an Egyptian,' a reflection of the common myth that existed in Europe that the Gypsies originated in Egypt."[11]

Evliyā Çelebī's remarks on gypsies are not limited to their alleged origin and the curse imposed upon them by Moses, that they should live outside of Egypt, homeless and poor. First, in Evliyā's discourse, "Gypsy" is not a homogenous category; Gypsies are categorized as Anatolian or Rumelian, each group with its distinctive dialect, professions, and religious practices. According to Evliyā Çelebī, Gypsies often speak the "languages of the countries where they are settled."[12] Nevertheless, both Gypsies of Anatolia and Gypsies of Rumelia have their own peculiar dialects, containing "thousands of . . . naughty expressions."[13] Nominal attachment to any religion, one of the most lasting stereotypes attributed to Gypsies in various societies, can also be read in Evliyā's account. For instance, at one point, Evliyā Çelebī represents the Gypsies of Anatolia as "quasi Muslims" and argues that "they pretend to be Muslims but are not even infidels!" "The Rumelian Gypsies," on the other hand, "celebrated Easter with the Christians, the Festival of Sacrifice with the Muslims, and Passover with the Jews. They do not accept any one religion, and therefore our imams refused to conduct funeral services for them but gave them a special cemetery outside Egri Qapu."[14]

About half a century later, Dimitrie Cantemir (d. 1723), appointed a prince of the Ottoman vassal state of Moldavia by the Ottomans, discusses the origins of the Gypsies, as well as on their reception by the Ottoman state and by society at large, in his *System of the Muhammadan Religion*, published in Russian in 1712. Having lived and been educated in Istanbul in the last decades of the seventeenth century—and being conversant in many languages, including the Turkish written and spoken at the

11 Ginio, "Neither Muslims nor *Zimmis*," 131. According to Ginio, not only *kıptî* but also *çingene* is in fact a designation that emanated from contemporary Greek terminology: *yiftos* (i.e., *ḳıpṭī*) and *atsingani* (i.e., *cingān*). Therefore, Ginio suggests, Ottoman adoption of the contemporary Greek terminology for "Gyspy" is related to appropriation of some of the Byzantine practices in the region. In fact, Ginio argues that the Ottomans appropriated not only the term but also other Byzantine practices concerning Gypsies, the most important being the levy of a poll tax on both Christian and Muslim Gypsies.

12 Friedman and Dankoff, "The Earliest Known Text in Balkan (Roumelian) Romani," 156.

13 Friedman and Dankoff, "The Earliest Known Text in Balkan (Roumelian) Romani," 156.

14 Friedman and Dankoff, "The Earliest Known Text in Balkan (Roumelian) Romani," 157.

time—Cantemir provides insights on Ottoman society in general, and gypsies in particular, that should not be overlooked. According to Cantemir,

> the Turks and together with them the other Muslims say that people of the Gypsies are related with Pharaohs, [. . .] having no knowledge of letters, books and any other divine human law, [they are] spread all over the world, by the mercy and the commandment of God. The Gypsies who believe in Muhammad consider themselves to be perfectly pious by this only title, but beside this; they do not look for the commandments and the conditions of the Law; they ignore all of it without doing or preserving the Law says; there are no prayers of any kind, no fasts and they do not want to even hear about Mecca; instead of sympathy they commit larcenies, frauds, charms and witch crafts [. . .].[15]

One of the significant issues that emerges from this account is the similarity it bears to the ways in which the origin and perceptions of Gypsies had been approached in the narratives mentioned above. While Sedefkār Meḥmed Agha's biographer constructs a morally appropriated origin story for Gypsies, Cantemir, like Evliyā Çelebī, contends that Gypsies are related to the pharaohs, thus hinting at Egypt as their "homeland." Nevertheless, within all of these narratives, Gypsies are represented as belonging to an ignorant community, indulging in various immoral activities, and portrayed as only nominally Muslim, straying from the normative Muslim code of conduct.

As I have explained elsewhere in detail, writing on Ottoman Gypsies, especially in the early modern period, is a daunting task for a number of reasons, the most important being the extant sources.[16] While we have many accounts concerning Gypsy lifestyles in the nineteenth and early twentieth centuries of the Ottoman realm, the available literary and narrative sources are rather limited for the early modern period. The narrative sources at hand are not only very limited but also were produced by the learned hierarchy and the male elites of Ottoman society, and as such reflect their authors' prejudices and perceptions. Thus, throughout the rest of this study, I would like to consider another genre: court records. The reason for this selection is twofold. First, court records provide us with a

15 Cantemir, as quoted in Oprişan, "An Overview of the Romanlar in Turkey," 167.
16 See Çelik, "'Community in Motion,'" 1–7.

sizeable body of information toward reconstructing a "social, economic and mental map" of a particular community, against which the position of Gypsies can be considered. To be more precise, when court records are read as "texts" rather than mere "documents," they disclose parameters of social stratifications—including, but not limited to, religion, gender, and ethnicity—and networks of power embedded in early Ottoman society. For this reason, they are invaluable sources for exploring what constituted normativity and difference in the early modern Ottoman world. Second, although the "facts" that the court records document are framed through certain legal categories and formularies, which privilege some values while silencing others, they offer us glimpses into not only how Gypsies were viewed by the communities in which they lived, but also the ways in which Gypsies themselves resisted and acted upon some of the prejudices directed toward them in everyday life.

THE *ÇINGĀNE* OR *ḲIBṬĪ* (GYPSY) IN OTTOMAN COURT RECORDS

The ways in which gypsies are identified in court records reveal how they were positioned in the socio-economic and moral landscape produced by the Ottoman legal elite. Gypsy clients of the court—Muslim and non-Muslim; men and women; nomadic, seminomadic, or (recently) settled—were always labeled through their communal affiliations, drawn on the basis of their "ethnicity" rather than their religious affiliation, while the latter appears to have been the more common marker used for various other communities. In the case of Gypsies, the scribes meticulously identified them by one of two means. Before or after the name of the individual, including the standard patronymic marker, they added either *çingāne* or *ḳıbṭī* (*ḳıbṭiyye* for women).[17] Or, rather than marking the individual as either *çingāne* or *ḳıbṭī/ḳıbṭiyye*, the scribes would identify them with the name of the community to which they belonged (*ḳıbṭī tāʾifesinden*).[18]

17 See, for example, USS 56 / 3b / 2: *Ḳıbṭī Ḥüseyin b. Maḥmūd* (Ḥüseyin the Gypsy, son of Maḥmūd); USS 17 / 46a / 2: *Yūnus b. ᶜAbdullāh nām çingene* (Gypsy named Yūnus, son of ᶜAbdullāh); USS 56 / 33a / 2: *Āltūn bt. Ḥüseyin nām çingene* (Gypsy named Āltūn, daughter of Ḥüseyin); and USS 84 / 115a / 4: *Cevher bt. Dervīş nām ḳıbṭiyye* (Gypsy named Cevher, daughter of Dervīş named). USS stands for Üsküdar Court Records (*Üsküdar Şerᶜiyye Sicilleri*), followed by volume number, folio number, and entry number.

18 See, for example, USS 17 / 8b / 3: *Ḳıbṭī tāʾifesinden Dimo b. Koçi* (Dimo, son of Koçi, from the community of Gypsies); USS 56 / 3b / 1: *Ḳıbṭīyān tāʾifesinden Pazarlı*

How should we conceptualize the category *çingāne* or *ḳıbṭī* in the court's discursive practice? Although for a modern reader this label may appear to be a marker of "ethnic" identification, it should not be construed as the politically constructed "ethnicity" of modernity, and hence needs to be qualified. Unfortunately, current research on Ottoman understandings of "ethnicity" in the early modern period is very limited, despite the existence of various genres of sources that include minute details pertaining to the "qualities" ascribed to certain "ethnic" groups, including (but not limited to) Turks, Kurds, Arabs, Persians, and Albanians.[19] Leslie Peirce suggests that the ways in which "ethnic" designations were used within the discourse of court registers can teach us about the Ottomans' understanding of "ethnicity." According to Peirce, in Aintab's sixteenth-century court lexicon, "ethnic" designations were used as markers of differentiation for those nomadic and tribal communities unassimilated into urban culture. In the case of Aintab, these groups were Kurds, Turcomans, and Arabic-speaking Bedouins.[20] In eighteenth-century Salonico, Ginio observes that groups who were labeled by their "ethnicity" included Gypsies, Blacks (*ᶜArab*), and migrant Albanians (*Arnāvud*).[21] Yet in sixteenth-century Üsküdar, these groups included Gypsies, Blacks (most of whom were either freed or fugitive slaves), and recent immigrant communities, such as Tatars and Albanians (these recent immigrants are increasingly visible in the records dating to the 1580s and after).

Therefore, I would like to suggest that by employing *çingāne* or *ḳıbṭī* as a marker of identity, the court seems to highlight the Gypsies' hybrid lifestyle—nomadic, seminomadic, and recently settled—and their "as yet unassimilated" position in "civilized" urban settings.

OBJECTIFYING GYPSIES AS "EVIL-DOERS"

The question that I would like to address next is whether the court records can help us heterogenize the "Gypsy" image epitomized in the narrative

---

b. Muṣṭafā (Pazarlı, son of Muṣṭafā, from the community of Gypsies); and USS 84 / 16b / 4: *Zümre-i ḳıbṭīyāndan Ḥasan b. Ṣādıḳ* (Ḥasan, son of Ṣādıḳ from the community of Gypsies).

19 See, for example, Kunt, "Ethnic-Regional (Cins) Solidarity in the Seventeenth-Century Ottoman Establishment"; Lewis, *Race and Slavery in the Middle East*; Tezcan, "Dispelling the Darkness"; Casale, "The Ethnic Composition of Ottoman Ship Crews and the 'Rumi Challenge' to Portuguese Identity," 122; and Kafadar, "A Rome of One's Own."

20 Peirce, *Morality Tales*, 146.

21 Ginio, "Neither Muslims nor *Zimmis*."

sources quoted above. In other words, can the various stigmatizations that the narrative sources attribute to Gypsies as a *community* also be found in the court records?

As I have discussed elsewhere, encountering itinerant Gypsy musicians in registers of important affairs (*mühimme*) from the second half of the sixteenth century is not uncommon.[22] Nevertheless, within these state-generated documents—which were dispatched in response to petitions submitted by either local power holders or by ordinary subjects hoping to resolve certain problems—neither Gypsies' mastery of music nor their mobile lifestyle is romanticized. On the contrary, as is expected from this genre of sources, which more often than not mirror the socio-economic and moral concerns of the petitioners, itinerant Gypsy musicians are accused of organizing parties for the public and of seducing bachelors and married men by providing occasions for prostitution (*fiᶜl-i şenīᶜ*). Due to their alleged engagement in such "vice trades," others often despised Gypsies, and brought their complaints before the authorities, asking for Gypsies' expulsion from their communities.[23] Furthermore, in the registers some itinerant Gypsy communities are accused of engaging in other criminal activities, damaging individual and public property as well as causing insecurity for travelers.[24] In the formulaic parlance of these documents, those Gypsies who engaged in illicit activities, harming individual and public property as well as violating public morality, were labeled as *ehl-i fesād* (people of corruption), a generic term that the Ottomans used for habitual criminals.

First, it should be stated that we have no indication in the court records that Gypsies, whether as individuals or as itinerant groups, played music to make a living in sixteenth-century Üsküdar. We do, however, find some cases (though extremely few in number) that cast light on the ways Gypsies were perceived by the larger community in which they lived. For instance, sometime in the very late sixteenth century, a certain Meḥmed Subaşı, the police superintendent who was charged with controlling the rebels (*eşḳıyāyı ḥıfẓ içün taᶜyīn buyrulan*) in Üsküdar, asked Arslan b. Ḳurd, Meḥmed b. Şucaᶜ, and Ḳaplan b. ᶜAbdullāh from the community of Gypsies (*ḳıbṭī tā'ifesinden*) to come to the court, claiming that

22 Çelik, "Limits of Tolerance"; Çelik, "Exploring Marginality in the Ottoman Empire"; and Çelik, "Probing the Margins."

23 See, for instance, BOA, MD 7, no. 100; and BOA, MD 5, no. 186. See also Akdağ, *Türk Halkının Dirlik ve Düzenlik Kavgası*, 150.

24 BOA, MD 7, no. 66 and no. 100.

"many *sipāhī*s informed me that these Gypsies—who happened to wear janissary uniform—consumed alcohol (*şürb-i ḫamr idüb*) and assaulted Muslim women who were passing by and hence I want them to be interrogated and the result to be registered." Upon being questioned at the court, the Gypsies declared, "We are caulkers of imperial navy and we did not assault any Muslim women but we were at a wedding and we drank [alcohol] and at that moment we were drunk."[25] The case does not end here. In a subsequent entry, we learn that it was actually the janissaries and some "trustworthy" Muslims who had brought the case to Meḥmed Subaşı's attention. When Meḥmed Subaşı arrived at the scene, the fight between these Gypsies (men and women) and the janissaries had already begun. Apparently, the janissaries had asked the organizers of the wedding—husbands and wives—why they were drinking with their wives on such a sacred day. Then, their wives—whose Gypsy identity is underlined in the record—replied that "we drink wine and do whatever you want." They swore at the janissaries, saying, "you are ignorant day laborers (*boz ırġādlarsız*) and who are you to interfere with our business?" Despite the fact that there are some details missing from the register, we can assume that, having been unable to control the situation himself, Meḥmed Subaşı ordered these Gypsies to be taken to the town immediately and brought to the sharia court. Once questioned at the court, the Gypsies acknowledged the charges against them and, in the presence of the judge, further cursed and attacked the janissaries who had directed charges against them in the first place. After that, the trustworthy and righteous Muslims (*ṣuleḥā*) of Üsküdar who were present at the court hearing argued that "their actions and attitudes are always like that: they always consume alcohol and they do not refrain from talking and swearing at unrelated men/women (with whom marriage is not forbidden) and if they are not punished, they might commit further evil acts."[26]

This case is significant for a number of reasons. First, it documents the fact that some Gypsies were employed in the imperial navy and obtained a privileged position. This privileged position can be deduced not only from how they dressed but also from the manner in which they resisted the janissaries who brought charges against them. By calling the

25 USS 84 / 35 a / 3.

26 See USS 84 / 35 a / 4: "bunlaruŋ efᶜāl ve evżāᶜı böyledür dāᵓimā şürb-i ḫamr edüb nā-maḥrem ile muṣāḥabet ve münāzaᶜātdan ḫālī degillerdür bunlaruŋ ḥaḳlarından gelinmezse fesād etmeleri muḳarrerdür."

janissaries "ignorant day laborers" and by asking them "who are you to interfere in our business?," the Gypsies not only denigrated the janissaries but also challenged their authority. Second, being "Gypsy" does not seem to have constituted an obstacle to attaining a position in the higher echelons of the Ottoman administrative machinery. As epitomized in this case, what created tension in society was deviation from a way of life deemed morally appropriate and from commitment to performing normative Muslim behaviors (at least in public). But what constitutes normative Muslim behavior? Are the court records the correct historical sources to consult for references to normative behaviors expected of Gypsies? In the next section, I will present cases that not only demonstrate what being Muslim entailed in everyday life but also highlight the main consequences that Gypsies faced once they were considered as deviating from these normative practices.

RESISTING "NOMINALLY MUSLIM" STATUS

As highlighted above, Gypsies' indifference to "orthodox" practices of Islam—from conversion to gender segregation—was an important element in their perception by contemporary Ottomans as suspicious, less than trustworthy, and only nominally Muslim. From the seventeenth century onward, the court records provide significant insights into how this nominally Muslim status was translated into state practice in the sphere of taxation, and how some Gypsies who professed to be Muslim resisted this practice and negotiated their status.

It should be stressed at the outset that excessive and unfair taxation seems to have been one of the reasons why Gypsies used the channels of the Ottoman judicial system.[27] In the court records of Üsküdar are various examples in which nomadic Gypsies used the local court to obtain a certificate (*temessük*) confirming that they had paid their taxes

27 For telling examples, see, for instance, BOA, KK–67, 356/1 (imperial edict dated 1572, which addresses the judges and governors of Gümülcine and Karasu, written in response to a petition submitted by Gypsies who claimed that they were excessively taxed by the tax collectors); BOA, KK–67, 488/2 (imperial edict dated the same year, written in response to a petition submitted by Gypsies living in Gümülcine who complained about tax collectors excessively taxing Gypsies in the surroundings of Gümülcine, Karasu Yenicesi, and Siroz); and BOA, KK–67, 1258/1 (imperial edict addressing the judge of Motalice, concerning the excessive taxation of Gypsies).

elsewhere, so they could not be harassed by tax collectors while they were in Üsküdar.[28] Similarly, and more interestingly, starting from the very beginning of the seventeenth century we come across cases in which *Muslim* Gypsies resorted to local and imperial courts to petition against "unjust" taxation.[29] Their main argument was centered on the fact that, despite being Muslim, they were asked to pay a poll tax (*cizye*), which was contrary to the sharia. For instance, sometime in the year 1690, a certain Muṣṭafā, son of el-Ḥacc ᶜOs̱mān (literally, son of ᶜOs̱mān the pilgrim), and other gypsies from among the residents of Balat submitted, through the imperial court, a petition to the sultan in order to obtain an imperial decree favorable to their claim.[30] Apparently they were granted an imperial decree, which was later sent to the judge of Istanbul and registered in the court records to serve as a precedent for later cases. In the decree, the sultan informs the judge of Istanbul:

> despite the fact that they [that is, son of el-Ḥacc ᶜOs̱mān and the other Gypsies residing in Balat] are from the community of Muslims (*cemāᶜat-i müslimīn*), following the rules of gender segregation (*ehl-i perde*), praying five times a day, reciting *salawat-i sharifa* and reading the Koran properly (*tilāvet-i Ḳurʾān*) as well as protecting their family and household members from forbidden acts (*ehl ü ᶜiyāllerini ḥarāmdan ḥıfẓ edüb*) and some of them have even completed their hajj duty and indeed they even have a fatwa to prove their claim, they were still asked to pay poll-tax against the sharia and hence were humiliated and degraded by the tax-collectors.[31]

Accordingly, the sultan commands the judge of Istanbul that "if the Gypsies [who happen to come to the sharia courts] are from the community of Muslims, follow the gender segregation rules, pray five times a day, and are considered from the people of Islam [by the communities in which they reside], then they should not be required to pay poll-tax against the sharia and should not be humiliated."[32] Similarly, sometime in 1664, almost three decades before the imperial edict cited above, el-Ḥacc

28 See, for instance, USS 17 / 79b / 2; and USS 17 / 87a / 7.
29 Examples include ISS 3 / 94b /2; ISS 12 / 114b / 2; ISS 12 / 114b / 3; and BAB 54 / 95b/2.
30 BAB 54 / 95b / 2.
31 BAB 54 / 95b / 2.
32 BAB 54 / 95b / 2.

Meḥmed b. Bālī (literally, Meḥmed, the pilgrim son of Bālī), who happened to be muezzin at the mosque of Muṣṭafā Pasha and a resident of the Muṣṭafā Pasha neighborhood in the suburb of Eyüp, came to the local court and stated:

> [Despite the fact that] I am a Muslim and from the community of Prophet Muḥammad (*ehl-i sünnet*), residing in a Muslim neighborhood, praying five times a day with my community, fasting and preventing my family and children from having relationship with unrelated people in accordance with the sharia (*ehl ü ᶜiyālimi nā-maḥrem olan eşḫāṣdan ber-mūceb-i şerᶜ-i ḳavm ḳaçırub*) as well as already completed my hajj duty, I am still asked to pay poll-tax and constantly humiliated by the tax-collectors on the ground that my father, Bālī, was a Gypsy and his name is listed in the register of poll-tax payers.[33]

As in the case of Meḥmed and his friends, el-Ḥacc Meḥmed provided a fatwa to the court to support his claim.[34] Furthermore, his status as a trustworthy and practicing Muslim (*ṣāliḥ ve mütedeyyin*) was confirmed by other residents of his neighborhood. After having considered the fatwa and hearing the testimonies of the neighbors, the judge decided that Meḥmed, as a Muslim, was not obliged to pay a poll tax, on the grounds that his and his father's names were included in the poll-tax register of the Gypsies.[35]

The taxation of Gypsies—particularly the taxation of Muslim Gypsies by the Ottoman imperial state—is a point of contention among the few scholars who have written on the subject. Various interpretations respond to the fact that the Ottoman imperial state taxed Muslim Gypsies illegally, imposing a poll tax on them despite the fact that the amount of *cizye* that Muslim Gypsies paid was lower than the amount prescribed for non-Muslim Gypsies. According to İsmail Altınöz, the reason for this difference is related to Gypsies' perceived nominal attachment to Islam.[36] Eyal Ginio, on the other hand, argues that the root cause of this discriminatory policy

33 ISS 12 / 114b / 2.

34 Indeed, this particular fatwa was issued by Şeyḫü'l-islām Yaḥyā Efendi, one of the most reputable jurists of the seventeenth century, and is cited in extenso within the case.

35 ISS 12 / 114b / 3.

36 Altınöz, "Osmanlı Toplumunda Çingeneler," 204.

was not the Gypsies' otherness—the dominant explanation in the field—but rather is to be found in the local customs that prevailed in the Balkans before the Ottomans. He suggests that, because the poll tax was levied on Gypsies in the Balkans before the arrival of the Ottomans, the Ottomans continued collecting this tax and named it *bedel-i mektūʾ*—"the equivalent of the fixed tax." However, he contends that this was in fact a poll tax, and that *bedel-i mektūʾ* was merely a semantic device used to legitimize imposing the poll tax on a Muslim group.[37] I will not resolve this contested issue here. Nevertheless, both earlier scholarship and my rather preliminary readings of the seventeenth-century court records of Istanbul suggest three significant points. First, toward the end of the late sixteenth century we see the emergence of a new category of Gypsy in the imperial decrees related to taxation: "Gypsies with Muslim names." Second, these Gypsies were explicitly obliged to pay poll tax (*cizye*), despite the fact that the amount they paid was less than that paid by non-Muslim Gypsies. Third, despite the existence of such decrees dating from the seventeenth century onward, it is difficult to categorically state that Ottomans did in fact collect poll tax from *all* Gypsies who professed to be Muslim. These cases suggest that once Gypsies were settled and assimilated into the urban culture, followed gender segregation rules, and socialized with other Muslims rather than with their "Gypsy" brethren, most frequently the judge or the sultan himself responded to their petitions and acknowledged their right, as Muslims, not to pay the poll tax.

WERE ALL GYPSIES SEEN AS "EVIL-DOERS"?

To further heterogenize this narrative, I would like to look at certain roles that some Gypsies assumed at the court or in the administration of their communities. This will give us an opportunity to see that not all Gypsies were considered "morally slippery," at least from the perspective of local courts and tax-collecting officials who represented state authority at the local level. Gypsies at the court of Üsküdar appeared in various capacities—defendants and litigants, bail agents and fiscal guarantors (*kefīl bi'l-māl*) in credit and property transactions, guarantors for a person's whereabouts (*kefīl bi'l-nefs*), proxies (*vekīl*) to represent a client at the court or to collect imperial taxes in the vicinities of their own communities, guardians

37 Ginio, "Neither Muslims nor *Zimmis*," 130.

of minors (*vāṣī*),[38] and witnesses (*ṣuhūdu'l-ḥāl*)—mostly in cases related their own communities. Once they appeared at the court as witnesses, the "Gypsy" tag after their names was removed, except in cases in which all witnesses were gypsies.[39] Among the gypsies who sat at the court as expert witnesses, Durmuş b. Pazarlı and Ḳoçi b. Çaḳır are most noticeable. The court records provide ample evidence for the various roles they assumed in their community beyond sitting as witnesses at the court.

THE CASE OF DURMUŞ B. PAZARLI

In a copy of the imperial fiscal register found in a court register in the Üsküdar court records, Durmuş b. Pazarlı was originally registered in Istanbul and at some point came to Üsküdar.[40] From the same registration we see that he belonged to the community (*cemāᶜat*) of Yolcu, which was attached to the *imaret* waqf of the late Sultan Bāyezīd II (r. 1481–1512), along with Fotini veled-i ... (?), Ḳoçi veled-i Çaḳır, and Çavuş veled-i ᶜAbdullāh.[41] Despite the fact that Durmuş was identified as Durmuş veled-i Pazarlı in the fiscal survey, in the documents drafted by the court he was almost exclusively recorded as Durmuş b. Pazarlı, indicating that, at least from the court's perspective, he was Muslim.[42] As to his resident status, Durmuş b. Pazarlı was most likely a seminomadic Gypsy. He is consistently identified as being from the community of Gypsies, with no further tag, such as the name of a neighborhood or a village, attached to his identification. It seems that he served his community in several capacities. First, he appears to have been a major creditor. He often gave loans using gold (coins).[43] Although he was mostly a creditor to individuals from his own community, there are also instances in which he was involved with individuals from different communities. Court records also suggest that Durmuş b. Pazarlı was involved in the administration of his own community. He was appointed as proxy and

38 See, for instance, USS 27 / 58 / 4.

39 USS 56 / 40a / 3.

40 USS 17/ 79b / 2; for a similar type of registration, see also USS 17 / 87a / 7.

41 USS 17 / 79b / 2.

42 It should be noted that the *bin* and *veled* formula, which was deployed as a textual technology to differentiate between Muslims and non-Muslims in legal practices that we encounter in the later centuries of Ottoman rule, had not yet been established systematically in sixteenth-century Üsküdar.

43 See, for instance, USS 20 / 97b / 3; and USS 22 / 42b / 5.

nā'ib-i menāb to collect taxes from gypsies living in Üsküdar.[44] In this capacity, he brought individuals who failed to pay their taxes to the attention of the court. For instance, in 1556 he brought Ḥasan b. Ḳaya, from the community of Gypsies, and accused him of not paying his obligatory tax, called *kesim*, for the previous three years, when he was traveling with a group of Gypsies (*üç yıldır ḳatana ile göçüb ḳonub*). As Ḥasan b. Ḳaya did not have an official certificate (*temessük*) claiming otherwise, he was required to pay fifty silver aspers (*aḳçe*) for each year he was missing.[45] Furthermore, he brought many individual Gypsies to the court for various transgressions, together with other local officials who represented imperial authority. For instance, in 1562, together with Alagöz Bey b. ᶜAbdullāh, the proxy of the police superintendent (*subaşı*) of Üsküdar, Ḥasan brought to the court Şamli b. Kulfāl, from the community of the "Crazy Gypsy" (*Deli Çingāne tā'ifesinden*), accusing him of being publicly intoxicated.[46] He also acted as guarantor for criminal suspects (*kefīl bi'l-nefs*). In this capacity, his role entailed ensuring that suspects did not evade the law by simply disappearing. For instance, in 1550 he provided guarantee for the presence of a Gypsy nicknamed Poyraz whenever he might be requested by the court.[47] Yet, most significantly, he served as a witness in cases related to Gypsies. Among 233 entries that mention at least one Gypsy, Durmuş b. Pazarlı appears within the ranks of witnesses (*şuhūdu'l-ḥāl*) at least ten times.[48] When he is registered as a witness, as in the cases of many non-Muslims, his Gypsy tag is omitted.

There were two levels at which witnesses served at court: "circumstantial/occurrence witnesses" (*ᶜudūl-ımuslimūn*) and "instrumental witnesses" (*şuhūdu'l-ḥāl*).[49] In the former capacity, they bore witness to happenings or facts pertaining to a case and often spoke in support of a litigant, verifying his or her testimony. Indeed, "*ᶜudūl* testified for the plaintiff

44 USS 20 / 105b / 4.

45 USS 18 / 27a / 2.

46 USS 25 / 34a / 295.

47 USS 27 / 97 / last entry.

48 Examples include USS 15 / 51b / 5; USS 15 /56b / 3; USS 17 / 28b / 3; USS 17 / 35b / 3; USS 22 / 50b / 2; USS 22 / 51a / 1; and USS 25 / 32b / 5.

49 Hülya Canbakal translates *şuhūdu'l-ḥāl* as "instrumental witnesses" and *ᶜudūl-u müslimūn* as "circumstantial/occurrence witnesses." Leslie Peirce, on the other hand, prefers to use "case witnesses" for *şuhūdu'l-ḥāl*. See Canbakal, "Ayntab at the End of the Seventeenth-Century," 201; and Peirce, *Morality Tales*, 97. Following Canbakal, in this study I use "witnesses" for both *şuhūdu'l-ḥāl* and *ᶜudūl-u müslimūn*.

(occasionally, for the defendant) and were introduced by the litigants themselves as 'evidence' (*beyyine*)."[50] In the latter capacity, they testified to the soundness of the proceedings as a whole. "Instrumental" witnesses for a particular case were members of the community, usually three or four in number, whose names were inscribed in court registers following the record of the case.

Durmuş b. Pazarlı served at court in both of these capacities. In one instance, a Gypsy named ᶜArab b. Ḳosta denied being bailiff (*kefīl bi'l-māl*) for another Gypsy in a credit transaction case. Durmuş b. Pazarlı and Ḳoca b. Ḳaragöz (both registered as being from the community of Gypsies) were brought to the court as witnesses by the defendant, Ḳoçi b. Resūl (again from the community of Gypsies), and they substantiated the defendant's claim.[51] Similarly, as we saw above, a certain ᶜAbdī b. Ḥasan, from the city of Üsküdar, brought a Gypsy woman, Fāṭima bt. ᶜAbdullāh, to court for pickpocketing; Ḳoçi b. Çingāne was registered among the "righteous Muslims" (*ᶜudūl-u müslimūn*). Along with three other Muslim males, he substantiated the defendant's claim by testifying against Fāṭima bt. ᶜAbdullāh. It is significant to note that once Ḳoçi b. Çaḳır was registered among the "righteous Muslims," his Gypsy identity was not mentioned.[52] Nevertheless, whenever he came to the court, as litigant or defendant, his Gypsy identity was clearly spelled out.[53]

Both Ḳoçi b. Çaḳır and Durmuş b. Pazarlı sat in the court as witnesses for cases related to their own communities. Whether they also sat as witnesses for other communities is a question that must be addressed. In a fatwa issued by a famous jurist and grand mufti of the sixteenth century, İbn Kemāl (d. 1535), we see that the testimony of Gypsies (along with that of many others) was deemed invalid.[54] Nevertheless, those Gypsies who pursued a settled life, were Muslim in creed, and were well established in the communities where they lived occasionally sat as witnesses for cases not necessarily related to Gypsies. My examples are

50 Canbakal, "Ayntab at the End of the Seventeenth Century," 205.

51 USS 15 / 93a / 1.

52 USS 29 / 80a / 4. For the full translation of this case, see Çelik, "'Community in Motion,'" 285.

53 See, for instance, USS 22 / 47 a / 2; USS 22 / 50b / 3; and USS 22 / 52b / 1.

54 This fatwa is quoted and translated partly in Peirce, *Morality Tales*, 160. Its transcribed version in the modern Turkish alphabet can be found in İnanır, "İbn Kemal'in Fetvaları Işığında Osmanlı'da İslâm Hukuku," 142. For its English translation and annotation, see Çelik, "'Community in Motion,'" 207–10.

very few in number at this point, but they are significant nonetheless. For instance, in 1544, a certain Ḥasan b. Eşref, from the village of Viran, was brought to the court, where he confessed, "I have a loan of two hundred sixty five *aḳçe* to be paid back to this Ramażān b. Yaᶜḳūb." Apparently Ramażān b. Yaᶜḳūb had inherited this money from his late father, with whom Ḥasan b. Eşref had a credit relationship. In this inheritance case, Maḥmūd, a Gypsy, sat among the *şuhūdu'l-ḥāl*, along with Mesᶜūd b. Bāyezīd, Ḥüseyin b. Babacıḳ, and others.[55] Although those males who served as witnesses along with Maḥmūd were inscribed into the record only as being Muslim, in Maḥmūd's case the scribe underscored his "ethnicity" by spelling out *ḳıbṭī* (Gypsy) before his name. Notable also is the fact that neither Ramażān b. Yaᶜḳūb nor Ḥasan b. Eşref seems to have been from the community of Gypsies. Therefore, Maḥmūd's involvement in the court procedure makes one wonder about his status in the community. In a registration entry recorded six years after this inheritance case, we come across Maḥmūd again. This time, the case is related to the taxation of those Gypsies who were registered in Istanbul in the imperial registry but resided in Üsküdar. In this registration, the ways in which Maḥmūd is mentioned suggest that he was an important figure in the community, in that he was charged with collecting taxes from Gypsies living in Istanbul and Edirne.[56]

Similarly, in a court register from seventeenth-century Manisa, we find Cingen Ḥüseyin (literally, Ḥüseyin the Gypsy) among the *şuhūdu'l-ḥāl*, along with other Muslims, in a divorce case between Nesliḫān bt. Meḥmed Çelebī, from the neighborhood of Bölüçek-i Cedid, and Mūsā b. Aḥmed.[57] Why did Cingen Ḥüseyin testify in a case not related to his own community? Unfortunately, the manner in which the case is registered provides no further information about either his profession or his wealth. Yet we come across Cingen Ḥüseyin's name again once because his daughter, Fāṭima, came to the court to register her marriage to Aḥmed b. Ḥüseyin, an adult male from the community of Gypsies. Apparently Cingen Ḥüseyin and his family were settled Muslim Gypsies living in the neighborhood of Bektaş in the city of Manisa. The rather high amount of *mihr-i müᵓeccel*, along with other household items, offered to his

55 USS 13 / 21b / 260.

56 USS 17/ 87a / 7.

57 MSS 124 / 105b / 3. MSS stands for Manisa Court Records (*Manisa Şerᶜiyye Sicilleri*), followed by volume number, folio number, and entry number.

daughter by her husband as dowry might be indicative of the family's status in the community.[58]

CONCLUSIONS

To write a history of Gypsies in the early modern Ottoman Empire is a daunting task that requires overcoming a number of historical, theoretical, and methodological challenges. These challenges stem from the limitations of the historical sources on Gypsies, the variety of narratives—shifting from popular to academic, from politically engaged to "objective"—produced on the history of Gypsies, and the deployment of contested concepts such as "marginality," "ethnicity," and "race" with almost no problematization, contextualization, or historicization in contemporary scholarship.[59] In this study, I have endeavored to underline challenges regarding sources. While we have many accounts—memories and travelogues, or, later, novels and short stories—produced not only by European travelers and consuls but also by the Ottomans themselves concerning Gypsy lifestyles in the nineteenth and early twentieth centuries, the available literary and narrative sources are rather limited as far as the early modern period is concerned. In addition to being limited in number, these sources, as we have seen, were written by the learned male elite who belonged to the upper echelons of Ottoman society, and, as such, they represent upper-class perceptions and biases toward Gypsies. These challenges pertaining to narrative sources led me to read them in concert with Ottoman sharia court records, considered by Ottomanists to be the most reliable sources for reconstructing the everyday life and survival tactics of various subaltern groups. Despite their limitations as historical sources, which have already been identified by numerous Ottomanists,[60] court records at once read as both text and document, providing us with not only the ways in which Gypsies were identified, categorized, and perceived by those who held power at the local or imperial level but also how they were seen and approached by the larger

58 MSS 124 / 113b / 4 and 114 b / 1.

59 Further on this scholarship, see Çelik, "'Community in Motion,'" 48–92.

60 Examples include Ze'evi, "The Use of Ottoman Sharīᶜa Court Records as a Source of Middle Eastern Social History"; Agmon, "Women's History and Ottoman *Sharīᶜa* Court Records"; and Agmon and Shahar, "Shifting Perspectives in the Study of Sharīᶜa Courts."

community in which they lived. Moreover, court records are invaluable for revealing Gypsies' socio-economic resources as well as the various responsibilities that they undertook in managing their communities, not to mention some of the roles they assumed as witnesses (*ṣuhūdu'l-ḥāl* or *ᶜudūl-u muslimūn*) in the adjudication process. More significantly, albeit in certain translations,[61] the court records provide us occasions to hear the voices of Gypsies themselves and to learn how they resisted, acted upon, and negotiated their status vis-à-vis the unlawful practices directed against them.

One of the main questions of this study was how the category of *çingāne* or *ḳıbṭī* was understood and represented by early modern Ottomans. The modern conception of Gypsies as constituting an ethnic group whose origin dates back to India was absent in early modern Ottoman discourse. As we have seen, Ottomans in different times constructed various origin stories for Gypsies; yet, up until the late nineteenth century, these origin stories had nothing to do with India. While in the dream of Sedefkār Meḥmed Agha, "Gypsy" was associated with *jinns* and demons, in the accounts of the celebrated seventeenth-century traveler Evliyā Çelebī and the famous Moldavian nobleman Dimitrie Cantemir, Gypsies were thought to be from Egypt. As interesting as these origin stories may be, what makes these three narratives worth exploring further is the manner in which Gypsies were represented: in all three accounts, Gypsies are presumed to be poor, dirty, illiterate, morally inferior, and nominally Muslim but talented musicians and dancers.

Another question that this study seeks to answer is whether court records can help us heterogenize the "Gypsy" image epitomized in narrative sources? In other words, can various stigmatizations attributed to Gypsies as a *community* in narrative sources also be read in court records, or do such documents help us to undo this image in any way? First, what emerges from the sixteenth-and early seventeenth-century court records of Üsküdar (on which this study is primarily based) is that, like other inhabitants of Üsküdar, local Gypsies were clients of the sharia court, though perhaps to lesser degree. They came to the court to submit claims against

61 Court records translate certain words against the framework of legal categories and court recording procedure. In doing so, they privilege specific terminologies, values, and meanings while remaining silent on others. For detailed discussions of these issues, see Ergene, *Local Court, Provincial Society, and Justice in the Ottoman Empire*, 125–141; al-Qattan, "Dhimmis in the Muslim Court," especially 142–145.

others, or were obliged to appear in court to defend themselves against allegations; they registered all kinds of agreements and also appeared as taxpayers. Gypsy clients of the court—men or women, nomadic, semi-nomadic, or (recently) settled—were always labeled as *çingāne* or *ḳıbṭī*, an affiliation drawn on the basis of "ethnicity" rather than "religion," which was, until recently, considered to be the main category that marked one's status in Ottoman society. Nevertheless, this reference to "ethnicity" must be qualified. In the textual world of the court records, I suggest (following Leslie Pierce), that "ethnicity" was a label used for those who had yet to be assimilated into the settled urban life of the empire, including (but not only) Gypsies.

Second, despite being tagged as "Gypsy"—which (in the textual world of the court records) eventually differentiated them from the larger Muslim and non-Muslim communities—in the legal processes that they encountered and the justice they received, Gypsies were no more disadvantaged than their Muslim and non-Muslim counterparts.[62] Claims and petitions submitted by *Muslim* Gypsies regarding unjust poll-tax collections by a Muslim community are a case in point. Though presently very few in number, these cases demonstrate that once Gypsies were settled and assimilated into the urban culture, and once their conversion to Islam was complete and their "good Muslim" status was confirmed by other residents of their neighborhoods, the judge or the sultan himself responded to their petitions and acknowledged their right, as Muslims, not to pay the poll tax.

Finally, contrary to the images drawn from the available narratives and the many decrees found in the *mühimme* registers of the period, court records also suggest that not all Gypsies were considered "evil-doers" or "morally slippery" in everyday practices. As the examples I provide from the court records suggest, some Gypsies were well established in terms of wealth and social status in their own communities, and some even proved sufficiently morally upright to sit as witnesses in cases involving the broader Muslim community.

62 Hallaq makes the same observation for women and non-Muslims. See Hallaq, *Sharīʿa*, especially Chapter 4.

BIBLIOGRAPHY

Sources

Court Records

Üsküdar Mahkemesi Şer^ciyye Sicilleri (USS): Vols. 7–20, 22–23, 25–29, 51, 56, 84.

Manisa Mahkemesi Şer^ciyye Sicilleri (MSS): Vol. 124.

BOA

Istanbul, Başbakanlık Osmanlı Arşivi. Mühimme Defteri (MD) 3–60.

Istanbul, Başbakanlık Osmanlı Arşivi. KK–67, 356/1.

Istanbul, Başbakanlık Osmanlı Arşivi. KK–67, 488/2.

Istanbul, Başbakanlık Osmanlı Arşivi. KK–67, 1258/1.

3 Numaralı Mühimme Defteri (966–968 / 1558–1560). 2 vols. [Vol. 1: Facsimile; Vol. 2: Summary and Transcription]. Edited by İsmet Binark, Necati Aktaş, and Necati Gültepe. Ankara: T. C. Başbakanlık Devlet Arşivleri Genel Müdürlüğü, 1993.

5 Numaralı Mühimme Defteri (973 / 1565–1566). 2 vols. [Vol. 1: Summary and Index; Vol. 2: Facsimile]. Edited by İsmet Binark, Necati Aktaş, and Necati Gültepe. Ankara: T. C. Başbakanlık Devlet Arşivleri Genel Müdürlüğü, 1994.

6 Numaralı Mühimme Defteri (972 / 1564–1565). 3 vols. [Vol. 1–2: Summary, Transcription, and Index; Vol. 3: Facsimile]. Edited by İsmet Binark, Necati Aktaş, and Necati Gültepe. Ankara: T. C. Başbakanlık Devlet Arşivleri Genel Müdürlüğü, 1995.

7 Numaralı Mühimme Defteri (975–976 /1567–1569). 4 vols. [Vol. 1–2: Facsimile; Vol. 3–4: Summary, Transcription, and Index]. Edited by Murat Şener, Nurullah İşler, and H. Osman Yıldırım. Ankara: T. C. Başbakanlık Devlet Arşivleri Genel Müdürlüğü, 1997.

12 Numaralı Mühimme Defteri (978–979 / 1570–1572). 3 vols. [Vol. 1–2: Summary, Transcription, and Index; Vol. 3: Facsimile]. Edited by İsmet Binark, Necati Aktaş, and Necati Gültepe. Ankara: T. C. Başbakanlık Devlet Arşivleri Genel Müdürlüğü, 1996.

Ca^cfer Efendi. *Risāle-i mi^cmāriyye*. Edited by Howard Crane as *Risāle-i mi^cmāriyye: An Early-Seventeenth-Century Ottoman Treatise on Architecture: Facsimile with Translation and Notes*. Leiden: Brill, 1987.

İstanbul Kadı Sicilleri Bâb Mahkemesi 54 Numaralı Sicil (H. 1102 / M. 1691). Edited by Yılmaz Karaca, Rasim Erol, Salih Kahriman, Fuat Recep, Sabri Atay, and Hüseyin Kılıç. Istanbul: İSAM, 2010.

İstanbul Kadı Sicilleri İstanbul Mahkemesi 3 Numaralı Sicil (H. 1027 / M. 1618). Edited by Yılmaz Karaca, Rasim Erol, Salih Kahriman, Fuat Recep, Sabri Atay, and Hüseyin Kılıç. Istanbul: İSAM, 2010.

İstanbul Kadı Sicilleri İstanbul Mahkemesi 12 Numaralı Sicil (H. 1073–1074 / M. 1663–1664). Edited by Yılmaz Karaca, Rasim Erol, Salih Kahriman, Fuat Recep, Sabri Atay, and Hüseyin Kılıç. Istanbul: İSAM, 2010.

İstanbul Kadı Sicilleri Üsküdar Mahkemesi 1 Numaralı Sicil (H. 919–927 / M. 1513–1521). Edited by Bilgin Aydın and Ekrem Tak. Istanbul: İSAM, 2010.

İstanbul Kadı Sicilleri Üsküdar Mahkemesi 9 Numaralı Sicil (H. 940–942 / M. 1534–1536). Edited by Kenan Yıldız. Istanbul: İSAM, 2010.

İstanbul Kadı Sicilleri Üsküdar Mahkemesi 14 Numaralı Sicil (H. 953–955 / M. 1546–1549). Edited by Nuray Güler. Istanbul: İSAM, 2010.

İstanbul Kadı Sicilleri Üsküdar Mahkemesi 17 Numaralı Sicil (H. 956–963 / M. 1549–1556). Edited by Orhan Gültekin. Istanbul: İSAM, 2010.

İstanbul Kadı Sicilleri Üsküdar Mahkemesi 26 Numaralı Sicil (H. 970–971 / M. 1562–1563). Edited by Rıfat Günalan. Istanbul: İSAM, 2010.

İstanbul Kadı Sicilleri Üsküdar Mahkemesi 51 Numaralı Sicil (H. 987–988 / M. 1579–1580). Edited by Rıfat Günalan. Istanbul: İSAM, 2010.

İstanbul Kadı Sicilleri Üsküdar Mahkemesi 56 Numaralı Sicil (H. 990–991 / M. 1582–1583). Edited by Hilal Kazan and Kenan Yıldız. Istanbul: İSAM, 2010.

İstanbul Kadı Sicilleri Üsküdar Mahkemesi 84 Numaralı Sicil (H. 999–1000 / M. 1590–1591). Edited by Rıfat Günalan. Istanbul: İSAM, 2010.

Studies

Agmon, Iris. "Women's History and Ottoman *Sharīʿa* Court Records: Shifting Perspectives in Social History." *Hawwa* 2 (2004): 172–209.

Agmon, Iris, and Ido Shahar. "Theme Issue: Shifting Perspectives in the Study of Shariʿa Courts: Methodologies and Paradigms." *Islamic Law and Society* 15 (2008): 1–19.

Akdağ, Mustafa. *Celâlî İsyanları (1550–1603)*. Ankara: Ankara Üniversitesi, Dil ve Tarih-Coğrafya Fakültesi, 1963.

Akdağ, Mustafa. *Türk Halkının Dirlik ve Düzenlik Kavgası*. Ankara: Bilgi Yayınevi, 1975.

Aksu, Mustafa. *Türkiye'de Çingene Olmak*. Istanbul: Ozan Yayıncılık, 2003.

Alpman, Nazım. *Başka Dünyanın İnsanları Çingeneler*. Istanbul: Ozan Yayıncılık, 1997.

Altınöz, İsmail Haşim. "Osmanlı Toplumunda Çingeneler." Ph.D. diss., Istanbul University, 2005.

Attridge, Derek. "Language as History/History as Language: Saussure and the Romance of Etymology." In *Post-Structuralism and the Question of History*, edited by Derek Attridge, Geoff Bennington, and Robert Young, 183–211. Cambridge: Cambridge University Press, 1989.

Barany, Zoltan. *The East European Gypsies: Regime Change, Marginality, and Ethnopolitics*. Cambridge: Cambridge University Press, 2002.

Barany, Zoltan. "The Poverty of Gypsy Studies." *News Net* 40, no. 003 (2000): 1–4.

Braude, Benjamin, and Bernard Lewis, eds. *Christians and Jews in the Ottoman Empire: The Functioning of a Plural Society*. 2 vols. New York: Holmes & Meier, 1982.

Campbell, Gordon, ed. *The Oxford Dictionary of the Renaissance*. Oxford: Oxford University Press, 2003.

Canbakal, Hülya. "Ayntab at the End of the Seventeenth Century: A Study of Notables and Urban Politics." Ph.D. diss., Harvard University, 1999.

Canbakal, Hülya. *Society and Politics in an Ottoman Town: ᶜAyntāb in the 17th Century*. Leiden: Brill, 2007.

Casale, Giancarlo. "The Ethnic Composition of Ottoman Ship Crews and the 'Rumi Challenge' to Portuguese Identity." *Medieval Encounters* 13, no. 1 (2007): 122–44.

Crowe, David M. "Roma: The Gypsies." In *Encyclopedia of European Social History: From 1350–2000*, 5:449. New York: Scribner, 2001.

Çelik, Faika. "'Civilizing Mission' in the Late Ottoman Discourse: The Case of Gypsies." *Oriento Moderno* 93 (2013): 577–97.

Çelik, Faika. "'Community in Motion': Gypsies in Ottoman Imperial State Policy, Public Morality and at the Sharia Court of Üsküdar (1530s–1585s)." Ph.D. diss., McGill University, 2013.

Çelik, Faika. "Exploring Marginality in the Ottoman Empire: Gypsies or People of Malice (*Ehl-i Fesad*) as Viewed by the Ottomans." *European University Institute Working Papers* 39 (2004): 1–21.

Çelik, Faika. "Gypsies (Roma) in the Orbit of Islam: The Ottoman Experience (1450–1600)." M. A. thesis, McGill University, 2003.

Çelik, Faika. "The Limits of Tolerance: The Status of Gypsies (*Roma*) in the Ottoman Empire." *Studies in Contemporary Islam* 5, nos. 1–2 (2003): 161–82.

Çelik, Faika. "Probing the Margins: Gypsies (Roma) in the Sixteenth Century Ottoman Society." In *Subalterns and Social Protest: History from Below in the Middle East and North Africa*, edited by Stephanie Cronin, 173–99. London: Routledge, 2007.

Dankoff, Robert, and Victor Friedman. "The Earliest Text in Balkan (Rumelian) Romani: A Passage from Evliya Çelebi's *Seyaḥāt nāmeh*." *Journal of the Gypsy Lore Society* (1991): 1–20.

De Tapia, Stéphane. "Le lexique anatolien de la mobilité et de la migration (göçebe, yörük, yaylaci, muhacir, göçmen, gurbetçi. . .)." *Turcica* 42 (2010): 89–140.

Ergene, Boğaç A. *Local Court, Provincial Society, and Justice in the Ottoman Empire: Legal Practice and Dispute Resolution in Çankırı and Kastamonu (1652–1744)*. Leiden: Brill, 2003.

Fraser, Angus M. *The Gypsies*. Oxford: Blackwell, 1992.

Ginio, Eyal. "Neither Muslims nor *Zimmi*s: The Gypsies (Roma) in the Ottoman Empire." *Romani Studies* 5 (2004): 117–44.

Gökbuğa, Ferdi. "1075–1076/M. 1665–1666 Tarihli 124 No'lu Manisa Şerᶜiyye Sicili Transkripsiyonu ve Değerlendirilmesi." M. A. thesis, Celal Bayar University, 2008.

Hallaq, Wael B. *Sharīᶜa: Theory, Practice, Transformations*. Cambridge: Cambridge University Press, 2009.

Hanna, Nabil Sobhi. *Ghagar of Sett Guiranha: A Study of a Gypsy Community in Egypt.* Cairo: American University of Cairo, 1982.

Hasluck, Margaret. "Firman of A. H. 1013–14 (A.D. 1604–5) Regarding Gypsies in the Western Balkans." *Journal of the Gypsy Lore Society* (Third Series) 27, nos. 1–2 (1948): 1–12.

İnalcık, Halil. *The Ottoman Empire: The Classical Age, 1300–1600.* London: Weidenfeld & Nicolson, 1973.

İnanır, Ahmet. "İbn Kemal'in Fetvaları Işığında Osmanlı'da İslâm Hukuku." M. A. thesis, Istanbul University, 2008.

Kafadar, Cemal. "Janissaries and Other Riffraff of Ottoman Istanbul: Rebels without a Cause?." In *Identity and Identity Formation in the Ottoman World,* edited by Baki Tezcan and Karl K. Barbir, 113–34. Madison: University of Wisconsin Press, 2007.

Kafadar, Cemal. "A Rome of One's Own: Reflections on Cultural Geography and Identity in the Lands of Rum." *Muqarnas* 24 (2007): 7–25.

Kasaba, Reşat. *A Moveable Empire: Ottoman Nomads, Migrants, and Refugees.* Seattle: University of Washington Press, 2009.

Kenrick, Donald. *From India to the Mediterranean: The Migration of the Gypsies.* Toulouse: Gypsy Research Centre CRDP Midi Pyrénées, 1993.

Kunt, Metin. "Ethnic-Regional (*Cins*) Solidarity in the Seventeenth-Century Ottoman Establishment." *International Journal of Middle East Studies* 5, no. 3 (1974): 233–39.

Levy, Juliette de Bairacli. "The Gypsies of Turkey." *Journal of the Gypsy Lore Society* (Third series) 31 (1952): 5–13.

Lewis, Bernard. *Race and Slavery in the Middle East: A Historical Enquiry.* Oxford: Oxford University Press, 1992.

Lucassen, Leo, and Wim Willems. "The Weakness of Well-Ordered Societies: Gypsies in Western Europe, the Ottoman Empire, and India, 1400–1914." *Review (Fernand Braudel Center)* (2003): 283–313.

Lucassen, Leo, Wim Willems, and Annemaried Cottaar, eds. *Gypsies and Other Itinerant Groups: A Socio-Historical Approach.* Basingstoke: Macmillan, 1998.

Marsh, Adrian. "No Promised Land: History, Historiography and the Origins of Gypsies." Ph.D. diss., University of Greenwich, 2008.

Marsh, Adrian, and Elin Strand, eds. *Gypsies and the Problem of Identities: Contextual, Constructed and Contested.* Istanbul: Swedish Research Institute in Istanbul, 2006.

Marushiakova, Elena, and Veselin Popov. *Gypsies in the Ottoman Empire: A Contribution to the History of the Balkans.* Edited by Donald Kenrick. Paris: Centre de recherches tsiganes, 2001.

Mayall, David. *Gypsy Identities 1500–2000: From Egipcyans and Moon-men to the Ethnic Romany.* London: Routledge, 2004.

Niyazioğlu, Aslı. "Dreams, Ottoman Biography Writing, and the Halveti-Sünbüli Sheikhs of Sixteenth Century Istanbul." In *Many Ways of Speaking about the Self, Middle*

Eastern Ego-Documents in Arabic, Persian and Turkish (14th–20th Century), edited by Ralph Elger and Yavuz Erköse, 171–85. Wiesbaden: Harrassowitz, 2010.

Niyazioğlu, Aslı. "How to Read an Ottoman Poet's Dream? Friends, Patrons and the Execution of Fiġānī (d. 938/1532)." *Middle Eastern Literatures* 16, no. 1 (2013): 48–59.

Niyazioğlu, Aslı. "The Very Special Dead and a Seventeenth-Century Ottoman Poet: Nevʾīzāde ʿAṭāʾī's Reasons for Composing his *Mes̱nevīs*." *Archivum Ottomanicum* 25 (2008): 221–32.

Okely, Judith. *The Traveller Gypsies*. Cambridge: Cambridge University Press, 1983.

Oprişan, Ana. "An Overview of the Romanlar in Turkey." In *Gypsies and the Problem of Identities: Contextual, Constructed and Contested*, edited by Adrian Marsh and Elin Strand, 163–70. Istanbul: Swedish Research Institute in Istanbul, 2006.

Özkan, Ali Rafet. *Türkiye Çingeneleri*. Ankara: Kültür Bakanlıgı, 2000.

Paspatēs, Alexandros Geōrgios. *Études sur les Tchinghianés; ou, Bohémiens de l'Empire ottoman*. Constantinople: Impr. A. Koroméla, 1870.

Peirce, Leslie. *Morality Tales: Law and Gender in the Ottoman Court of Aintab*. Berkeley: University of California Press, 2003.

Pym, Richard. *The Gypsies of Early Modern Spain, 1425–1783*. Basingstoke: Palgrave Macmillan, 2007.

al-Qattan, Najwa. "Dhimmis in the Muslim Court: Documenting Justice in Ottoman Damascus 1775–1860." Ph.D. diss., Harvard University, 1996.

al-Qattan, Najwa. "Textual Differentiation in the Damascus Sijill: Religious Discrimination or Politics of Gender?" In *Women, the Family, and Divorce Laws in Islamic History*, edited by A. E. A. Sonbol, 191–201. Syracuse: Syracuse University Press, 1997.

Sariyanis, Marinos. "Mob, Scamps and Rebels in Seventeenth Century Istanbul: Some Remarks on Ottoman Social Vocabulary." *International Journal of Turkish Studies* 11 (2005): 1–15.

Soulis, George C. "The Gypsies in the Byzantine Empire and the Balkans in the late Middle Ages." *Dumbarton Oaks Papers* 15 (1961): 141–65.

Şerifgil, Enver M. "XVI. Yüzyılda Rumeli Eyaleti'ndeki Çingeneler." *Türk Dünyasındaki Araştırmalar Dergisi* 15 (1981): 117–44.

Tamdoğan, Işık. "L'écrit comme échec de l'oral? L'oralité des engagements et des règlements à travers les registres de cadis d'Adana au XVIIIe siècle." *Revue du monde Musulman et de la Mediterrenée* 75–76 (1995): 155–65.

Tezcan, Baki. "Dispelling the Darkness: The Politics of 'Race' in the Early Seventeenth-Century Ottoman Empire in the Light of the Life and Work of Mullah Ali." *International Journal of Turkish Studies* 13 (2007): 73–95.

Tietze, Andreas. *Tarihi ve Etimolojik Türkiye Türkçesi Lugatı = Sprachgeschichtliches und etymologisches Wörterbuch des Türkei-Türkischen*. Istanbul: Simurg, 2002.

Trumpener, Katie. "The Time of the Gypsies: A "People without History" in the Narratives of the West." *Critical Inquiry* 18 (1992): 843–84.

Willems, Wim. *In Search of the True Gypsy: From Enlightenment to Final Solution.* London: Frank Cass, 1997.

Yıldız, Hüseyin. "Türkçede Çingeneler İçin Kullanılan Kelimeler ve Bunların Etimolojileri." *Dil Araştırmaları Dergisi* 1, no. 1 (2007): 61–82.

Ze'evi, Dror. "The Use of Ottoman Sharīʿa Court Records as a Source of Middle Eastern Social History: A Reappraisal." *Islamic Law and Society* 5, no. 1 (1998): 35–56.

Gendered Infidels in Fiction: A Case Study on Ṣābit's *Ḥikāye-i H̱ᵛāce Fesād*

İpek Hüner-Cora

This article centers on Ṣābit's *Ḥikāye-i H̱ᵛāce Fesād*, the seventeenth-century fictional story of an Armenian couple and two male tricksters, told in verse form (*meṣnevī*).[1] It aims to underline the significance of gender as a crucial factor in understanding ethno-religious representations and prejudices in Ottoman fiction by drawing attention to the representation of different genders throughout the narration. Over the following pages, after introducing the story and its author, I will discuss the church and Christianity as a setting for Ottoman fiction, with a focus on humorous and mocking representations of Christianity and of non-Muslims in literature. I will then focus on the narration of the rape of the Armenian woman as a fictional moment to discuss gender roles in representations of non-Muslims. My close reading, as one possible reading among many, suggests that the trick and the rape primarily target the Armenian husband, who is described with pejorative references to

---

* I am grateful to the editors, the members of the Early Modern Workshop at the University of Chicago, Kara A. Peruccio, Yaşar Tolga Cora, and the two anonymous reviewers for their very useful comments on previous drafts of this study. I owe special thanks to Helga Anetshofer, who read Ṣābit's *meṣnevī*s with me.

1 This *meṣnevī* is titled *Ḥikāye-i H̱ᵛāce Fesād* in some manuscripts and *Derenāme* in others. Turgut Karacan published it as *Derenāme ya da Hāce Fesad ve Söz Ebesi.* Throughout this paper, I refer to the manuscript copy titled *Ḥikāyet-i H̱ᵛāce Fesād* in Süleymaniye Library, Ali Nihat Tarlan 2/3 [100a–103b]. Unless otherwise noted, all translations are mine.

his ethno-religious background. The victim of the rape, the Armenian woman, is of secondary importance to the narration, as is her ethno-religious background.

THE STORY: ḤİKĀYE-İ H̬ᵛĀCE FESĀD

The protagonist of the *Ḥikāye-i H̬ᵛāce Fesād* is a man of evil nature (*söz ebesi*) who has fallen in love with a married Armenian woman. The "lover" in this story is not a man of virtue, nor does his love change him into a better man. Furthermore, this is not a story of conversion or high morals, pointing the readers or the audience toward the right path, but rather an obscene story about worldly desires. The man is described as a mad and untrustworthy trickster who is prone to inducing sedition and seduction. He is portrayed as both a womanizer and a pederast, showing a strong desire for male slaves and dancers.[2] In S̱ābit's words, "his place was ready in every hell."[3] He attempts to reach the Armenian woman through several means, yet all of his efforts are in vain. He decides to seek help from his trickster friend, the master of sedition (*h̬ᵛāce fesād*). Upon hearing that the Armenian woman has gone with her husband to their orchard, the evil man and the master of sedition also go there. At the master's suggestion, the evil man cross-dresses as a pregnant woman who is going into labor. Then, pretending to be helpless, the master runs to the Armenian couple. He asks for the Armenian woman's help for his pregnant wife. The Armenian woman rushes to the "pregnant wife" to help with the delivery, but she finds only the evil man, agitated and ready to rape her. She calls to her husband for help, saying, "Come here, it is a male"—rendered in Ottoman Turkish as, "It is a man."[4] Upon hearing this, the husband assumes that she is talking about the sex of the baby and does nothing. When the master of sedition joins the evil man to seize the opportunity, the Armenian woman yells that there are two men, but the husband simply thinks that the "pregnant woman" has given birth to twins. At the end of the story, the men sneak away, and the husband has no clue as to what has happened to his wife. The readers do not learn what becomes of the Armenian woman or the two men.

---

2 S̱ābit, *Ḥikāye-i H̬ᵛāce Fesād*, 100a12–21.
3 S̱ābit, *Ḥikāye-i H̬ᵛāce Fesād*, 100a19: "her cehennemde yeri ḥāżır idi."
4 S̱ābit, *Ḥikāye-i H̬ᵛāce Fesād*, 103a12: "erine dedi ki be gel erkek imiş / dişi ṣandımdı meger erkek imiş."

The author of this story, S̱ābit, was born in Užice, Bosnia (modern-day Serbia), in the mid-seventeenth century and died in the early 1710s.[5] In addition to the *Ḥikāye-i Ḫᵛāce Fesād*, he compiled a collection of poetry (*Dīvān*) and wrote *mes̱nevīs* titled *Ẓafernāme*, *Edhem ü Hümā*, *Berbernāme*, and *ᶜAmr ü Leys̱*. It is widely accepted that S̱ābit introduced a new set of vocabulary and images to Ottoman classical poetry.[6] It is safe to assume that S̱ābit's *mes̱nevīs* were very popular during the eighteenth century, as numerous copies from this time period can be found in manuscript libraries in Turkey, as well as in collections throughout Europe.[7] With the modernization of the Ottoman Empire and the emergence of the Republic of Turkey, S̱ābit became a marginal figure in the study of Ottoman literature.[8] His themes, choice of words, and the obscenity of his stories are openly despised by most modern Turkish scholars; yet, paradoxically, he is given some credit as a pioneer of "pure" Turkish who used "local language" as well as many adages and proverbs.[9] Very few

5 The date of Ṣabit's death is given in the biographical dictionaries (*teẕkire*) compiled by Belīġ and Sālim as 1124/1712–13, and in that compiled by Ṣafāyī as 1125/1713–14. See İpekten, Haluk, et al., "Sabit." For a list of earlier sources on Sabit, see Rypka, *Beiträge zur Biographie, Charakteristik und Interpretation des türkischen Dichters Sábit*, x. For an introduction to Sabit, see *DİA*, s.v. "Sabit." (T. Karacan).

6 Turgut Karacan has published his *Dīvān* in addition to some of his *mes̱nevīs*. See Sabit. *Dīvān*. For a critique of Karacan's approach, see Özyıldırım, "Sabit'in Türk Edebiyatındaki Yeri Üzerine Bazı Sorular," 5.

7 For the purposes of my research, six manuscripts were consulted: Istanbul, Süleymaniye Library, Ali Nihat Tarlan 2/3, 100a–103b, Esad Efendi 3484, 26b–27b; Istanbul, Büyükşehir Belediyesi Atatürk Kitaplığı OE Yz 1946, 18a–21b; Ankara, Milli Yazmalar Koleksiyonu 1603, 100b–103b; Paris, Bibliothèque nationale de France, Supp. Turc 1256, fol. 142v–146r, Supp. Turc 753, 213r–217v.

8 Özyıldırım, "Sabit'in Türk Edebiyatındaki Yeri Üzerine Bazı Sorular," 1–10. For a discussion of the Ottoman canon and marginalized figures in scholarship, see Schmidt, "Sünbülzāde Vehbī's Şevk-Engīz," 10. In his studies referring to the Ottoman literary canon, Selim Kuru points out the same shift in the nineteenth century, with special reference to texts about sex or texts with pornographic elements. See Kuru, "Sex in the Text 160." On sexuality as a common topic in classical Ottoman literature, see Usluer, "Aşk Mesnevilerinde Cinsellik Mazmunları."

9 On the local elements in Sabit's *Dīvān*, see Kaplan, "Sabit Divanı'nda Mahallileşme ve 17. Yüzyıl Sosyal Hayat Unsurları." For examples of secondary literature critical of the "ugly," "low," and "obscene" language and content, see Karacan, *Derenāme ya da Hāce Fesad ve Söz Ebesi*, 3–18. Özyıldırım's remarks on Karacan nicely summarize the problem: "It is unfortunate that Karacan ends the conclusion part of the analysis of Sabit's *Dīvān* as follows: 'With these features, Sabit is a personal, original and a powerful poet. However, his presence was not felt among the great poets of his age, like, for example, Nābī.' This sentence, and many other remarks

scholars hold S̲ābit in high esteem for his literary achievements. One who does is Özyıldırım, who questions the use of "localization movement" as a reference to the style of a group of poets, including S̲ābit, in the eighteenth and nineteenth centuries. Due to S̲ābit's influence on the defining poets of the period, Özyıldırım further suggests to name this period "the age of S̲ābit."[10]

Whether a "localization movement" actually existed, and, if it did, how it should be defined and delineated are not matters on which scholars agree. The criteria of localization are commonly defined as using colloquial and proverbial phrases, choosing quotidian incidents as themes, and selecting characters and topics from local neighborhoods.[11] Tülay Artan and Irvin Schick treat localization in a broader context, referring to this literary process of localization and vernacularization as "Ottomanization." They argue that this new mode of literary expression, epitomized by Nedīm's (d. 1730) poetry, created a form of erotica: the idealized beloved was replaced with a beloved in flesh and blood.[12]

This article claims neither that S̲ābit was unique in striving to introduce a new vocabulary or images, nor that he was unique in his choice of worldly characters and mundane topics. Nevertheless, S̲ābit's *mes̲nevīs* are indeed good examples in following the criteria of localization and discussing gender as a category. First, although S̲ābit did not use a "pure" local language, his *mes̲nevīs* are full of colloquial and proverbial phrases. While using a great deal of imagery from classical poetry, especially in his descriptions of the beloved, he also employs many proverbial expressions and local themes. The second feature that may link S̲ābit to the localization movement is his choice of characters,

---

and comments in his study are significant because they show that even Karacan who wrote his Ph.D. Dissertation on Sabit's *Dīvān* and published his *mes̲nevīs* cannot go beyond conventional judgments." See Özyıldırım, "Sabit'in Türk Edebiyatındaki Yeri Üzerine Bazı Sorular," 5n13.

10 For a discussion of Sabit, his style, and his impact on different poets, see Özyıldırım, "Sābit'in Türk Edebiyatındaki Yeri Üzerine Bazı Sorular."

11 Demirel, "XVIII. Yüzyıl Klasik Türk Şiirinin Anlam Boyutunda Meydana Gelen Üslup Hareketleri," 295. On localization and its impact on the language in Sabit's *Dīvān*, see Kaplan, "Sabit Divanı'nda Mahallileşme ve 17. Yüzyıl Sosyal Hayat Unsurları." On the use of proverbial sayings, proverbs, and the localization movement, see Tanyıldız, "Klasik Dönem Türk Şiirinde Atasözü ve Deyim Kullanımı Bir Akımın Göstergesi midir?"

12 Artan and Schick, "Ottomanizing Pornotopia," 163.

who are all too human; both the lover and the beloved are in "flesh and blood." It is also significant that Ṣābit chose settings from daily life, namely a church and an orchard. These make his works suitable for examining character traits and tracing his readers' world. In the following sections, I will focus on the setting and the characters in order to understand the humorous and mocking representations of church, Christianity, and non-Muslim characters.

READING THE CHURCH AND CHRISTIANITY AS A SETTING FOR FICTION

In order to express the evil man's desire for the Armenian woman, Ṣābit successfully uses the church and Christianity as a source of literary metaphors. The couplets narrating the evil man's insatiable desire provide readers with a colorful (and distorted) image of Christian customs, seen and represented by a mocking and playful poet aiming to entertain his readers and, toward that end, not hesitating to distort reality to his own ends.

A set of images related to Christianity is used to describe the condition of the vile lover who cannot reach the Armenian beloved: the man, upon seeing the Armenian woman passing by coquettishly, is petrified like an idol, as if he were a monk before the figure of Mary. As he sighs with longing, his chest is torn apart like the gates of a church. The heat of longing withers him away, turning him into one of the mere skeletons in the Christian church. In Ṣābit's metaphoric language, this is probably a reference to Christian asceticism. Hopelessly, he opens his arms in the form of a cross, seeking a pretext under which to be crucified. "The man was supposedly a monk, but really a pig," says Ṣābit, comparing his hopeless situation to that of a pig about to be sacrificed for the Armenian religious holiday.[13]

The evil man's desires are also narrated with Christian images: he obsessively thinks of the locks of the Armenian woman's hair, and the nights become longer and longer, like those during the Great Lent. His moaning sounds like church bells. The desire for the woman's neck leads this man to light white camphor candles in the Armenian church. To try

13 Pigs were not sacrificed, and this mention of pigs as sacrifices and Armenian holidays will be discussed later in detail. Ṣābit, *Ḥikāye-i Ḫ^vāce Fesād*, 100b13–18.

to reach his beloved, he grants gifts to the priests and offers sacrifices to monasteries. Every Sunday, he waits at the door of the church—like Satan. He settles there and does not leave, as if he were the latch of the church gate. When he becomes petrified like an idol, the priests make noises and poke fun at him. The reaction of the Armenian woman is narrated in the same vein: the beloved, the Armenian beauty, is stone-hearted, like a stone monastery. It is impossible to soften her heart. The infidel woman receives all of his gifts with ingratitude.[14]

References to Christians are common in Persian literature dating to early periods; Christianity and allusions to Christian beliefs and stories are found in various genres.[15] The image of the infidel is also common in Ottoman poetry, especially through the characterization of the beloved as *kāfir* or *tersā* ("infidel" or "Christian, non-Muslim").[16] Taken from Persian poetry, this element was adapted into Ottoman culture and underwent further changes over time in both Persian and Ottoman contexts.[17]

Poets in the early modern Ottoman world used Christianity as a theme, too—either as a setting for or as the central theme of a story. For example, in ᶜAṭāᵓī's *Ḫamse,* there is the story of a young Muslim boy and a Christian girl falling in love. Both convert in their last breath to the other's religion—out of fear that they would not find union on the Day of Judgment—and then die of lovesickness. Like Ṣābit, ᶜAṭāᵓī uses vocabulary related to Christianity: for instance, the length of Great Lent appears as a metaphor.[18] Another text using this shared vocabulary, but richer than the *Ḥikāye-i Ḫᵛāce Fesād* in its references to Christianity, is the "Humorous Letter from Nābī to Armenian Aşuġ Ḥakkī Mosis."[19] In a

14 Ṣābit, *Ḥikāye-i Ḫᵛāce Fesād*, 100b18–101a11.

15 For an example of using Christian images "with a positive aura and an insider's knowledge of Christianity," one can look at the works of the twelfth-century Persian poet Khāqānī (d. 1190). See Lewis, "Sexual Occidentation," 712–13. See also Āryān, "Christianity in Persian Literature."

16 Hüseyin Gönel argues that Christian imagery was more commonly used by Rumelian poets, as they were living in closer contact with Christians. See Gönel, "15.–16. Yüzyıl Divanlarına göre Divan Şiirinde Sevgili," 157. Although this observation might be correct, there is no solid evidence to prove it. It is important to remember that Christians and non-Muslims were not only in the Rumelian parts of the Empire, and that in both Arabic and Persian poetry the image of the infidel was commonly used in a similar fashion. See, for example, Āryān, "Christianity in Persian Literature."

17 Demir, "Osmanlı Şiirinde Öteki ve Başkası Olarak Kafir İmgesi," 431, 434.

18 Kortantamer, *Nev'i-zāde Atayi ve Hamse'si*, 64.

19 Aşuġ Mosis was an Armenian minstrel, jeweler, and engraver, who recited folk poetry

different genre, a letter, Nābī makes very thorough use of Christian imagery and relevant vocabulary, continuously referring to Christian customs in order to mock the Armenian *aşuġ* in his reply.[20]

In most other examples in the literature, the lover, although called *kāfir*, is not actually an "infidel," but the lover's cruelty, intoxicating nature, inclination to sin, and otherness make the metaphor of the infidel suitable, as Matthias Kappler has discussed in detail. Kappler underlines that the repeated use of "infidel" in poetry denotes "a form of otherness worth examining," and he identifies "three clichés of infidel" recurring in Ottoman classical poetry. The first cliché is that infidels drink, often indulging in wine. As a consequence, the image of the infidel is commonly used in conjunction with the image of the beloved as a cupbearer (*sāqī*). Second, imagery relates infidels to violence and oppression, and thus infidels are considered to be cruel—this in turn corresponds to the warrior infidel figure in literature. The third image is stimulated by the belief that infidels cannot go to Paradise but are destined for Hell. Consequently, they are represented as being inclined to sin. Kappler argues that these three images create the three most common stereotypes of the beloved: with an intoxicating nature, a heartless character, and an inclination to sin—regardless of whether the beloved is actually an infidel or not.[21] The references to the *kāfir* are sometimes based on material conditions as well. For instance, the recognition that infidels were capable of constructing strong buildings is related to their stone-hearted natures.[22] Some of these stereotypes can also be found in the *Ḥikāye-i Ḫᵛāce Fesād*. For example, "[the Armenian woman] was of candid and jovial temperament, like a goblet of wine,"[23] and "she was stone-hearted like a stone monastery."[24]

---

in Turkish under the pen-name Ḥakkī. He exchanged letters with the famous poet Nābī. For further information, see Dağlar, "Nābī'den Ermeni Aşuğ Hakkī Mosis'e Mizahī Mektup."

20 For the whole text and its analysis, see Dağlar, "Nābī'den Ermeni Aşuğ Hakkī Mosis'e Mizahī Mektup."

21 Kappler, "The Beloved and His Otherness," 40–42. For couplets depicting the tyrant and cruel infidel image, see, for example, the couplets by Emrī and ᶜAvnī in Demir, "Osmanlı Şiirinde Öteki ve Başkası Olarak Kafir İmgesi," 436.

22 Demir, "Osmanlı Şiirinde Öteki ve Başkası Olarak Kafir İmgesi," 440. For further examples of similar uses, see Onay, *Açıklamalı Divan Şiiri Sözlüğü*, 237.

23 S̲ābit, *Ḥikāye-i Ḫᵛāce Fesād*, 100b5: "cām-ı mey gibi küşāde-meşreb."

24 S̲ābit, *Ḥikāye-i Ḫᵛāce Fesād*, 101a4: "ṭaş manastır gibi sengīn-dil idi."

One might find different motives behind S̱ābit's references to Christianity. Considering the rich imagery S̱ābit uses in his work, it is plausible that they were not intended to have a different impact than any other image-set used in his *mes̱nevīs*. For instance, in another of his *mes̱nevīs*, *Berbernāme*, S̱ābit places the barbershop at the center/foundation of his imagery, just as he does the church in *Ḥikāye-i H̱ᵛāce Fesād*. In *Ḥikāye-i H̱ᵛāce Fesād*, the metaphors revolve around the church and Christianity, as the beloved is Armenian. In *Berbernāme*, all of the metaphors about passionate love and the beloved revolve around the shop and the tools of the barber, as the beloved is a barber boy.[25]

Nevertheless, S̱ābit's allusions to Christianity could also be seen in a different light—as tools for creating a humorous setting in which non-Muslims could be mocked. In this regard, his reference to "the pigs that will be sacrificed for the Armenian religious holiday" proves to be a fertile example.[26] This quote allows for different readings. As pigs were not sacrificed in the Armenian religious holiday, the audience may deduce that S̱ābit does not have a deep knowledge of Christianity and the customs of Armenians. They may also interpret this as a reference to the common people's beliefs about Christianity, rather than the true observance of the belief. Another possibility is that it is a reference to eating pork as an identity marker for Christian Armenians, since eating pork was religiously prohibited for both Muslims and Jews in the Ottoman lands.[27] This reference can also be perceived as a pejorative joke intended to insult Armenians—to Muslims, pigs are one of the most detestable animals. For historians, it is impossible to single out either the motivation or the outcome of this and similar references in the text; nevertheless, it is safe to claim that this fictional imagery creates a humorous effect, intended to entertain the audience while mocking non-Muslims and their customs.

The mocking of non-Muslims—or, more generally, of other religious communities—was certainly not unique to S̱ābit's *mes̱nevīs* or to the writings of other Muslim authors of the Ottoman lands. Another

25 Karacan, "Berbername Mesnevisi," 41.

26 S̱ābit, *Ḥikāye-i H̱ᵛāce Fesād*, 100b18: "özge ḫınzīr idi ruhbān olacaḳ / Ermenī ᶜīdine ḳurbān olacaḳ."

27 A sixteenth-century Armenian author emphasizes the importance of eating pork as an identity marker for Christian Armenians. See Goshgarian, "Blending In and Separating Out," 49, 60–62.

seventeenth-century text,—namely, Eremya Çelebi Kömürjian's Armeno-Turkish poem titled *The Jewish Bride*,—gives further insight into the representation of inter-communal tensions in contemporaneous literature.[28] *The Jewish Bride* narrates the story of the elopement of a Jewish girl, Mrkada, with the Christian baker, Dimo, upon agreeing to convert to Christianity and to live with him in Albania. The tale does not end with their successful departure from Istanbul and glorious marriage, however. Instead, it continues with the plight of the Jewish mother and the two communities' public confrontation through songs and lamentations. The protagonists—Dimo, Mrkada, and her mother—get lost in their larger communities, since both their and their respective communities' honors are at stake.[29] The few Muslim characters mentioned in the text are Ottoman officials, who are approached to restore justice. The Greek community's mockery gives a rather negative portrayal of the Jewish population while simultaneously highlighting the multi-ethnic and -religious character of seventeenth-century Istanbul, where communities were close enough not only to know each other's customs and habits but also to fall in love with members of other communities.

Looking back at the many examples in *Ḥikāye-i Ḫ^vāce Fesād*, the Christian setting does not seem unfamiliar to S̱ābit or his readership. He has at least some familiarity with Christianity, and he assumes that the reader is also familiar with the church, crucifixion, candle lighting, fasting, the appearance and habits of monks, etc. Only through this shared imagery do his metaphors and images become accessible to his readers and create a humorous effect. While the references to the church and Christianity prepare the setting in which the desires of the lover are

28 For a transliteration and translation of the poem with a comprehensive introduction to its context and versions, see Eremya Çelebi Kömürjian, "The Jewish Bride." For a discussion placing *The Jewish Bride* within the seventeenth-century Ottoman literature, especially in *mes̱nevī* tradition, see Sancak, "Eremya Çelebi Kömürciyan'ın *Yahudi Gelini*'ni 17. Yüzyıl Edebiyatlarında Konumlandırmaya Çalışmak."

29 An emphasis on honor (both personal and communal) can be found throughout the text. Noticeable examples are found in the subsections, "The chant sung by the Jews against the Turks: Ne dur bu zhulum," (114–16) and "The mother's tragic lament in diverse ways" (130–38). In the former, the Jews refer to the bride as "our girl" and call the events an "atrocity done to us." In the latter, the most striking quote is from the mother, who states that the Albanian baker "Made her a disgrace for me and my people / So that our story will be told like a fairy tale / For [all] times, for [all] times (131). See Eremya Çelebi Kömürjian, "The Jewish Bride." All translations quoted from the text are by A. Tietze.

described, they also serve to portray a mocking image of the Armenian characters' daily life. Neither the church nor the Armenian characters appear in the most positive light, as in the example of the priests compared to pigs—but neither do the evil men. We assume that both men who raped the Armenian woman are Muslim, as they are not defined otherwise.[30] The evil Muslim men are the most deplorable characters.

READING RAPE

The rape of the Armenian woman by two evil men is the climax of the story. How rape in literature should be read and interpreted has been the focus of scholarly discussion, and there is no short, straightforward answer to the question.[31] Another difficult—and related—question is how contemporaneous readers would have read and perceived a narration of rape. Was the narration of an Armenian woman's rape a trope for mocking and laughter, as was the narration concerning the church and Christianity? Was it a misogynist and/or xenophobic rendering? Or both?[32] Did the authors narrating rape reproduce existing social values, such as the subordination of women, or was literature a means of social critique? These and similar questions are tackled by scholars with reference to both legal and literary works of the early modern world.[33] To understand how rape was defined, read, and perceived, historians have consulted legal and/or literary/fictional sources. Each type of source has its advantages and pitfalls, yet, as remarked upon by some scholars, rape is always "represented" through writing and narration. Thus, "rape" is always a representation.[34] Keeping this in mind, I will also use legal sources to understand the representation and perception of rape in the Ottoman context in general, and in Ṣābit's narrative in particular.

Defining or classifying rape in the Ottoman legal system is complicated and will be beyond the scope of this discussion. Suffice it to say

30 For the "default" being Muslim, see Peirce, "Seniority, Sexuality and Social Order," 171.

31 See, for example, Robertson and Rose, *Representing Rape in Medieval and Early Modern Literature*; Catty, *Writing Rape, Writing Women in Early Modern England*; and Gravdal, *Ravishing Maidens*.

32 For an outline of this discussion, see Vitz, "Rereading Rape in Medieval Literature"; and Robertson and Rose, *Representing Rape in Medieval and Early Modern Literature*, 6–8.

33 See, for example, Gravdal, *Ravishing Maidens*, 122–40.

34 Catty, *Writing Rape*, 11.

that rape was considered to be under the larger category of *zināʾ* (illicit sex)—and thus categorized with *ḥadd* crimes. In both legal opinions and court records it is further distinguished by the adjective "forced" (*cebren zināʾ*), to distinguish it from *zināʾ* per se.[35]

In a rape case, to be given the *ḥadd* punishment—*recm* (stoning)—the man had to belong to the legal category *muḥṣan*, meaning that he was married (and the marriage was consummated), free, and Muslim.[36] Examples from *Fetāvā-yı Feyżiyye*, a collection of the chief jurisconsult (*şeyḫülislām*) Feyżullāh Efendi's *fetvā*s dating from the late seventeenth century, provide useful insights. The standard legal procedure is exemplified by the following *fetvā*:

> If Zeyd commits *zināʾ* by force (*cebren*) to Hind, what must be done to Zeyd?
> Answer: If Zeyd is *muḥṣan,* he will be stoned (*recm olunur*); if not, he is flogged a hundred times (*degnek urulur*).[37]

For slaves, the punishment was half that for a *non-muḥṣan*, that is, fifty floggings.[38] Hind, the female, is not described in either case. Presumably she is a free Muslim, as slaves and non-Muslims were dealt with in other cases, such as the one below:

> If Zeyd, who is Muslim and *muḥṣan*, commits *zināʾ* by force (*cebren*) to Hind, who is non-Muslim (*ẕımmiyye*), what must be done to Zeyd?
> Answer: Stoning (*recm*).[39]

According to this example, forced *zināʾ* with a non-Muslim woman had the same consequences as that with a Muslim woman, so long as the male

35 For "rape" in the Ottoman context, see *Encyclopedia of Women & Islamic Cultures*, s.v. "Rape: Overview" (E. Semerdjian); Semerdjian, *"Off the Straight Path,"* especially 3–28 and 29–58; Sonbol, "Rape and Law in Ottoman and Modern Egypt"; and *Encyclopedia of Women & Islamic Cultures*, s.v. "Rape: Ottoman Empire" (L. Peirce). For the discrepancy between legal ideals and court records, see Peirce, *Morality Tales*, especially 111 and 353–54.

36 A discussion of the extent of the category of *muḥsan* according to different schools of Islam and scholars of jurisprudence (*fiqh*) is beyond the scope of this paper. For an introduction to the topic, see *DİA*, s.v. "İhsan" (Ş. Dağcı); *EI*², s.v. "Muḥṣan" (J. Burton).

37 Feyżullāh Efendi, *Fetāvā-yı Feyżiyye*, 113, fetvā no. 751.

38 Feyżullāh Efendi, *Fetāvā-yı Feyżiyye*, 113; fetvā no. 752.

39 Feyżullāh Efendi, *Fetāvā-yı Feyżiyye*, 114; fetvā no. 758. For *cebren zināʾ* cases committed against slaves, also see other examples on the same page.

was *muḥsan*—the qualifications of the perpetrator were primary to the case. Likewise, if a slave committed *cebren zinā*ᵓ against Hind (who is not defined as a slave or non-Muslim), the punishment was based primarily on the perpetrator's status as a slave, not on the status of the victim.[40]

Scholars working on court records have emphasized discrepancies between theory and practice. The practice of law in courts deviated from the ideals of sharia law.[41] Studies based on court records show that the religion of the rapist, the age of the victim (a minor/a virgin/an adult woman), the status of the victim (married/free/slave), and the gender of the victim mattered.[42] In addition to the fact that real-life cases were more complicated than theoretical renderings, further points make the study of rape reports difficult. First, for *zinā*ᵓ allegations, accusations that could not be proven were strictly punished.[43] Second, scholars observe that reported rape cases usually dealt with pregnant women or with women who had lost their virginity. This observation gives the impression that other women may have kept their complaints to themselves.[44]

If we look again at S̱ābit's narration in light of this background, a few observations are possible. First, the narration focuses on rape itself. The rape scene is narrated primarily through a description of the male body rather than by following the male gaze. S̱ābit keeps both the woman and the reader in suspense while describing the erect penis of the rapist with various metaphors. The center of attention is the man's penis and its actions. References to the Armenian woman describe her desperation and her cries to her husband, who is unaware of the rape.

40 See, for example, Feyżullāh Efendi, *Fetāvā-yı Feyżiyye*, 114, fetvā no. 755.

41 On the necessity of considering both theory and practice, see El-Rouayheb, "Review of Elyse Semerdjian, *Off the Straight Path*."

42 Sonbol, "Rape and Law in Ottoman and Modern Egypt," 221–22; and Peirce, *Morality Tales*, 111.

43 For information on witnesses and allegations, see Peirce, *Morality Tales*, 353. *Fetāvā-yı Feyżiyye* includes examples on the status of female witnesses; women cannot be witnesses in a rape case: "If Hind litigates against Zeyd claiming that he committed *zinā*ᵓ by force, and if Zeyd denies the claim, and if some women act as witnesses to Hind's claim, would their testimonies be accepted? Answer: No." See Feyżullāh Efendi, *Fetāvā-yı Feyżiyye*, 246; fetvā no. 1536. This *fetvā* is followed by a more general example about female witnesses in *zinā*ᵓ cases, stating that their testimonies are void. Feyżullāh Efendi, *Fetāvā-yı Feyżiyye*, 246; fetvā no. 1537.

44 Peirce, *Morality Tales*, 373. About motivations to go to court, see also Ergene, "Why Did Ümmü Gülsüm Go to Court?."

In *Ḥikāye-i Ḫ^v^āce Fesād*, the readers never learn what happens to the perpetrators or to the victim. We do not know about the men's eligibility to be punished by *ḥadd*—that is, if they were *muḥṣan.* The fact that the victim was an Armenian woman would not have changed the punishment for the rape, as the *fetvā* quoted above suggests. Ṣābit's choice of punishment is not what is described as *ḥadd* punishment for *cebren zinā'*, yet the author underlines the necessity of punishment, as he declares that the men ought to be exiled and shot to death.[45] It is also possible that he was uninterested in the legal intricacies, or was aware of the difficulties of proving a rape case.

GENDER: A USEFUL CATEGORY OF ANALYSIS FOR ETHNIC STEREOTYPES

From a gendered perspective, references to rape in legal literature commonly categorize and punish rape from a male-centered view: the primary determining factor in punishment was the man's qualifications. A woman's status made a difference only in relation to men: if she was someone's daughter, wife, or widow.[46] Comparably, in Ṣābit's narrative men's decisions and actions matter significantly, whereas the Armenian woman is merely the object of the male gaze and desire. As such, it is possible to read the trick and the rape as an interaction between the evil men and the Armenian husband, instead of a violation of the Armenian woman.[47]

Despite her central role to the plot, the Armenian woman is not a central figure. In the beginning, she is subject to the gaze of the evil man, yet the readers never know whether she is aware of him or his love. Vague hints indicate that he attempted to reach her and was not

45 Ṣābit, *Ḥikāye-i Ḫ^v^āce Fesād*, 103b1: "iki müfsid ki şehirden sürecek / çifte ḳurşunla urub öldürecek." (Those two mischief-makers are to be exiled from the city, they should be killed with a double-barreled gun.)

46 See, for example, the case discussed in Sonbol, "Rape and Law in Ottoman and Modern Egypt," 221.

47 Christine M. Rose suggests a similar approach: "[Chaucer's] use of rape so often in his poetry is integral to the discourse of his own, and to some extent our, cultural inheritance; it objectifies and removes the women as victim, focusing instead on the empowerment of men and rape as trope, changing it from violence to women to interactions between men. It consistently reveals women's status as property." See Rose, "Reading Chaucer Reading Rape," 49.

successful in coaxing her, but Ṣābit makes no direct reference to such a confrontation. The reader only hears her voice when she calls on her husband to save her. Her cries are primarily important to the plot in order to emphasize her husband's inability to grasp the situation, not to reflect her feelings.[48] Throughout the story, she is described in a rather stereotypical fashion and praised for her beauty and attractiveness. She is a type, consistent with the "beloved" image of the classical canon.[49] She is described as a woman of joyful and lighthearted temperament; her body is like a rose, her mouth is like a rosebud, her cheeks are like tulips, and her height is compared to that of a cypress tree.[50] The stereotypical description is remarkable considering Ṣābit's tendency to seek original metaphors and similes, as well as his innovative use of imagery.[51] Ṣābit did not hesitate to use uncommon imagery in seeking new metaphors, yet he chose not to do so in the case of this female character.

After she is introduced to readers in this rather mundane fashion, the readers and the protagonist learn that she is actually "a cruel Armenian woman, adulterous with vile-ideas, [and she is] an infidel fairy."[52] Remarkably, the harshest judgment about her appears in the couplet in which her Armenian ethnicity is revealed. This couplet is also significant from another perspective: it is from this point on that the references and metaphors related to Christianity begin to appear. Nevertheless, it is important to note here that her Armenian background is not related to her beauty or sexuality in a direct way—that is, the narrator does not provide a consequential relationship saying that she was Armenian, and thus beautiful and sexually attractive. Her Armenian identity seems to provide

48 On the disappearance of female characters from fiction with the transformation of the Empire after the conquest of Constantinople, see *Encyclopedia of Women & Islamic Cultures*, s.v. "Representations: Poetry and Prose, Premodern" (S. Kuru).

49 For a concise summary of stereotypical images in Ottoman poetry, see Kappler, "The Beloved and His Otherness," 37.

50 Ṣābit, *Ḥikāye-i Ḫᵛāce Fesād*, 100b3–6.

51 For instance, in another *meṣnevī*, he feels free to compare the lover's eyes brimming with tears to an uncontrollable bladder. See Ṣābit, *Berbernāme*, 98b2: "dīde-i āġeşte-i eşk-i gül[g]ūn / mübtelā-yı selīsü'l-bevl-i füsūn" (The evil man was shedding tears as if he were suffering from a condition in which he could not control his bladder).

52 Ṣābit, *Ḥikāye-i Ḫᵛāce Fesād*, 100b10. On the similarity of Armenian and Ottoman women's dress, see *Encyclopedia of Women & Islamic Cultures*, s.v. "Armenian Women: Overview" (H. Berberian).

a useful setting for S̱ābit, allowing him to create a mocking and fictitious image of the church and Christianity.

Considering the whole narrative, although a significant section is dedicated to praise of the beloved and the evil man's longing for her, S̱ābit does not excuse the rapists' actions by referring to the protagonist's love or uncontrollable desire for the Armenian woman. Rape follows her being unreachable. As suggested above, there is no link between her beauty and her ethnic-religious background; only after he has fallen in love does the protagonist learn that she is Armenian. The few negative references to her, noting her ethnic-religious background—"a cruel Armenian woman, adulterous with vile-ideas, an infidel fairy"[53]—seem to comply with the fictitious infidel imagery of Ottoman/Persian literature rather than with stereotypes about a specific ethnic or religious group. Yet the tone of the narration suggests that her husband's Armenian identity does matter.

While the Armenian woman is praised for her beauty in a stereotypical fashion, S̱ābit depicts her husband in a pejorative tone and continually ridicules him. He is portrayed as a merry man, fond of indulging in food and drink. Moreover, he is referred to as Boḳçu Murād. Murād is a common name among Armenians, and *boḳçu* means "dung dealer," a reference indicating that he is Armenian, that he is a sewer worker, or both. *Risāle-i Ġarībe*, a treatise that provides us with invaluable information about seventeenth-century daily life and perceptions in Ottoman Istanbul, informs us that in Istanbul all sewer workers were Armenians, and, as a consequence, "*boḳçu*" was used to refer to Armenians.[54] Evliyā Çelebi describes the Armenian sewer workers in detail: "It is true that they are blameworthy and filthy people; yet, they are necessary in Egypt and Istanbul. With the service of these filthy people Istanbul becomes clean."[55] The author of

---

53 S̱ābit, *Ḥikāye-i Ḫ^vāce Fesād*, 100b10.

54 *Risāle-i Ġarībe*, 97. Another possible meaning of "*boḳçu*" is "sodomite," and couplets from the *Derenāme* (that is, *Ḥikāye-i Ḫ^vāce Fesād*) are given as examples. See Bingölçe, *(Tanıklarıyla) Osmanlı Argosu Sözlüğü*. However, neither is there an indication of the sexual inclination of the Armenian husband nor does the context imply a sexual reference. Considering his Armenian identity, the explanation of *boḳçu* in *Risāle-i Ġarībe* is more plausible. This usage also appears in one of the Armeno-Turkish writings of Eremya Çelebi, titled "Rumlar Ermenilere bokdzi dedikleri ichün jevabname el hakir Iremya." For a list of his polemical works, see Eremya Çelebi Kömürjian, *The Jewish Bride*, 37.

55 Evliyā Çelebi, *Seyāḥatnāme*, 1:341: "Gerçi mez̠mūm ü mülevves̠ ḳavmdir, ammā Mıṣır ile İslāmbol'da lāzımlı ḳavmdir. Bu mülevves̠ ḳavmiŋ ḫiz̠metiyle İslāmbol pāk olur."

Risāle-i Ġarībe curses the Armenians who attempt to gain better status or jobs, for example as poets, and suggests that they should deal only with dung.[56] Whether Murād was actually a sewer worker or not, *boḳçu* is clearly a pejorative term indicating his filthiness as an Armenian.

Additionally, he is portrayed as a "stupid ass" who is completely unaware of his wife's situation and is not properly responsive to her cries. He is ridiculed further as he talks to himself for several couplets, proclaiming himself to be quick-witted, as he "knew" upon seeing the "pregnant woman" that she was to give birth to twins.[57] The narrator clearly holds him and his absentmindedness responsible for his wife's plight. He is blamed for letting his wife be taken by strangers and for his inability to ensure her proper conduct.[58]

It would be anachronistic to read and perceive ethnic stereotypes with modern sensibilities; yet reading this story as merely a mocking description of the church and Christianity, as well as the bullying of an Armenian husband through the rape of his wife, is too simplified.[59] While this and similar stories were meant to entertain their readers and cause laughter,[60] they certainly reflect possible perceptions of the time periods in which they were narrated and retold. My reading of the story suggests that the trick and the rape were directed by the evil men against the Armenian husband, and through him, against the larger Armenian community. The Armenian woman, due to her gender, was of secondary importance, as was her ethnic background. The Armenian man was ridiculed not only for his inability to protect his wife, but also with ethnic-religious references.

56 *Risāle-i Ġarībe*, 41: "ve poḳçuluḳ yėterken her şeyʾe ve her ṣanʿata ḳarışan Ermenīler; ve ṣulu boḳçuluḳ ile boḫ olmış iken şāʿirliğe yeltenen Ermenīler."

57 Ṡābit, *Ḥikāye-i Ḫ*^{v}*āce Fesād*, 103b4–7.

58 Various references in *Risāle-i Ġarībe* denote the significance of segregating women from men, and mention husbands' responsibilities for proper conduct. See especially *Risāle-i Ġarībe*, 28, 29, 36. Peirce observes that there are examples of court cases in which rape occurs outside of the home, whereas the legal ideal of *fetvā* collections presumes gender segregation and seclusion of women in their homes. Peirce, *Morality Tales*, 354.

59 For an example of such a simplistic attitude in the European context, see Vitz, "Rereading Rape in Medieval Literature."

60 Another possible question is whether these stories aim to titillate the reader and serve the interests of voyeurism. This question is beyond the scope of this paper, but knowing more about how these stories were read, performed, and circulated will help scholars to imagine how they were consumed and reproduced.

An analysis of the aforementioned story entitled *The Jewish Bride* both complements and complicates possible gendered readings of ethnic and religious stereotypes. Like the beloved in the *Ḥikāyet-i Ḫᵛāce Fesād*, the Jewish bride herself is not at the center of the public scolding or shame. It is her mother who is held responsible and ridiculed, because she was unable to protect her daughter.[61] She is chastised by her own community and the Greeks—for different reasons. Her own community blames her for allowing Dimo access to her daughter,[62] and the Greeks scold her in their songs for her relentless attempts to bring her daughter back. The Greek song creates a contrast between the amorous and happy condition of the new bride and the miserable circumstances of the mother, who is referred to as a "dirty witch" and similar epiphets throughout the song.[63] The song makes clear that all her attempts are in vain and criticizes her public appearances—claiming that the event is becoming more famous than that of Sabatai Tzevi, referring to her calls at the offices of the pashas, and simply by calling her a "street broom."[64]

As it was the husband's responsibility to protect his wife in *Ḥikāyet-i Ḫᵛāce Fesād*, it was the mother's duty to protect her unmarried daughter in the absence of her father in *The Jewish Bride*. In *Ḥikāyet-i Ḫᵛāce Fesād*, the disparity between the representation of the Armenian husband and that of his wife points at the importance of gender as a crucial and embedded criterion when questioning perceptions and stereotypes based on ethnicity and religious background. In *The Jewish Bride*, the community puts the blame on the mother. The bride is not reproached by her own community; the father, as head of the household, is not reprimanded for being absent either. In this example, a gendered reading requires transgressing the male-female dichotomy and obliges the reader to consider further nuances such as hierarchies within

61 The readers learn from the mother's lament that the father is in Egypt and does not know about the events. See Eremya Çelebi Kömürjian, "The Jewish Bride," 134.

62 See especially the subsection titled "Some relatives of Mrkada's mother, who had come to console her, reproached her for allowing into her home the Albanian who had caused her daughter's loss and who had brought insult to her (Jewish) people" in Eremya Çelebi Kömürjian, "The Jewish Bride," 128–30.

63 See especially the subsection titled "The Greeks and Jews bear a grudge against each other. The Greek *zurafa*s chanted songs when they confronted the Jews" in Eremya Çelebi Kömürjian, "The Jewish Bride," 122–28.

64 Eremya Çelebi Kömürjian, "The Jewish Bride," 122–23.

the institutions of marriage and family, including seniority.[65] That said, in both cases, a focus on gender not only allows readers to see beyond common ethnic stereotypes but also makes them aware of the gendered perceptions and representations of the seventeenth-century Ottoman literary world.

BIBLIOGRAPHY

Sources

Eremya Çelebi Kömürjian. *The Jewish Bride.* Edited and transliterated by Avedis K. Sanjian and Andreas Tietze as *Eremya Chelebi Kömürjian's Armeno Turkish Poem "The Jewish Bride."* Wiesbaden: Otto Harrasowitz, 1981.

Evliyā Çelebi [Meḥmed Ẓıllī b. Dervīş]. *Seyāḥatnāme.* Edited and transliterated by Robert Dankoff and Yücel Dağlı. In *Evliyâ Çelebi Seyahatnâmesi.* Vol. 1. Istanbul: Yapı Kredi Yayınları, 2006.

Risāle-i Ġarībe. Edited and transliterated by Hayati Develi as *XVIII. Yüzyıl İstanbul Hayatına Dair Risâle-i Garîbe.* Istanbul: Kitabevi, 1998.

S̱ābit. *Berbernāme.* Istanbul: Süleymaniye Library, Ali Nihat Tarlan 2/2, 97b–100a.

S̱ābit. *Berbernāme.* Edited and transliterated by Turgut Karacan as "Berbername Mesnevisi." *Çevren Bilim Kültür Dergisi* XVII, no. 76 (1990): 37–44.

S̱ābit. *Dīvān.* Edited and transliterated by Turgut Karacan. In *Divan (Sabit Alaeddin Ali).* Sivas: Cumhuriyet Üniversitesi, 1991.

S̱ābit. *Ḥikāyet-i Ḫ*ᵛ*āce Fesād.* Istanbul: Süleymaniye Library, Ali Nihat Tarlan 2/3, 100a–103b.

S̱ābit. *Ḥikāyet-i Ḫ*ᵛ*āce Fesād.* Edited and transliterated by Turgut Karacan as *Derenāme ya da Hāce Fesad ve Söz Ebesi.* Sivas: Dilek Basımevi, 1990.

Feyżullāh Efendi. *Fetāvā-yı Feyżiyye.* Edited by Süleyman Kaya. Istanbul: Klasik, 2009.

Studies

Artan, Tülay, and Irvin Cemil Schick. "Ottomanizing Pornotopia: Changing Visual Codes in Eighteenth-Century Ottoman Erotic Miniatures." In *Eros and Sexuality in Islamic Art*, edited by Francesca Leoni and Mika Natif, 157–207. Surrey, England; Burlington, VT: Ashgate, 2013.

Āryān, Qamar. "Christianity in Persian Literature." In *Encyclopaedia Iranica* 5 (1991).

Bingölçe, Filiz. *(Tanıklarıyla) Osmanlı Argosu Sözlüğü.* Ankara: AltÜst, 2011.

65 For a very insightful discussion of different life-stages and their significance in Ottoman society, see Peirce, "Seniority, Sexuality and Social Order."

Catty, Jocelyn. *Writing Rape, Writing Women in Early Modern England; Unbridled Speech*. Basingstoke; New York: Palgrave Macmillan, 2011.

Dağlar, Abdülkadir. "Nābī'den Ermeni Aşuğ Hakkī Mosis'e Mizahī Mektup." *Milli Folklor* 95 (2012): 83–95.

Demir, Recep. "Osmanlı Şiirinde Öteki ve Başkası Olarak Kafir İmgesi." *Turkish Studies* 8 (2013): 431–45.

Demirel, Şener. "XVIII. Yüzyıl Klasik Türk Şiirinin Anlam Boyutunda Meydana Gelen Üslup Hareketleri: Klasik Üslup – Sebk-i Hindī – Hikemī Tarz – Mahallileşme." *Turkish Studies* 4, no. 2 (2009): 279–306.

El-Rouayheb, Khaled. "Review of Elyse Semerdjian, *Off the Straight Path*: Illicit Sex, Law, and Community in Ottoman Aleppo." *The American Historical Review* 114, no. 5 (2009): 1574.

Ergene, Boğaç A. "Why Did Ümmü Gülsüm Go to Court? Ottoman Legal Practice between History and Anthropology." *Islamic Law and Society* 17 (2010): 215–44.

Goshgarian, Rachel. "Blending In and Separating Out: Sixteenth-Century Anatolian Armenian Food and Feasts." In *Starting with Food: Culinary Approaches to Ottoman History*, edited by Amy Singer, 49–68. Princeton: Markus Wiener Publishers, 2011.

Gönel, Hüseyin. "15.–16. Yüzyıl Divanlarına göre Divan Şiirinde Sevgili." Ph.D. diss., Gazi University, 2010.

Gravdal, Kathryn. *Ravishing Maidens: Writing Rape in Medieval French Literature and Law*. Philadelphia: University of Pennsylvania Press, 1991.

İpekten, Haluk, et al. "Sabit." In *Tezkirelere Göre Divan Edebiyatı İsimler Sözlüğü*. Ankara: Kültür ve Turizm Bakanlığı, 1988.

Kaplan, Yunus. "Sabit Divanı'nda Mahallileşme ve 17. Yüzyıl Sosyal Hayat Unsurları." *Turkish Studies* 4, no. 5 (2009): 209–48.

Kappler, Matthias. "The Beloved and His Otherness; Reflections on Ethnic and Religious Stereotypes in Ottoman Love Poetry." In *Intercultural Aspects in and around Turkic Literatures; Proceedings of the International Conference held on October 11th–12th 2003 in Nicosia*, edited by Matthias Kappler, 37–48. Wiesbaden: Harrasowitz, 2006.

Kortantamer, Tunca. *Nev'i-zāde Atayi ve Hamse'si*. Izmir: Ege Üniversitesi Edebiyat Fakültesi, 1997.

Kuru, Selim S. "Sex in the Text: Deli Birader's *Dâfi*ᶜ*ü'l-gumûm ve Râfi*ᶜ*ü'l-humûm* and the Ottoman Literary Canon." *Middle Eastern Literatures* 10, no. 2 (2007): 157–74.

Lewis, Franklin. "Sexual Occidentation: The Politics of Conversion, Christian-Love and Boy-Love in ᶜAttār." *Iranian Studies* 42, no. 5 (2009): 693–723.

Onay, Talât. *Açıklamalı Divan Şiiri Sözlüğü: Eski Türk Edebiyatında Mazmunlar ve İzahı*. Edited by Cemâl Kurnaz. Ankara: Kurgan Edebiyat, 2013.

Özyıldırım, Ali Emre. "Sabit'in Türk Edebiyatındaki Yeri Üzerine Bazı Sorular." *Türkbilig* 23 (2012): 1–10.

Peirce, Leslie P. *Morality Tales: Law and Gender in the Ottoman Court of Aintab*. Berkeley: University of California Press, 2003.

Peirce, Leslie P. "Seniority, Sexuality and Social Order: The Vocabulary of Gender in Early Modern Ottoman Society." In *Women in the Ottoman Empire: Middle Eastern Women in the Early Modern Era*, edited by Madeline C. Zilfi, 169–96. Leiden, New York, Cologne: Brill, 1997.

Robertson, Elizabeth, and Christine M. Rose, eds. *Representing Rape in Medieval and Early Modern Literature*. New York: Palgrave, 2001.

Rose, Christine M. "Reading Chaucer Reading Rape." In *Representing Rape in Medieval and Early Modern Literature*, edited by Elizabeth Robertson and Christine M. Rose, 21–60. New York: Palgrave, 2001.

Rypka, Jan. *Beiträge zur Biographie, Charakteristik und Interpretation des türkischen Dichters Sâbit*. 1. Teil, vol. 8. Prague: Náklad Filosofické Fakulty Univerzity Karlovy; v komisi F. Řivnáče, 1924.

Sancak, Azra. "Eremya Çelebi Kömürciyan'ın *Yahudi Gelini*'ni 17. Yüzyıl Edebiyatlarında Konumlandırmaya Çalışmak." *Monograf* 6 (2016): 87–109.

Schmidt, Jan. "Sünbülzāde Vehbī's Şevk-Engīz, an Ottoman Pornographic Poem." *Turcica* 25 (1993): 9–37.

Scott, Joan W. "Gender: A Useful Category of Historical Analysis." *The American Historical Review* 91:5 (1986): 1053–75.

Semerdjian, Elyse. *"Off the Straight Path": Illicit Sex, Law, and Community in Ottoman Aleppo*. Syracuse, NY: Syracuse University Press, 2008.

Sonbol, Amira. "Rape and Law in Ottoman and Modern Egypt." In *Women in the Ottoman Empire: Middle Eastern Women in the Early Modern Era*, edited by Madeline C. Zilfi, 214–31. Leiden, New York, Cologne: Brill, 1997.

Tanyıldız, Ahmet. "Klasik Dönem Türk Şiirinde Atasözü ve Deyim Kullanımı Bir Akımın Göstergesi midir?" *Türkiyat Araştırmaları* 4, no. 6 (2007): 93–104.

Usluer, Fatih. "Aşk Mesnevilerinde Cinsellik Mazmunları." *Turkish Studies* 2, no. 4 (2007): 795–822.

Vitz, Evelyn Birge. "Rereading Rape in Medieval Literature: Literary, Historical, and Theoretical Reflections." *The Romanic Review* 88, no. 1 (1997): 1–26.

"The Greatest of Tribulations": Constructions of Femininity in Sixteenth-Century Ottoman Physiognomy

Emin Lelić

Life is no good without them
Yet, they are the greatest of tribulations[1]
Love of women ruins lands
For female deception is a deep sea[2]

In the late sixteenth century Ḥasan Kāfī el-Aḳḥiṣārī (d. 1616), an Ottoman scholar and judge, wrote a popular treatise on statecraft, *Uṣūl al-ḥikam fī niẓām al-ᶜālam* (Foundations of Wisdom on the Ordering of the World),[3] in which he claimed that the problems of the Ottoman governance system in 1596 could ultimately be ascribed to two causes: venality (*rüşvet*) and a male desire (*raġbet*) for women that led

1 Taᶜlīḳīzāde, *Firāsetnāme*, 30b: "lā yuṭību'l-ᶜīş bilāhunna / va aşaddu'l-belā hunna.

2 Taᶜlīḳīzāde, *Firāsetnāme*, 30a: "ḥubbu'n-nisā yuḫarribu'l-avṭān / baḥr ᶜamīḳ ḥīletu' n-nisvān."

3 See Ḥasan Kāfī el-Aḳḥiṣārī, *Uṣūl al-ḥikam fī niẓām al-ᶜālam*. *Uṣūl al-ḥikam* was received very favorably at court at the time of its composition (1595), and it has remained a great favorite in studies on Ottoman statecraft. The reason for its popularity was not so much the originality of its ideas but rather its ability to summarize with elegance and precision what was considered to be more or less common wisdom. As such, it lends itself very well to our purposes, in that it provides a lucid and succinct summary of what were thought to be the major causes of the problems faced by the Ottoman state in the late sixteenth century.

to acting upon their advice.[4] The text was written a year after the death of Murād III (r. 1574–95) and was dedicated to his son and successor, Mehmed III. It was, if anything, a scathing assessment of Murād III's two-decade-long reign, claiming that the moral fabric of the ruling elite—and, as a direct consequence, the whole imperial order—was being torn to shreds by the two (intertwined?) social ills of venality and female involvement in governance. Similar, or identical, assessments of the downturn in the fortunes of the House of ᶜO̱smān were voiced by like-minded Ottomans,[5] and the beginnings of the twin evils of the "Sultanate of Women"[6] and of Ottoman "decline"[7] are generally situated in the reign of Murād III.[8]

---

4 In fact, Ḥasan Kāfī listed four causes, all of which ultimately originated in bribery and the desire for women. The first cause for the breakdown of order was negligence in carrying out justice and in implementing proper political relationships; this occurred because state affairs were not assigned to those properly qualified to carry them out. The second cause was negligence in seeking consultation, due to the vanity and haughtiness of the grandees (*ekābir ve aᶜyān*) who declined to consult with scholars and sages (*ᶜulemā ve ḥukemā*). The third cause was negligence in administering the army and maintaining it in a state of preparedness; the cause was that soldiers had no fear of their officers. The fourth cause, fountainhead to the other three, was rampant covetousness and insatiable desire for women (*raġbet*) as well as the habit of acting upon their advice (*nisā ṭāᵓifesine raġbet idüb sözleriyle ᶜamel eylemekdür*). See Ḥasan Kāfī, *Uṣūl al-ḥikam fī niẓām al-ᶜālam*, 249–50.

5 In 1599, mufti Ṣunᶜullāh Efendi included the influence of women "in matters of government and sovereignty" in his criticism of the disruptions in Ottoman society. See Selānikī, *Tārīḫ-i Selānikī*, 826, as quoted in Peirce, *The Imperial Harem*, vii, 179. A quarter century after Ḥasan Kāfī's *Uṣūl al-ḥikam*, the *Kitāb-ı müsteṭāb* came to a similar conclusion regarding the root of the problems besetting the Ottoman Empire: assigning offices to unqualified individuals through bribery and "acting according to the wishes of women." See Anonymous, *Kitāb-ı müsteṭāb*, 31, as quoted in Peirce, *The Imperial Harem*, 179.

6 It was, in fact, during the reign of Murād III that the sultan's mother acquired the formal title of *valide sultan*: "With her formal title, the *valide sultan* joined the ranks of the most exalted officials of the empire, whose status was acknowledged by the omission of their personal names from their titles." Enjoying an officially established role, "the public persona of" Murād III's "*valide sultan* gained expression in a number of ways. . . . Nurbanu established a paradigm for the careers of the *valide sultans* of the century following her death." See Peirce, *The Imperial Harem*, 187.

7 Regarding the so-called Ottoman "decline" paradigm, see Abou-El-Haj, *Formation of the Modern State*; Kafadar, "The Question of Ottoman Decline"; Fleischer, "From Şeyhzade Korkud to Mustafa Âli"; and Howard, "Genre and Myth in the Ottoman Advice for Kings Literature," 137–66.

8 Recent historical works have challenged the notion that the involvement of women in affairs of state was a catalyst for Ottoman decline. Instead, some historians have

In part, such claims may be seen as a direct critique of Murād III and, by extension, his court—both as the sedentary sultan who did not lead his troops into battle (and thus failed to live up to the gazi-warrior ideal of his predecessors) and as the sexually imbalanced sultan who had acquired a reputation for irredeemable lechery "with a record number of consorts," which, incidentally, was preceded by an equally commented upon bout of impotence.[9] The two critiques in fact seemed to work hand in hand, as illustrated by the fact that Murād III had broken the tradition of his predecessors by moving his private chambers into the women's quarters,[10] thus effectively exchanging the battlefield for the harem. Murād III's pathological lechery, coupled with the unprecedentedly influential role in state politics played by his mother and his harem officials, bore an eloquent testimony to the apparent ascendancy of the harem over the traditional imperial elites, particularly the martial elements. In fact, this was precisely the issue with which the critiques found fault; they reacted censoriously to Murād III's attempts to destabilize traditional centers of power, such as the vizier households and the judicial elites, in order to further his absolutist agenda through the creation of alternative foci of power within the court, which included women and harem servants.[11]

---

argued that contemporary or near-contemporary Ottoman attacks on the increasing role of women at court composed a myopic reaction by men who failed to see the larger transformations taking place in their society and thus found the increased and more visible role of women in governance to be an easy target for their frustrations. Consider, for example, Leslie Peirce's argument: "The sedentarization of the sultanate," and with it the increasing role of women, "was part of a whole web of changing circumstances and institutional accommodations, a phenomenon the commentators lacked the perspective of time and distance to appreciate." See Peirce, *The Imperial Harem*, 168. Whatever the motivations behind charges against female participation in government, there seems to have been a general prejudice against it, which could be drawn upon by the commentators.

9 Peirce, *The Imperial Harem*, 94. On Murād's impotence, see Muṣṭafā ᶜĀlī, *Künhü'l-aḫbār*, 289a–b; and Peçevī, *Tārīḫ-i Peçevī*, 2:4–5, as quoted in Peirce, *The Imperial Harem*, 94. For a more detailed discussion of Murād III's impotence, and his sexual life more generally see Felek, "Re-Creating Image and Identity," 5–44.

10 Necipoğlu, *Architecture, Ceremonial, and Power*, 164–65.

11 The creation of alternative centers of power opened up new circulations of resources, which Ḥasan Kāfī and like-minded Ottomans condemned, seemingly equating them with venality. One alternative locus of power became the newly created office of the black eunuch, the chief officer of the harem. See Tezcan, "The Politics of Early Modern Ottoman Historiography," 177–78.

Although these critiques of increased female involvement in governance were voiced within a very specific political context, they also drew on much deeper notions of femininity and masculinity prevalent in the Ottoman intellectual and cultural tradition. This raises important questions: Was the influence of women in government considered to be corrupting by definition? If so, why?

Two physiognomical treatises (*Firāsetnāme* or *Ḳıyāfetnāme*)[12] composed for Murād III, in honor of his accession to the Ottoman throne, might shed some light on these questions. Physiognomy (*ᶜilm-i firāset*, literally the "science of discernment") was considered a legitimate science (*ᶜilm*), and, as such, claimed to offer a scientific explanation for the differences between men and women. It is in physiognomy's analysis of the fundamental makeup of inborn male and female dispositions that contemporaneous Ottoman thoughts on the suitability of women as holders of political power—or lack thereof—may be found.

PHYSIOGNOMY

The reign of Murād III (r. 1574–95) witnessed an increased interest in the science of physiognomy.[13] It was marked not only by a quantitative

12 The terms *firāsetnāme* and *ḳıyāfetnāme* seem to have been used interchangeably to designate Ottoman physiognomical treatises. For example, in the top margin of the first page of Taᶜlīḳīzāde's treatise is written both *firāsetnāme* and *ḳıyāfetnāme*, in Arabic script. However, because in his treatise Taᶜlīḳīzāde refers to physiognomy as *firāset*, I have chosen to refer to his treatise as *Firāsetnāme*. Technically speaking, the science of *firāset* (*ᶜilm-i firāset*) designates what is known as physiognomy in the Western context. Although the term *ḳıyāfet* seems to have been used to mean the same thing, in fact the science of *ḳıyāfet* (*ᶜilm-i ḳıyāfet*), from which the term *ḳıyāfetnāme* is derived, was a tradition that traced morphoscopic or genealogical lines and connections. According to Bālīzāde Muṣṭafā, "*Ḳıyāfet-i beşer* is a tradition through which one who practices it (*ḳāyif*) can ascertain men's grandeur of genealogy and nobility by examining (*naẓar*) them." See Muṣṭafā b. Bālī, *Risāle-i Ḳiyāset-i Firāset*, MS Nuruosmaniye 4100, 14a. Furthermore, Bālīzāde classifies *ḳıyāfet-i beşer* as one of the eight occult sciences (*ᶜulūm-ı ġarībe*) that resemble *ᶜilm-i firāset*. These related traditions, or sciences (*ᶜulūm*), were based on the same principle of acquiring knowledge of the imperceptible through perceptible signs. The first type is based on tracking (*ḳıyāfet*), and it consists of two different arts of *ḳıyāfet*: (1) tracking genealogy (*ḳıyāfet-i beşer*) and (2) tracking traces (*ḳıyāfet-ı i̱sr*) (14a–16a).

13 Although the beginnings of an Ottoman (-Turkish) physiognomical tradition are traceable to the fifteenth century, physiognomy's visibility in the Ottoman corpus

increase in the composition of Ottoman physiognomical treatises—four physiognomical texts were composed within the first few years of his reign—but also by a qualitative change, an expanded understanding of what constituted a physiognomical treatise. In particular, two treatises composed specifically for Murād III transformed the genre of Ottoman physiognomy.[14] The first treatise, *Firāsetnāme,* was composed in 1574 by Taᶜlīḳīzāde (d. 1600), formerly a *kātib* in Murād's princely household.[15] The second treatise, *Risāle-i Ḳiyāset-i Firāset,* was composed in 1576, just over a year later, by Bālīzāde Muṣṭafā (d. 1618), a high-ranking *müderris* and judge.[16]

By definition, physiognomy "consists of inferring the inner character (*aḫlāḳ-ı bāṭıne*) from the exterior state (*aḥvāl-ı ẓāhire*)."[17] It is generally conveyed through a list of *protasis* and *apodosis* between particular shapes and sizes of body parts and their equivalents in terms of

---

ebbed and flowed over the centuries. Interest in physiognomy at the Ottoman court seems to have enjoyed a period of comparatively great intensity during the reign of Murād III, as witnessed by the increased production of physiognomical texts—at least four within the first few years of his reign. For a more detailed treatment of the Ottoman physiognomical tradition during the sixteenth century and its ties to Murād III's reign, see my article, "Physiognomy (ᶜilm-i firāsat) and Ottoman Statecraft: Discerning Morality and Justice," *Arabica* 64 (2017): 609–646.

14 While addressed specifically to the reigning sultan, the treatises must be regarded as part of the broader literary and pictorial blossoming at the Ottoman court during this time—both in terms of qualitative maturation as well as quantitative expansion. The audience of this new literary-artistic explosion far exceeded the person of the sovereign to include the imperial court as a whole. Immense resources were allocated to support this surge, which, aside from its artistic and literary merits, also functioned as an Ottoman imperial acculturation program. It was "instrumental in forming the perspective of their elite audience—the current and future members of the Ottoman court," by disseminating "a particular vision of empire and a shared understanding of the past to the inhabitants of the Topkapı and other imperial palaces and grandee households, both in the capital and beyond." See Fetvacı, *Picturing History at the Ottoman Court*, 4–5.

15 Taᶜlīḳīzāde, *Firāsetnāme*, BnF, MS Turc. 1055. Taᶜlīḳīzāde was a *kātib* in Murād's princely household and openly dedicated his treatise to Murād III. For more on Taᶜlīḳīzāde, see Woodhead, "From Scribe to Litterateur"; and Afyoncu, "Talîkîzâde Mehmed Subhî'nin hayatı hakkında notlar."

16 For Bālīzāde Muṣṭafā, see ᶜAṭāʾī, *Ḥadāʾiḳü'l-ḥaḳāʾiḳ*, 2:620. See also Introduction to Muṣṭafā b. Bālī, *Risāle-i Ḳiyāset-i Firāset* (Sarıçiçek edition).

17 Muṣṭafā b. Bālī, *Risāle-i Ḳiyāset-i Firāset*, MS Nuruosmaniye 4100, 4b. From here on, Muṣṭafā b. Bālī, *Risāle.* Unless otherwise noted, all references to Bālīzāde Muṣṭafā's *Risāle-i Ḳiyāset-i Firāset* are from this specific manuscript copy.

moral character.[18] Taᶜlīḳīzāde and Bālīzāde Muṣṭafā did not neglect that fundamental and defining aspect of Ottoman physiognomy in their treatises. However, they expanded (and redefined) it by listing physiognomy's related sciences[19] and by introducing different "methods" (*ṭuruḳ*) of physiognomy.[20] These methods transcended immediate physical appearance to include a person's gender and life stage, as well as background factors such as social estate/class (*eṣnāf*), race/ethnicity, and clime.[21] Physiognomy was undergirded by humoral theory.

18 An example, selected at random, that establishes a connection between a person's hue and aspects of inner character: "A reddish hue is a sign of quick-bloodedness / A dusky tint signifies good judgment." See Muṣṭafā b. Bālī, *Risāle*, 51a; taken directly from an earlier Ottoman physiognomical treatise: Ḥamdullāh Ḥamdī (d. 1503), *Ḳıyāfetnāme*, 2a.

19 The related traditions, or sciences (*ᶜulūm*), were based on the same principle of acquiring knowledge of the imperceptible through perceptible signs and included, among others, tracking (*ḳıyāfet*), further subdivided into tracking genealogy (*ḳıyāfet-i beşer*) and tracking traces (*ḳıyāfet-ı iṣr*); divination (*ᶜilm-i ᶜirāfet*); palmistry, or, literally, the science of palm and foot sole lineaments (*ᶜilm-i huṭūṭ-i ekuff u aḳdām*); the tradition of deducing particular states based on, for example, palpitating a pupil or moles; the tradition of discerning the states of the higher world based on reading the signs made by rays of light hitting sheep withers; predicting rainfall or absence thereof based on observing clouds, thunder, and lighting; dowsing for water; extracting valuable minerals and metals from mines. See Muṣṭafā b. Bālī, *Risāle*, 14a–21a.

20 The different "methods" (*ṭuruḳ*) of physiognomy were divided into seven by Bālīzāde Muṣṭafā: the first method is based on a predictable correspondence between limbs and characteristics; it rests on the presupposition that the inborn disposition matches its reflection in a person's appearance and has not changed or been transformed through training or self-discipline. The second method is based on predictable correspondences between sounds and character. The third method is based on zoological physiognomy. The fourth method is based on social estate/caste and racial/ethnic background. The fifth method is based on gender. The sixth method is based on the fact that certain characteristics appear together in groupings, and if one (for example, shamelessness) is discerned in a person it may be assumed that its associate characteristics (for example, abjectness, pilferage, parsimony) will also predominate in that person. See Muṣṭafā b. Bālī, *Risāle*, 21a–27a.

21 The new physiognomical methods were, in fact, as old as physiognomy itself. They are found in the first Greek treatises and, not surprisingly, also in the earliest Arabic physiognomical treatises, which were based on their Greek predecessors. Interestingly, it was not until the sixteenth century that the full breadth and complexity of the physiognomical tradition was translated into Ottoman.

GENDER PHYSIOGNOMY IN THEORY

One of the physiognomical methods was gender. Just as particular shapes of human limbs were thought to reflect specific sets of characteristics, so, too, was each gender thought to be reflective of particular character traits. The basis for the characterization of the genders was humoral theory. The archetypal male temperament (*mizāc*) was described as warm and dry (that is, choleric), while the archetypal female temperament was described as cold and moist (that is, phlegmatic).[22] A temperament (*mizāc*) was described as a dynamic "combination of contraries"—the four elemental qualities: warm, cold, moist, and dry.[23] In most human beings, one element—or, more commonly, a combination of two elements—tends to predominate. The ideal, however, is an equable or balanced temperament[24]: "if the quality and quantity of the four elements, of which it

---

22 The four humors were originally based on "concrete, visible and tangible parts of the body," black bile, phlegm, yellow (or red) bile, and blood, each of which acquired particular physiological and psychological characteristics. "Humours corresponded, it was held, to the cosmic elements and to the divisions of time; they controlled the whole existence and behaviour of mankind, and, according to the manner in which they were combined, determined the character of the individual." See Klibansky, Panofsky, and Saxl, *Saturn and Melancholy*, 3.

The following schema summarizes the basis of humoral theory:

Humor	*Season*	*(Ages of Man)*	*Qualities*
Blood	Spring	Boyhood/Youth	Warm and Moist
Yellow Bile	Summer	Youth/Prime	Warm and Dry
Black Bile	Autumn	Manhood/Decline	Cold and Dry
Phlegm	Winter	Old Age	Cold and Moist

It must be noted that this particular application of humors to males (warm and dry) and females (wet and humid), respectively, is as old as physiognomy itself and can be traced to the beginnings of the Islamic physiognomical tradition. See, for example, Fakhruddīn Rāzī's physiognomical treatise *Kitāb al-firāsa*, on which both Bālīzāde Muṣṭafā's *Risāle-i Ḳiyāset-i Firāset* and Taᶜlīḳīzāde's *Firāsetnāme* are based. See Mourad, *La Physiognomie Arabe et le Kitâb al-Firâsa de Fakhr al-dîn al-Râzî*, 24 (Arabic), 89 (French).

23 "Temperament is the quality produced from the interaction of opposing qualities that stabilize at a certain point." See Ibn Sīnā, *al-Qānūn fī'l-ṭibb* (1993), 1:19, as translated in Abu-Asab, Amri, and Micozzi, *Avicenna's Medicine*, 54.

24 In his *al-Qānūn fī'l-ṭibb*, Ibn Sīnā mentions nine types of temperament, "classified into eight *unequables* and one *equable* (balanced). Unequables are products of the inequality of the opposite qualities; they are comprised of four single temperaments: hot, cold, wet, and dry; and four composites: hot and dry, hot and wet, cold and dry, and cold and wet." See Abu-Asab, Amri, and Micozzi, *Avicenna's Medicine*, 51.

is made up, have the proper ratio [to each other], the temperament is well-proportioned and equable (*muᶜtedil*). If the four elements do not have the proper ratios, the temperament is inequable (*ġayr-i muᶜtedil*)."[25] An equable combination of contraries in a temperament is, according to Bālīzāde Muṣṭafā, the "cause of perfection" (*bāᶜiṡ-i kemāl*), while a combination which is "excessive or deficient" (*zāyid ü nāḳıṣ*) in certain elements "is a cause of defectiveness (*mūcib-i iḫtilāl*)."[26]

The natural temperamental makeups of the two genders, which are described as warm-dry and cold-moist, are thus in reality markers of defectiveness (*iḫtilāl*), for only an equable or perfectly balanced temperament is "the cause of perfection." Understanding the stylized, perfectly opposite portrayal of the two genders can, however, also be seen as a way of bringing to light their complementary natures. All the characteristics which the male, choleric humor lacks are found in the female, phlegmatic humor, and vice versa. Thus, the two genders, when properly united, can form a complete whole with an equable proportion of elements—the "cause of perfection." This suggests that acquaintance with one's opposite gender could highlight and bring into focus the deficiencies and excesses of an individual's own particular temperament. Intimate acquaintance between the genders is presented as an intensified interaction between the warm-dry male and cold-moist female humors, which are imbalanced in opposite ways; this interaction allows for the possibility of balance.

On the other hand, if the physiognomical descriptions of archetypal choleric males and phlegmatic females are taken as being less descriptive of reality and more prescriptive of an imagined reality, then the male–female relationship becomes an important setting in which the prescriptive choleric-male and phlegmatic-female characteristics are honed and perfected. Such a setting creates tension between the two opposites,

25 Muṣṭafā b. Bālī, *Risāle*, 29a: "Eger ᶜanāṣır-ı erbaᶜadan ḥāṣıl olan keyf ü kemmde vech-i lāyıḳ üzere olursa mizāc muᶜtedildür. Eger ᶜanaṣır-ı erbaᶜadan ḥāṣıl olan vech-i lāyıḳ üzere olmazsa mizāc ġayr-ı muᶜtedildür." According to Ibn Sīnā, the temperate, or balanced, temperament "is not derived from quantitative equality but rather from fairness in distribution, and that is, when in the body of a healthy individual the temperament components have the optimum quantity and quality for a human temperament at the best distribution and ratio." See Ibn Sīnā, *al-Qānūn fī'l-ṭibb*, 19, as translated in Abu-Asab, Amri, and Micozzi, *Avicenna's Medicine*, 54.

26 Muṣṭafā b. Bālī, *Risāle*, 29b.

which in turn brings out and intensifies (what are considered to be) the essential character traits of each.

The gender types constructed by Bālīzāde Muṣṭafā and Taᶜlīḳīzāde should not be taken too literally. Rather, the attribution of specific traits to each of the genders seems to indicate that females and males differ in the frequency of appearance and intensity of particular traits. Bālīzāde adds, rather matter-of-factly,

> If the form and shape which are necessitated by the specific character (*aḫlāḳ*) of women are seen in a man, we can determine that he possesses characteristics of a feminine inner nature (*ḫulḳ*). In the same way, if the form and shape which are necessitated by the specific masculine inner nature (*ḫulḳ*) are observed in women, it can be determined that they possess characteristics of the male nature. And God knows best.[27]

Thus, the feminine and masculine inner natures seem to be polar opposites on an abstract level; in reality, they can manifest in either gender.

Furthermore, not all men are considered to be of a choleric humor, nor all women of a phlegmatic humor; the treatises themselves speak of different types of temperaments regardless of gender. Indeed, the generalizations made in the name of gender physiognomy seem to be meant only within the specific context of the male–female dichotomy. The dichotomy introduced by gender physiognomy should—without completely undermining its descriptive possibilities, for the divide between description and prescription of social norms is rarely very clear—furthermore be seen as a manual in *performativity*,[28] which encapsulates socially

---

27 Muṣṭafā b. Bālī, *Risāle*, 26a–26b: "Cins-i nisāda olan aḫlāḳ-ı maḫṣūṣa ne şekl ü ne hey'et iḳtiżā ederse erlerden birisinde ol şekli müşāhede edicek ᶜavretlerde olan ḫulḳ ile ittiṣāfına ḥükm ederiz. Ve ke-ẕālik erlerde olan ḫulḳ-ı maḫṣūṣ ne şekl ve ne hey'et iḳtiżā ederse ol şekli ᶜavretlerde göricek ricālde olan ḫulḳ ile ittiṣāflarına ḥükm olunur. Va Allāhu aᶜlem."

28 Consider, for example, Michael Herzfield's insightful observation about a Cretan village: "In Glendiot idiom, there is less focus on 'being a good man' than on 'being *good at* being a man'—a stance that stresses *performative excellence*, the ability to foreground manhood by means of deeds that strikingly 'speak for themselves.'" See Herzfeld, *The Poetics of Manhood*, 16. See also Gilmore, *Manhood in the Making*, 9–29.

and culturally agreed-upon contours of expected behavior for men and women.[29]

Scholars have pointed out the strongly developed gender roles, to the point of "gender polarity," prevalent in the Mediterranean basin, in which opposing character traits, such as timidity in women and assertiveness in men, are valued and taken as defining standards.[30] El-Rouayheb's examination of sexuality in the Ottoman Arab provinces between 1500 and 1800, for example, argues that

> the early Ottoman Arab East evidently belonged to the latter category [of "gender polarity"], with its separate and clearly demarcated male and female spheres, which legitimately overlapped only in certain well-defined contexts. Merely by virtue of his biological sex, a man was expected to participate in a world from which women were in principle excluded. This was the public world in which men competed and cooperated in the pursuit of money, status, and power. Succeeding in this world was to succeed as a male, to live up to the demands of masculinity, and was thus on the symbolic level linked to virility. Defeat, on the other hand, was symbolically equivalent to calling into question male gender identity, to emasculation.[31]

This apt description of the Ottoman Arab East, which is rooted in more general observations about the Mediterranean basin, seems to provide a fitting context for the dichotomous gender characterizations made in sixteenth century Ottoman physiognomy. The social context of "gender polarity" created particular expectations of men and women, which stood at the heart of the envisioned social and political order. Any transgression of the established expectations in *performativity* could be considered a serious breach of the social covenant and was sure to trigger repercussions.

---

29 At the risk of stating the obvious, it should be noted that the physiognomical treatises were written by men, for men and the degree of their objectivity, or lack thereof, must be kept in mind accordingly.

30 For an insightful study of honor and gender in contemporary Mediterranean culture, see Gilmore, "Introduction: The Shame of Dishonour."

31 El-Rouayheb, *Before Homosexuality in the Arab-Islamic World*, 25–26.

GENDER PHYSIOGNOMY IN PRACTICE

According to Bālīzāde Muṣṭafā's physiognomical treatise, the warm and dry male temperament, in every species (that is, not only human), is stronger (*eḳvā*) and more perfect (*ekmel*) than its cold and moist female counterpart. "Yet," adds Bālīzāde, "it happens at times that a perfect individual (*ferd-i kāmil*) is found amongst the female gender, who has few counterparts amongst the male gender."[32] The reason that the male temperament (*mizāc*) was thought of as being stronger and more perfect than the female is its humoral composition, which dictates the states of both soul (*nüfūs*) and body (*ebdān*).[33] Yet, as Bālīzāde makes sure to point out, this is a general rule, which does not necessarily apply to every single individual; it may well happen that a woman is superior to most men. However, such a woman, who has become a perfect or complete individual (*ferd-i kāmil*) and is thus superior to most men, seems, in the greater scheme of things, to be the exception that proves the general rule of female inferiority.

Bālīzāde Muṣṭafā continues with a systematic elaboration of the precise physical and character-based manifestations of the archetypal male temperament, based on the choleric humor:

> First sign: male bodies are firm and taut (*ṣıḳışmış*), the chest and nerves (*siŋir*) are strong, the feet are large and thick; the face and skin are even more lacking in slenderness (*leṭāfet*) [than the aforementioned limbs].
>
> Second sign: the appetite and digestion of males is greater and their endurance (*taḥammül*) in movement and hardships is vaster.
>
> Third sign: males have a stronger and more powerful pulse (*nabż*). They have greater courage, perseverance (*iḳdām*) and irascibility (*ġażab*).
>
> Fourth sign: males are stronger than females in acts of the spirit (*efᶜāl-i nefsāniyye*), that is, they are stronger in excellence of intellect, in beauty of reflection and thought, and in learning the sciences.
>
> Fifth sign: in generosity and improvement of moral qualities (*maḥāsin-i aḫlāḳ*) males are superior to females.[34]

32 Muṣṭafā b. Bālī, *Risāle*, 54a: "Fa-ammā gāh olur cins-i ināṡdan baᶜżı ferd-i kāmil bulunur ki cins-i ricālde aŋa muᶜādil az bulunur."

33 Muṣṭafā b. Bālī, *Risāle*, 54a.

34 Muṣṭafā b. Bālī, *Risāle*, 54a: "Delāyil-i ẕukūr. Delīl-i evvel: er cinsiniŋ bedenleri berk ve ṣıḳışmış olur ve göğüsleri ḳavī olur ve sinirleri ḳavī ve ayaḳları kebīr ü ġalīẓ olur ve

Conversely, the archetypal female temperament, based on the phlegmatic humor, with its combination of cold and moist qualities, is the exact opposite of the typically male choleric humor, and thus, predictably, exhibits qualities opposite the above-listed male characteristics:

> First sign: female bodies are soft (*gevşek*) and fleshy (*etli*). Their thighs are fleshy (*uyluḳları etli*), their faces are fine and slender (*laṭīf*), their chests weak. Their ribs are slender (*laṭīf*) and small and their feet, too, are fine and slender (*laṭīf*). Their nerves are mild and soft (*mülāyim*). Because the meat that contains the soft tissues (tendons, sinews, nerves) of the body (*āᶜṣablar*) is predominantly humid the body's soft tissues are also soft (*līnet*).
>
> Second sign: the female of every species has a small head. Furthermore, their hips and thighs are fleshy (*ucaları ve uyluḳları etli*), and their calves are thick (*sāḳı kalın olur*).
>
> Third sign: women are passive (*sükūn*) and move little. Their souls (*nefs*) are inert (*murde*) and they lack strength and vigor (*ḳuvvet u şiddet*). They easily submit and obey (*inḳiyād*).
>
> Fourth sign: they lack irascibility (*ġażab*) and have little inclination for vengeance (*intiḳām*). However, deception (*mekr*), brazenness (*bī-ḥayālik*) and transgression of every ordered prohibition are predominant (*artuḳ*) amongst[35] women.
>
> Fifth sign: they are deficient (*eksik*) in acts of the spirit (*efᶜāl-i nefsāniyye*), in the improvement of moral qualities (*maḥāsin-i aẖlāḳ*), and in the ennoblement of actions (*mekārim-i efᶜāl*).[36]

---

yüzleri vesāyir beşereleri leṭāfetde anlardan eksik olur. İkinci delīl: erkek cinsiniŋ iştihāları ziyāde ve hażmları artuḳ ve ḥareket ü meşaḳḳate taḥammülleri ziyāde olur. Üçünci delīl: erkek cinsiniŋ nabżları ḳavī ve ᶜaẓīm olur ve şecāᶜat u iḳdām u ġażabları ziyāde olur. Dördünci delīl: erkek cinsi efᶜāl-i nefsāniyyede ünṣā cinsinden ḳavīdir, yaᶜnī cevdet-i ẕihn ü ḥüsn-ü reviyyet ü fikr ve taḥṣīl-i ᶜulūmda bunlar ḳavīdir. Beşinci delīl: kerem ve meḥāsin-i aẖlāḳda cins-i ricāl nisāndan artuḳdur."

35 In the second (and only other extant) manuscript copy of Muṣṭafā b. Bālī's *Risāle*, the author adds that this is true for "all women" (*ḳamu ᶜavretler*). See Muṣṭafā b. Bālī, *Risāle*, MS Izmirli Hakkı 1926, 54a.

36 Muṣṭafā b. Bālī, *Risāle*, 54b: "Delīl-i evvel: ᶜavretleriŋ bedenleri gevşek olur ve etli olurlar ve uyluḳları etli ve yüzleri laṭīf ve gögüsleri żaᶜīf ve egegileri leṭāfet üzere ve küçük olur ve ayaḳları daẖi laṭīf olur ve siŋirleri mülāyim olur zīrā aᶜṣābların iḥāṭa iden laḥm ruṭūbet üzere olmağla aᶜṣābları daẖi līnet üzere olur. İkinci delīl: her cinsiŋ dişisiniŋ başı küçük olur fa-ammā ucaları ve uyluḳları etli olur ve ᶜavretleriŋ sāḳı ḳalın olur. Üçünci delīl: ᶜavretler sükūn üzere olur ve ḥareketleri az olur ve nefsleri

Bālīzāde Muṣṭafā's comparatively short entry on gender physiognomy is very straightforward and strictly based on the scientific theory of the humors: particular humoral combinations dictate a predictable range of outcomes, both physiologically and psychologically.[37] In short, the warm and dry choleric humor, which rules the male gender, is marked by physical and mental strength and irascibility. It is complemented by a capacity for generosity and high moral character. The female gender, on the other hand, is dominated by the cold and moist phlegmatic humor. It is by nature weak in body and in spirit, as well as docile and passive. Female physiological and psychological weakness is complemented by moral weakness; unlike men, women lack the capacity for great moral improvement.

The major themes that define Bālīzāde Muṣṭafā's dichotomous separation of the two genders also mark Taᶜlīḳīzāde's description. There is, however, a difference in emphasis. Taᶜlīḳīzāde opens his section on gender physiognomy with a brief catalog of the predominant male and female characteristics:

---

mürde olur ve ḳuvvet ü şiddet üzere olmazlar. İnḳıyādları sehl olur. Dördünci delīl: bunlarıŋ ġażabları eksik ve intiḳāma raġbetleri az olur. Fa-ammā ḳamu ᶜavretlerde mekr ü bī-ḥayālıḳ ve her emrde ḥadden tecāvüz artuḳ olur. Bu ẕikr olunan umūr delālet eder ki mizācları żaᶜīf ola. Beşinci delīl budur ki efᶜāl-i nefsāniyyede ve meḥāsin-i aḫlāḳ ve mekārim-i efᶜālda bunlar eksik olur."

37 It is also very similar to the gender entry in the earliest extant Greek physiognomical treatise: "Of all the animals which we attempt to breed the females are tamer and gentler in disposition than the males, but less powerful, and more susceptible to rearing and handling. This being their character, they have less spirit than the males. This is perhaps obvious from our own case, for when we are overcome by temper, we become less submissive and are more determined in no circumstance to yield to anyone, but we are inclined to violence and to act in any direction to which our temper impels us. But it seems to me that the female sex has a more evil disposition than the male, is more forward and less courageous. Women and the female animals bred by us are evidently so; and all shepherds and hunters admit that they are such as we have already described in their natural state. Moreover, this is also obvious, that in each class each female has a smaller head, a narrower face and a more slender neck than the male, as well as a weaker chest and smaller ribs, and that the loins and thighs are more covered with flesh than in the males, that the female has knock-knees and spindly calves, neater feet, and the whole shape of the body built for charm rather than for nobility, with less strong sinews and with softer, moister flesh. The males are in every respect opposite to this; their nature is as a class braver and more honest, that of the female being more cowardly and less honest." See Ps.-Aristotle, *Physiognomy*, 109–10; 809a–809b. It is worth adding that Ps.-Aristotle's *Physiognomy* was not at all based on humoral theory, which in turn raises questions about the precise nature of the relationship between humoral theory and physiognomy in Taᶜlīḳīzāde and Bālīzāde Muṣṭafā's treatises.

> Masculinity is dominated by heat[38] and necessitates the following: a hard and strong body (*bedeni ṣulb ve muḥkem*), firm (*berk*) bone and marrow.
>
> Femininity is dominated by coldness and moistness; [female] bodies are tender (*süst*) and exceedingly fleshy (*eti ziyāde*). Females of all species have smaller heads than males. Their faces are exceptionally beautiful (*beġāyet güzel*), their necks are slender (*ince*), their bosoms pure (*ṣāf*), their thighs are fleshy (*etli*), soft (*mülāyim*) and elegant (*nāzik*), their legs are thick (*ġalīẓ*), their feet are slender and thin (*nerm ü laṭīf*), with tender (*raḳīḳ*) soles.
>
> However, they are incapable of enduring frightful affairs (*umūr-ı muḫavvife*) and anything that causes fatigue and misery (*matāᶜib-i ṣāḳe*). They lack the strength for continued movement (*ḥarekāt-i müstemirre*).[39]

Taᶜlīḳīzāde presents a set of characteristics that first focuses exclusively on the physical aspects of men and women, especially on the notion that men are strong and women are beautiful.[40] He then introduces two further characteristics that distinguish the male and female types from each other: "In truth, courage for women is fear and their generosity is avarice."[41] It is, in other words, perfectly normal for women to be timid and covetous, but these same characteristics are shameful for men.[42] In this respect, Taᶜlīḳīzāde and Bālīzāde Muṣṭafā are in full agreement—

---

38 Taᶜlīḳīzāde omits, or forgets to mention, dryness here. Given that for femininity he lists both moistness and coldness, it would seem to be an insignificant omission, especially as he clearly followed the same patterns elaborated above by Bālīzāde Muṣṭafā.

39 Taᶜlīḳīzāde, *Firāsetnāme*, 29a–29b: "Ẕukūret istilāyı ḥarāret sebebile buni iḳtiżā eyler ki bedeni ṣulb ve muḥkem ola ve maġz u ustuḫᵛāni ziyāde berk ola. Ve unūs̱et ġalebe-yi burūdet ve ruṭūbet sebebiyle bedenleri süst ve eti ziyāde olur ve nisvānıŋ her çendiniŋ başı ẕukūrden küçük olur. Ammā yüzleri be-ġāyet güzel ve boyunları ince ve sīneleri ṣāf ve rānları etli ve mülāyim ve nāzik ve sāḳları ġalīẓ ve ḳademleriniŋ yüzi nerm ve laṭīf ve altı raḳīḳ olur. Ammā umūr-ı muḫavvife ve matāᶜib-i ṣāḳeye müteḥammil olmayub ḥarekāt-i müstemirreye iḳtidārları yoḳdur."

40 Although it should be noted that Bālīzāde Muṣṭafā also stressed the elegant beauty (*leṭāfet*) of females, in contrast to males.

41 Taᶜlīḳīzāde, *Firāsetnāme*, 29b: "Fī'l-ḥaḳīḳa ᶜavrete tarsnāk olmaḳ şecāᶜat ve imsāk saḫāvetdir."

42 Taᶜlīḳīzāde, *Firāsetnāme*, 29b.

courage and generosity are defining characteristics, and possession of them, or lack thereof, marks the male and female genders, respectively.[43]

Taᶜlīḳīzāde adds another layer of defining female characteristics through a very interesting play on the creation parable. As is known, writes Taᶜlīḳīzāde, man was created from dust, and woman was created from man's left rib. Hence, they both carry within them the strength (*himmet*) of their source of origin: man's power (*himmet*) is that of dust, while woman's power (*himmet*) is that of the human being. "Thus," continues Taᶜlīḳīzāde, "because women lack corporeal and bodily strength, their power is their world-conquering intellect (*ᶜaḳl*)."[44] Women, Taᶜlīḳīzāde argues, have been endowed with superior intelligence as a counterweight to man's overwhelming physical (and moral?) superiority. Interestingly, Bālīzāde Muṣṭafā never mentions the superiority of female intellect, unless female deception (*mekr*) was meant as a degenerate form of what Taᶜlīḳīzāde describes as intelligence (*ᶜaḳl*).[45] Ultimately, however, Taᶜlīḳīzāde's initially positive portrayal of female intelligence takes on a more negative tone. He concludes that female intelligence, if turned to scheming, can be of great danger to men, and he seeks refuge in God from the snares of women, which "incline towards guile like the coquettish *dunyā* and towards deception like the *nefs-i emmāre*."[46] Women's interest in men, he continues, is driven by one of two things: noble background (*şeref-i neseb*) or wealth (*māl*). Yet, adds the author, such money as attracts a woman is cursed, as is the woman who covets it.[47]

---

43 Neither of the two physiognomical treatises takes for granted that all men are endowed with the defining male characteristics of courage and generosity, thus complicating this neat binary opposition between the two genders.

44 Taᶜlīḳīzāde, *Firāsetnāme*, 30a: "Ammā çünkim ḳuvvet-i cismāniye ve ḳuvvet-i cüsmāniyeleri yoḳdur himmetlerin nīrū-yi ᶜaḳl-ı kure-kuşāye ṣarf ederler."

45 In fact, Taᶜlīḳīzāde himself, just a few lines prior, speaks of female stratagems (*ḥīle*), which he equates to bottomless seas (*baḥr ᶜamīḳ*), and quotes a hadith that compares women to satanic snares (*inne'n-nisā ḥabā'ilu'ş-şeyṭān*). See Taᶜlīḳīzāde, *Firāsetnāme*, 30a.

46 Taᶜlīḳīzāde, *Firāsetnāme*, 31b–32a: "Nastaᶜīẕullāh min ḳaydı'n-nisā, şöyle ki Dalla-i dünyā gibi muḥtāle ve nefs-i emmāre gibi muḳāyede meyyāle."

47 Taᶜlīḳīzāde, *Firāsetnāme*, 32a.

GENDER PHYSIOGNOMY IN CONTEXT: HUMORAL THEORY

The two lists of gender physiognomy, particularly the one created with Bālīzāde Muṣṭafā's methodical approach, create a dichotomous opposition between the two genders and their sets of dominant characteristics, and thus present the male and female genders as mirror opposites of each other. A closer look into humoral theory more generally, however, reveals that this particular articulation of the two humors—as seen, for example, in Bālīzāde Muṣṭafā's deliberate exclusion of the superiority of feminine intelligence—is often uneven; it is rather ungenerous toward the female phlegmatic humor and exceedingly generous toward the male choleric humor. While the choleric humor, whose symbol is fire, is indeed characterized by an extremely high level of energy, aggressiveness, and physical and mental fitness, its darker side is a violently vengeful, resentfully envious, acrid, and negative character, possessed by uncontrolled rage. On the other hand, a more positive dimension of the phlegmatic humor is a person who, while admittedly sluggish, pallid, and timid, is also peaceful, controlled, reliable, even-tempered, and calm.[48] Thus, it becomes apparent that the authors of these treatises have selected very specific combinations of possible character traits to construct specific choleric-male and phlegmatic-female types.

Because humoral theory, according to the treatises, forms the scientific underpinnings for physiognomy, it is addressed in some detail by both treatises. Bālīzāde Muṣṭafā even explores the workings of the different temperaments within the larger medical–philosophical tripartite division of the soul into vegetative, animal, and human aspects.[49] This general

48 For more on the humors, see Arikha, *Passions and Tempers*.

49 Classical Ottoman medicine and philosophy divided the soul into three parts: vegetative soul, animal soul, and human soul. Each of these souls has several faculties. The four faculties of the vegetative soul (*nefs-i nebātī*) are (1) the nutritive faculty (*ḳuvvet-i ġadiye*), by which the organism supplies nourishment for the body; (2) the faculty of augmentation (*ḳuvvet-i nāmiye*), by which, up to a certain period of life, the organism grows, that is, increases in length, breadth, and depth; (3) the faculty of generation (*ḳuvvet-i müvellide*), by which the organism, by detaching a portion of itself, produces another similar individual; (4) the informative faculty (*ḳuvvet-i muṣavvire*), by which the aforesaid detached portion, if it fall into a suitable place, is molded into its proper form and fashioned into a similar individual. These four faculties are served by four others: (1) the attractive faculty (*ḳuvvet-i cāẕibe*), by which the organism draws to itself the material proper for its nourishment; (2) the retentive faculty (*ḳuvvet-i māsike*), by which it retains the food in the proper place

description of the temperaments,[50] beyond the male–female dichotomy, makes for an interesting comparison with the particular manifestations of the temperaments in gender physiognomy. The choleric humor, according to Bālīzāde Muṣṭafā, is recognizable by the following signs,

> signs of psychic actions (*efʿāl-i nefsāniyye*)[51]: intelligence (*ẕekā*) and excellent mind (*ẕihn*). However, the power of mind (that is, memory) is stronger than the power of thought (*fikr*), because dryness gives rise to perfect memory (*ḥıfẓ*). Thought, which consists of moving from one form (*ṣūret*) to another, reaches its perfection with moistness. The senses are clear (*ṣafā*) and the faculty of movement (*ḳuvvet-i muḥarrike*), or the practical faculty (*ḳuvvet-i ʿāmile*), is exceptionally perfect (*kemāl*).
>
> Signs of the animal faculty (*ḳuvvet-i ḥayvāniyye*): courage, strength, boldness and temerity are strong and each one is close to being permanently fixed. Pulse and breath are strong and quick.
>
> Signs of the informative faculty (*ḳuvvet-i müṣavvire*): the chest is wide, the arteries are wide; joint bones are visible.
>
> Signs of the generative faculty (*ḳuvvet-i müvellide*): lust for intercourse (*şehvet-i cimāʿ*), but also a shortage of seminal fluid.
>
> Signs of the nutritive faculty (*ḳuvvet-i ġadiyye*): leanness.
>
> Sings of the digestive faculty (*ḳuvvet-i hāẓime*): digests heavy (*ġalīẓ*) foods well, light (*laṭīf*) foods not so well.

---

until digested; (3) the digestive faculty (*ḳuvvet-i hāżime*), by which it converts the food into matter proper for the reparation of the waste of the body; (4) the expulsive faculty (*ḳuvvet-i dāfiʿa*), by which it casts forth what is superfluous. The animal soul (*nefs-i ḥayvānī*), which contains all the faculties of the vegetative soul, is defined by the faculty of organic perception and the faculty of voluntary motion. The faculty of organic perception directs the five external senses (sight, hearing, smell, taste, and touch) and the five internal senses (common sense, fantasy, reflection, estimation, and recollection). The faculty of voluntary motion is also divided into two: that which attracts beneficial things, called the concupiscible faculty (*ḳuvvet-i şeheviyye*), and that which repels harmful things, named the irascible faculty (*ḳuvvet-i ġażabiyye*). The human soul (*nefs-i insānī*), which contains all the faculties of the vegetative and animal souls, is mainly distinguished from the other two through possession of the faculty of rationality. See Muṣṭafā b. Bālī, *Risāle*, 29b–32a.

50 Gender here seems to be irrelevant, although one does get the vague impression that in fact it is only concerned with the male gender.

51 The psychic faculty (*ḳuvvet-i nefsāniye*), as Bālīzāde Muṣṭafā explains in the introduction to this chapter of the treatise, is the equivalent in Ottoman medical parlance of what philosophers call the human soul. See Muṣṭafā b. Bālī, *Risāle*, 29b–30a.

Signs of the expulsive faculty (*ḳuvvet-i dāfiᶜa*): sparse discharge of sweat, urine, excrement or other remnants. The body is very hairy. Shaved hair grows fast. The hair on the head is black and dense. With the passing of time the front of the head becomes hairless. Complexion is olive-complexioned, with a strong dark shade.

Things that it is affected by (*infiᶜālāt*): the constitution is warm and firm. It benefits from cold and moist objects. Warm and dry things are harmful to it.[52]

This general description of the choleric humor—which nearly resembles a beast of prey: highly acute senses, exceptionally agile body, strong, bold, and courageous, lean with a wide chest and highly lascivious—more or less matches the description of the male choleric humor.

The major difference between this general description of the choleric humor and the description of the specifically male choleric humor is the stress on a diminished capacity for thought (*fikr*)—one might even say, diminished mental capacity or intelligence—in the general description. Instead, the general choleric humor is endowed with a strong memory (*ḥıfẓ*). Interestingly, this is in direct contrast to the description of the male choleric humor, which, as mentioned above, Bālīzāde Muṣṭafā describes as being "stronger in excellence of intellect, in beauty of reflection and thought, and in learning the sciences" than its female phlegmatic counterpart.[53] According to the above-quoted general description of the choleric

52 Muṣṭafā b. Bālī, *Risāle*, 33b–34a: "Delāyil-i mizāc-ı ḥarr-ı yābis. Delāyil-i efᶜāl-i nefsāniyye: ẕekā ve cevdet-i ẕihn fa-ammā ḳuvvet-i ẕihni ḳuvvet-i fikrden aḳvā ola zīrā ḥıfẓ yubūset ile kāmil olur ve fikr ki bir ṣūretden ṣūret-i uḫrāya intiḳālden ᶜibāretdir ruṭūbet ile kāmil olur ve ḥavāssi ṣafā üzerine olmaḳ ve ḳuvvet-i muḥarrikesi yaᶜnī ḳuvvet-i ᶜāmilesi be-ġāyet kemālde olmaḳ. Delāyil-i ḳuvvet-i ḥayvāniyye: şecāᶜat ve şiddet ve iḳdām ve tehevvür ḳavī fa-ammā her biri s̱ebāta maḳrūn ola ve nabż u nefesi ḳuvvet ü sürᶜat üzere olmaḳ. Delāyil-i ḳuvvet-i muṣavvire: gögsi giŋ olmaḳ ve ṭamarları giŋ olmaḳ ve eŋ kemikleri ẓāhir olmaḳ. Delāyil-i ḳuvvet-i müvellide: şehvet-i cimāᶜ fa-ammā menī ḳıllet üzere ola. Delāyil-i ġadiyye naḥāfet. Delāyil-i hāżima: ġalīẓ ġıdāları eyü hażm etmek ve laṭīf ġıdāları hażmi redāᵓet üzerine olmaḳ. Delāyil-i ḳuvvet-i dāfiᶜa: ḳıllet-i istifrāġ yaᶜnī ᶜaraḳ ile ve bevl ü berāz vesāyir fażalāt ile ve bedeni ġāyet ile ḳıllı ola ve tirāşı ġāyet tīz gelmek ve başınıŋ ḳılları siyāh olmaḳ ve bitdügi zamān da sıḳ bitmek ve eger zamān geçerse başınıŋ öŋi ḳılsız ola ve beŋzi buġday eŋlü ola fa-ammā ḳarası ḳatı artuḳ ola. İnfiᶜālāt: yapışılması ısıcaḳ olmaḳ ve berk olmaḳ ve bārid-i raṭb nesnelerden müntefiᶜ olmaḳ ve ḥārr-i yābis eşyādan müteᵓez̠z̠ī olmaḳ."

53 Muṣṭafā b. Bālī, *Risāle*, 54a.

humor, however, it is precisely the moist-cold phlegmatic humor that, by virtue of being moist, is endowed with the capacity for thought. Thus, Bālīzāde's general description of the choleric humor confirms Taᶜlīḳīzāde's claim of superior female intelligence.[54] Unfortunately, Bālīzāde Muṣṭafā does not provide the same detailed description of the phlegmatic humor; he merely adds that it is the exact opposite of the choleric humor.

Another major difference between Bālīzāde Muṣṭafā's general choleric and male choleric descriptions is the omission of the lust for intercourse (*şehvet-i cimāᶜ*) in the specifically male choleric characterization. Although the major and dominant characteristic of the fiery choleric humor is irascibility (*ġażab*)—or, put differently, a predominance of the irascible faculty (*ḳuvvet-i ġażabiyye*)—it seems, based on Bālīzāde's description of the general choleric humor, that the choleric humor was not immune to the desires of the concupiscible faculty (*ḳuvvet-i şeheviyye*). This might in fact shed some light on the problem that contemporary or near-contemporary Ottomans found with Murād III's lasciviousness: his excessive lust for intercourse would seem to have sapped his irascible energies.[55] As a result, the head of the Ottoman *devlet* failed to live up to his martial expectations and betrayed the defining characteristic of the choleric humor, which was the fundamental prerequisite for membership in the *ᶜaskerī,* or warrior class—the Ottoman military-administrative elite—to which the sultan belonged.[56]

---

54 Taᶜlīḳīzāde's description of the humors, however, further complicates things immensely. According to Taᶜlīḳīzāde, the person dominated by the choleric humor "has an excellent mind (*al-ḫāṭir*), accurate thinking (*ṣādiḳ al-fikr*), acute vision (*al-naẓar*), excellent memory, penetrating vision (*raʾy*)...." See Taᶜlīḳīzāde, *Firāsetnāme*, 39a–39b.

55 It is well known that athletes and soldiers are discouraged from sexual intercourse, especially before major events, because it is thought to diminish their irascible energies. Thus, for example, in the *sirr al-asrār* (*Secretum Secretorum*), Aristotle counsels Alexander the Great: "O Alexander, lean not towards lechery, for it is a habit of swine. And what glory is there in a thing in which brutes excel thee? It emaciates the body, destroys life, corrupts the constitution, causes effeminacy." See *Secretum Secretorum*, 186.

56 As will be discussed below, some Ottoman treatises, such as Ḳınalızāde ᶜAlī Çelebi's *Aḫlāḳ-ı Alāʾī*, placed the ruler above society and its different segments. See Ḳınalızāde, *Aḫlāḳ-ı Alāʾī*. The older tradition of Ottoman political thought, however, tended to consider the ruler as one of the men of the sword. Technically, of course, the Ottoman *ᶜaskerī* class extended beyond men of the sword to include the ulema and men of the pen (the early modern version of state bureaucrats). While in reality the distinctions among men

HUMORAL THEORY IN OTTOMAN POLITICAL THOUGHT

A new layer of complexity was added to humoral theory with its integration into Ottoman political thought. Ḳınalızāde's *Aḫlāḳ-ı Alāʾī*—written in 1565, a decade before Bālīzāde Muṣṭafā and Taʿlīḳīzāde's physiognomical treatises—applied humoral theory to theories of governance and socio-political organization.[57] It divided society into four estates, or classes.[58] Each of the four estates was equated with one of the four primary elements (fire, water, air, earth): first, men of the pen resemble water; second, men of the sword resemble fire; third, men of trade and commerce resemble air; fourth, men of agriculture resemble earth.[59]

The primary element of the choleric humor, which, according to the physiognomical treatises, dominates both the male gender and the men of the sword, is fire. The predominant characteristic of men of the sword, according to Ottoman political thought, is irascibility, as their defining purpose is securing property and religion, fighting against intruders, and preserving the kingdom's frontiers.[60] The irascible faculty (*ḳuvvet-i ġażabiyye*)—unlike its counterpart, the concupiscible faculty (*ḳuvvet-i*

---

of the sword, men of the pen, and ulema could be very blurry, early modern Ottoman political theory, as will be seen, did propose a theoretical division and envisioned a military–administrative elite made up of men of the sword.

57 The application of humoral theory in theories of state and social organization dates to long before the sixteenth century. It can be traced to Celāleddīn Devānī's (d. 1502) famous Persian *aḫlāḳ* treatise *Akhlāq-i Jalālī*. See Thompson, *The Practical Philosophy of the Muhammadan People*, 388–90. The same model of the four classes, without reference to the humors, was followed by Ḥasan Kāfī el-Aḳḥiṣārī (d. 1616) in *Uṣūl al-ḥikam fī niẓām al-ʿālam* (1596). See Ḥasan Kāfī, *Uṣūl al-ḥikam fī niẓām al-ʿālam*, 251–53. Kātib Çelebi (d. 1657) also adapted the analogy of the four humors to the division of society. It became the thematic underpinning for his treatise on governance, *Düstūrü'l-amel*. It should be pointed out, however, that Katip Çelebi changed the correspondences between humors and estates. See Katip Çelebi, *Düstūrü'l-ʿamel li-ıṣlāḥi'l-ḫalel* (Behrnauer translation), 120–24. See also Hagen, "Legitimacy and World Order," 64. Often, instead of mentioning the four humors directly, the texts speak of them in terms of their primary elements: fire is associated with yellow bile or the choleric humor, air is associated with blood or the sanguine humor, water is associated with phlegm or the phlegmatic humor, earth is associated with black bile or the melancholic humor. For an overview, see Stelmack and Stalikas, "Galen and the Humour Theory of Temperament," 258.

58 This division is based on occupation but generally determined by a combination of heredity and proclivity.

59 Ḳınalızāde, *Aḫlāḳ-ı Alāʾī*, 479.

60 Ḳınalızāde, *Aḫlāḳ-ı Alāʾī*, 479.

şeheviyye)—is active and externally oriented. At its best, the irascible faculty is courageous and generous, thus matching the above-quoted characteristics of the male choleric characterizations.[61] Courage, which is the defining characteristic of a balanced irascible soul, is necessary for keeping the kingdom in order by protecting it against threats from inside and out. Generosity, which blunts the sharp edge of irascibility, is its balancing characteristic. The irascible faculty, by its nature, is turned outward, toward repelling undesirables, through its courage, and rewarding desirables, through its generosity. Its counterpart, the concupiscible faculty, is turned inward; its function is attracting and retaining desirables, which is reminiscent of the above-quoted female phlegmatic characteristics of timidity and covetousness. Because of its timid nature and lack of assertiveness, the female phlegmatic character, according to Taᶜlīḳīzāde, is forced to rely on its intelligence and to resort to stratagems.[62]

The phlegmatic temperament, which dominates the female gender, is symbolized by water; in the four-tiered division of society, water is the primary element of the scholarly estate, or men of the pen. They are the custodians of knowledge (*ᶜilm*), which, according to Ḳınalızāde, gives life to souls, just as water gives life to bodies.[63] The learning of knowledge and its transmission, which is the purpose of the scholarly estate, requires a developed mental capacity and intelligence (*ᶜaḳl*).[64] The association of the phlegmatic humor with the characteristic of intelligence, or thinking *(fikr)*, is thus brought out to its fullest in the case of the men of the pen.[65]

---

61 The irascible soul or faculty is one of the three faculties—concupiscible, irascible, rational—that make up the human soul. A well-balanced concupiscible soul is moderate, a well-balanced irascible soul is courageous (an imbalanced irascible soul is either timid or temerarious), a well-balanced rational soul is wise. When all three souls are thus balanced, justice ensues. This is an ancient concept, traceable to the Greeks and prevalent in Islamic *aḫlāḳ*. See also Ḳınalızāde, *Aḫlāḳ-ı Alāʾī*, 95.

62 Taᶜlīḳīzāde, *Firāsetnāme*, 29b.

63 Ḳınalızāde, *Aḫlāḳ-ı Alāʾī*, 479. The human soul, according to Islamic teaching, is man's connection to the divine; its sole purpose is worshiping and contemplating the divine. Without knowledge of the divine, however, the soul fails to fulfill its purpose and is parched if its connection to the divine source is cut.

64 Learning and the transmission of knowledge also requires a strong memory, which, according to Bālīzāde Muṣṭafā, is a weakness of the phlegmatic humor. See Muṣṭafā b. Bālī, *Risāle*, 33b–34a.

65 Men of the pen and women seem to share two major characteristics of the phlegmatic humor: intelligence and passivity or inward-orientation. It has already been

The men of the sword and the men of the pen together made up the Ottoman ruling elite, also known as the *ᶜaskerī* estate. Nonetheless, it was, generally speaking, the men of the sword who ruled the empire.[66] The sultan, too, belonged to the general category of men of the sword,[67] especially according to the older tradition, which remembered the Ottoman sultan as *ġāzī* and warrior lord, and his court as a peripatetic warrior camp.[68] By the late sixteenth century, however, the nature of the Ottoman court had changed significantly; it was highly sophisticated, sedentary, secluded, and increasingly dominated by women and eunuchs. No longer was the Ottoman court governed by a purely choleric temperament. Instead, it seemed to be transforming into a mixture of the choleric and phlegmatic temperaments, a combination of male and female characteristics.

---

pointed out that intelligence and mental capacity are crucial for men of the pen in fulfilling their fundamental duty as custodians of knowledge. In the case of women, mental capacity is acknowledged in the physiognomical corpus, although often presented as scheming and deception. Both men of the pen and women, whose element is water, are non-impulsive and outwardly passive (in contrast to the impulsive choleric humor), as well as focused inward. The very nature of their occupation demands of the scholarly estate a certain degree of thoughtfulness and contemplation, in addition to great patience in the search for and acquisition of knowledge. The inward focus in the case of the female gender manifests somewhat differently. According to the physiognomical treatises, it is perceptible in the defining feminine characteristics of timidity and a selfish lack of generosity. Thus, two major characteristics of the phlegmatic humor—mental capacity and inward-orientation—take on very different manifestations in the female gender (scheming, timidity, and greed) and in the scholarly estate (knowledge, contemplation).

66 It must be pointed out, however, that the division between the two estates was often vague, and individuals crossed that divide. At the same time, chancellors and other men of the pen were highly influential in Ottoman governance. Yet, as an indicative example of a general rule, it was unthinkable, until the eighteenth century, that a man of the pen should occupy the position of grand vizier. See Itzkovitz, "Eighteenth Century Ottoman Realities," 86.

67 Ḥasan Kāfī and Ṭursun Beg counted the ruler as part of the military estate. See Ḥasan Kāfī, *Uṣūl al-ḥikam fī niẓām al-ᶜālam*, 251–52; and Hagen, "Legitimacy and World Order," 64. According to Ḳınalızāde, however, the ruler is above the four estates; he is a gardener who keeps the garden of his state fresh and prosperous. See Ḳınalızāde, *Aḫlāḳ-ı Alāʾī*, 479.

68 Gottfried Hagen has suggested that the inclusion of the ruler in the military estate is reflective of an older tradition which remembered the origins of the Ottoman sultans as *begs*, who were primus inter pares among the noblemen. See Hagen, "Legitimacy and World Order," 64.

AḪLĀḲ AND THE MATRYOSHKA DOLL OF EQUITY

In order to thoroughly examine the relationship between governance and gender, we must briefly turn to the Ottoman-Islamicate genre of ethics, or *aḫlāḳ*. The long and sophisticated Ottoman-Islamicate *aḫlāḳ* tradition divided *aḫlāḳ* into three dimensions: ethics (*aḫlāḳ*) of the soul, of economics or household management (*tedbīrü'l-menzil*), and of politics or governance of the polity (*tedbīrü'l-medīne*).[69] Each was seen as reflecting the other two. The ruler of a polity, the head of a household, and the rational faculty of the soul, stood at the heads of their respective hierarchies. As long as every element in each hierarchy knew and occupied its proper place, balance and justice prevailed. The three dimensions were deeply intertwined and, in the manner of a matryoshka doll, contained within each other: a justly governed polity depended on justly governed households, which in turn were dependent on properly balanced souls. A head of a household who did not possess a properly balanced soul was ignorant of the true meaning of justice, and consequently incapable of ordering his household with justice. A polity was seen as an extension of the dynastic household, and the dynast, as head of the royal household that governed the polity, was, above all men, expected to know justice by first developing it within his own soul.[70]

The *aḫlāḳ* tradition generally divided the soul into three parts: the concupiscible faculty, the irascible faculty, and the rational faculty. The prescribed goal of *aḫlāḳ* was to develop balance in each of the three faculties by removing their respective deficiencies and excesses. The concupiscible faculty, "which is the principle for the attraction of benefits and the quest of pleasures, by way of foods, drinks, . . . [lust] and the rest,"

69 The most prominent Ottoman *aḫlāḳ* treatise is Ḳınalızāde, *Aḫlāḳ-ı Alā'ī*. Perhaps the most prominent example of the genre is Nāṣīruddīn Tūsī's (d. 1274) *Akhlāq-i Nāṣiruddīn*. See Tūsī, *The Nasirean Ethics* (Wickens translation). The origins of the Ottoman, and more broadly Islamicate, *aḫlāḳ* tradition are essentially based on a combination of Aristotle's *Nicomachean Ethics* and Bryson's *Management of the Estate*. For Bryson's work, see Swain, *Economy, Family, and Society from Rome to Islam*.

70 Tūsī, *Nasirean Ethics*, 51–2: "The perfection of the Practical Faculty lies in organizing and ordering its own particular faculties and acts, so that they are in agreement and conformity, the one not seeking to dominate another. By their reconciliation its disposition grows in acceptability. Next, it should come to the degree of perfecting things other than itself, which is to regulate the affairs of households and cities; so that it orders those states falling within the purview of association, and all men arrive at a felicity shared by all."

was marked by self-restraint (*ᶜiffet*) in its balanced state. The irascible faculty, "which is the principle for repelling injuries, facing up to perils, and yearning after authority and exaltation," when balanced, was marked by courage (*şecāᶜat*). The rational faculty, "which is the faculty of perceiving intelligibles and distinguishing between good and evil actions," was marked by wisdom (*ḥikmet*) in its balanced state. Justice (*ᶜadālet*) ensued as a direct result of this tripartite balancing.[71]

Without putting too fine a point on it, the female-phlegmatic character type seems to share some of its defining characteristics (for example, frailty, timidity, covetousness) with descriptions of the concupiscible faculty, and the male-choleric character type seems to share some of its defining characteristics (for example, strength, assertiveness, irascibility) with descriptions of the irascible faculty. If that analogy is pursued further, the envisioned relationship between the female-phlegmatic and the male-choleric types would also be expected to correspond, in some ways at least, to the relationship between the concupiscible and irascible faculties as described by *aḫlāḳ* texts. According to *aḫlāḳ* literature, of the three faculties,

> only one possesses discipline and generosity in reality and in substance, and that is the Angelic Soul [rational faculty]; the second, although not possessed of discipline, is receptive thereof, and is submissive to the instructor at the time of schooling, and this is the Savage Soul [irascible faculty]; the third is devoid of discipline and unreceptive thereof, and this is the Bestial Soul [concupiscible faculty]. The reason for the existence of the Bestial Soul is (to ensure) the endurance of the body, which is the subject and vehicle of the Angelic Soul during the time in which it realizes its perfection and reaches its goal. Similarly, the reason for the existence of the Irascible Soul is to afflict and overcome the Bestial Soul, so as to ward off the corruption that may be expected from its ascendancy, for the bestial is not receptive of discipline.[72]

Ultimately, the concupiscible faculty's only purpose is its life-giving energy. That energy, however, if left unrestrained, lacks any discipline

71 Ṭūsī, *Nasirean Ethics*, 43; and Ḳınalızāde, *Aḫlāḳ-ı Alāʾī*, 95.

72 Ṭūsī, *Nasirean Ethics*, 57.

and generosity and generates corruption. Hence, the irascible faculty, which itself is capable of discipline, must "afflict and overcome" the concupiscible faculty. How, then (if at all), are these relationships among the soul's faculties reflected in interactions between the above-quoted character sketches of the archetypal male and female?

GENDER AND SEXUALITY

Taᶜlīḳīzāde relates two anecdotes to illustrate the negative, scheming, and cunning side of the superior female intellect (*ᶜaḳl*), when employed in the service of the *nefs-i emmāre* and its lower passions.[73] The first tells of a wealthy Baghdadi merchant who was tricked by his first wife into divorcing his second wife. Using her superior reflective faculties (*muṭālaᶜa-i ḫayāl*), the first wife outsmarted and manipulated her husband into submitting to her will.[74] The second anecdote tells of a new wife, married to the Prophet Muhammed, who falls prey to the deceptive trickery (*mekr-i efsā*) of the other wives and ends up being divorced from the Prophet.[75]

The ability of women to manipulate men's actions, even within the Prophet Muhammed's household, through scheming and deception, must have been the cause of great consternation among Ottoman men. Although the anecdotes seem ultimately harmless and are even marked by a humorous tone, they make a specific point, which is repeated in other anecdotes: women are generally motivated by their lower passions, mainly the characteristics of envy and covetousness. This underlines Taᶜlīḳīzāde's analogy between women and the *nefs-i emmāre*[76]—the Koranic term for the concupiscible faculty.[77] *Aḫlāḳ* teaches and trains man to control the deceptions of his concupiscible faculty, and, according to the physiognomical treatises, men also must not fall prey to the snares of female deception.

Taᶜlīḳīzāde further underscores the essential importance of controlling women with an Arabic distich:

73 Taᶜlīḳīzāde, *Firāsetnāme*, 31b–32a.
74 Taᶜlīḳīzāde, *Firāsetnāme*, 30a–30b.
75 Taᶜlīḳīzāde, *Firāsetnāme*, 30b.
76 Taᶜlīḳīzāde, *Firāsetnāme*, 31b–32a.
77 "Mention of these three souls is made in the Glorious Koran, under the titles of the Imperative Soul (*nefs-i emmāre*), the Reproachful Soul and the Peaceful Soul." See Ṭūsī, *Nasirean Ethics*, 57.

> The father of every girl, as she matures
> Entrusts her to three praiseworthy guardians:
> The mother, who watches her, the husband, who protects her
> And the grave, which conceals her; the grave being the most blessed of them all.[78]

Of the three guardians to which a happy father entrusts his daughter, the husband is fraught with the most danger and difficulty, for his protection occurs during the period of active sexuality. Thus, male control over the female sex during that life period must be rooted in control over female sexuality. Hence, the marrying of virgins is highly encouraged by Taᶜlīḳīzāde. Haste is from the devil, according to a saying quoted by Taᶜlīḳīzāde, except on three occasions, when it is in fact a prophetic tradition (*sünnet*); one such occasion is marrying a virgin.[79] Virgins, he continues, are filled with love for their husbands and have no secrets—and are thus easier to control.[80]

After bemoaning the absence of loyal and loving virgins in these "heart-frightening times,"[81] Taᶜlīḳīzāde tells a lengthy allegory about women in the Iranian town of Rasht, who have discovered the ways of sexual self-gratification (*saᶜterī, rass*).[82] The origins of female self-gratification, according to a story within the allegory, are attributed to Satan, who taught it to a group of women near Hadhramaut, so that they would know "the power of having no more need for men."[83] The men in the

78 Taᶜlīḳīzāde, *Firāsetnāme*, 30b–31a: "li-kull ab[ī] bint iz̲ā mā taraᶜraᶜat / s̲alās̲at aṣhār iz̲ā mā ḥamdu'ṣ-ṣihr // fa-umm yurāᶜīhā va baᶜl yaṣūnuhā / va ḳabr yuvārīhā fa-ḫayruhum al-ḳabr."

79 Taᶜlīḳīzāde, *Firāsetnāme*, 31a: "el-ᶜacele min ᶜameli'ş-şeytān illā fī s̲alās̲in fe-inne l-ᶜacele fīh sunnet: tezvīcu'l-bikr iz̲ā baliġat ve techīzu'l-meyyit iz̲ā māt ve teᶜcīl nazali'ż-żeyf iz̲ā nazal." (One should not rush, because haste is from the devil, except in three things when haste is *sunna*: marrying the virgin if she is marriageable, washing the corpse if it is dead, and receiving a visitor if he is traveling.)

80 Taᶜlīḳīzāde, *Firāsetnāme*, 32a.

81 Taᶜlīḳīzāde, *Firāsetnāme*, 32b: "bu zamān-ı dil-remānda böyle dürretü't-tāc şeb-i tārīk ü dācda aḫter-i raḫşān gibi bī-numūd bī-nişān olmuşdur." (In these heart-frightening times, such crown-adorning pearls have disappeared without appearance or sign, like a bright star in the darkness and obscurity of night.)

82 According to Taᶜlīḳīzāde, there are two types of female self-gratification, *saᶜterī* and *rass*. *Saᶜterī* is self-gratification with a male tool, while *rass* is rubbing the privates. See Taᶜlīḳīzāde, *Firāsetnāme*, 33a: "iki nevᶜ üzerinedir birine saᶜterī birine ress derler. Saᶜterī oldur ki ālet-i merdān peydā ederler ress oldur ki saḥḳ-ı furūc ederler."

83 Taᶜlīḳīzāde, *Firāsetnāme*, 33a: "İblīs-i bā-telbīs bir ᶜavret şeklinde aralarına ḳarışub

anecdote react by killing those women who would not submit to them, and the ensuing chaos could not be righted even by a prophet who, out of desperation, invoked God's vengeance and thus had the inhabitants of the cursed city turned into black rocks.[84] The moral of the story, it would seem, is that female sexual independence from men leads to the destruction of society.

The sexual relationship between men and women, as portrayed by Taᶜlīḳīzāde, is thus presented as a foundational and intensified basis for the male-female relationship as a whole. A breakdown of its interdependent nature has an unbalancing effect on the male-female relationship as a whole, and, consequently, a deeply destructive effect on the household and the social fabric that keeps it together. It is precisely in the sexual relationship that the choleric-phlegmatic, male-female dichotomy is reenacted; the man takes on the choleric characteristics of active dominance, and the woman takes on the phlegmatic characteristics of passive receptivity.[85] This is in tandem with Taᶜlīḳīzāde's dichotomy of the defining physiological and psychological differences between the genders: males are assertive and physically strong and sturdy, while females are timid and physically delicate and beautiful.[86] These defining gender roles within the sexual relationship, which are the fundamental building blocks for the male-female relationship as a whole, are further extended into the social realm to include timidity and covetousness for women and assertiveness and generosity for men.

The role of each gender is reflected in the sexual relationship between them, and, as Taᶜlīḳīzāde makes clear, veering away from those roles leads to sexual deviance and social disintegration. Social harmony is maintained only if each gender plays its role faithfully. According to both

---

ressi taᶜlīm eyledi çunki ᶜavretler erden mustaġniye olmanıŋ imkānın ḍuydular." (İblis, the deceiver, entered among them in the form of a woman and taught them self-gratification by rubbing the privates (*rass*), so that women may know the power of having no more need for men.)

84 Taᶜlīḳīzāde, *Firāsetnāme*, 33a–33b.

85 "The "active" and "insertive" role in sexual intercourse was uniquely appropriate to a man, and the "passive" or "receptive" role was uniquely appropriate to a woman." See El-Rouayheb, *Before Homosexuality*, 12.

86 Taᶜlīḳīzāde describes the perfect woman, and her behavior during moments of intimacy, as "always merry and joyful, her cheerful countenance *timid* (*cebīn*) and fresh. In her company is delight (*muṣāḥabetinde leẕẕet*), in her intimacy enjoyment (*muʾānesetinde ᶜişret*)." See Taᶜlīḳīzāde, *Firāsetnāme*, 35b (emphasis mine).

Ta^c^līḳīzāde and Bālīzāde Muṣṭafā, men have been endowed with the superior physical qualities (physical strength) and characteristics (courage, generosity) of the choleric humor, and thus it is their duty to maintain control, sexually and socially, over the phlegmatic female gender, which is the locus of the lower passional energies. As long as men play their assigned role and, especially in their capacity as heads of households, exert control over their households' womenfolk—"so as to ward off the corruption that may be expected from its ascendancy"[87]—balance and justice will prevail in the households. The same might then be said to apply to the royal household—and, by extension, to the state (*devlet*).

However, if men—especially the ruling elite and the sultan—fall prey to female wiles and coquettish manipulations, society and the state become deformed. The ruling elite takes on the character traits that mark the phlegmatic female gender, and, consequently, the state begins to unravel—a process reflected in Ḥasan Kāfī's four causes of Ottoman "decline." When men become covetous for wealth and for women, when they rely on female advice and hold women in high esteem, the fighting spirit of the military diminishes, the ruling elite fails to consult with the ulema, who are society's moral compass (and, incidentally, also defined by the phlegmatic humor), and unworthy candidates are appointed to high positions.[88]

CONCLUSION

One might perhaps speculate that Murād III's proclivities were known to the writers of the physiognomical treatises, especially to Ta^c^līḳīzāde, who was a *kātib* in Murād's princely household. In that case, their entries on gender physiognomy might be read as a warning to the new sultan and his court of the dangers of the fairer sex and an appeal to act more in the manner of the choleric male character. More broadly, however, the two physiognomical treatises inform us of a worldview in which the relationship between men and woman was envisioned in a very particular—and highly prescriptive and performative—way. Deviation from established

87 Ṭūsī's reference is to the concupiscible soul, but by analogy it is equally applicable to the phlegmatic–female characterization made in the physiognomical treatises. See Ṭūsī, *Nasirean Ethics*, 57.

88 Ḥasan Kāfī, *Uṣūl al-ḥikam fī niẓām al-^c^ālam*, 249–50.

norms, they cautioned, would be opposed to the very nature of things and thus would undermine the whole social and political structure.

It is clear that during the latter part of the sixteenth century the Ottoman Empire was undergoing a profound transformation, which was becoming particularly palpable during the reign of Murād III (r. 1574–1595). Perhaps the expansion of Ottoman physiognomy to numerous methods, including gender physiognomy, was the owl of Minerva spreading its wings at the twilight of an (imagined?) era. In that case, the codification of gender roles, as well as of social classes and ethnic and racial groups, in Taᶜlīḳīzāde and Bālīzāde Muṣṭafā's physiognomical treatises, might be seen as expressing a deeply unsettled reaction to the profound changes taking place around them.

The increased allocation of power to royal women and to harem servants was one of the more visible manifestations of the great transmutation—and an easy target for the swelling frustrations of many contemporaries. Yet, as I have tried to demonstrate, distaste for female participation in state politics, especially at the imperial level, was backed by a complex intellectual tradition, the roots of which stretched back to antiquity. It was furthermore intensely intertwined with Ottoman ethics. Although the physiognomical treatises made allowances for exceptions, they worked out a scientific system that essentially presented women as constitutionally unfit to justly wield power. Women's innate proclivity for submission to males was, however, immensely complicated by their intelligence, which, if turned to scheming, could garner them great power and thus threaten the most fundamental building block of the Ottoman socio-political fabric—justice. Justice, by definition, prevailed only when the male-choleric-irascible element disciplined the female-phlegmatic-concupiscible element and the two merged into a hierarchical whole. According to the Ottoman weltanschauung, which I have tried to reconstruct here, an inversion of this hierarchical power relationship was a deviation of the natural order and spelled disaster on both individual and collective levels.

BIBLIOGRAPHY

Sources

Anonymous. *Kitāb-ı müstetāb*. Edited and transliterated by Yaşar Yücel. In *Osmanlı Devlet Teşkilâtına Dair Kaynaklar*, part I. Ankara: Türk Tarih Kurumu Basımevi, 1988.

Ps.-Aristotle, *Physiognomy*. (1) Translated by W. S. Hett. In Aristotle, *Minor Works* (Loeb Classical Library Series). Cambridge, MA: Harvard University Press, 2014. (2) Translated by Simon Swain. In *Seeing the Face, Seeing the Soul: Polemon's* Physiognomy *from Classical Antiquity to Medieval Islam*, edited by Simon Swain. Oxford: Oxford University Press, 2007.

ᶜAṭāʾī, Nevᶜīzāde. *Ḥadāʾiķü'l-ḥaķāʾiķ*. In Aḥmed ibn Muṣṭafā Ṭāşköprīzāde, *Şakaik Nuᶜmaniye ve Zeyilleri*. Istanbul: Çağrı Yayınları, 1989.

Devānī, Celāleddīn (Davānī, Jalāluddīn). *Akhlāq-i Jalālī*. Translated by W. F. Thompson. In *The Practical Philosophy of the Muhammadan People: Being a Translation of the Akhlak-i Jalaly from the Persian of Fakir Jany Muhammad Assad*. Karachi: Karimsons, 1977.

Fakhruddīn (Faḫr al-dīn) Rāzī. *Kitāb al-firāsa*. In Youssef Mourad, *La Physiognomie Arabe et le Kitâb al-Firâsa de Fakhr al-dîn al-Râzî*. Paris: Librarie Orientaliste Paul Geuthner, 1939.

Ḥamdullāh Ḥamdī. *Ķıyāfetnāme*. Istanbul, Süleymaniye Kütüphanesi, MS Bağdatlı Vehbi 2162.

Ḥasan Kāfī [el-Aķḥiṣārī]. *Uṣūl al-ḥikam fī niẓām al-ᶜālam*. Edited and transliterated by Mehmet İpşirli. In "Hasan Kâfî el-Akhisarî ve Devlet Düzenine Ait Eseri *Usûlü'l-Hikem fî Nizâmi'l-Âlem*." *Tarih Enstitüsü Dergisi* 10–11 (1979–80): 239–78.

Ibn Sīnā. *al-Qānūn fī'l-ṭibb*. (1) Beirut: Jamīᶜ'l-ḥuqūq maḥfūẓa, 1993. (2) Translated in Mones Abu-Asab, Hakima Amri, and Marc S. Micozzi, *Avicenna's Medicine: A New Translation of the 11th Century Canon with Practical Applications for Integrative Health Care*. Rochester, Vermont: Healing Arts Press, 2013.

Kātib Çelebi [Ḫācī Ḫalīfe Muṣṭafā b. ᶜAbdullāh]. *Düstūrü'l-ᶜamel li-ıṣlāḥü'l-ḫalel*. Translated by W. F. A. Behrnauer, "Ḥâgi Chalfa's Dustûru'l-'amel." *Zeitschrift der Deutschen Morgenländischen Gesellschaft* 11, no. 1 (1857): 111–32.

Ķınalızāde [ᶜAlī Çelebi]. *Aḫlāķ-ı Alāʾī*. Edited by Mustafa Koç. Istanbul: Klasik, 2007.

Muṣṭafā ᶜĀlī. *Künhü'l-aḫbār*. Istanbul, Nuruosmaniye Library, MS. 3406.

Muṣṭafā b. Bālī (also Bālīzāde Muṣṭafā). *Risāle-i Ķiyāset-i Firāset*. (1) Istanbul, MS Nuruosmaniye 4100. (2) Istanbul, MS Izmirli Hakkı 1926. (3) Edited by Ramazan Sarıçiçek. In *Risâle-i Ķiyâset-i Firâset / İlm-i Firâset. Yüzler Hâli Söyler*. Istanbul: Büyüyenay Yayınları, 2014.

Nāṣīruddīn (Nāṣīr ad-Dīn) Tūsī. *Akhlāq-i Nāṣirī*. Translated by G. M. Wickens, *The Nasirean Ethics*. London: G. Allen & Unwin, 1964.

Peçevī (Peçūyī) İbrāhīm. *Tārīḫ-i Peçevī*. 2 vols. Istanbul: Matbaa-i Amire, 1281–84.
Selānikī [Muṣṭafā Efendi]. *Tārīḫ-i Selānikī*. Edited and transliterated by Mehmed İpşirli. In *Tarih-i Selânikî*. 2 vols. Istanbul: İstanbul Üniversitesi Edebiyat Fakültesi Basımevi, 1989.
Secretum Secretorum. Translated by A. S. Fulton. London: Oxford University Press, 1920.
Taᶜlīḳīzāde Meḥmed Ṣubḥī. *Firāsetnāme*. Paris, Bibliothèque nationale de France, MS Turc. 1055.

Studies

Abou-El-Haj, Rifaᵓat Ali. *Formation of the Modern State: The Ottoman Empire, Sixteenth to Eighteenth Centuries*. Albany: State University of New York Press, 1991.
Afyoncu, Erhan. "Talîkîzâde Mehmed Subhî'nin Hayatı Hakkında Notlar." *The Journal of Ottoman Studies* 21 (2001): 285–306.
Arikha, Noga. *Passions and Tempers, a History of the Humors*. New York: Ecco, 2007.
El-Rouayheb, Khaled. *Before Homosexuality in the Arab-Islamic World, 1500–1800*. Chicago: University of Chicago Press, 2005.
Felek, Özgen. "Re-Creating Image and Identity: Dreams and Visions as a Means of Murâd III's Self-Fashioning." Ph.D. diss., University of Michigan, 2010.
Fetvacı, Emine. *Picturing History at the Ottoman Court*. Bloomington: Indiana University Press, 2013.
Fleischer, Cornell. "From Şeyhzade Korkud to Mustafa Âli: Cultural Origins of the Ottoman *Nasihatname*." In *Third Congress on the Social and Economic History of Turkey*, edited by Heath W. Lowry and Ralph S. Hattox, 67–77. Istanbul: The Isis Press, 1990.
Gilmore, David. "Introduction: The Shame of Dishonour." In *Honor and Shame and the Unity of the Mediterranean*, edited by David Gilmore, 2–21. Washington, D.C.: American Anthropological Association, 1987.
Gilmore, David. *Manhood in the Making: Cultural Concepts of Masculinity*. New Heaven: Yale University Press, 1990.
Hagen, Gottfried. "Legitimacy and World Order." In *Legitimizing the Order: The Ottoman Rhetoric of State Power*, edited by Hakan Karateke and Maurus Reinkowski, 53–83. Leiden: Brill, 2005.
Herzfeld, Michael. *The Poetics of Manhood: Contest and Identity in a Cretan Mountain Village*. Princeton: Princeton University Press, 1985.
Howard, Douglas A. "Genre and Myth in the Ottoman Advice for Kings Literature." In *The Early Modern Ottomans: Remapping the Empire*, edited by Virginia H. Aksan and Daniel Goffman, 137–66. Cambridge: Cambridge University Press, 2007.
Itzkovitz, Norman. "Eighteenth Century Ottoman Realities." *Studia Islamica* 16 (1962): 73–94.

Kafadar, Cemal. "The Question of Ottoman Decline." *Harvard Middle Eastern and Islamic Review* 4, nos. 1–2 (1997–98): 30–75.

Klibansky, Raymond, Erwin Panofsky, and Fritz Saxl. *Saturn and Melancholy. Studies in the History of Natural Philosophy, Religion and Art*. London: Nelson, 1964.

Lelić, Emin. "Physiognomy and Ottoman Statecraft: Discerning Morality and Justice." In *Arabica: Journal of Arabic and Islamic Studies* (forthcoming).

Necipoğlu, Gülru. *Architecture, Ceremonial, and Power: The Topkapı Palace in the Fifteenth and Sixteenth Centuries*. Cambridge, MA: MIT Press, 1991.

Peirce, Leslie P. *The Imperial Harem: Women and Sovereignty in the Ottoman Empire*. Oxford: Oxford University Press, 1993.

Stelmack, Robert M., and Anastasios Stalikas. "Galen and the Humour Theory of Temperament." *Personality and Individual Differences* 12 (1991): 255–63.

Swain, Simon. *Economy, Family, and Society from Rome to Islam: A Critical Edition, English Translation, and Study of Bryson's Management of the Estate*. Cambridge: Cambridge University Press, 2013.

Tezcan, Baki. "The Politics of Early Modern Ottoman Historiography." In *The Early Modern Ottomans: Remapping the Empire*, edited by Virginia H. Aksan and Daniel Goffman, 167–98. Cambridge: Cambridge University Press, 2007.

Woodhead, Christine. "From Scribe to Litterateur: The Career of a Sixteenth-Century Ottoman *Kātib*." *Bulletin (British Society for Middle Eastern Studies)* 9, no. 1 (1982): 52–74.

Defining and Defaming the Other in Early Seventeenth-Century Ottoman Invective

Michael D. Sheridan

In October 1622 an envoy arrived in Istanbul from Isfahan with the annual Safavid tribute to the Ottoman Empire.[1] The grand vizier at the time was Meḥmed Pasha (d. 1626), also known as Gürcī ("the Georgian") or Ḫādım ("the eunuch"), as he was indeed a white eunuch of Georgian origin who had originally been presented to the Ottoman palace as a gift in the 1560s or 1570s. Some ninety years after the envoy's arrival, a miscellany—apparently compiled by the historian Muṣṭafā Naᶜīmā (d. 1716)[2]—recorded this anecdote about the grand vizier's reception of the Safavid envoy:

> When Gürcī Meḥmed Pasha was the grand vizier, a learned envoy came from Persia. His eminence the grand vizier prepared for the envoy a gathering in the style of a banquet, arranging for and having laid out all the foods and other necessities. The poet Nefᶜī—who was from Ḥasanḳalᶜası near Erżurūm—was present at the grand vizier's

---

1 Ḥüseyin Ṭūġī, *Muṣībetnāme*, 165, 169–70 and Kātib Çelebī, *Fezleke*, 693.

2 An inscription on the front flyleaf of this manuscript—University of Michigan, Isl. Ms. 409, of which I am currently preparing an edition and analysis—reads as follows: "Exquisite miscellany in the hand of the late and laudable Naᶜīmā of superior virtue, [may] God's mercy [be upon him]" (*mecmūᶜa-i nefīse bā-ḫaṭṭ-ı merḥūmu'l-mebrūr Naᶜīmā-yı bāhirü'l-feżāʾil, raḥmetü'l-lāh*).

> gathering, and he began to talk at such great length that no one else was able to say a word. Finally the pasha demeaned him by saying, "Now that you've found your long-lost brother, you're not giving anyone a chance to speak," upon which Nefᶜī expiated the embarrassment by replying, "My lord, while my father may have been a Ḳızılbaş, my mother was a Georgian."[3]

The anecdote is careful to emphasize Nefᶜī's (d. 1635) origins in Hasankale (the modern-day Pasinler) in eastern Anatolia, which at the time was not far from the border with Persia. On one level, this emphasis simply serves as the background to—or explanation for—Meḥmed Pasha's insulting suggestion that Nefᶜī may be a Safavid sympathizer, or Ḳızılbaş; on another level, it highlights Nefᶜī's perceived alterity, exactly the quality on which the grand vizier was playing in his insult, relying on a binary opposition between the Sunni Ottomans and the Shiite Safavids that was prevalent in contemporary discourses, both official and literary. Nefᶜī's response, although at a glance it might seem almost to flatter the Georgian grand vizier, in fact throws Meḥmed Pasha's own alterity, as a slave of non-Muslim origin, right back in his face—not to mention the sexual power implications of a Ḳızılbaş man siring a son on a Georgian woman.

Prior to the incident recounted here, Nefᶜī had been on cordial, or at least neutral, terms with Meḥmed Pasha, and had even written two panegyric *ḳaṣīde*s in his honor while the pasha was serving as deputy grand vizier (*ḳāʾim-maḳām*) several years earlier. After their clash at the banquet for the Safavid envoy, however, the relationship deteriorated. From this point on, Nefᶜī waged a war of words against the grand vizier, composing two long invective poems in *ḳaṣīde* form, slandering the pasha during the three short

3 Naᶜīmā (?), *ᶜUlāletü'l-mecālis, mecmūᶜātu'n-nefāʾis*, 62: "Laṭīfe: Gürcī Meḥmed Paşa ṣadr-ı aᶜẓam iken ᶜAcem'den bir ferzāne elçi gelüb ṣadr-ı ᶜālī ḥażretleri elçiye żiyāfet şeklinde tertīb-i meclis-i ṭaᶜām, temhīd-i levāzım u ikrām edüb şāᶜir Nefᶜī, ki Erżurūm ḳurbunda vāḳiᶜ Ḥasanḳalᶜası nām mevżiᶜden idi, ol meclis-i ᶜālīde bulunub elçi ile dūr u dirāz mükâlemeye āġāz edüb kimseye söz düşürmez. Paşa daḫı taᶜrīżen 'Hemşīreŋi bulunca kimseye fırṣat-ı kelâm vermez olduŋ' dedikde 'Sulṭānım, gerçi babam Ḳızılbaş idi lakin vālidem Gürcī idi' deyü cevāb edüb defᶜ-i ḫicālet eylemişdir." Unless otherwise noted, all translations are my own.

In a study of Nefᶜī, Abdülkadir Karahan refers, without providing the text itself, to another version of the same anecdote, in which the incident is described as having occurred a few years earlier, when Gürcī Meḥmed Pasha was serving as deputy grand vizier. See Karahan, *Nef'i*, 11.

months that the latter remained in his post before he was forced to step down by an uprising of *sipāhīs* and janissaries in February 1623.

By the time of his rift with Meḥmed Pasha, Nefᶜī had already developed a reputation as a notorious writer of invectives, and he would continue to produce poetry in this mode until it led to his execution a decade later, in 1635. The same Muṣṭafā Naᶜīmā who seems to have compiled the notebook with the anecdote mentioned above described Nefᶜī in his history: "In the field of invective, he was extremely foul-mouthed. Daring to defame the grandees of his time and to destroy the honor of great scholars and noble viziers, he lampooned the majority of the well-known figures of the day."[4] All in all, Nefᶜī wrote nearly 250 pieces of invective poetry attacking more than seventy people, up to and including such prominent figures as the grand vizier, the chief judges of Rumelia and Anatolia, and the chief finance minister. This corpus of invective dwarfs anything that had come before in Ottoman literature, and its like would not be seen again for another century or more.

One particularly salient feature of this invective corpus[5] is that it consistently uses a conscious, aggressive discourse of alterity that is similar in nature to that seen in the anecdote quoted above: typically, the target is first defined as an "other" by various rhetorical means, and that other is then defamed on the grounds thereby established. This article examines two such cases of othering taken from Nefᶜī's invective corpus. The first is the clash between Nefᶜī and the grand vizier Gürcī Meḥmed Pasha mentioned above, and the second involves the invectives Nefᶜī wrote against the chief finance minister Etmekçizāde Aḥmed Pasha (d. 1618). The former case focuses on methods of othering based on physical and sexual characteristics, whereas the latter concentrates on the ways in which the target's social background was used as a weapon

4 Naᶜīmā, *Tārīḫ-i Naᶜīmā*, 799: "[H]icv vâdîsinde gāyet bed-zebân olup asrında olan ekâbire harf-endâzlık ve ulemâ-i izâm ve vüzerâ-i kirâmın hedm-i ırzlarına cesâret edip meşâhîr-i vaktin ekserini hicv etmiş idi."

5 In this paper, the term "invective" translates the terms *hicv* or *hicāʾ*, but with a difference. As a literary mode rather than a genre as such, *hicv* has historically had a very broad application in studies of Islamicate literary traditions, being used to refer to everything from serious personal attack to playful ribbing among friends to broad social satire. I use the term "invective" to refer only to the first of these, serious personal attack (in verse), as the second emerges in quite different contexts while the third is more properly referred to as satire, with all the implications of conscious social criticism that that term entails.

against him in what may have been part of a smear campaign. In addition to these two cases, I investigate how the tactics employed by Nefᶜī in his invectives echo and parallel approaches taken by authors working in the genre of advice literature, as well as what these similarities can reveal about contemporary perceptions of the changing composition of the Ottoman elite in the late sixteenth and early seventeenth centuries.

NEFʿĪ AND GÜRCĪ MEḤMED PASHA

Shortly after Nefᶜī slandered Gürcī Meḥmed Pasha at the banquet held for the Safavid envoy, as described above, he appears to have been removed from his post as comptroller of mines (*maᶜden muḳāṭaᶜacısı*). Seeing this turn of events as Meḥmed Pasha's doing, Nefᶜī proceeded to write a long invective in *ḳaṣīde* form, personally attacking the grand vizier over the course of nearly sixty unrestrained couplets. The poem begins with the following lines, which set the tone for what was to follow:

> alas! it's the ruin of religion and state and the shame of Islam
> that a giant of a hermaphrodite holds the seal of Solomon
> not a giant but an unbridled gelding with an elephant face
> if he just had a cheap saddle I'd call him the Antichrist's ass[6]

There are two main points of attack in these lines. The first, and indeed the more prominent, is the insult leveled at Meḥmed Pasha for his physical size, calling him a demonic giant (*dīv*). In fact, throughout the poem, the grand vizier's girth remains among the dominant elements, often coupled with various associated concepts, such as appetite—both physical and political (as in the couplet, "he must have snapped off and swallowed his own balls out of ambition / or else why would they bother castrating such a torpid demon as him"[7])—as well as flatulence and defecation

6 Nefᶜī, *Sihām-ı Ḳażā* (Leiden), 2b: "zihī ḫüsrān-ı dīn [ü] devlet ve neng-i Müselmānī / k'ola bir dīv-i ḫunsā mālik-i mühr-i Süleymānī // ne dīv efsārı yoḳ bir bārgīr-i fīl-peyker kim / ḫar-ı Deccāl'dır derdim eger olaydı pālānı." There are approximately twenty extant manuscripts containing Nefᶜī's invective poetry either in full or in part. I have chosen to use, whenever possible, this Leiden University manuscript because, despite certain clear errors (many of which indicate that this manuscript was recorded at least partially orally), it is the earliest known copy—dating to January/February 1644, just nine years after Nefᶜī's death—and contains full vowel markings.

7 Nefᶜī, *Sihām-ı Ḳażā* (Leiden), 2b: "ḳoparmış kendü yudmuşdır ṭaşağın ḥırṣ ile yoḫsa / nice ḫādım ederler böyle ᶜifrīt-i girān-cānı."

(as in the couplet, "he's the solid frozen fart of the demon of Mount Damāvand / the bodily curdled turd of the patriarch of the Christians"[8]). While such blunt insults had long been the proverbial bread and butter of the Islamicate invective tradition, they also serve, in Nefᶜī's poem, as an effective rhetorical ploy to make an other of Meḥmed Pasha in physical terms, and also as the foundation for the somewhat more nuanced attack that is utilized throughout much of the poem.

The second point of attack is the grand vizier's identity as a eunuch. On one level, attacking Meḥmed Pasha for his eunuchism serves as a simple means of de-masculization, another standard rhetorical tactic in the Near Eastern invective tradition, dating back to pre-Islamic Arabic invective. On another level, however, this attack had profound political implications insofar as it suggested that a eunuch had no business governing the empire. Moreover, this assault on Meḥmed Pasha's eunuchism seems not to have been a personal preoccupation for Nefᶜī alone; when, several months after the poem was written, in February 1623, the *sipāhī*s and janissaries in Istanbul stormed the imperial council and removed Meḥmed from the grand vizierate, they are said to have called him a "false pasha" (*sāḫte paşa*)[9] and to have stated openly that they did not consent to a eunuch as, and would not allow a eunuch to be, grand vizier.[10] Although Meḥmed Pasha was by no means the first eunuch to serve as grand vizier, he *was* the first to be forcibly removed from the post and, more importantly, to have his very identity as a eunuch put forward as a reason for his deposition.[11]

Returning to Nefᶜī's invective, a later passage in the poem once again attacks the grand vizier on the grounds of identity, but from a rather different perspective:

---

8 Nefᶜī, *Sihām-ı Ḳażā* (Leiden), 3a: "mücessem żarṭa-i yaḫ-beste-i dīv-i Demāvendī / muṣavver yesteh-i efsürde-i baṭrīḳ-i Naṣrānī."

9 Peçevī, *Tārīḫ-i Peçevī*, 30.

10 Naᶜīmā, *Tārīḫ-i Naᶜīmā*, 507.

11 It should be noted, however, that anti-eunuch sentiment appears to have been on the rise among the Ottoman soldiery for some time. In a 1603 uprising, for instance, the *sipāhī*s and janissaries had claimed that the eunuch Ḫüsrev Pasha had been appointed as a military commander by the chief black eunuch (*dārü's-saᶜāde aġası*) and the deputy grand vizier, also a eunuch, solely because of his eunuchism. Thus, palace eunuchs appear to have been viewed by the soldiery as something of a corrupting faction of sorts. For the uprising, see Kātib Çelebī, *Fezleke*, 417–18. For analysis of the uprising, see Börekçi, "Factions and Favorites," 54–63.

look at what he's done! look at the sedition that has arisen
since he soiled the imperial council with his very body
so what if he *was* educated in the imperial harem
his unprecedented body still has no like in this world
can someone like him be a worthy vizier of the land of Islam,
this pigherd of a Georgian Armenian Turkish Gypsy?[12]

Although Nefᶜī does begrudgingly attest here to the fact that Meḥmed Pasha was well educated, within the poem's discourse education is trumped by identity, nurture by nature. What matters is not the system from which the pasha emerged, but his origins. The string of epithets in the last hemistich is clearly not concerned with accuracy, but rather with defining the grand vizier as an other who is categorically unfit for his post or for a place in the empire's ruling and cultural elite.

The ferocity of Nefᶜī's attack in this poem drove Meḥmed Pasha to attempt to have the poet executed, and he may even have requested that the grand mufti (*şeyḫü'l-İslām*), Yaḥyā Efendi (d. 1644), issue a fatwa authorizing such an execution—a request which, if it was indeed made, was denied.[13] The intention itself, however, provoked Nefᶜī to seek revenge through the composition of a second long invective in *ḳaṣīde* form, in which he again attacked the grand vizier's very identity. In this poem, in addition to voicing his complaint about the injustice of Meḥmed Pasha's attempt to have him executed, Nefᶜī used many of the same rhetorical tactics as in the first invective, attacking the grand vizier, for example, on the basis of his girth ("Gürcī, Georgian pig and massive mastiff, you dog!"[14]), his eunuchism and concomitant lack of masculinity ("how can the state remain in the hands of those without balls?"[15]), and so on. This time,

12 Nefᶜī, *Sihām-ı Ḳażā* (Leiden), 2b: "neler e[t]di ne deŋlü fitne peydā oldı ᶜālemde / edince tā vücūdıyla mülevveṡ ṣadr-ı dīvānı // ṭutalım ki ḥarīm-i muḥteremde perveriş bulmış / vücūdı bī-naẓīri kim bulunmaz aŋa bir s̱ānī // vezīr-i mülk-i İslām olmağa lāyıḳ mıdır andan / ṭoŋuz çobanı Gürcī Ermenīsi Türkī Çengânı."

13 No known official document records either the grand vizier's request or the grand mufti's refusal. The only evidence comes from Nefᶜī's own words in the poem in question: "even with so many crimes you are safe and sound, yet I / am deserving of death? you dark curse, you dog! // not even an infidel *ḳāḍı* would consent to this order / what has become of true Muslims, you dog?" (*bu ḳadar cürm ile sen ṣağ olasın da yine ben / vācibü'l-ḳatl olam ey baḫtek-i aẓlem* [*a köpek*] // *hele bu ḥükme kâfir ḳāḍısı olmaz rāżı / ḳande ḳaldı ki Müsülmān-ı müsellem a köpek*). See Nefᶜī, *Sihām-ı Ḳażā* (Leiden), 7a.

14 Nefᶜī, *Sihām-ı Ḳażā* (Leiden), 6b: "Gürcī ḫınzīri a şamsun-ı muᶜaẓẓam a köpek."

15 Nefᶜī, *Sihām-ı Ḳażā* (Leiden), 7a: "böyle ḳalur mı ṭaşaḳsızlar elinde devlet."

however, Nefᶜī also upped the ante considerably by making use of Meḥmed Pasha's *devşirme* origin to directly accuse him of being a crypto-Christian: "why should lampooning you be reason for execution? / if only I knew what you really were, you dubious infidel, you dog!"[16] He even went so far as to suggest that the grand vizier was deserving of death:

> if one considers how to bring order to the world
> above all else it requires killing you, you dog!
> you're an enemy of culture, a cursed one devoid of religion
> and if they kill you may your soul go to hell, you dog![17]

Overall, Nefᶜī's attacks on the grand vizier Meḥmed Pasha employ an aggressively othering discourse to define their target as an outsider who had usurped the highest office in the empire. The ultimate reason for this claim was the pasha's background as a converted Christian slave—and a eunuch slave at that. However, it should also be noted that during this period, as Metin Kunt has demonstrated, a rift was developing among the palace slaves, or *ḳul*s, with those of western origin, mainly Albanians and Bosnians, becoming increasingly dominant while those of eastern origin, like the Georgian Meḥmed Pasha, were beginning to become objects of derision.[18] Even the *sipāhī*s and janissaries, in their periodic uprisings against the state, tended to side with the western faction, as when they supported the Albanian Merre Ḥüseyin Pasha (d. 1624) in deposing Gürcī Meḥmed Pasha in February 1623. As will be shown, the western-eastern divide also extended beyond the *ḳul* class to a broader notion of center and periphery, and it also had an effect on Nefᶜī's relations with other poets within the context of the Ottoman cultural elite.

DEFINING THE OTHER IN CONTEMPORARY ADVICE LITERATURE

The othering discourse that animated Nefᶜī's invectives against Gürcī Meḥmed Pasha, as well as the fracturing of the Ottoman elite that

---

16 Nefᶜī, *Sihām-ı Ḳażā* (Leiden), 7a: "seni hicvetmekle ḳatle neden istiḥḳāḳ / sen nesin bilsem eyā kâfir-i mübhem a köpek."

17 Nefᶜī, *Sihām-ı Ḳażā* (Leiden), 7a: "ᶜadd olunsa eger esbāb-ı niẓām-ı ᶜālem / seni ḳatl eylemedir cümleden elzem a köpek // ehl-i dil düşmeni dīn yoḫsulı bir melᶜūnsun / öldürürlerse eger cān be-cehennem a köpek."

18 Kunt, "Ethnic-Regional (*Cins*) Solidarity," 237–39.

prompted it, was also a fundamental element used in the advice literature (*naṣīḥatnāme*, *lāyiḥa*) that began to proliferate in the second half of the sixteenth century and continued to be produced throughout the seventeenth century.[19] Much of this contemporary advice literature is shot through with resentment, particularly about the consequences of social mobility of various kinds. Ever-increasing mobility was effectively creating others *within* the ranks and circles of the administrative, military, and cultural elite, and, as their works clearly indicate, the authors of the advice literature saw this—or at least presented it—as a direct threat to their positions and aspirations.

Frequently, the social mobility so decried by the authors of the advice literature was framed in terms of the idea of mixture. For instance, in his 1581 *Nuṣḥatü's-selāṭīn* (Counsel for Sultans), Muṣṭafā ᶜĀlī of Gallipoli (d. 1600) compared this process to the dessert of mixed grains, fruit, and nuts called *ᶜaşūre*:

> The intrusion of the various classes into the different careers, and the permissiveness and accom[m]odating attitude of the highly-esteemed vezirs for these developments cause a complete disintegration and a dispersal of the people. It unfailingly has the effect that the food on the tables of government must become mixed up like the dish called *ᶜashūrā* and the nourishment of the tribes of perfect living becomes—God forbid!—disgusting like vomited matter and utterly confused.[20]

Muṣṭafā ᶜĀlī directly posits this social and professional "mixture" (*iḫtilāṭ*, here translated as "intrusion") as a cause of disturbance and disorder (*iḫtilāl*, here translated as "disintegration") in the empire's social fabric. Ultimately, as he elaborates, this mixture corrodes the government's very ability to govern effectively inasmuch as it encourages a glut of bribery and the buying and selling of government offices.

19 For a detailed overview of the period's advice literature, see Öz, *Kanun-ı Kadimin Peşinde*.

20 Muṣṭafā ᶜĀlī, *Nuṣḥatü's-selāṭīn*, 66, 163: "[E]cnās-ı muḫtelifenüŋ ṭuruḳ-ı mütenevviᶜeye iḫtilāṭı ve vüzerāᵓ-i maᶜālī-miḳdāruŋ bu maḳūle umūra ruḫṣat u inbisāṭı iḫtilāl-ı tāmma ve infiṣāl-ı enāma bāᶜi̱s olub niᶜmet-i simāṭ-ı devlet ᶜāşūrā aşı gibi maḫluṭ olmaḳ ve ᶜişret-i ᶜaşāyir-i mükemmel-maᶜīşet ḥāşā ḳusındı gibi müstekreh olub ḳarış murış bulunmaḳ bi'ż-żarūreti lāzım gelür." Translation by Andreas Tietze. Please note that Tietze's transcription of Muṣṭafā ᶜĀlī's text has been slightly adjusted to accord with the style used in this volume.

A similar claim was put forth in the anonymous *Kitāb-ı Müsteṭāb* (The Agreeable Book), which was likely composed around the year 1620 and presented to Sultan ᶜO̱smān II (r. 1618–22). The author—who was probably of *devşirme* origin and educated in the palace—details the ways in which the grand vizier's annual departure from Istanbul on campaign results, due to the relative vacuum of strict control, in a veritable orgy of buying and selling revenued administrative and military positions:

> Ever since the campaigns against Persia conducted in the happy time of Sultan Murad Khan [III, r. 1574–95], on the very day when the commander-in-chief crosses over to Üsküdar [for a campaign in the east] or goes out through the Edirne gate for a campaign in Rumelia, the provincial governors and district governors and other such office holders immediately begin taking bribes, that curse brought down on the world, to make transfers and reassignments and dismissals and new appointments, and so many revenued positions—such as butlers, miscellaneous officers, heralds, cavalry posts, wardens, artillerymen, waggoners, and armorers—are distributed and so many advancements made that it is not clear who has bestowed them and who has bought and sold them. It is such a busy buying and selling and back-and-forth exchange that it is impossible to fully describe. As a result, by the time the commander-in-chief returns from campaign, so many revenues and offices have been bought and sold that the public treasury lies in ruins. From among the subjects, Turks and Kurds and Gypsies and Anatolian Iranians and Persians and, in sum, anyone who wants can come right up, whether it be on campaign or in the capital, and use *aḳçe*s to obtain a revenued position. In this manner, outsiders have mixed with the slaves of the Porte and brought turmoil and chaos.[21]

21 Anonymous, *Kitāb-ı müstetāb*, ٧–٨: "Sulṭān Murād Ḫān ḥażretleriniŋ zamān-ı saᶜādetlerinde vāḳiᶜ ᶜAcem seferleriniŋ ibtidāsından bu āna gelince serdār olanlar hemān Üsküdār'a geçdikleri gün veyāḫūd Rum ili seferi ise Edrene ḳapusından ṭaşra çıḳdıḳları günden hemān beglerbegileri ve sancāḳ beglerini ve sāᵓir manṣıb nāmında olanlara ᶜāleme belā nāzil olan rüşvet sebebiyle tebdīl ü taġyīr ü ᶜazl u naṣb etmege mübāşeret ederler ve sāᵓir dirlikler ḫod mes̱elā çāşnīgīrlik ve müteferriḳa ve çavuş ve sipāhīlikler ve ḳapucı ve ṭopcı ve ᶜarabacı ve cebeci dirlikleri vermek ve teraḳḳīler verilmek gibi ne veren bellü ve ne alan ve ne ṣatan bellü hemān bir alış-veriş ve bir alım-ṣatım edinmişlerdir ki taᶜbīr ü taḥrīri mümkin degildir. El-ḥāṣıl bir serdār sefere varub gelinceye degin dirlikler ve manṣıblar bu vechle alınmaḳ ve ṣatılmaḳ ile beytü'l-māl-ı Müslimīn

Here, bribery is presented as opening the floodgates to a social "mixing" (*ḳarışmaḳ*)—that is, to an influx of, especially, non-*ḳul* individuals into governmental positions. Corruption, then, leads to what is effectively an actual contamination of the state's elite by "outsiders" (*ecnebī*) who, in a sense, serve as the others of the ideal state elite envisioned by—and, in fact, significantly, personally represented by—the authors of the advice literature.

In many cases, as in the *Kitāb-ı Müsteṭāb*, this influx of outsiders or others is specifically framed as comprising Ottoman "subjects" (*reᶜāyā*), typically but not exclusively those of Muslim origin, purchasing their way into the elite administrative classes that had traditionally been stocked by *ḳul*s of *devşirme* origin who, owing to the process of their education and training, were ideally considered to be more loyal to the state than to any familial or regional ties.[22] This is a point upon which Muṣṭafā ᶜĀlī expounded in some detail in another passage from the *Nuṣḥatu's-selāṭīn*, specifically in relation to Kurds and Turks (by the latter he likely meant nomadic and semi-nomadic Turkmens):

> [T]here are certain nations among the various races that are definitely not suitable for an administrative position and do not have capability and qualifications enough to become a refuge of the people. . . . One of these (nations) are the perfidious Kurds whose character is nothing but obstinacy and stubbornness. The other is the disunited Turks whose hearts are full of malice and mischief. That is why under the previous sultans the office of a *beglerbegi* was never given to Kurds or Turks, and even the office of a *beg* was not seen [as] proper to be given to any of them but to the son of a *beg* whose ancestors had been holding the title for many generations. But at our time such an observation of class distinctions is totally abandoned. Turks and Kurds, if they possess silver and gold coins, are rated higher even than the champions of the Hashimites.[23]

---

ber-bād olub ve reᶜāyā olanlardan Etrāk ve Ekrād ve Çengāne ve Ṭāt ve Aᶜcām el-ḥāṣıl her isteyen ilāu'l-ān varub eger seferlerde ve eger Āsitāne'de aḳçe ile dirliklere geçmek ile ḳūl ṭāʾifesine bu sebeb ile ecnebī ḳarışub herc ü merc olmışlardır."

22 As Metin Kunt has shown, this was indeed an ideal, as in reality many *ḳul*s did retain close familial and regional ties throughout their lives; see Kunt, "Ethnic-Regional (*Cins*) Solidarity," 234–37.

23 Muṣṭafā ᶜĀlī, *Nuṣḥatü's-selāṭīn*, 63, 158: "Ve ṭavāyif-i muḫtelifeden baᶜżı milel-i mütenevviᶜe vardur ki mutlaḳā ḥükūmete lāyıḳ olmazlar ve melaẕ-ı nās olacaḳlayın devlete liyāḳat u istiḥḳāḳ bulmazlar. . . . Ol zümreden biri Ekrād-ı bed-nihāddur

Here, we can observe Muṣṭafā ᶜĀlī conflating classes (*ṭabaḳāt*) and cultures in a manner that implicitly posits a more closed group—namely, the *ḳul* class, comprising the so-called "slaves of the Porte," or what Cornell Fleischer rather more accurately calls "the 'Palace' class of true Ottomans"[24]—as the only one capable of being relied upon to rule.

The same trepidations and much the same approach are also apparent in the treatises of Ḳoçi Beg (d. ca. 1650), himself a *ḳul* of *devşirme* origin. In his first treatise, for instance, which was composed in 1630 and presented to Sultan Murād IV (r. 1623–1640), Ḳoçi Beg focused in particular on how a degeneration based in social mobility was infecting the *devşirme*-based janissary corps:

> People of unknown origin and religious affiliation like urban riffraff, Turks, Gypsies, Anatolian Iranians, Kurds, outsiders, Laz, Yörüks, muleteers, camel drivers, porters, body waxers, bandits, pickpockets, and all sorts of other types have all joined different ranks [of the janissaries] and the traditions and ways have been corrupted and the customary laws and rules done away with.[25]

The equation here of class-based categories with such criminal—and, indeed, seditious—actors as bandits (*ḳuṭṭāᶜ-ı ṭarīḳ*) and pickpockets (*yan kesici*) is telling. The declinist tendencies of the late sixteenth- and early seventeenth-century advice literature were intimately linked to the elite background—that is, highly educated and trained for government service, and primarily but not exclusively *ḳul*s—of that literature's producers, as they perceived or constructed in their works a novel social mobility that threatened the status quo.

---

ki cibilletleri maḥż-ı lecc u ᶜināddur. İkinci Etrāk-ı ḳalīlü'l-ittiḥāddur ki ḫilḳatleri maḥż-ı şirret ü fesāddur. Bāᶜi<u>s</u> budur ki selāṭīn-i sābıḳa zamānlarında Ekrād u Etrāk'a beglerbegilikler verilmezdi ve eben ᶜan ced begzādelerinden ġayrisine beglik bile lāyıḳ görülmezdi. Ammā fī zamāninā ol gūne ṭabaḳāt riᶜāyeti meslūbdur, Etrāk u Ekrād mālik-i sīm ü dīnār olduġı taḳdīrce dilīrān-ı Hāşimīden bile merġūbdur." Translation by Andreas Tietze.

24 Fleischer, *Bureaucrat and Intellectual*, 209.

25 Ḳoçi Beg, *Ḳoçi Beg Risālesi*, 61: "Ve bi'l-cümle her zümreye … millet ü me<u>z</u>hebi nā-maᶜlūm şehir oġlanı ve Türk ve Çengâne ve Ṭāt ve Kürd ve ecnebī ve Lāz ve Yörük ve ḳatırcı ve deveci ve ḥammāl ve aġdacı ve ḳuṭṭāᶜ-ı ṭarīḳ ve yan kesici ve sā'ir ecnās-ı muḫtelife mülḥaḳḳ olub āyīn ü erkān bozuldı ve ḳānūn u ḳāᶜide ḳalḳdı."

Recent historiography has begun to reveal that, quantitatively speaking, the notion of such social mobility as a phenomenon new to the late sixteenth century and onward, and even as a real phenomenon at all, is historically inaccurate.[26] With this caveat in mind, however, the very proliferation during this period of advice literature emphasizing the influx of "outsiders"—that is, of others—is by no means coincidental and is in fact quite revealing. It suggests that the administrators and bureaucrats—*ḳul*s like Ḳoçi Beg and the anonymous author of the *Kitāb-ı Müsteṭāb*, as well as disillusioned men of letters like Muṣṭafā ᶜĀlī—not only penned their treatises from a center that was conceptual if not necessarily geographical in nature, but also, and more importantly, projected what they were experiencing and seeing around them, or at least what they feared to be the case at the center, out onto the periphery on an empire-wide scale, and especially onto the military classes that were in many ways the state's primary concern. In the center, at the highest administrative levels as well as within the cultural elite (including patrons), there were in fact new actors and factional configurations emerging.[27] Accordingly, the "old guard" that the authors of the advice literature presumed to represent did in fact, as their works make abundantly clear, feel threatened by what they saw as a process of peripheral others "contaminating" the center that they had considered to be largely their own prerogative.

NEFʿĪ AND ETMEKÇIZĀDE AḤMED PASHA

Many of the concerns that the advice literature presents in a typically restrained and reasoned manner also animated the period's invective, where they emerged in a much more vitriolic voice—one that revealed, from the inside (as it were), how intensely contemporary actors were reacting to what was happening around them. This is the case in the second example of invective that I will examine—namely, Nefᶜī's assault on Etmekçizāde Aḥmed Pasha, who served as the chief finance minister (*başdefterdār*) for most of the reign of Sultan Aḥmed I (r. 1603–17)—in which we can observe the same concerns that are expressed in the advice

26 See, for example, Darling, "Nasihatnameler, İcmal Defterleri, and the Timar-Holding Ottoman Elite," 203–9.

27 For a detailed study of the factional changes occurring at this time, see Börekçi, "Factions and Favorites."

literature regarding social mobility destabilizing the Ottoman center, and indeed the empire as a whole.

Aḥmed Pasha, the target of Nefᶜī's invective, was a living example of such mobility, as, in the context of his time, he had quite an unconventional background for a person in his post. His Muslim Albanian father was the head of Edirne's bakers' guild—hence the name Etmekçizāde, or "son of the baker"—and Aḥmed became a *sipāhī* while also accumulating enough capital to buy his way into the tax-farming system, obtaining a position as a collector of taxes (*ᶜāmil*) from the city's Roma. From here, he steadily rose through the ranks, eventually becoming the military treasurer (*sefer defterdārı*) in 1597, during the Long War with the Habsburgs, and finally chief finance minister in June 1606. He was thus, remarkably, a Muslim-born financial entrepreneur from an *ᶜaskerī,* or military, background, as compared to previous ministers, who had almost uniformly come up through either the educational-judicial or the scribal career tracks.[28]

A number of contemporary sources remark on Aḥmed Pasha's uncustomary background and rise to power—but never in a positive light. For instance, a report (*telḫīṣ*) drawn up a few years after the pasha's death in 1618 stresses the fact that he was the first chief finance minister to be given the rank of vizier:

> Formerly, [chief] finance ministers were not of the rank of vizier, and if an imperial decree was writ regarding imperial possessions, it would pass through four or five hands, with three [other] finance ministers setting their seal on it. Any previously written decree would have been registered by the council's senior clerks, the *muḳāṭaᶜacıs* and accountants, and so they would be aware of what was written therein. Moreover, revenue would come directly to the imperial gate. In this manner, it was not possible to secrete away any possessions rightfully belonging to the sultan. In the year 1015 [1606/07], the late Sultan Aḥmed [I] Khan made Etmekçizāde Aḥmed Pasha the chief finance minister with the rank of vizier. Since that time, finance ministers have been granted viziership. As a result, the condition of the treasury has been disturbed and disordered and has not been free

28 For more on Etmekçizāde Aḥmed Pasha and the unique nature of his background, see Tezcan, *The Second Ottoman Empire*, 14–17.

> of destruction and ruin. For now that finance ministers are viziers, whenever it is necessary to write an imperial decree, they have a scribe of their very own write it and then affix it with their signature and seal without anyone being aware of what is written therein. With the finance ministers of former times, even if they were traitorous thieves, they still did not have the power to steal even one *aḳçe*. But now that they have viziership, they are able to steal whatever amount they desire. In sum, the granting of the rank of vizier to finance ministers is immensely harmful to the treasury.[29]

This detailed analysis—chronicling the elimination of certain bureaucratic checks and its negative effect on the Ottoman treasury—situates Aḥmed Pasha, and specifically the novelty of his viziership, at the very advent of this process. Despite the insinuation, however, the report stops short of directly and specifically accusing Aḥmed Pasha *himself* of the corruption that it criticizes.

Such discretion is perhaps to be expected in a report meant for submission to the sultan. Others, though, writing in different genres for different audiences, could afford to be, and in fact were, rather less circumspect. For instance, a chronogram written in the margins of a miscellany by a scribe named ^{c}Ömer on the occasion of Aḥmed Pasha's death describes its subject in the following manner:

> I wonder if he now repents
> the injustice he wreaked on the people

29 Murphey, "The Veliyyuddin Telhis," 561: "Ve defterdārlar muḳaddemā vezāret pāyesiyle olmadan māl-ı pādişāhī içün bir emr-i şerīf yazılsa dört beş elden geçüb üç defterdār daḫı birer nişān çekerdi. Ve evvel yazılan ḥükmi Ḳubbealtı'nda olan dīvān ḫ^{v}āceleri ki muḳāṭa^{c}acılar ve muḥāsebeciler der-ḳayd edüb ol ḥükmiŋ mażmūnına vāḳıflar idi. Ve māl-ı mīrī ṭoğrı bāb-ı hümāyūna gelürdi. Bu ṭarīḳ ile māl-ı pādişāhī ketm olunmaḳ mümkin degil idi. Merḥūm Sulṭān Aḥmed Ḫān biŋ onbeş tārīḫinde Etmekçizāde Aḥmed Paşa'yı vezāret ile başdefterdār eyledi. Ol zamāndan berü defterdārlar vezāret ile olur idi. Bu sebebden beytü'l-māl aḥvāli muḫtel ü müşevveş olub żāyi^{c} ü telef olmaḳdan ḫālī degildir. Zīrā defterdārlar vezīr olmaġla bir emr-i şerīf yazılmaḳ lāzım geldikde kendüye maḫṣūṣ bir kātibe yazdırub kendüsi imżāsın ve ṭuğrasın çeküb mażmūnına bir ferd vāḳıf olmaz. Muḳaddemā olan defterdārlar ḫā$^{\circ}$in ve ḫırsız olsalar daḫı bir aḳçe sirḳat eylemeğe ḳādir değiller idi. Lakin vezāret olıcaḳ murād eyledüği miḳdārı sirḳaya ḳādir olur. Ḥāṣıl-ı kelâm, defterdārlarıŋ vezāret ile olması beytü'l-māla küllī żarardır. . . ."

he turned Rumelia to wrack and ruin
but now they're once again safe and sound
yet he was corrupt since his rise began
none were so tenacious in *bid^cah*[30]

The emphasis here is on injustice (*ẓulm*), which in the context seems to refer primarily to corruption and theft. In fact, the poem also goes on to declare that Aḥmed Pasha's possessions should immediately be confiscated by the government: "all his goods must be taken for the treasury / indeed, the sultan should have spilled his blood."[31] Though the pasha's blood was never spilled—he appears to have died of natural causes—his possessions were seized for the imperial treasury following his death; they amounted to the immense total value of 1,000 *yük*s, or 100 million *aḳçe*s.[32] The poem also claims, however, that Aḥmed Pasha had been corrupt from the very start of his career (*fürū^c*), and, much like the report mentioned above, it also hints at the sheer novelty (*bid^cah*) of his rise to power, implying that his very background was a preliminary to corruption.

This approach by the scribe ^cÖmer echoes the contemporary advice literature's claims—both implicit and explicit—that any governmental official or soldier who did not advance to his position through the traditional channels would be more subject to corruption. This was also the approach that Nef^cī adopted in the numerous invectives, both short quatrains (*ḳıṭ^ca*) and long *ḳaṣīde*s, that he wrote against Aḥmed Pasha, in which the link between the pasha's nontraditional background and his corruption serves as the primary linchpin. The quatrains, in particular, were an easily recalled form that could feed slander more effectively and widely into the rumor mill of oral distribution, a process of which Nef^cī took advantage

30 Alkan, "Ekmekçizâde Ahmet Paşa," 46 (374): "Halka ettikleri zulümlerine / Aceb oldu mu şimdi ol nâdim / Rum ilini harabe vermiş idi / Şimdiden sonra oldular sâlim/ Gerçi fürûunda zâlim idi / Olmadı böyle bid'ate âzim". Please note that, lacking access to the original manuscript, which is in Alkan's private collection, I have here reproduced his transcription of the poem as published.

31 Alkan, "Ekmekçizâde Ahmet Paşa," 46 (374): "Cümle malını miriye almak / Padişaha hele kanı lâzım."

32 Kātib Çelebī, *Fezleke*, 642.

in casting aspersions on Aḥmed Pasha's origins.[33] Take, for instance, the following poem:

> hey, lowly baker! what insolent grace is this?
> a Gypsy tax collector, you waltzed to a viziership
> now you've turned the treasury to your own fortune
> you were just a miserly merchant selling worn-out rags[34]

Here, just as in the report described above, there is a complaint about Aḥmed Pasha being granted vizieral status. Moreover, Nefʿī connects this promotion not only to the pasha's own personal corruption, describing him as enriching himself at the treasury's expense, but also, and even more significantly, to his relatively common origins: this pasha is in fact a "lowly baker" (*ḫabbāz-ı dūn*) and "a miserly merchant selling worn-out rags" (*eski püski ṣatıcı bir cimrī bāzirgān*) who nevertheless managed to easily obtain the rank of vizier.

The essentialist implications of this line of attack were made even more explicit in a long invective—nearly seventy distichs in the *terkīb-i bend* stanzaic form—that Nefʿī wrote against the pasha. The poem was produced in the spring of 1609, and may have played a part in the concentrated smear campaign conducted by the grand vizier Ḳuyucu Murād Pasha (d. 1611), a possible patron of Nefʿī during this period. Murād Pasha openly held a grudge against Aḥmed Pasha because the latter had refused

33 Unfortunately, relatively little is known about how invectives circulated during this period, as the main source for such information, the contemporary biographical dictionaries of poets (*teẕkīre-i şuʿarā*), are not forthcoming on the matter. However, drawing from the (still limited) information of earlier biographical dictionaries, it can be hypothesized that invectives were rarely if ever read or sent to their targets directly. Instead, they were most often read out among a circle of friends, generally fellow poets, and subsequently remembered and/or noted down, to be later recounted and/or read out in different circles. In this way, the target—whether it was another poet or a state official—would eventually come to hear, or at least hear of, the invective in question. In the biographical dictionary of ʿĀşıḳ Çelebi (d. 1572), for instance, most examples of invective are accompanied by the verb *demek* ("say, tell"), and in some cases the target is later said to have heard (*işidmek*, *şāyiʿ*) the invective and responded (*cevāb*, *muḳābelede*), sometimes by means of an invective; see, for example, ʿĀşıḳ Çelebi, *Meşāʿirü'ş-şuʿarā*, II: 938; III: 1552–57.

34 Nefʿī, *Sihām-ı Ḳażā* (Leiden), 15b: "bu ne küstāḫāne himmetdir eyā ḫabbāz-ı dūn / bī-[tekellüf] ṣadra geçdiŋ ʿāmil-i Çengân iken / eylediŋ sermāye şimdi beytü'l-mālı hep / eski püski ṣatıcı bir cimrī bāzirgân iken."

to grant him financial assistance several years earlier, when Murād had been experiencing financial difficulties as the governor of Diyarbakır. After Murād was appointed grand vizier in December 1606, several months following Aḥmed's own appointment to chief finance minister, the tension between the two men seems to have merely simmered for two years while the grand vizier was campaigning against rebels in Anatolia. But then, in early October 1608, Aḥmed Pasha found himself in Bayburt, the same city as the grand vizier; Murād had come there to winter his army, while the chief finance minister had been sent there with a consignment of money and troops. Immediately upon his arrival, Aḥmed Pasha began to fear for his life and arranged to be recalled to Istanbul. His fears seem not to have been unfounded, because the very next spring, when the grand vizier was back in Istanbul—or, more precisely, Üsküdar—preparing for a campaign against the Safavids, he asked for and received Sultan Aḥmed I's permission to have Aḥmed Pasha killed, ostensibly for laying waste to the treasury. Soon afterward, however, the sultan appears to have changed his mind—or had it changed for him—and he spared Aḥmed Pasha, upon which the latter immediately joined with the chief black eunuch, Muṣṭafā Agha (d. 1624), to suggest to the sultan that Murād Pasha should be removed from his position because he was a frail old man, unwilling and unable to campaign against the Safavids now that the threat from rebels had been quelled. Aḥmed I, however, dismissed such ideas and maintained the grand vizier in his post.[35]

It was into the midst of this clash that Nefᶜī dropped his long invective against the chief finance minister. The poem begins with a highly complex and obscure stanza, replete with arcane astrological references, connecting the troubles of the times and the rise of Aḥmed Pasha to a variety of inauspicious astrological events. In the next stanza, Nefᶜī announces how the rest of the poem will proceed: "let me begin the description of that unscrupulous tyrant / see if there's ever been such a blameworthy person."[36] The poem goes on to list and comment on one quality after another, and it is structured as a list of Aḥmed Pasha's faults, which make

35 This abbreviated outline of events is taken from Kātib Çelebī, *Fezleke*, 537, 549–52, 561–69. The same information is to be found in the chronicle of Muṣṭafā Naᶜīmā, *Tārīḫ-i Naᶜīmā*, 339, 350, 355–56, 369, 374–76; however, Naᶜīmā's account is copied verbatim from Kātib Çelebī's.

36 Nefᶜī, *Sihām-ı Ḳażā* (Leiden), 4b: "başlayam vaṣfına ol ẓālim-i bī-pervā / böyle meẕmūmı olur mı göriŋüz insānıŋ."

him unfit not only for the position of chief finance minister but for any governmental position whatsoever. The basic faults as listed fall into four broad categories as follows.

First is his corruption, which Nefᶜī—much like the aforementioned scribe ᶜÖmer, whose chronogram implies that Aḥmed Pasha had been siphoning off money from the very beginning of his career—claims to have already been in full force when the pasha was serving as military treasurer at the end of the 1590s:

> for all those years that he was out on campaign
> would anything go right for the commander sent there?
> he would become close to every commander
> on the front before killing him and devouring his goods
> the soldiers on the front saw none of their stipends
> and the goods coming to the sultan were always few[37]

The second point of attack is Aḥmed Pasha's imputed lack of education and culture; Nefᶜī describes everything from his illegible handwriting and poor spelling ("his abominable handwriting looked just like his face / whatever he wrote was full of flaws in spelling"[38]) to his inappropriate and dishonest manner of speaking ("when he came with a chair to the council to report / the viziers all thought some storyteller had come to the square"[39]).

Third, Nefᶜī attacks Aḥmed Pasha's association with and patronage of disreputable and ignorant people, saying that "his disgraceful friends and fellow drinkers / are, like him, vile and wicked and pointless."[40] He even names some of the pasha's associates and proceeds to insult them as well.

Finally, and perhaps most bluntly, Nefᶜī repeatedly and extensively attacks Aḥmed Pasha's sheer ugliness and unmasculine inelegance, likening, for example, his pale face to a chamber pot ("whoever sees his

37 Nefᶜī, *Sihām-ı Ḳażā* (Leiden), 4b: "bunca yıllar seferde idi serdār evvel / hiç işi rāst gelür miydi varan paşanıŋ / ḳangı serdāra ḳarīn oldıysa ser-ḥadde / yedi başını bütün mālı ile hep anıŋ / görmez olmışdı mevācib yüzin ehl-i ser-ḥadd / hep kem alurdı varan mālı şeh-i devrānıŋ."

38 Nefᶜī, *Sihām-ı Ḳażā* (Leiden), 5a: "ḫaṭṭ-ı müstekrehi de şekline beŋzerdi hemān / yazsa başdan başa imlāda ḳuṣūrı ne idi."

39 Nefᶜī, *Sihām-ı Ḳażā* (Leiden), 6a: "varıcaḳ ᶜarż içün iskemle ile [dīvāna] / ḳıṣṣa-ḫᵛ[ā]n geldi ṣanurdı vüzerā meydāna."

40 Nefᶜī, *Sihām-ı Ḳażā* (Leiden), 6a: "hem-dem ü hem-ḳadeḥi olan erāẕiller de / bir alay kendü gibi dūn u ḫabīs̱ ü mühmel."

yellow face and shit-stained mouth / says it's like a copper chamber pot all polished up"[41]) and his mincing, affected walk to someone struggling not to defecate all over himself ("if he took one step he'd crap himself from daintiness"[42]).

These four points of attack are relatively standard approaches in the Ottoman invective tradition. What is novel, however, is the way in which Nefʿī consistently and directly links all of these faults to Aḥmed Pasha's relatively undistinguished social background. For instance, in the midst of describing both how the pasha has stolen goods and money while collecting taxes in Rumelia ("if he goes, it's to collect taxes, and if he comes it's with a treasure / none can know the coercion that the poor were subjected to"[43]) and how poor his handwriting and spelling are, Nefʿī pens this couplet:

> his mother's a slave-girl cook, his father a baker,
> so what could he possibly know of affairs of state?[44]

In the same stanza, he criticizes Aḥmed Pasha's supposedly meteoric rise from a nobody to a power broker:

> he had in this world no trace of name or claim to fame,
> so how'd he just appear like that in one or two days?[45]

Lines like these voice many of the same complaints that can be observed in the contemporary advice literature, but in a visceral way that reveals even more clearly the intensity of the fractures that were developing within the elite circles of the time. If, for instance, we recall the aforementioned report's tame and carefully reasoned complaint against granting viziership to finance ministers, we can compare it with the harsh

41 Nefʿī, *Sihām-ı Ḳażā* (Leiden), 6a: "der gören çehre-i zerdī ile boḳlı ağzın / bir baḳır ḥāvruza gūyā ki urulmuş ṣayḳal."

42 Nefʿī, *Sihām-ı Ḳażā* (Leiden), 5a: "bir adım yürise yestehler idi nāzından."

43 Nefʿī, *Sihām-ı Ḳażā* (Leiden), 5a: "çıḳsa taḥṣīle çıḳar gelse ḫazīneyle gelür / kimse bilmez fuḳarā çekdüği zorı ne idi." Cf. the scribe ʿÖmer's hemistich, "the injustice he wreaked on the people" ([ḫ]*alḳa ettikleri ẓulümler*), quoted above.

44 Nefʿī, *Sihām-ı Ḳażā* (Leiden), 5a: "anası aşcı kenīzek babası etmekçi / kendünüŋ devlet umūrında şuʿūrı ne idi."

45 Nefʿī, *Sihām-ı Ḳażā* (Leiden), 5a: "dehrde ẕerre ḳadar nām [u] nişānı yoğiken / bir iki günde gelüb böyle ẓuhūrı ne idi."

aggression of a similar complaint made by Nefᶜī in a quatrain directed against Aḥmed Pasha:

> you kill the seller for one bit of bread that's missing
> there's you, you yellow dog, and then there's viziership
> who would see you and think you were a vizier?
> viziership was a pure gem, and now it's turned to shit[46]

Considering these lines in the light of Nefᶜī's other criticisms of Aḥmed Pasha, it is clear that it was not the pasha's appearance—not his pale skin and blond hair—that made him unfit for viziership, no matter how many lines the poet devoted to describing it in intimate detail. Instead—just as in the case of Nefᶜī's invectives against Gürcī Meḥmed Pasha, in which the grand vizier's girth and eunuchism were used to paint him as an other in order to provide a ground for much more serious defamation—so too in the case of Etmekçizāde Aḥmed Pasha does Nefᶜī use unflattering descriptions of the finance minister's physical features as, effectively, an external manifestation of an inner, fundamental corruption.[47] The real complaint, much as in the advice literature, was the sheer uncommonality of Aḥmed Pasha's background: he was, in effect, an other intruding into the space of the Ottoman elite.

CONCLUSION

By its very nature as a mode of poetry that denigrates and castigates, invective necessarily defines its target or targets as others: in order to more effectively defame the target, any given invective must present him or her as a figure replete with faults, while at least implicitly casting the poet as one capable of discerning and exposing those faults. This holds true regardless of whether an invective is a "vertical" one targeting a superior, as in the case of Nefᶜī's invectives against Gürcī

46 Nefᶜī, *Sihām-ı Ḳażā* (Leiden), 15b: "bir etmeğiŋ eksik ṣatıcı öldüreceksin / sen ḳande eyā ṣarı köpek ḳande vezāret / kim görse o ṣūretle vezīr olduğuŋ[u der] / bir cevher-i pāk idi boḳa düşdi vezāret."

47 It might also be noted in this context that Etmekçizāde Aḥmed Pasha apparently had no eyebrows, a large and crooked nose, blue eyes, and a pale beard: "with those plucked eyebrows and that crooked packsaddle of a nose / with those Persian blue eyes and that beard like yellow arsenic" ("o yoluḳ ḳaşlar ile ol semerī eğri burun / o ᶜAcem māʾīsi gözlerle o zırnıḫī ṣaḳal"). See Nefᶜī, *Sihām-ı Ḳażā* (Leiden), 6a.

Meḥmed Pasha and Etmekçizāde Aḥmed Pasha, or a "horizontal" one targeting a peer.[48] As such, on one level the invectives of Nefʿī very much represent a continuation of the Islamicate and earlier Ottoman invective tradition, utilizing many of the same tools (for example, caricaturization) within the same forms (that is, primarily quatrains, with the occasional more extended piece) to achieve largely similar ends (for example, loss of prestige for the target, with a concomitant rise in prestige for the poet).

At the same time, however, there is much that is novel about Nefʿī's invectives as well, and indeed about the early seventeenth-century Ottoman invective corpus as a whole, as compared particularly to the invectives of the so-called "classic" era from the late fifteenth to the mid-sixteenth centuries.It is important to remember in this context that not only those poets engaged in the production of invective, but also their targets, considered themselves to be "Rūmī," a term connoting those who represented the Ottoman social, cultural, and to some extent political center of "Rūm."[49] Cemal Kafadar has rightly pointed out that "Rūmī" was a concept that was paired both with "Turk" in terms of social class[50] and with "Persian" and "Arab" in terms of cultural achievement and identity.[51] As he phrases it, "'Rumi' . . . was used in large measure to designate a novel social and cultural constellation, namely the identity of those from a variety of backgrounds but with a shared disposition toward a certain style of expression in the arts as well as quotidian life."[52] It was, effectively, a way of assimilating multiple peoples under one avowedly

48 The notion of "vertical" and "horizontal" invective used here is borrowed from Thomas Conley's analysis of the scenarios within which insults are made; see Conley, *Toward a Rhetoric of Insult*, 3–4. While Conley's vertical-horizontal differentiation is based in individual vs. group distinctions, I have adjusted it here to accord, especially, with Islamicate invective written in the context of a patronage system: "vertical" invective is that which is directed at a superior (that is, a potential patron), while "horizontal" invective is that which is directed at a peer (that is, a rival for patronage, typically another poet).

49 While attempting to delineate precise geographic boundaries for the abstract concept of "Rūm" would be an exercise in futility, it would not be entirely inaccurate to claim that, around the turn of the seventeenth century, it encompassed Istanbul and environs, Rumelia or the Balkans, and western Anatolia.

50 "'Rumi vs. Turk' . . . resonated with a social class distinction and had connotations similar to 'bourgeois vs. rustic.'" Kafadar, "A Rome of One's Own," 11. One particularly stark example of this opposition is to be found in a social satire composed by the poet Faḳīrī (d. 1526), in which he gently mocks both the Rūmī and the Turk; see Ambros, "Six Lampoons," 34–35.

51 Kafadar, "A Rome of One's Own," 15.

52 Kafadar, "A Rome of One's Own," 15.

elite rubric, creating a sociocultural center that was primarily based in the geographical center but could appear anywhere a self-styled "Rūmī" was present. In terms of poetry specifically, it was a major animating force behind the numerous biographical dictionaries of poets of the sixteenth century, which sought to establish and canonize a distinctly Ottoman poetic identity.[53]

Once the vicissitudes of the late sixteenth century had set in and begun to inform and hence alter notions of elite self-identity, however, the by now established sense of what a "Rūmī" was began to ossify in response, a process that was only exacerbated by the massive influx into Istanbul and environs of rural peasants fleeing both high taxes and rebel depredation in what later became known as the "Great Flight" (*Büyük Ḳaçġun*).[54] In the invective corpus, this period's insularization of the Ottoman elite is nowhere more clear than in the use of ethnonyms, with all their associated sociocultural baggage. Prior to the late sixteenth and early seventeenth centuries, epithets such as "Turk" or "Armenian" were rarely used in invective of an openly personal nature (that is, aimed at a specified individual target). In the case of terms like the latter (that is, those relating to a more or less verifiable origin rather than an explicitly socially loaded epithet like "Turk"), they were used accurately in the sense that those of a given origin would typically be attacked through that origin.[55] However, a line such as Nefᶜī's aforementioned "pigherd of a Georgian Armenian Turkish Gypsy" presents a rather different phenomenon: on the one hand, "pigherd," "Georgian," and "Armenian" serve as explicitly Christian references, thereby casting the target, Gürcī Meḥmed Pasha, out of the (Sunni) Muslim aspect integral to Ottoman identity; on the other hand, "Turkish" serves to cast him out of the "Rūmī" elite,[56]

53 See Kafadar, "A Rome of One's Own," 15, and Kuru, "The Literature of Rum."

54 For an overview of the "Great Flight," see Akdağ, "Büyük Kaçgunluk."

55 While treatment of the topic of such socially based invective in this earlier period lies beyond the scope of this paper, some preliminary work has been done in the area. See, for example, Öztürk, "Divan Şairinin Nimet ve İktidar Ekseninde"; Ambros, "'The Other' (Non-Muslim, Non-Ottoman) in Ottoman Literary Humour"; and the anthological study by Güven, "Klâsik Türk Şiirinde Hiciv." Unfortunately, since all these studies are in the nature of literary surveys, they lack a historical perspective on the development of Ottoman invective over time and in contemporary context. For a different approach, see Erdem Çıpa's contribution in this volume.

56 A similar double expulsion can be seen in, for instance, the poet Ravżī's (d. after 1600) *murabbaᶜ* against the Albanians, where he describes the people of Lezhë as follows: "Some of the people are infidels, some are Turks" (*Ḫalḳınuŋ kimisi kāfir kimisi Türkeş'dür*). See Ravżī, *Dīvān*, 64.

as does the epithet "Gypsy," which also works as a variety of wild card through reference to one of the most marginalized and ostracized Ottoman communities of all.

This difference can be especially clearly seen in the invectives that were written against Nefᶜī. In this context, it is worth recalling that however much he may have positioned himself against "outsiders" and "upstarts" like Gürcī Meḥmed Pasha and Etmekçizāde Aḥmed Pasha, Nefᶜī was *himself* something of an outsider and upstart, an other who had originally come from a periphery (Hasankale in eastern Anatolia) to the center in Istanbul. Here, even as he set about fashioning himself as a poet and cultural representative of the center, he found himself in the midst of—and indeed facing off against—a readymade faction of western Anatolian and Rumelian scholar-poets, men like Nevᶜīzāde ᶜAṭāʾī (d. 1635), Ganīzāde Meḥmed Nādirī (d. 1626), Ḳāfzāde Fāʾizī (d. 1622), Veysī (d. 1628), and Riyāżī (d. 1644). All of these men had long-standing familial and *intisāb* connections with one another, all implicitly or explicitly saw themselves as representatives of "Rūmī" elite culture, and all penned invectives against Nefᶜī in which they used much the same othering discourse as he did in an attempt to keep out someone they saw as an upstart from the provinces. And in the process of thus attacking Nefᶜī, they employed the full gamut of derogatory ethnonyms, none of them actually applicable to the target, in order to distinctly mark him off as their other. He was, for instance, labeled "a converted Armenian cuckold" (*Ermeniden dönme gidi*) owing to his origins in eastern Anatolia.[57] Likewise, he was called "the son of a Jewish bitch" (*Çıfıt ḳaḥpeniŋ oğlı*)[58] in reference to his supposed shirking of religious duties, a "Jewish pimp" (*Çıfıt gidi*)[59] in reference to his wife's imputed extracurricular sexual activities, an "Abyssinian ass" (*Ḥabeşī ḫar*)[60] in reference to his dark skin, and a "Jewish Gypsy" (*Cehūd Çengenesi*)[61] in reference to his supposedly dirty and mixed origins. Most frequently, however, he was simply called a "Gypsy" (*Çengāne*), both because of his dark complexion and so as to associate him with that severely marginalized group of people. But, significantly, even as they were attacking Nefᶜī through such a discourse, this coterie of scholar-poets was cultivating connections with emerging administrative and political actors like Gürcī Meḥmed Pasha

57 Anonymous, *Mecmūᶜa*, 47b.
58 Nefᶜī, *Sihām-ı Ḳażā* (Istanbul), 88b.
59 Anonymous, *Mecmūᶜa*, 48b.
60 Nefᶜī, *Sihām-ı Ḳażā* (Istanbul), 92b.
61 Anonymous, *Mecmūᶜa*, 48b.

and Etmekçizāde Aḥmed Pasha—the very figures against whom Nefʿī had set himself. Both sides in this poetic rivalry, then, effectively appointed themselves gatekeepers to the "Rūmī" Ottoman elite, to the center, by consciously foisting a discourse of "otherness" or alterity on their opponents.

Ultimately, Nefʿī and his opponents were not only products of the othering that was beginning to fracture the Ottoman elite during this period but also contributors to the continuation of this process of defining and defaming the other as such. Much like the advice literature that proliferated during the same time, but to an even greater degree, the invectives that emerged from this process demonstrate that this othering was tearing apart the very center of the empire, and they reveal, with a sometimes disturbing clarity, how extreme these internal divisions had actually become.

BIBLIOGRAPHY

Sources

Anonymous. *Kitāb-ı müstetāb*. Edited by Yaşar Yücel. Ankara: Ankara Üniversitesi Basımevi, 1974.

Anonymous. *Mecmūʿa*. Istanbul University Library TY 3004.

Āşıḳ Çelebi. *Meşāʿirü'ş-şuʿarā*. Edited by Filiz Kılıç. In *Meşâʿirü'ş-Şuʿarâ: İnceleme – Metin*. 3 vols. Istanbul: Istanbul Araştırmaları Enstitüsü Yayınları, 2010.

Ḥüseyin Ṭūġī. *Muṣībetnāme*. Edited by Şevki Nezihi Aykut. In *Musîbetnâme: Tahlil – Metin ve İndeks*. Ankara: Türk Tarih Kurumu Basımevi, 2010.

Kātib Çelebī. *Fezleke*. Edited by Zeynep Aycibin in "Fezleke: Tahlil ve Metin." Ph.D. diss., Mimar Sinan Güzel Sanatlar University, 2007.

Ḳoçi Beg. *Ḳoçi Beg Risālesi*. Istanbul: Maṭbaʿa-i Ebū'ż-żiyā, 1303 (1885/86).

Muṣṭafā ʿĀlī. *Nuṣḥatü's-selāṭīn*. Edited and translated by Andreas Tietze. In *Muṣṭafā ʿĀlī's Counsel for Sultans of 1581*. 2 vols. Vienna: Verlag der Österreichischen Akademie der Wissenschaften, 1979–82.

Muṣṭafā Naʿīmā. *Tārīḫ-i Naʿīmā*. Edited and transliterated by Mehmet İpşirli. Vol. 2. Ankara: Türk Tarih Kurumu, 2007.

Muṣṭafā Naʿīmā (?). *ʿUlāletü'l-mecālis, mecmūʿātu'n-nefāʾis*. Ann Arbor, University of Michigan Isl. Ms. 409. [ca. 1708–12.]

Nefʿī. *Sihām-ı Ḳażā*. Istanbul University Library TY 511, 61b–94a.

Nefʿī. *Sihām-ı Ḳażā*. Leiden Cod. Or. 662.

[İbrāhīm] Peçevī. *Tārīḫ-i Peçevī*. Edited by Zuhal Kayakurt. In "Peçevî Tarihi (317b–351a: Metin, Dizin, Özel Adlar Sözlüğü)." M.A. thesis, Marmara University, 2005.

Ravżī. *Dīvān*. Edited by Yaşar Aydemir. In *Ravzî Divanı*. Ankara: T.C. Kültür ve Turizm Bakanlığı, 2009.

Studies

Akdağ, Mustafa. "Celâli İsyanlarından Büyük Kaçgunluk, 1603–1606." *Ankara Üniversitesi Dil ve Tarih-Coğrafya Fakültesi Tarih Bölümü Tarih Araştırmaları Dergisi* 2, no. 2–3 (1964): 1–49.

Alkan, A. Turan. "Ekmekçizâde Ahmet Paşa'nın Ölümüne Düşürülmüş Bir Tarih ve Cennetle Müjdelenen Bir Zâlim." *Tarih ve Toplum* 9, no. 54 (June 1988): 46 (374)–49 (377).

Ambros, Edith Gülçin. "Six Lampoons out of Faqīrī's *Risāle-i taʿrīfāt*." *Wiener Zeitschrift für die Kunde des Morgenlandes* 82 (1992): 27–36.

Ambros, Edith Gülçin. "'The Other' (Non-Muslim, Non-Ottoman) in Ottoman Literary Humour." *Journal of Turkish Studies / Türklük Bilgisi Araştırmaları* 44 (December 2015): 85–100.

Börekçi, Günhan. "Factions and Favorites at the Courts of Sultan Ahmed I (r. 1603–17) and His Immediate Predecessors." PhD diss., The Ohio State University, 2010.

Conley, Thomas. *Toward a Rhetoric of Insult*. Chicago and London: The University of Chicago Press, 2010.

Darling, Linda T. "Nasihatnameler, İcmal Defterleri, and the Timar-Holding Ottoman Elite in the Late Sixteenth Century." *Osmanlı Araştırmaları/The Journal of Ottoman Studies* XLIII (2014): 193–226.

Fleischer, Cornell. *Bureaucrat and Intellectual in the Ottoman Empire: The Historian Mustafa Âlî (1541–1600)*. Princeton: Princeton University Press, 1986.

Güven, Hikmet Feridun. "Klâsik Türk Şiirinde Hiciv." Ph.D. diss., Gazi University, 1997.

Kafadar, Cemal. "A Rome of One's Own: Reflections on Cultural Geography and Identity in the Lands of Rum." *Muqarnas* 24 (2007): 7–25.

Karahan, Abdülkadir. *Nef'i: Hayatı, Sanatı, Şiirleri*. Istanbul: Varlık Yayınevi, 1967.

Kunt, Metin İbrahim. "Ethnic-Regional (*Cins*) Solidarity in the Seventeenth-Century Ottoman Establishment." *International Journal of Middle East Studies* 5, no. 3 (June 1974): 233–39.

Kuru, Selim S. "The Literature of Rum: The Making of a Literary Tradition (1450–1600)." In *The Cambridge History of Turkey, Vol. 2: The Ottoman Empire as a World Power (1453–1603)*. Edited by Suraiya N. Faroqhi and Kate Fleet. Cambridge: Cambridge University Press, 2013. 548–592.

Murphey, Rhoads. "The Veliyyuddin Telhis: Notes on the Sources and Interrelations between Koçi Bey and Contemporary Writers of Advice to Kings." *Belleten* XLIII, no. 171 (1979): 547–71.

Öz, Mehmet. *Kanun-ı Kadimin Peşinde: Osmanlı'da "Çözülme" ve Gelenekçi Yorumcuları (XVI. Yüzyıldan XVIII. Yüzyıl Başlarına)*. Istanbul: Dergâh Yayınları, 2013.

Öztürk, Murat. "Divan Şairinin Nimet ve İktidar Ekseninde Ulusları Ötekileştirmesi." *Atatürk Üniversitesi Türkiyat Araştırmaları Enstitüsü Dergisi* 51 (2014): 63–88.

Tezcan, Baki. *The Second Ottoman Empire: Political and Social Transformation in the Early Modern World*. New York: Cambridge University Press, 2010.

"Are You From Çorum?": Derogatory Attitudes Toward the "Unruly Mob" of the Provinces as Reflected in a Proverbial Saying

Helga Anetshofer

This paper focuses on the history and implications of a Turkish proverbial expression of contempt—basically an insult—directed toward the people of Çorum, a city in northern Anatolia. Using the case of Çorum, I examine the background of the denigration of residents of provincial places via proverbial sayings, a form of alterophobia. I argue that not only historical and political contexts but also sound associations, rhymes, and word play are involved in the creation and development of derogatory sayings based on toponyms or demonyms.

The modern Turkish proverbial saying *Çorumlu musun?* ("Are you from Çorum?")[1] is recorded in an Ottoman text from the late sixteenth century. Muṣṭafā ᶜĀlī (d. 1600), the well-known historian and bureaucrat, uses it in his unfavorable account of Çorum, which is unexpectedly inserted into his linguistically updated version of the fourteenth-century

1 The Turkish denominal suffix *+li* makes adjectives and nouns (e.g., *şekerli* "sugary, with sugar" < *şeker* "sugar") and transforms a toponym, e.g., İstanbul or Çorum, into a demonym, *İstanbullu* "Istanbulite" or *Çorumlu* "Chorumian." In this paper I use the Turkish derivative *Çorumlu*, designating a person from or living in Çorum.

epic romance *Dānişmendnāme*. The saying has kept negative and disparaging sentiments toward the inhabitants of Çorum alive to the present day; the original motivation for the saying apparently has been forgotten over time, and the words are charged with new meanings according to more current notions about the people of Çorum—but the saying's highly insulting character has been preserved. Finally, I will argue, in the case of Çorum the name of the city itself, or rather its folk-etymological interpretation through sound association, plays a major role in the creation of the negative sentiment.

Located in northern Anatolia, the city of Çorum today is considered a rather unattractive and still underdeveloped provincial capital (*Çorum ilinin merkezi*), with an urban population of 250,464, according to the 2015 census.[2] Among other features, the province of Çorum prides itself on important Hittite archaeological sites,[3] the production of *leblebi* (roasted chickpeas), and pleasant picnic areas in the countryside—which Muṣṭafā ᶜĀlī visited for his camping holiday at the end of the sixteenth century. The development of adult literacy in the twentieth century lagged behind Turkey's average; the literacy rate was 5.1% in 1927, according to the first census of the Turkish Republic,[4] and 53.7% in 1975.[5] Çorum is frequently hit by earthquakes; several earthquake faults run near Çorum, and an etiological story about an earthquake in Çorum, as recorded in the Old Anatolian Turkish epic romance, is related to our proverbial saying.

Historically, the city of Çorum has been almost exclusively Turkish-speaking and Muslim.[6] However, the fairly large, predominantly rural Alevi population of the province of Çorum represents a historically disadvantaged minority group. Sentiments against this group partially account for the development of the derogatory saying in question. Because they are Turkish speakers and are subsumed under the general category of

2 Türkiye İstatisik Kurumu (TÜİK), "Adrese Dayalı Nüfus Kayıt Sistemi Sonuçları, 2015."

3 For example, Ḫattusa (Turkish Hattuşa – Yazılıkaya), the capital of the Hittites near Boğazkale (earlier Boğazköy).

4 Kodal, "Ilk Genel Nüfus Sayımında Çorum Vilâyeti," 246.

5 The literacy rate for Turkey in general in 1975 was 62% ("Çorum," 2074).

6 *EI³*, s.v. "Çorum" (H. Unbehaun). For the extremely low number of non-Muslims ("Gypsies" [*Ḳıbṭī*], Armenians, Greeks, Protestants) in the province (*sancaḳ*) of Çorum, according to the censuses between 1831 and 1914, see Kodal, "Ilk Genel Nüfus Sayımında Çorum Vilâyeti," 236–39.

Muslims, the Alevis are not listed separately in the Turkish censuses. Since the early twentieth century, the term "Alevi" has been used to denote those socio-religious communities in Anatolia that share certain medieval Islamic mystical traditions as opposed to sharia-centered versions of Islam (popularly called "orthodox").[7] The term "Alevi" has replaced the negatively loaded historical term "Ḳızılbaş" ("Redhead"), but notions of the Alevis' otherness continue to prevail.[8] The well-known clash in Çorum in 1980, between Nationalist Sunni Muslims and Alevis, left more than fifty Alevis killed and more than one hundred wounded.

Today, we know of many proverbial phrases that use toponyms (for example, Kayseri) or demonyms (for example, *Kayserili*, a person from Kayseri) and are offensive to the inhabitants of certain places. Note the following examples, among others:

> *Kayserili Yahudi'den cimridir.*
> "A person from Kayseri is stingier than a Jew."
>
> *Kastamonu'dan / Adana'dan adam çıkmaz.*
> "No good man comes out of Kastamonu / Adana."
>
> *Afyon'un kaymağı, Konya'nın manyağı.*
> "While Afyon is famous for its clotted cream, Konya is famous for its crazy men."

The phrase "Are you a Çorumlu?"—or its longer version, "Not even a Çorumlu would do what you did (*Senin yaptığını Çorumlu bile yapmaz*)"—is less transparent in its meaning but apparently is regarded as a stronger insult. It is not recorded in any modern Turkish dictionary or collection of proverbial sayings—probably because of its insulting character, or because it was not well enough known to be regarded as a fixed saying.[9] Nevertheless, it is apparently part of the collective memory

7 On Alevi-Bektaşi historiography and the emergence of the Ḳızılbaş movement in the fifteenth century, see Karakaya-Stump, *Vefailik, Bektaşilik, Kızılbaşlık*, 1–12, 79–84.

8 *EI*[3], s.v. "Alevīs" (M. Dressler). For the debate surrounding the religious identity of Turkey's Alevis, and the process of otherizing the Alevis by subscribing heterodoxy to them, see Dressler, "Turkish Politics of Doxa."

9 Ahmet Özcan's blog *Ayrımcı Sözlük* (or, *Dictionary of Discriminative Sayings, Proverbs, and Idioms*) lists *Senin bu yaptığını Çorumlu bile yapmaz* and addresses the issue of collecting denigrating, racist, and sexist sayings (Özcan, "Diğer Türkçe Ayrımcı Deyiş, Deyim ve Atasözleri").

of Turkish speakers from Anatolia, though less so for Turkish speakers from Istanbul. The websites of Turkish collaborative hypertext dictionaries (such as *Ekşi Sözlük* and *Uludağ Sözlük*) are forums in which users share information and commentaries on any subject. In some entries users discuss the image of Çorum, exploring the meaning and origin of the derogatory phrase. There is agreement that the phrase is highly insulting.[10] The contributors report stories that illustrate the character of people from Çorum in order to explain the reason for the saying. Generally, two major character traits come forward:

1. the Çorumlu is stingy and cheap; he always considers his own economic advantage[11]
2. the Çorumlu is disloyal and unsubmissive; he does not feel bound by the rules of public law and order[12]

Both modern senses of the saying, stingy and self-seeking as well as disloyal and unruly, are also described in Muṣṭafā ᶜĀlī's account, albeit with different references. Muṣṭafā ᶜĀlī's *Mirḳātü'l-Cihād* (The Staircase of Holy War) is one of his less known works.[13] It is a reworking of the

---

10 Contributors to *Ekşi Sözlük* say, "That's a really strong word (*amma agir laf yahu*). May well result in a fight," and "A Çorumlu calling another Çorumlu Çorumlu is actually much like a black man (*zenci*) calling another black man (*zenci*) a black man (*zenci*)." See *Ekşi Sözlük*, "Senin bu yaptığını çorumlu bile yapmaz" and "Çorumlunun bir çorumluya çorumlu demesi." Also see *Uludağ Sözlük*, "Çorumlu," "Çorumlu olmak," and "Senin bu yaptığını çorumlu yapmaz"; and *İTÜ Sözlük*, "Çorumlu musun" and "Senin yaptığını çorumlu yapmaz."

11 "They asked a Çorumlu, 'Would you like to go to heaven?' The Çorumlu answered, 'What's the daily wage (*yewmiye* [!]) there?'" See *Ekşi Sözlük*, "Çorumlu." Another story goes: "This phrase ('Not even a Çorumlu . . .') is based on a story that a Çorumlu, in order to not pay taxes for his donkey, hid the donkey in his bed and told the tax inspector 'This is my mother'; it must mean: Like a Çorumlu you simply do everything that's to your advantage." See *Ekşi Sözlük*, "Senin bu yaptığını çorumlu bile yapmaz."

12 "A farmer employs a Çorumlu as his steward (*kahya*). One day the Çorumlu takes off with the farmer's favorite horse; the new steward is from Kayseri, and one day he takes off with the farmer's favorite horse and his wife, leaving the farmer to say, 'Not even the Çorumlu did what you did.'" See *Ekşi Sözlük*, "Senin bu yaptığını çorumlu bile yapmaz." Another association with Çorum is, "people that walk on the street while there is a sidewalk." See *Uludağ Sözlük*, "Çorum denince akla gelenler."

13 My references to ᶜĀlī's *Mirḳātü'l-Cihād* are based on the Istanbul manuscript that was copied by ᶜĀlī's youngest brother İbniyāmīn between Rajab 997/May 1589 and Rajab 1000/April 1592—within three years after ᶜĀlī composed it. Cf. Fleischer, *Bureaucrat and Intellectual in the Ottoman Empire*, 20–21. During the final stages of

Dānişmendnāme, a pre-Ottoman Turkish epic romance whose plot is set in the eleventh and early twelfth centuries.[14] Muṣṭafā ᶜĀlī, who read the legendary narrative as a historical account of early Turkish history in Anatolia, accomplished his reworking within a period of just forty days in the spring of 1589.[15] At that time he was at a low point in his career. He had just been dismissed from the position of finance director of Sivas (*defterdār-ı ḫazīne-i Rūm*), which was already a post unworthy of his learning and accomplishment. He laments this fact in prose and poetry in the introduction to his *Mirḳātü'l-Cihād*.[16] He also tells us that he wrote his book in the spring—following his dismissal—while camping in the green pastures around Çorum.[17] We hear again, and in more detail, about Çorum and the faults of its inhabitants when the epic narrative comes to the point at which the hero King Dānişmend, the eponymous founder of the Danishmendid dynasty, and his ghazi warriors deal with the disloyal and criminal inhabitants of Çorum.

This narrative passage in the fourteenth-century epic romance involves two connected etiological stories: the first explains the reason for an earthquake in Çorum (as Çorum has continuously been hit by earthquakes), and the other explains the meaning of the name Çorum itself. The reason for both the earthquakes and the name was the disloyalty and wickedness of the people of Çorum, in this case Byzantine Christians (*kāfirler*, infidels). According to the story in the *Dānişmendnāme*, the newly converted inhabitants (*yeŋi müslümānlar*, new Muslims) of Çorum, which is called "Yanḳoniya" by the Byzantines, renounced their Islamic faith and plotted to poison King Dānişmend.[18] However, the Prophet Muhammed appeared to King Dānişmend in a dream, alerting

the preparation of this article Ali Akar published an edition, which I did not have the chance to consult: *Mirkâtü'l-cihâd: Dil İncelemesi–Metin–Dizin / Gelibolu Mustafa ᶜAli*, edited by Ali Akar (Ankara: Türk Dil Kurumu, 2016).

14 See *EI*[3], s.v. "Danişmendname" (H. Anetshofer). My references to *Dānişmendnāme* are based on the editions by Irène Mélikoff and Necati Demir. Mélikoff's primary source—the unpublished Paris manuscript titled *Ḳıṣṣa-ı Melik Dānişmend*, copied in 985/1577—has also been consulted.

15 Muṣṭafā ᶜĀlī, *Mirḳātü'l-Cihād*, 9a.

16 Muṣṭafā ᶜĀlī, *Mirḳātü'l-Cihād*, 5a–6a.

17 Muṣṭafā ᶜĀlī, *Mirḳātü'l-Cihād*, 6b: *Elli gün tamām Çorum muḳābilindeki çayırlar tevābiᶜümüze muḫayyam ḫıyām ḳılınub* ("For fifty days a tent camp was set up for my entourage in the pastures opposite of Çorum").

18 *Dānişmendnāme* (Mélikoff), 2:241; and *Dānişmendnāme* (*Ḳıṣṣa-ı Melik Dānişmend*), 154a.

him to their treason; he evacuated his warriors from Çorum before the earthquake hit and destroyed the city. (The earthquake was followed by heavy rain and flooding for forty days.) Upon his ghazis' inquiry, King Dānişmend explained that God punished the city because its inhabitants wanted to poison him. That is also the reason why the city is called Çorum—because the inhabitants committed a "crime," or an "act of disobedience" (Turkicized چُرم *çur(u)m* < Arabic جرم *jurm*).[19]

> The King explained to them that he had seen the Prophet—may God bless and preserve him—in his dream, and that he said: The infidels want to poison you; that is why God, the Exalted, will destroy them. That is how this city was called Çorum, because the city's inhabitants have committed a crime (*çur(u)m* < *jurm*), therefore they call it Çorum. King Dānişmend explained this circumstance to the ghazis.[20]

The Istanbul manuscript copy of the *Dānişmendnāme*, edited by Necati Demir, includes the wording, "They named the city Çorum because the inhabitants were rebellious and criminal (Arabic *mujrim*, from the same root as *jurm*)."[21] Thus, according to this associative etymology or folk etymology, the toponym Çorum is based on the "disobedience, crime" of the inhabitants of the city. In fact, the etymology of the toponym Çorum remains unresolved. We know from Ibn Bībī's (d. 1285?) *History of the Seljuks*, and from early Ottoman administrative documents, that the city's name was initially Çorumlu, which later, in the course of the sixteenth century, was shortened to Çorum.[22]

---

19 Irène Mélikoff acknowledges the folk etymology associating the place name Çorum with the word چُرم. She reads it as *çürüm* and gives the meaning "péché [sin, offense, trespass]," albeit without mentioning the Arabic origin. See *Dānişmendnāme* (Mélikoff), 1:422n3.

20 *Dānişmendnāme* (Mélikoff), 2:242: *Melik daḫı peyġāmberi ṣallā Allāhu ʿaleyhi vesellem düşinde görüb kāfirler size ağu vėrmek isterler. Ḥaḳ taʿālā ol sebebden bunları helāk ėder dėdügini bunlara beyān eyledi. Ol şehre Çorum* (چُورُمْ) *dėmege vecih bu dur ki ol şehrüŋ ḳavmı çur(u)m* (چُرم) *ėtdiler anuŋ içün Çorum* (چُورُم) *dėrler. Bu aḥvāli Melik Dānişmend ġāzīlere beyān eyledi.* Cf. the French translation in *Dānişmendnāme* (Mélikoff), 1:422; and *Dānişmendnāme* (*Ḳıṣṣa-ı Melik Dānişmend*), 155b.

21 *Dānişmendnāme* (Demir), 1:176 (text), 4:220a (facsimile): *Ol ḳavm ʿāṣī ve mücrim olduḳlarıyçün ol şehre Corum* (جُرْم) *dėyü ad ḳodılar.*

22 One of the oldest known Ottoman tax registers (*taḥrīr defterleri*), dated 860/1455–56, mentions the city of Çorum as *şehr-i Çorumlu*. See Faroqhi, "Fatih Döneminden

While the rebellion of the infidels of Yanḳoniya (or Çorum) in the eleventh century belongs to the realm of legend, the equation of Çorum with "disobedience, crime" most likely reflects the fact that Çorum and its environs had a reputation for being disloyal and rebellious already in the fourteenth century, when the *Dānişmendnāme* was written down. In fact, the Turkmen shaykh Bābā İlyās-i Ḫorāsānī, who led a major religio-political uprising against the Anatolian Seljuq establishment—the Revolt of the Bābāʾīs of 1240, was located in Amasya and had followers in Çorum. The Bābāʾī Revolt ultimately facilitated the Mongol takeover of much of eastern and central Anatolia, in 1243.[23] Since the thirteenth century, Çorum has been a place of conflicts, shifting loyalties, and rebellious beys; as seen from the viewpoint of centralized Seljukid or Ottoman power, Çorum's environs were involved in the most important socio-political and socio-economic uprisings in central and northern Anatolia. Çorum initially was part of the Danişmendid and Seljukid states, the Eretna principality, and Ḳāḍı Burhāneddīn's principality; only in 1427 it was incorporated into the recently created Ottoman province of Rūm (*Vilāyet-i Rūm*), together with Amasya, Sivas, and Tokat. Subsequently, supporters in Çorum had a role in the pro-Safavid Şāh Ḳulu ("Slave of the Shah") rebellion in 1511, as well as the uprisings of the socially and economically underprivileged *madrasa* students (*suḫte*) from about 1575 to 1597.[24]

What does Muṣṭafā ᶜĀlī say about the Çorumlus toward the end of the sixteenth century, which was marked by the Ottoman–Safavid conflict? It was at that time that the Ottoman religious elites developed a discourse of a strict Shiᶜi/Sunni and orthodox/heterodox dichotomy as a political tool of socio-religious defamation.[25] Muṣṭafā ᶜĀlī utilizes this standard Ottoman anti-Ḳızılbaş rhetoric against the Çorumlus but also adds new generalizations of his own. His narrative follows the *Dānişmendnāme* closely, but he departs from it twice, inserting lengthy incursions on the

---

Evliya Çelebi Seyahatine Kadar Çorum," 82. On the unresolved etymology of Çorumlu/Çorum and Evliya Çelebi's folk etymology for Çorum, see Anetshofer, "Folk Etymologies," 108–10.

23 See Pfeiffer, "Mevlevi-Bektashi Rivalries and the Islamisation of the Public Space in Late Seljuq Anatolia," 317; Ocak, "Zaviyeler," 255–56; and *EI*[3], s.v. "Babai" (A. Y. Ocak).

24 "Çorum," 2032–35. For the Şāh Ḳulu rebellion, see Imber, *The Ottoman Empire, 1300–1650*, 37–39. For the uprisings of the religious students, see Barkey, *Bandits and Bureaucrats*, 156–63.

25 Dressler, *Writing Religion*, 226.

character of the current population of Çorum. His report is based on the forty to fifty days he spent camping in the green pastures near the city.

Following the original text of the *Dānişmendnāme* romance, ᶜĀlī narrates that the people from Çorum were called *cur(u)mlu* ("guilty, criminal") because they had committed so many crimes and sins (*curm u günāh*). He also repeatedly calls them *mücrim* ("criminal"), as was also seen in the Istanbul copy of the *Dānişmendnāme*. ᶜĀlī further explains that, in the "vulgar pronunciation of the peasants," the Arabic-based *cur(u)mlu* has turned into Çorumlu.[26] Here, ᶜĀlī apparently is reminded of the contemporary derogatory saying *Sen-de Çorumlı mısın?* ("Are you a Çorumlu?") and inserts the following comment:

> To this day the disposition of the population [of Çorum] has been quite infamous with the rulers. So, if an obstinate people display malice and villainy, they say, "Are you a Çorumlu?" Or if a group of sons of bitches demonstrates a lack of obedience and all kinds of opposition and obstinacy against the rulers, they say, "Are you one of the Çorumlu sinners, or what?"[27]

In what follows, Muṣṭafā ᶜĀlī elaborates on the deficiencies of the character of the Çorumlus. However, he makes rather moderate use of the prevailing anti-Ḳızılbaş rhetoric of the time when he discusses the Çorumlus' disloyalty. He primarily focuses on two issues that are crucial

26 Muṣṭafā ᶜĀlī, *Mirḳātü'l-Cihād*, 226b9–16: *Yanḳoniya dedikleri kişver ki ḥālā* چورم *Çorum dedikleri yerdir . . . sābiḳan ḳavminden bu maqūle ḫıyānet ve* جرم *curm ṣādir olub Melik Dānişmend Ġāziye zehr içürmek istedüklerini ve baᶜde şerefi'l-islām mürted olub curm u günāhı ḳat ḳat etdüklerini maᶜlūm edindikde ol şehriŋ yerlüsine* جرملو *cur(u)mlu nām ḳomışlar giderek ṣarf-ı rūstāyīler taṣarrufına giderken* چورملو *çorumlu deyü edā-ı ġalīẓ etmişler ki tarḫīminde* چُورُم *Çorum ḳalmışdır* ("The land called Yanḳoniya, which is the place they now call Çorum. … In time past its inhabitants committed such a perfidy and sin. When it transpired that they wanted to poison Melik Danişmend Ghazi, and that they became apostates—after having embraced Islam—and committed numerous sins and crimes the locals were called 'criminal, sinner' (*cur(u)mlu*). When the name was more and more utilized by peasants, they would pronounce it in a vulgar way as 'Çorumlu'—and in the end it became 'Çorum' through apocope [loss of the last syllable]."

27 Muṣṭafā ᶜĀlī, *Mirḳātü'l-Cihād*, 226b17–21: *Ve-ammā ilā hāẕe'l-ān ḫalḳınuŋ ṭabᶜı ᶜinde'l-ḥükkām bir mertebede iştihār-ı tām bulmışdur ki meṡelā bir ḳavm-i ᶜanīdüŋ şirret ü şaḳāları ẓāhir olsa 'Sen-de* چورملی *Çorumlı mısın?' derler ve bir zümre-i pelīd-i pelīdüŋ ḥākimlere ᶜadem-i inḳıyādı ve dürlü dürlü muḫālefet ve ᶜinādı taḥaḳḳuḳ bulsa 'Yoḫsa* چورملو *Çorumlu günahkārlarından mısın?' deyü söylerler.*

to him: the Çorumlus are greedy and corrupt, always seeking personal financial gain, and the ulema of Çorum—the qadis in particular—are ignorant and corrupt. ᶜĀlī dwells on incompetent officials as the lead actors for the chaos in provincial administration in his other works as well.[28]

Concerning the Çorumlus' disloyalty, ᶜĀlī says that he had heard of their "Shiᶜi sectarianism" and "heresy"—he uses the current terms *rafż* and *ilḥād*—even before he took up his post in Sivas. But he had thought it to be exaggeration and had not believed in the rumors.[29] He reports three cases in which the Çorumlus unite in large gatherings (*cemᶜiyyet*) and reach unjust agreements. However, all three cases display an economic motivation rather than a political or ideological one. Only the first case implies a causal relationship between the reported lack of hospitality and greediness of the Çorumlus and their affinity with the Ḳızılbaş: when a traveler, who is an Ottoman soldier (*leşker-i celīlden biri*), is passing through Çorum on his return from a campaign (*sefer-i hümāyūn*)—presumably against the Safavids—he has some fodder cut from nearby fields for his hungry horse, for which he must pay the owner of the field.[30] This unfriendliness and lack of hospitality (of the Çorumlus toward the Ottoman soldier) is ᶜĀlī's basis for later calling the Çorumlus Ḳızılbaş supporters; he sums up in verse that they do not like the Ottoman cavalry or any visitor from outside, but they adore the Ḳızılbaş:

> They [that is, the Çorumlus] have always been lovers of the Ḳızılbaş,
> if you ask their grandees.
> They do not like the Ottoman cavalry,
> they do not want incoming travelers.
> [But] whenever one of them sees a Redhead (*Sürḫ-ser*),
> They bring their wives as a present of honor.
> They dress up their daughters and wives,
> and generously give their jewelry.
> When an [Ottoman] cavalryman (*sipāhī*) stops over they don't give
> him fodder,

28 Fleischer, *Bureaucrat and Intellectual in the Ottoman Empire*, 131. For the oppression and injustice of unqualified high officers in outlying areas, see Muṣṭafā ᶜĀlī, *Nuṣḥatü's-selāṭīn*, 1:80 (translation), 181 (text).

29 Muṣṭafā ᶜĀlī, *Mirḳātü'l-Cihād*, 227b–228a.

30 Muṣṭafā ᶜĀlī, *Mirḳātü'l-Cihād*, 227a6–9.

They rather scare his swift (horse), which flies like a falcon.
Whereas to a Ḳızılbaş—every scum
liberally gives whatever rare things he has.[31]

In the two other reported cases, ᶜĀlī likewise portrays the Çorumlus as unwelcoming to strangers and greedy for money—however, without any reference to an Ottoman-Ḳızılbaş background. The cases involve the Çorumlus' stingy attitude toward another traveler (*misāfir*) and an outsider grandee (*aṣḥāb-ı cāh u celālden biri*) who put the people of the city at a financial disadvantage.[32] ᶜĀlī also blames the Çorumlus for frequently appealing to the Porte in trivial matters and thus causing unrest.[33] Furthermore, he is very critical of the large number of incompetent and corrupt ulema in Çorum; he mentions thirty qadis who hardly know how to write.[34] Thus, the focus of ᶜĀlī's critique of the Çorumlus is their supposed moral and intellectual deficiencies, especially their greed, disloyalty, and lawlessness, which is described by partially applying the terminology of anti-Ḳızılbaş rhetoric.

In conclusion, Çorum's involvement in the anti-Seljukid rebellion in the thirteenth century, the Bābā'ī Revolt, may have been an initial factor in defaming and denigrating the inhabitants of the city. Over time, however, the original motivation was lost, and only the notion of the Çorumlus' disloyalty and villainy remained. In the sixteenth century, the derogatory saying "Are you from Çorum?"—meaning, "You are an obstinate and disloyal prick"—was already in common use. In his *Mirḳātü'l-Cihād*, ᶜĀlī inflected the words with new meaning by reading them against the backdrop of Çorum's involvement in the Ottoman–Safavid conflict. At the same time, ᶜĀlī records the notion of the Çorumlus' greed, and thus adds a new aspect to the saying. Both consecutive characteristics, disloyalty and greed, were retained locally into the twenty-first century, when they were furnished with new stories to give them meaning, as documented in online collaborative Turkish dictionaries.

---

31 Muṣṭafā ᶜĀlī, *Mirḳātü'l-Cihād*, 227b14–19: *Heb hevādārıdur Ḳızılbaşuŋ / Yoḳlasaŋ anlarıŋ ekābirini // Ḫayl-i ᶜOsmāniyānı sevmezler / İstemezler gelen misāfirini // Sürḫ-ser görse her biri ay(y)ā / Tuḥfe ilter ᶜayāl-ı fāḫirini // Ḍonadub ḳızlariyle zenlerini / kerem-i ᶜām ėder cevāhirini // Bir sipāhī ḳonarsa yem vėrmez / Ürkidür bāzṭabᶜ ṭāyırını // Bir Ḳızılbaşa līk her evbāş / Bez̲l ėder varınıŋ nevādirini.*

32 Muṣṭafā ᶜĀlī, *Mirḳātü'l-Cihād*, 227a9–19.

33 Muṣṭafā ᶜĀlī, *Mirḳātü'l-Cihād*, 228a21–228b1.

34 Muṣṭafā ᶜĀlī, *Mirḳātü'l-Cihād*, 229a1–9.

Although a history of rebellion and unruliness is not unique to Çorum, these features did not give rise to similarly strong derogatory sayings about other cities. Apparently, the sound of place names, with their related associative meanings and word plays, play a significant role in the creation of derogatory sayings. Here I have demonstrated that fact through the case of the toponym Çorum, for which the etymologically opaque demonym Çorumlu at some point became associated with the Arabic-Turkish *cur(u)mlu* ("with sin; disobedient criminal, sinner").[35] Examples of derogatory sayings regarding toponyms that are based on rhyme patterns include proverbial sayings about Konya and Tokat; cf. *Afyon'un kaymağı, Konya'nın manyağı* and *Tokat içine bir kürek bok at* ("Throw a shovel of shit into Tokat!").[36]

Ultimately, in the Ottoman and Turkish context the creation of derogatory sayings—derived from toponyms or demonyms, by using sound associations, rhyme and word play—is based on the othering of the provincial Anatolian, described as being uncivilized, uneducated (hence greedy and corrupt), far from Istanbul (the center of power), and therefore potentially disloyal and unruly.

BIBLIOGRAPHY

Sources

Dānişmendnāme. Edited by Necati Demir as *Dānişmend-nāme: Tenkidli Metin, Türkiye Türkçesine Aktarılış, Dil Özellikleri, Sözlük, Tıpkıbasım*. Cambridge, MA: Harvard University, Department of Near Eastern Languages and Civilizations, 2002.

Dānişmendnāme. Edited by Irène Mélikoff as *La geste de Melik Dānişmend: étude critique du Dānişmendnāme*. 2 vols. Paris: A. Maisonneuve, 1960.

Dānişmendnāme. Ḳıṣṣa-ı Melik Dānişmend Ġāzī Aḥmed bin ᶜAlī. Paris: Bibliothèque nationale de France, Turc 317. 985/1577.

35 For an associative word play using a toponym in American English, cf. the pejorative term "masshole" (< Massachusetts + asshole), which is frequently used by New Hampshire residents to refer to those from Massachusetts (particularly Boston) (Nagy and Irwin, "Boston (r)", 270n6).

36 Apparently a reference to the lowliness and insignificance of Tokat, this derogatory saying has a background and usage that are unknown to me. It is documented in a few online sources, such as *Ekşi Sözlük*, where the user says that he has heard the rhytmic rhyme (*tekerleme*) from the notables of Tokat themselves: *"tokat, içine bi kürek bok at" kafiyeli tek ellemesini* (sic) *de bizzat tokat eşrafından duymuşumdur* (*Ekşi Sözlük*, "Tokat").

Muṣṭafā ʿĀlī. *Mirḳātü'l-Cihād*. Istanbul, Süleymaniye Kütüphanesi Reşit Efendi, 678. 997/1589–1000/1592. *Mirkâtü'l-cihâd: Dil İncelemesi–Metin–Dizin* / Gelibolu Mustafa 'Ali, edited by Ali Akar, Ankara: Türk Dil Kurumu, 2016).

Muṣṭafā ʿĀlī. *Nuṣḥatü's-selāṭīn*. Edited by Andreas Tietze as *Muṣṭafā ʿĀlī's Counsel for Sultans of 1581*. 2 vols. Vienna: Verlag der Österreichischen Akademie der Wissenschaften, 1979–82.

Studies

Anetshofer, Helga. "Folk Etymologies and Stories of Toponyms from Danishmendid Territory in Evliya Çelebi's Seyahatname." *Journal of Turkish Studies* 44 (2015): 101–23.

Barkey, Karen. *Bandits and Bureaucrats: The Ottoman Route to State Centralization*. Ithaca: Cornell University Press, 1994.

"Çorum." In *Yurt Ansiklopedisi: Türkiye, İl İl, Dünü, Bugünü, Yarını*, vol. 3, 2009–14. Istanbul: Anadolu Yayıncılık, 1982.

Dressler, Markus. *Writing Religion: The Making of Turkish Alevi İslam*. New York: Oxford University Press, 2013.

Dressler, Markus. "Turkish Politics of Doxa: Otherizing the Alevis as Heterodox." *Philosophy and Social Criticism* 41, no. 4–5 (2015): 445–51.

Ekşi Sözlük. "Çorumlu," "Çorumlunun bir çorumluya çorumlu demesi," and "Senin bu yaptığını çorumlu bile yapmaz." <https://eksisozluk.com>. Accessed May 2, 2016.

Ekşi Sözlük. "Tokat." Accessed June 7, 2016.

Faroqhi, Suraiya. "Fatih Döneminden Evliya Çelebi Seyahatine Kadar Çorum." In *Çorum Tarihi*, 79–120. [Ankara?]: 5. Hitit Festival Komitesi, [198–?].

Fleischer, Cornell H. *Bureaucrat and Intellectual in the Ottoman Empire: The Historian Mustafa Âli (1541–1600)*. Princeton: Princeton University Press, 1986.

Imber, Colin. *The Ottoman Empire, 1300–1650: The Structure of Power*. 2nd ed. Houndmills, Basingstoke, Hampshire; New York: Palgrave Macmillan, 2009.

İTÜ Sözlük. "Çorumlu musun" and "Senin yaptığını çorumlu yapmaz." <https://www.itusozluk.com>. Accessed May 2, 2016.

Karakaya-Stump, Ayfer. *Vefailik, Bektaşilik, Kızılbaşlık: Alevi Kaynaklarını, Tarihini ve Tarih Yazımını Yeniden Düşünmek*. Istanbul: Bilgi Üniversitesi Yayınları, 2015.

Kodal, Tahir. "Türkiye Cumhuriyeti'nin Ilk Genel Nüfus Sayımında Çorum Vilâyeti'nin Nüfus Özellikleri." *Fırat Üniversitesi Sosyal Bilimler Dergisi* 19, no. 1 (2009): 233–58.

Nagy, Naomi, and Patricia Irwin. "Boston (r): Neighbo(r)s nea(r) and fa(r)." *Language Variation and Change* 22, no. 2 (July 2010): 241–78.

Ocak, Ahmet Yaşar. "Zaviyeler." *Vakıflar Dergisi* 12 (1978): 255–56.

Özcan, Ahmet. "Diğer Türkçe Ayrımcı Deyiş, Deyim ve Atasözleri." In *Ayrımcı Sözlük = Dictionary of Discriminative Sayings, Proverbs, and Idioms*. <http://ayrimcisozluk.blogspot.com>. Accessed September 15, 2016.

Pfeiffer, Judith. "Mevlevi-Bektashi Rivalries and the Islamisation of the Public Space in Late Seljuq Anatolia." In *Islam and Christianity in Medieval Anatolia*, edited by A. C. S. Peacock, Bruno De Nicola, and Sara Nur Yıldız, 312–27. Farnham, Surrey, England; Burlington, VT: Ashgate, 2015.

Türkiye İstatisik Kurumu (TÜİK). "Adrese Dayalı Nüfus Kayıt Sistemi Sonuçları, 2015." <https://biruni.tuik.gov.tr/medas/?kn=95&locale=tr>. Accessed April 5, 2016.

Uludağ Sözlük. "Çorumlu," "Çorum denince akla gelenler," "Çorumlu olmak," "Senin bu yaptığını çorumlu yapmaz." <http://www.uludagsozluk.com>. Accessed May 2, 2016.

Index

A

Abaza ("Abkhazian") Meḥmed Pasha (d. 1634), 30–32, 133n15
Abaza Ḥasan Pasha (d. 1659), 30–31
ᶜAbdullāh, Dervīş (author of *Halberdier's Treatise*), 44–59, 61–62, 68–71
ᶜAbdullāh Çelebī (Rıḍvān Paşazāde, fl. 1639), 25
Abkhazians, 2, 29–32, 39
African characters in Islamic history, 51–53
aḫlāḳ tradition, 286–288
Aḥmed I, Sultan (r. 1603–1617), 12–13, 59, 69, 133n15, 144, 307, 312
Aḥmed III, Sultan (r. 1703–1730), 38, 54–55
Aḥmed Çelebī, 38n54
ᶜAjā'ib al-Makhlūqāt wa Gharā'ib al-Mawjūdāt (Wonders of Creation and Oddities of Existence), *see* al-Qazwīnī, Zakariyyā
Alexandru Iliaş (r. 1616–1618 and 1628–1629), 191, 193–194
ᶜAlī Mekkī, *see* Black Africans
ᶜAlī Pasha ("Şehīd," d. 1716), 54
ᶜAmber Meḥmed Agha, chief eunuch, 54
anti-Circassian bias, 24
anti-Greek sentiments (graecophobia), 188
  anti-Greek discourse, 204–208
  composition of social elite and power distribution, 195–199
  in Danubian principalities, 190–195
  Greeks in political position and, 199–204
  "Greek takeover" and, 195–199 *History of the Events in Wallchia* (by Matthew of Myra), 190–193
  negative characteristics attributed to Greeks, 193
  in Wallachia and Moldavia, 190, 195–199
anti-Judaism in premodern Ottoman society, 107–108
  beglerbegi incident, 112–113
  blood libel cases, 118–122
  expressions of distrust, 118
  Iberian Jews' experience, 109 imperial orders against Jews, 118–119
  by grand viziers of *devşirme* origin, 115–118, 122–124
  looting of Jewish homes, 110–111
  murder of Esperanza Malchi, 114–115
  reasons, 108–109
  street violence and lynching, 110
  targeting by janissaries and cavalry forces, 110–115
anti-*ḳul* sentiments
  in Ottoman historiography, 4–10
  in Ottoman advice literature (*naṣīḥatnāme*), 10–14
ᶜĀşıḳpaşazāde Dervīş Aḥmed (d. after 1484), 7–8

B

Bābā'ī Revolt (1240), 327, 330
Bahrām Gūr (r. 420–438), 83, 84f4
Baličević, Bishop Franjo (d. 1615), 151–152
Bālīzāde Muṣṭafā, (d. 1618), 267n12, 268–269, 269n20, 270n22, 271–272, 274, 276–283, 284n64, 291–292
Bāyezīd II, Sultan (r. 1481–1512), 9, 15–16, 23–24, 112, 231
Benić, Fr. Bono (d. 1785), 156–158, 159n50, 162–163, 166, 169, 171–172, 173n123, 175–176
Beşīr Agha (chief eunuch, d. 1746), 35, 54–55, 57–59, 69–70
al-Bīrūnī (d. 1048), 66
Black Africans
  ᶜAbdullāh's treatise, 43–59, 70
  ᶜAlī Mekkī's *Ḥabeşler Āyinesi* (The Mirror for Ethiopians), 59–70

Mollā ᶜAlī's *Dispelling the Darkness*, 63–68, 70–71
skin color of Africans, 61–64, 67–68
Bogdanović, Fr. Marijan (d. 1772), 156–157, 161–165, 168, 171, 179
Bosnian Catholics, 155

C

Cantacuzino, Constantin (d. 1716), 201–202, 204
Cantacuzino, Dumitraşco (Dimitrie) (r. 1673–1675, 1684–1685), 205
Cantemir, Dimitrie (d. 1723), 221, 236
Capsali, Elijah (d. after 1550), 112
Celālzāde Muṣṭafā (d. 1567), 14–16
Me'āṡir-i Selīm Ḫānī (Illustrious Acts of Selīm Khan), 15–16
Chardin, Jean de (d. 1713), 33
Charles VI, Emperor (r. 1711–1740), 38
Christians, resentment towards
as *devşirme* recruits, 13
in Ottoman historiography, 4–10
in Ottoman advice literature, 10–14
Cingen Ḥüseyin (17th cent.), 234
Circassian Mamluks, xiv, 22–39
as elite slaves, 22
ethnic pride of, 33–35
Evliyā's description of, 32–33, 35
Ottoman attitude toward, 23–25
reintroduction in Egypt, 29–30
Constantinopolite Greeks, 201–202, 204
Çorum
anti-Seljukid rebellion, 330–331
city of, 322, 326
newly converted inhabitants of, 325
people of, 322, 324, 328–329
as a place of conflicts and rebellious beys, 327
Çorumlus, 321–331

D

Dānişmendnāme, 322, 325–328
devşirme, 5–7, 9, 11n38, 12–14, 16, 22, 27, 29–31, 39, 108, 115–116, 122–124, 160, 164, 302, 304–306
Durmuş b. Pazarlı, 231–235

E

Egyptian beys, 28
Eremya Çelebī Kömürjian (d. 1695), 252, 258n54
The Jewish Bride, 252, 258n54
Etmekçizāde Aḥmed Pasha (d. 1618), 298, 307–316, 318–319
Europeans
in Ottoman cosmographies, 95–101
in Qazwīnī's *ᶜAjā'ib*, 95–96, 99–100
Evliyā Çelebī (d. 1682), 23, 29, 32–35, 128–146, 220–222, 236, 258, 237n22
antagonisms towards Jews, 136–138
blood libel cases, 134–136
canards about Jews, 134–136
casual reference to Jews as crucifiers of Christ, 130–134
character traits and derogatory attributes, 138–141
description of Christians, 145
Jews as alchemists, 141–143
Jews as murder of prophets (*nebī*), 130–134
omission of Jewish immigration, 143–144
pedigree of Salonika Jews, 144
Seyāḥatnāme (Book of Travels), 32–35, 128, 130–144

F

Faqārīs, 31, 34, 37
Ferdinand of Aragon (d. 1516), 118
Ferdowsī, Abū al-Qāsim (d. 1020), 83, 84f4
Shāhnāmeh (Book of Kings), 83, 84f4
Feyżullāh Efendi (d. 1708), 254
Franciscan chronicles
antagonism between Franciscans and Orthodox Christians, 176
Catholicism in Ottoman Bosnia, 149–157
confessionalization, 155
Franciscans' conciliatory and submissive attitude toward Ottomans, 152–153
Franciscan sympathies toward Catholics and Ottoman retaliation, 152–154
"Greek schismatic" carpenter, 179
history of suffering for faith, 158–159
Islamization and conversion to Islam, 167–170
official relation between Ottoman state and Franciscans, 150–151
Orthodox–Catholic Church conflict, 172–178
rights and privileges of Franciscans, 150

Turks, 157–167, 170–172
Vlachs and Vlachisation, 172–179
Frenkbeg-oğlı Meḥmed Agha, né Marcantonio Querini (d. 1602), 114

G

Ġazanfer Agha (d. 1603), 113, 114
al-Gharnāṭī, Abū Ḥāmid (d. 1169–1170), 78–80, 92
Georgescu, Valentin, 198
Georgian *mamlūks*, 29–30, 36
Gerlach, Stephan (d. 1612), 116
Ginio, Eyal, 220, 221n11, 224, 229
Grazziani, Gaspar (r. 1619–1620), 200
Greaves, John (d. 1652),
Pyramidographia, 98
Greek influence on Romanian society and culture, 189–190, 203
Gürcī Meḥmed Pasha (d. 1626), 296–302, 315–318
Gypsy (*çingāne*), 215–237
in court of Üsküdar, 230–231
nominally Muslim status, 227–230
origin of, 219–223
in Ottoman court records, 223–224
perceived as evil-doers, 224–227
taxation of, 227–230

H

Ham, Curse of, 46–50, 61, 64, 66–69
Halberdier's Treatise, 43–59, 71
ᶜAbdullāh's construction of Noah's family, 45–48
advice for sultan, 56–57
Beşīr Agha, 55, 58
biological inheritance between children of Cain and children of Seth, 46
black eunuchs, 45, 53–54, 57–58
Curse of Ham, 46–50
genealogy of evil, 51–53
Harsányi Nagy, Jakab (d. after 1679), 1–3
Ḥasan Begzāde Aḥmed Pasha (d. 1636 or 1637), 111n2, 115
Ḥasan Kāfī el-Aḳḥiṣārī (d. 1616), 12, 264, 265n4–5, 266n11, 283n57, 285n67, 291
Uṣūl al-ḥikam fī niẓām al-ᶜālam (Foundations of Wisdom on the Ordering of the World), 264
Ḥikāye-i Ḫᵛāce Fesād, *see* Ṣābit
human-frog hybrid Jew, 76–91
humoral theory, 269–270, 274, 276, 279–285, *see also* physiognomy

I-İ

Ibn ᶜAbd al-Bāqī
The Colored Brocade, 60n58, 61, 63n64–65, 65–68
Ibn ᶜAbd al-Ḥakam (d. 871)
The History of the Conquest of Egypt, North Africa, and Spain, 66
Ibn al-Jawzī, Abū al-Faraj (d. 1201), 61, 63, 66
Ibn Bībī (d. after 1285), 326
History of the Seljuks, 326
İbn Kemāl (d. 1534), 233
Ibn Khaldūn (d. 1406), 55
Ibrāhīm Bey Abū Shanab (d. 1718), 36, 39
İbrāhīm Pasha (d. 1536), 26, 28, 54, 116
İbrāhīm I, Sultan (r. 1640–1648), 53
Imām Muḥammad Badakhshānī, 50, 51n28
Gulshan-i Tavārīkh, 50
infra-communal alterophobia, 187–188
Isabella of Castile (d. 1504), 118
Ismāᶜīl Bey ibn Ivāẓ Bey (d. 1724), 36, 37, 39
Ismāᶜīl I, Shāh (r. 1501–1524), 24

J

Jewish identity,
in Ottoman cosmographies, 76–91
in Abū al-Qāsim Ferdowsī's *Shāhnāmeh*, 83
Jewish observance of Sabbath and its impact, 79, 82, 89
Jewish *shaykh* creature, 76–91, 95, 99
in Gharnāṭī's treatise, 79–80
in Qazwīnī's *ᶜAjāᵓib*, 76–83, 86, 88–90
John Zápolya (r. 1526–1540), 163

K

Ḳāḍīzādeli movement, 63n64, 155, 161–162, 168
Ḳamış, tribe of, 32
Karacan, Turgut, 244n1, 246n6, 246–247n9
Kātib Çelebī (d. 1657), 283n57
Ḳavānīn-i yeŋiçeriyān (Laws of the Janissaries, ca. 1609–1617), 11n38, 13
Keşfī Meḥmed Çelebī (d. 1524), 24
Khūshqadam (Ḫoşḳadem, r. 1461–1467), 34
Ḳınalızāde ᶜAlī Çelebī (d. 1572), 282n56
Aḫlāḳ-ı Alāᵓī, 282n56

Kitāb-ı Müsteṭāb (The Agreeable/Pleasant Book, ca. 1620), 11n38, 13, 265n5, 304–305, 307
Ḳoçi Beg (d. ca. 1650), 11n38, 306–307
Ḳoçi b. Çaḳır, 231, 233
Köprülü Meḥmed Pasha (d. 1661), 30–31
Kösem Sultan (d. 1651), 53
ḳuls, 4–10, 27, 305–306
anti-*ḳul* sentiments, 7–10
*mamlūk*s as alternatives to, 29–30
Ottoman universal order (*niẓām-ı ᶜālem*), 12 problem in Egypt, 27–30
rebellion, 111–112
Kunt, Metin, 5n12, 23, 30, 302, 305n22,
Kuru, Selim, 246n8

L

Lastrić, Filip (Philippo ab Occhevia, d. 1783), 157–159, 161, 170n105, 173–176
Lašvanin, Fr. Nikola (d. 1750), 156–160, 163, 165, 168–169, 171–176, 178
Leon Tomşa (d. 1632), 194, 195, 199, 201, 202n55
Lubenau, Reinhold (d. 1613), 111
Lukmān, 64–65
Luṭfī Pasha (d. 1563), 11n38, 12

M

Malchi, Kira Esperanza (d. 1600), 113–115
Maḥmūd I, Sultan (r. 1730–1754), 53, 55
Maḥmūd Çelebī (d. 1589), 111–112, 115
Matei Basarab (r. 1632–1654), 200
Matthew of Myra (d. 1624), *see* anti-Greek sentiments (graecophobia)
Meḥmed Bey, Çerkes (d. 1730), 35–39
Meḥmed II (r. 1444–1446 and 1451–1481), 5–8, 17, 112, 120–122, 149–151
centralizing policies, 7
College of, 60, 69
court culture, 5
fratricide clause, 5
imperial project, 6
patronage of arts, 6
Meḥmed III (r. 1595–1603), 12, 265
Meḥmed IV (r. 1648–87), 53
Meḥmed Pasha (d. 1774), son of Muḥsinzāde ᶜAbdullāh Pasha, 171
Meḥmed Pasha (d. 1551), governor of Buda, 135
Melek Aḥmed Pasha (d. 1662), 29–32
*merdümzāde*s, 14–16
Merre Ḥüseyin Pasha (d. 1624), 302
Mollā ᶜAlī (d. 1622), 43, 59, 63–71
Rāfiᶜü'l-ġubūş fī feżāyili'l-ḥubūş (Dispelling the Darkness on the Merits of the Ethiopians), 43, 59, 63–71
Muḥammad, Jarkas (Muḥammad Bey Jarkas), *see* Meḥmed Bey, Çerkes
Muḥammad, Prophet, 25, 34, 47–50, 65, 89n42, 136, 142, 143, 158, 161, 222, 229
Murād III, Sultan (r. 1574–1595), 58, 95, 117, 216, 265–268, 282, 291–292, 304
Murād IV, Sultan (r. 1623–1640), 29, 306
Murād Bey ("the *defterdār*"), 36
Muṣṭafā, Prince (d. 1553), 27, 116, 121
Muṣṭafā I (r. 1617–1618 and 1622–1623), 54, 59
Muṣṭafā ᶜĀlī (d. 1600), 9, 12, 14, 25, 58, 111–112, 135n21, 303, 305–307, 321–322, 324–325, 327–328
Mirḳātü'l-cihād (The Staircase of Holy War), 324–325, 328–330
Nuṣḥatu's-selāṭīn (Counsel for Sultans, 1581), 12, 303, 305
Muṣṭafā Agha (chief eunuch, d. 1624), 59–60, 63, 69–70, 312
Muṣṭafā Başeski, Mollā (d. 1809), 161–162, 167–168
Muṣṭafā Naᶜīmā (d. 1716), 114, 296, 289, 312n35
Muṣṭafā Efendi, Cenābī (d. 1590), 51n28
Muṣṭafā Ṣafī (d. 1616), 28
müteferriḳa corps, 26–28

N

Naᶜīmā, Muṣṭafā (d. 1716), 114, 133n15, 296, 298, 312n35
Naqshbandīs, 45, 51n28, 56
naṣīḥatnāme (advice literature), 4, 10–14, 17, 53
Nefᶜī (d. 1635)
invective corpus, 296–319
against Etmekçizāde Aḥmed Pasha, 298, 307–315
against Gürcī Meḥmed Pasha, 297–302
Nogmov, Shora Bekmursin, 34

O-Ö

Öküz Meḥmed Pasha (d. 1619), 28, 30
Özbek (Azbak) Bey, 34–36
ᶜÖmer Agha, 113–114
Orhonlu, Cengiz, 44, 54, 58n53

Orthodox Christians
in Ottoman cosmographies, 91–95, 101
Church of the Raven, 93–94
Qazwīnī's text, 92
tension between Ottomans and Orthodox Church, 92–94
ᶜOsmān II, Sultan (r. 1618–1622), 28–30, 304
othering discourse
Kitāb-ı Müsteṭāb (The Agreeable/Pleasant Book), 304–305, 307
Nefᶜī's invective corpus, 296–302, 307–315
Nuṣḥatu's-selāṭīn, 305
social mobility and, 303
Ottoman–Mamluk wars, 23–25

P

Passi, David (fl. after 1593), 117–118
Pax Ottomanica, xi, 2, 180
Pīrī Reʾīs (d. 1553), 27–28
Pīrīzāde Meḥmed Ṣāḥib (d. 1749), 55–58, 70
Phanariot regime (*also* Phanariot Greeks), 178, 188–190
physiognomy, 267–292, *see also* humoral theory
characterization of gender, 270–273
definition, 268
different "methods" (*ṭurūḳ*) of, 269n20
terms *firāsetnāme* and *ḳıyāfetnāme*, 267n12
Ottoman physiognomical treatises, 268

Q

Qānṣūh al-Ghūrī, Sultan (r. 1501–1516), 24–26
Qāsimīs, 31, 33, 35–36
Qāytbāy, Sultan (r. 1468–1496), 23
al-Qazwīnī, Zakariyā (d. 1283)
ᶜAjāʾib al-Makhlūqāt wa Gharāʾib al-Mawjūdāt (Wonders of Creation and Oddities of Existence), 75–101

R

Radu Leon (r. 1665–1669), 200–201
al-Ramlī, Khayr al-Dīn (d. 1671), 50, 50–51n28
Tabyīn Milal, 50
Rıḍvān Bey Abū'l-Shawārib, 31, 33–36, 38
Risāle-i Ġarībe, 258–259
Rūm Meḥmed Pasha (d. ca. 1470), 7–8
Rūmī/Rūmīs, 9, 34, 39, 142, 316–319
Rüstem Pasha (d. 1561), 116

S

S̱ābit (d. after 1712), 244–261
choice of words and obscenity of stories, 246–247
Ḥikāye-i Ḫᵛāce Fesād, 244–261
church and Christianity, references to, 248–253
clichés of infidel, 250
ḥadd punishment, 256
kāfir, references to, 250
rape of Armenian woman, 253–256
story, 245–248
woman's status and men's decisions and actions, 256–261
localization movement, 247
*mesnevī*s, 247
metaphoric language, 248
mocking of non-Muslims, 251–252
narration of rape, 253–256
references to Church and Christianity, 248–253
woman's status and men's decisions and actions, 256–261
Ṣafiyye Sultan (d. 1619), 113–114
Saka, Pınar, 45, 45n9, 47n12, 52n31, 54, 58n52
Sambari, Yosef (d. ca. 1700s), 116
Sandys, George, 98
A Relation of a Journey (1615), 98, 99
Sedefkār Meḥmed Agha (d. 1617), 215, 217–219, 222, 236
Selānikī Muṣṭafā Efendi (d. ca. 1600), 111, 114
Selīm I (r. 1512–1520), 15–16, 24–26, 134
Selīm II (r. 1566–1574), 27
Şerban, Constantin (r. 1654–1658, 1660), 200
Şāh Ḳulu rebellion ("Slave of the Shah," 1511), 327
Sinān Pasha ("Ḳoca," d. 1596), 116–118
Sinān ("Miᶜmār," d. 1588), 93
"slave-servants" of Ottoman sultan, *see ḳuls*
Soḳollu Meḥmed Pasha (Sokolović, d. 579), 160

Süleymān I (r. 1520–1566), 4, 11, 15, 26, 27, 53, 57, 63, 116, 120, 121, 137, 151n9, 176
Süleymān Agha (d. 1715), 54
Ṣunᶜullāh Efendi (d. 1612), 265n5

T
Tāhmāsb I, Shah (r. 1524–1576), 137
Taᶜlīḳīzāde Meḥmed (d. 1600), 1–3, 267n12, 268–269, 272, 276–278, 282–284, 288–292
Toledano, Ehud R., 4n12, 5
Trabzon incident, 134–135
"Turkish-Islamic Synthesis" doctrine, 3

V
Vişne Meḥmed Efendi, 216–217, 219–220

Y
Yaḥyā Efendi (d. 1644), 229n34, 301
Yaḥya İnāl, 25

Z
Zülfiḳār Bey, 37–38
Zvi, Sabbatai (d. 1676), 144
Zvizdović, Fr. Anđeo (d. 1498), 149–150, 170

www.ingramcontent.com/pod-product-compliance
Lightning Source LLC
Chambersburg PA
CBHW071359300426
44114CB00016B/2117
9798897830947